The Total Politics Guide to

tʰ

Edited by

The Total Politics Guide to the 2010 General Election

Edited by Greg Callus and Iain Dale
In association with ComRes

biteback

First published in Great Britain in 2009 by
Biteback Publishing Ltd
Heal House
375 Kennington Lane
London
SE11 5QY

ISBN 978-1-84954-028-5 (hardback)
ISBN 978-1-84954-005-6 (paperback)

A CIP catalogue record for this book is available from the British Library.

Set in Kepler and Trade Gothic by Soapbox
Printed and bound in Great Britain by TJ International, Padstow, Cornwall

Contents

REGIONAL AND CONSTITUENCY PROFILES

Regional profiles by Robert Waller; constituency profiles by Dan Hamilton

Editors' introduction & acknowledgements

Greg Callus and Iain Dale

Editing a book like this is, as you can imagine, a pleasure for political enthusiasts like the two of us. We have tried to cater for the political enthusiast as well as the casual observer of the political scene, and hopefully both will be satisfied.

We have tried to give a blend of material – ranging from lists and statistics, through to thematic essays, mixing detailed opinion polling and electoral law with insightful chapters on the media and the hidden party 'machines'. No book like this could cover every aspect of the next election, but hopefully this will prove a useful and thought-provoking tome to accompany what is promising to be an exciting year in British politics.

Such a project requires the effort of many talented people who have been as patient with our requests as they have been generous with their time. All our contributors have given us interesting and well-written material for which we are very grateful, but some individuals merit a special mention.

First such thanks go to Andrew Hawkins, CEO of ComRes, for co-sponsoring the publication of this guide, as well as for writing one of the articles. The generosity of ComRes also extended to providing us with the remarkable Dan Hamilton, whose encyclopaedic knowledge was matched only by his industry in profiling 200 seats in the final section of the book. We are also indebted to Robert Waller for his regional profiles, which have appeared in each issue of *Total Politics* magazine. His book *The Almanac of British Politics* is an invaluable resource for everyone involved in electoral politics.

We would also like to extend our sincere gratitude to Professors Colin Rallings and Michael Thrasher from the Elections Centre at the University of Plymouth. Most of the election statistics which appear in this book are courtesy of their great work, and appear with their permission. Their *Media Guide to the New Parliamentary Constituencies* is rightly considered a psephological bible. Biteback Publishing will be publishing a paperback of their book, British Electoral Facts, in late 2009.

Our gratitude is also due to John Owens, Francesca Wilski, Jonathan Wadman and James Stephens at Biteback Publishing for their skill and dexterity in researching, editing and marketing this book.

In a book of this scope there are bound to be a few errors, and some necessary omissions (parliamentary candidates yet to be chosen, black swans yet to be spotted etc.). We take full responsibility, of course, but hope that any such instances will be so few and marginal as not to detract from the book as a whole.

Foreword

Peter Riddell

The 2010 general election promises to be very different from any of the other seventeen contests since 1945. It looks set to produce the largest turnover of MPs since then thanks to the coincidence of several different factors. Some have been present before, such as a change in parliamentary constituency boundaries, which occurs every ten to fifteen years. Big swings against the incumbent government have occurred roughly five times since 1945. But what is new and unpredictable is the turmoil caused by the expenses scandal. A large number of MPs have already announced they will stand down at the election, with many more expected to follow. Finally, there is the impact of the most severe recession for over seventy years and the associated fiscal hangover, which are likely to affect British politics for much of the next decade.

First, boundary changes. A majority of constituencies in England and Wales (Scotland changed in 2005) will have new boundaries. This reflects shifts of people away from inner cities to suburbs and adjoining rural areas. As before, there will be a net benefit to the Conservatives and a net loss to Labour. The changes, already approved by Parliament, will see the creation of thirteen new seats and the disappearance of nine. But a larger number of MPs face significant changes in their boundaries, in some cases turning a safe seat into a marginal one, or in twenty cases changing party control. In a few cases that puts sitting MP against sitting MP to fight for a new seat. In many more it will lead to a decision to step down. The size of the House of Commons will rise by four to 650. This makes 326 the finishing line for an overall majority.

It is impossible to be precise about the impact, but the most widely used assessment, by Colin Rallings and Michael Thrasher of Plymouth University, suggests that, on the basis of votes at the 2005 election, the Labour majority on the new boundaries would have been thirty-six, rather than the sixty-four won on the day. Looked at another way, this means that while, on the old boundaries, the Conservatives would require a switch in votes, or swing, of 2.2 per cent from Labour to remove Gordon Brown's overall majority, they now require a swing of just 1.5 per cent. This means that it will be very hard for Labour to retain an overall majority even if there is only a small adverse swing – and, at the time of writing, it looks much, much worse for them than that. However, a swing of 4.6 per cent is still required for the Tories to become the largest single party and 7.1 per cent to gain an overall majority of just one. That assumes a uniform swing across the country and ignores any gain from targeting key seats or tactical voting against Labour.

Second, anti-government swing. Recent local and parliamentary by-election results, let alone national opinion polls, point to considerable losses by Labour and gains by the Conservatives, amounting to a small but clear-cut Conservative overall majority. However, despite the boundary changes, the electoral system still favours Labour. This means the Tories still have to gain a higher percentage of the vote than Labour to win the same number of MPs. This is not because of some deliberate plot, but because Labour's vote is more efficiently distributed to win seats, whereas the Conservatives pile up a lot of very big majorities in safe seats. A further bias comes from the backward-looking nature of the boundary changes, which are based on the 2001 census.

Unlike previous big swings, in 1945, 1964, 1970 and 1979, it is not just a simple two-party switch. There is a sizeable third party in the Liberal Democrats, as well as a growing vote, if not representation, for other parties and independents. So, as noted above, it would still require a very large swing for the Tories to win outright, on a scale seen only once since 1945, in 1997, when half the sitting Conservative MPs were defeated.

Third, the expenses row. A wave of MPs have said they will stand down at the coming general election following disclosures over their expenses. Some, especially those aged over sixty, might have been intending to go anyway, as often happens after a long period of one-party rule when government MPs fear defeat. MPs now tend to retire earlier than in the past because of more generous pension arrangements and because it is now much harder to be only a semi-active MP. But the expenses factor has unquestionably boosted the total in two ways. First, and most obvious, has been the announcements from those named and shamed, who have been forced to stand down. Second, several MPs have privately admitted that the pressures of disclosure and local criticism have tilted the balance against them standing again.

Each of these factors on its own could have a big impact. Together, they could produce seismic changes. The number of MPs announcing their retirement has, at the time of writing, already reached three figures, but looks almost certain to exceed the previous peaks of 125 in 1945 (at the end of the war and after a ten-year parliament) and 117 in 1997. So between a fifth and a quarter of MPs could leave the Commons before taking account of the defeat of any incumbent Labour MPs. This could easily mean that between a third and two-fifths of the next Commons consists of new MPs. In particular, a half, or even more, of the post-election Conservative parliamentary party could consist of new MPs. Indeed, it is bound to do so if the party is to form a government with an overall majority. At the last election, there were 198 Tory MPs—many fewer than the 271 that Labour had before its big surge in 1997. If you deduct voluntary and involuntary retirements, this means that half the minimum 326 MPs needed for an overall majority would be new to the Commons. This would have a profound effect not just on the Commons itself but also on David Cameron's task as a party leader.

A clear Conservative victory is still possible, even likely according to opinion polls, but a lot can happen in the run-up to the election. While there is no invariable electoral law of a swing back to the incumbent government, Labour could be helped if signs emerge of a bottoming out in the economy, or even of a start to recovery. A hung parliament cannot therefore be ruled out. Much of the inevitable speculation about possible deals and coalitions is mistaken. The February 1974 general election, and the 2007 Scottish election, show that what matters is direction and momentum, rather than notional combinations. In February 1974, Ted Heath was seen as the loser, having called the election and lost seats, which is why the Liberals would not back him to carry on as Prime Minister, and he resigned on the Monday after the election. In Scotland in 2007, even though the Scottish Nationalists were only one seat ahead of Labour, they were clearly seen as the winners, having gained twenty seats. That gave the SNP the initiative in forming a minority government, as Alex Salmond successfully did. Similarly, if the Conservatives oust Labour to become the largest single party, but fail to win an overall majority, David Cameron will be seen as the winner and Gordon Brown the loser. Even if, mathematically, Labour and the Liberal Democrats could combine to have an overall majority, Nick Clegg may be reluctant to be associated with the losing leader and party. More likely is a period of minority government under Mr Cameron until he calculates the Tories can win an overall majority. In these circumstances, the key election would be the second one: if there is no clear result then, all bets are off about coalitions and electoral reform.

How will the revolt against MPs caught in the expenses revelations work out? Will independents oust tarnished incumbents? With the party leaderships eagerly moving to dump any MP caught up in expenses charges, there may be fewer targets for independents. The evidence from the past is that only in very exceptional circumstances can a true independent win. After all, the success of Martin Bell in 1997 was because not only did the controversial Neil Hamilton stay and fight, but the two other parties, Labour and the Liberal Democrats, agreed to stand down. In other cases, only a genuinely local candidate, such as Dr Richard Taylor, fighting to save a local hospital, has a hope of winning. So do not bet on more a handful of independents succeeding.

A more important question may be whether the Liberal Democrats can hang onto their threescore block, or will they be caught by the Tory resurgence, as the third party was before in 1970 and 1979? Worryingly for Nick Clegg, the Conservatives did very well in Liberal Democrat-held seats in the south-west in the May 2009 local elections. And, will other parties (the UK Independence Party, the Greens and the British National Party), that expanding footnote at the bottom of the opinion polls, resist their usual general election squeeze and not only affect the outcome but also even gain seats?

The campaign itself is likely to move even further away from the familiar model of the past forty-five years of national press conferences. The national media will be bypassed even more than in 2005, not just through the increased use of the new media but also by focusing on marginal constituencies. Targeting of resources on key marginal seats, especially by the Conservatives, has already been under way for several years, but will be taken even further in the campaign.

We may also, at long last, see a national televised debate, or debates, among the three main party leaders (with variations in Scotland, Wales and Northern Ireland). That will become a major talking point of the campaign as the tactics and personalities are endlessly discussed. But the experience in the United States and in Europe is that the leaders invariably play safe and the debates very seldom change the outcome.

The drama of election night itself may be longer drawn out than in the past. The increased checking now required of postal votes may delay counting and the announcement of results. Of course, if there is a big swing, we should still be clear about the overall outcome. But there will be lots of mini-dramas along the way. If the defeat of Michael Portillo in Enfield, Southgate by Stephen Twigg was the most memorable moment of the 1997 election, what will be the equivalent in 2010? There will be a lot of focus on high-profile celebrity independents, and possibly also on Greens, the BNP and UKIP. But the most likely personality stories may involve former Cabinet ministers such as Jacqui Smith, Charles Clarke and Andrew Smith. Labour would really be in trouble if a current minister like John Denham or Ben Bradshaw lost.

The whole election will be fought against the background of the deepest recession for seventy years. Even if the worst of the downturn is over, few economists expect more than a gradual and weak recovery as confidence remains low and banks still have a lot to do to rebuild their balance sheets. Unemployment, especially amongst young people, is likely to remain very high, and will probably still be rising, with real incomes squeezed. Moreover, the public finances have deteriorated and drastic action, cutbacks in spending plans and higher taxes, and probably a combination of the two, will be necessary in the next parliament.

The political impact is double edged. At one level, the Brown government gets the most blame. But the uncertainty and doubts have also made Mr Cameron's task harder. No politician likes to promise austerity rather than hope of improvement. The election campaign will turn, in part, on arguments about which party is better able to manage recovery and the necessary changes in public services and in the role of the state. In that respect, there are closer parallels to the post-Winter of Discontent election of 1979 than the 'things can only get better' election of 1997. Yet, unlike 1979, there is not yet a sense of a change in the direction of policy: nothing comparable to the rejection of the post-war economic and welfare settlement that even then was implicit, though not yet explicit, in Margaret Thatcher's appeal. Talking about the post-bureaucratic state and scrapping quangos does not have the same ring. We may be at a turning point in the electoral cycle but it is unclear whether the pro-market globalisation era of the past two to three decades is about to change radically. Throwing the rascals out is always the easiest part of elections, and politics.

Peter Riddell is chief political commentator of The Times *and a senior fellow of the Institute for Government, as well as chairman of the Hansard Society and author of six books on British politics.*

The pollster's perspective:
key moments and trends in the 54th parliament

Andrew Hawkins

If the 2005 parliament were to be characterised by a single figure, it would be a 45 degree slope, denoting the gradual but apparently inexorable decline of Labour's popularity.

Like the twitching of a recently deceased corpse, there were a couple of moments when Labour support appeared to lurch back to life: when Tony Blair swapped places with Gordon Brown, and then again during the second phase of the recession, when the public sought the comfort of political leadership which offered the most experience at a time of acute crisis.

Labour lead since 2005 general election

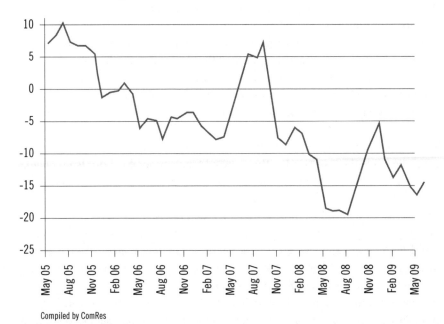

Compiled by ComRes

In retrospect, Gordon Brown was hardly a popular choice of leader. The question asking how people would vote if a candidate were leading their party is a hypothetical one, but provides a reasonable indicator of likely popularity when that imagined leader has been Chancellor of the Exchequer for the past ten years.

Voting intention November 2005–May 2007

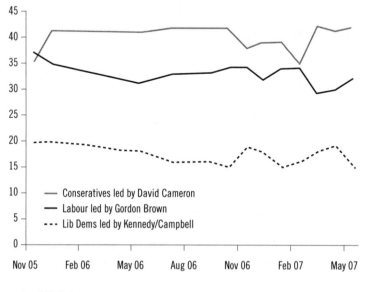

Compiled by ComRes

On 7 September 2006, Tony Blair said he would stand down within a year. Fortunately for pollsters and the media, this allowed plenty of time to explore the virtues of the respective candidates for the leadership. However, for Gordon Brown it also exposed the underlying perceptions of the electorate, which explains why he was always going to struggle to shine against David Cameron. In January 2007, just six months before Brown assumed the top job, most people thought that 'a rising star' should be chosen as Labour leader. Brown was the choice of only 33 per cent of the public.

In April of that year, two months before he became Prime Minister, only one in four (25 per cent) thought Gordon Brown would make a good Labour leader while 42 per cent said he would be bad. In the following month, 62 per cent disagreed that a Gordon Brown succession would 'make the Labour Party more appealing'.

However, after a decade in power, Labour were always going to be at their most vulnerable at the point where voters decide that it's time for a change. Ominously, in April 2007, more than seven in ten people expressed concern that Gordon Brown would represent 'more of the same' and only 22 per cent thought he would represent the fresh start the country was looking for.

There was, though, an important upside in Gordon Brown's pre-Downing Street polling. At Labour's party conference in September 2008 Brown said in respect of the rapidly worsening economic situation that 'it is no time for a novice'. Doubtless the party's strategists were homing in on the massive contrast in perceived experience between him and David Cameron. In May 2007 the soon-to-be Prime Minister outdid the Leader of the Opposition on being the more competent and stronger leader, and he led his younger opponent on being 'experienced' by fully 85 per cent to 7 per cent.

Where Cameron was appealing, though, was in the qualities needed of an empathetic leader: in being likeable, inspiring, forward-looking and caring.

Thus were the seeds sown for Gordon Brown to emerge relatively well through the crucible of economic crisis. But will those be the qualities people want in their leader by the time the election comes around?

The honeymoon

It is easily forgotten that Gordon Brown did enjoy a honeymoon, albeit for a couple of months until he stopped teasing the media into thinking he might call an early election.

The first crisis he had to tackle was the failed terrorist attack on Glasgow airport, to which more than three-quarters of people think he responded well. Significantly, given the frustration with his predecessor, 60 per cent disagreed that Tony Blair should be leading the country rather than Gordon Brown.

Expectations were high too: almost twice as many people expected the government would perform better under Brown than it had under Blair. By the time the 2007 party conference season was under way, Brown was a happy man, enjoying both the job he had craved all his political life and a broad level of satisfaction with his leadership of Labour, according to 67 per cent of the public.

The first signs in the UK that the impending financial crisis would have a serious impact was the run on Northern Rock in September 2007. Here was a crisis tailor-made for the Iron Chancellor, who, one month earlier, had out-polled David Cameron on being 'best in a crisis' by a whopping 69 per cent to 17 per cent.

There the story might have ended, had Brown paid closer attention to those of his advisers who were urging him to call that early election.

The fall from grace

Labour's demise following the phantom election ('cancelled' on 6 October 2007) was fast and dramatic. The party's biggest poll lead over the Conservatives, registered immediately prior to their annual conference, was an impressive 13 percentage points. Before the end of the following month, the Conservatives scored a poll lead of 8 percentage points over Labour.

What caused the decline?

The period from September to November 2007 saw a retreat into the previous gradient of Labour's decline evident since 1997 that even Tony Blair could not stem. It was as if the electorate had woken up to find that the emperor with the clunking fist was as naked as any other unclothed potentate. To put it another way, the misgivings expressed by voters prior to Gordon Brown taking over, which they had suspended during the honeymoon, were being proved right.

Within four months of the new leader being installed, six in ten people disagreed that he had brought 'freshness, change and renewal'. There was a sudden wave of pessimism about the future direction of the government. And, just two months after half of voters said Northern Rock had been handled well, 54 per cent were now saying it was managed badly.

Of course, this rapid decline in popularity was caused by more than just a run on a minor bank. The main issue was that in appearing to let the phantom election story run on throughout the Labour conference, Brown allowed voters to regard him as like all the rest – he was just an opportunist after all. Worse still, the government was shortly afterwards responsible for losing data discs containing personal bank records of half of all households in Britain, prompting a tidal wave of warning letters from banks asking people to keep a close eye on their statements.

Was the decline inevitable? In short, yes.

Labour lead 1997–2010

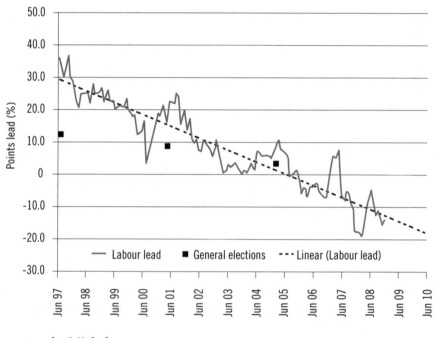

Compiled by ComRes

The above chart plots the average Labour poll lead since 1997, together with an arithmetically generated best fit line to show the historical and ex ante trend line, plus the election results themselves.

The gradient confirms what academic Dr Timothy Heppell proposes about the nature of longer periods of government. His study 'The Degenerative Tendencies of Long-term Governments' suggests this Labour government has shown classic signs of degeneration, highlighting that similar patterns were seen in the 1960s and again in the 1990s. These are:

1. governing competence ebbs away
2. leadership credibility fails
3. ideological divisions appear
4. there is an appearance of abuse of power
5. the appearance of a renewed opposition.

In assessing perceptions of governing competence, perhaps the most important measure is which economic team is trusted most to steer Britain's economy through difficult times. In September Gordon Brown and Alistair Darling enjoyed a clear lead over David Cameron and George Osborne on this measure, with almost three times the percentage of endorsement. Having seen this measure reversed to the Conservatives' advantage, the Labour team regained a smaller lead during part of 2008 before the Conservative economic team took the lead once more in early 2009, where it has remained.

The credibility of Labour's leadership followed a similar pattern: during that brief honeymoon Brown led Cameron by a massive margin as the man who 'would make the best Prime Minister'. The Conservative leader took the lead in the autumn of 2007 and, with the exception of a blip towards the end of 2008, remains ahead – in fact, the gap has been widening more recently.

Labour is also regarded as more divided than the Conservatives. Several polls have shockingly placed Labour under Gordon Brown as being more divided than the Conservatives were under John Major. For those who remember what the last Conservative Prime Minister called his 'eighteen-month winter' the reality will be somewhat different. But in electoral politics, perception is often more important than the reality. The events surrounding Labour's disastrous European elections in June 2009 will only have served to reinforce this visage.

Then there is the expenses crisis. This apparent abuse of position has hit all major parties to some extent. While the Conservatives have not escaped scot free, Labour's handling of the scandal was heavily criticised – not least by MPs such as Dr Ian Gibson, who felt he had been singled out unfairly. For Labour, the expenses scandal came hot on the heels of a rather unpleasant episode involving the Prime Minister's special adviser, Damian McBride, who was exposed for fabricating stories about prominent Conservatives. Although the emails were circulated among only a small group, they called into question the integrity of people very close to the heart of Labour's leadership.

The fifth criterion, a renewed opposition, had been increasingly evident since David Cameron was elected leader of his party in December 2005. However, it did take fully three years for the Conservative to regroup to the point where they became a serious and likely threat to Labour, especially in light of the large swing required to achieve an overall majority.

The modernising Conservative leadership has faced several challenges. First, they have long been regarded by most voters as 'not yet ready for government'. Second, they face the problem of brittle support: people want to ditch Labour but they know so little of what the Conservatives, and in particular Cameron, stand for, that their vote is inevitably more to indicate the belief that it is time for a change rather than reflecting a zeal for what the opposition have to offer.

Of course, the biggest issue for all the political parties is the economy. Aside from perceptions of which party has the best economic team, the Conservatives have consistently struggled to convince voters that they 'have the right ideas about how to get Britain out of recession' (April 2009 – 49 per cent disagree, 38 per cent agree). Indeed, in April 2009 some 79 per cent of voters said Cameron needed to be clearer about what he would do about the economy if he were Prime Minister.

The three electoral drivers
The economy
The biggest determining issue for the next election will without doubt be the economy. It is the defining moment in Gordon Brown's premiership and plays to his main strengths in terms of economic competence, following a decade as Chancellor during a period of benign economic growth, and in terms of his experience. And it appeals to the man's view of the state: he believes it can deliver. His interventionist approach to the credit crunch also has resonance with Labour MPs, at a time when it is important for him to be able to rally their support.

In the latest longitudinal surveys looking at 'the most important issues facing the country', the economy has been scoring record highs of 70 per cent plus. The importance of this issue cannot be overstated, which bodes well for Brown in that the net satisfaction scores (the percentage of voters who are satisfied minus those who are dissatisfied) for Chancellor Alistair Darling are *only* at minus 16 per cent, and for the government's economic policies are *only* minus 35 per cent.

These scores actually compare rather favourably with those achieved (if that is the right word) during the darkest days of the Major government. Chancellor Norman Lamont, in the wake of Black Wednesday, managed a whopping negative rating of minus 52 per cent on the same measure. But king of them all was Ken Clarke, whose lowest satisfaction rating hit rock bottom at minus 53 per cent. So much for all those who said David Cameron should have made him Shadow Chancellor.

The speed with which the economy recovers is likely to be the single most important factor in determining the extent of Tory victory, or at least Labour defeat.

'I expect the economy will start showing signs of improvement soon'

	MARCH	JUNE
Agree	39%	67%
Disagree	58%	27%

The stakes for Labour are high and they face double jeopardy. If the economy fails to improve before the next election, perceptions of the party's competence, and that of its leader, will take a serious knock. In the meantime, as the above chart shows, the public expect the economy to improve soon. If it doesn't, the government will face a further backlash having raised hopes only to disappoint.

Public service cuts

Evidence of whether the public understands the need for public spending cuts is inconclusive. If it were otherwise, it would be an obvious choice for the parties whether or not to 'come clean' on the need for them.

However, there are some pointers. The claim by Labour that the Conservatives cannot be trusted with where public spending cuts should be made does not wash with voters. The Conservatives are more trusted than Labour on this issue, as the table below shows.

Which party do you trust most to decide where spending cuts should be made?

Conservative	31%
Labour	21%
Lib Dem	14%
Other	7%
None	16%
Don't know	10%

ComRes/Independent, 30 June 2009

That more than one in four voters trust none of the parties most on this measure, or do not know, suggests there is still much to play for, but the negative message 'don't trust the Tories' will be a very hard one for Labour to succeed with.

When the economy first hit the buffers, the polls showed a certain resonance with the suggestion that Labour had failed to mend the roof when the sun was shining. By extension, this has become an effective message when decisions are to be made about where to cut public services.

Cleaning up the expenses scandal

The Westminster village can be woefully wrong in its instinctive reading of public opinion. One notable example was the arrest of Damian Green MP in November 2008, when the noisy outrage in Parliament contrasted with the low-key public reaction. People simply didn't care.

By stark contrast, the public was livid over the *Telegraph*'s expenses stories, strung out over four weeks to deliver maximum impact. And deliver they did: by the end of May, 80 per cent of voters felt 'the main political parties in Westminster have let the country down'. They made this feeling felt in more practical terms a few days later, in the European elections, by staying at home (especially Labour voters) or voting for smaller parties. For example, the UK Independence Party beat Labour into third place. The Conservatives polled 4.2 million votes yet the smaller parties' combined voters were more than 50 per cent higher than those for the Conservatives.

Although the British National Party's vote share was up by less than 2 per cent, they put shock waves through the political establishment by sending two MEPs to Brussels. In the North West region, however, the election of the party's leader, Nick Griffin, was despite an actual reduction in the number of votes cast compared with 2004. Griffin, and his colleague in Yorkshire, won because Labour voters stayed at home.

The challenge for the parties is how to respond to the expenses scandal and the corresponding fallout. The response was truly chaotic: having brought forward an inquiry by the Committee on Standards in Public Life into MPs' expenses, the government then pushed forward with what looked like emergency legislation which, if implemented in its original form, would have had far-reaching constitutional implications.

The public certainly wanted something to change in the wake of the scandal. Support for proportional representation, for instance, shot up to almost 70 per cent in its immediate aftermath. Support for fixed-term parliaments was even higher, at 79 per cent, while David Cameron's flagship policy of a 'significant reduction' in the number of MPs at Westminster was supported by 73 per cent of voters.

The appetite for reform is clear, but the details are hazy. Coming towards the end of the parliamentary session, the expenses scandal opened up a chasm into which a confusing pile of regulatory and constitutional reforms has been flung. But there has been no clear, strategically considered answer to the problem of MPs' remuneration.

Worse still for the parties, MPs have been standing down in their droves. There is likely to be turnover at a scale not seen since 1945 which, unless the Conservatives can win a substantial majority, will cause nightmares for the whips.

The path to 2010

The last date constitutionally when the election can be held is 3 June 2010. The challenge faced by the Conservatives is the scale of the mountain they face, having piled up votes in the wrong places.

Purely in terms of national swing, and measured rather crudely, a Conservative lead of up to 6 per cent on polling day will result in a Labour-dominated hung parliament. A Conservative lead of between 6 per cent and 9 per cent would result in a Conservative-dominated hung parliament. The Conservatives only creep into overall majority territory with a lead greater than this, on such an analysis.

However, this is of course analytical fiction. The House of Commons majority will be won or lost in the targeting of marginal seats and persuading people not to waste their votes supporting candidates who cannot win.

The balance sheet

On the Conservatives' side, they have the powerful appeal of 'time for a change', a helpful revision of parliamentary boundaries, freedom from blame for the financial crisis, and a leader with the empathetic qualities needed to reassure a nation worried about its economic future.

Labour benefit from the advantage of incumbency and the levers of power at its disposal. It has a leader who is considered best in a crisis with clearly more experience than his opposite number. They also have the electoral maths stacked highly in their favour.

However, Labour have two aces up their sleeve. The first of these is the economy. All it will take is one quarter's economic growth for Gordon Brown to argue that he delivered a decade of growth, the world plunged us into recession, but he – and only he – had the wisdom and courage to introduce the biggest economic rescue package since the Great Depression. Importantly, the 2009 Q4 economic growth figures are likely to be published towards the end of March 2010. Even if unemployment continues to rise, as doubtless it will, the Conservatives would be faced with an obvious question: what would they have done differently?

The second ace is a further change of leader. As has been demonstrated here, Labour enjoyed a substantial honeymoon in the polls when Gordon Brown took over, ostensibly not because of any inherent qualities he possessed, but merely because he was not Tony Blair.

Although many alternative Labour leaders are unrecognisable to many voters, the patterns revealed by polling show a clear likelihood that the senior figures of Jack Straw, or especially Alan Johnson, would lead to an immediate and significant boost to Labour's fortunes. In one poll conducted immediately after the European elections, Johnson was the only potential candidate who could deny David Cameron a majority.

Labour MPs may be many things but they are not stupid. They know that to precipitate a change of leader too soon risks a premature general election, before better economic news has a chance to filter through. That said, these are already desperate times for the party.

Without a change of leader, it is difficult to see how Labour can win. With a change of Labour leader, it becomes possible to see how the Conservatives could be denied a majority.

Andrew Hawkins is the CEO of the opinion pollster ComRes.

Deaths, resignations and retirements: the by-elections of the 54th parliament

Mike Smithson

There have been two overwhelming themes in the series of Westminster by-elections during the 2005 parliament: the intertwined stories of the re-emergence of the Conservatives as a party capable of winning seats and the difficulties that the Liberal Democrats have had in maintaining their historically excellent record in this form of contest.

For the latter, Westminster by-elections had over the years become the oxygen that had kept the party alive when the two-party contest between the reds and the blues seemed to dominate everything. They had an approach, perfected in battle after battle, that saw them go from one sensational win to another over several decades.

By the summer of 2009, however, it seemed that the old Liberal Democrat by-election magic had evaporated and they simply were not the force that they once had been.

How different it was in the first year of the 2005 parliament, where the by-election series began with a very unusual contest – a Liberal Democrat defence against the Conservatives in the leafy outer Manchester suburb of **Cheadle**. This had been a Liberal Democrat hold in the general election but the MP, Patsy Calton, sadly died less than four weeks later. Apart from Winchester in 1997, where the general election result had been annulled by the courts, Cheadle was the only Liberal Democrat defence of a seat since the party's foundation in 1987.

The Conservatives, who had then started their prolonged leadership battle, were keen to prove that after their general election defeat they were still a fighting force and they put everything into the battle. The Liberal Democrats did the same and the result was a big squeeze on the Labour vote. In the end the Liberal Democrat candidate saw his vote rise by 3.3 per cent and the Conservative up by 2.2 per cent, all at the expense of Labour, which failed to achieve the 5 per cent threshold needed to save the party's deposit.

The next contest was at **Livingston**, caused by the death of the former Foreign Secretary who had resigned from the Cabinet over Iraq, Robin Cook. Here, it was the SNP that saw the biggest increase: their share rose by 11.1 per cent to come just 2,680 votes behind Labour.

By the time of the next by-election, also in Scotland at **Dunfermline & West Fife**, the political climate in the UK had changed entirely. On 6 December 2005, David Cameron had been elected Conservative leader and the first polls had the party level-pegging with Labour for the first time since the early 1990s. One month and one day later, the Liberal Democrat leader resigned after reports of his drinking problems and the by-election was held bang in the middle of the contest to find his replacement. The Liberal Democrats then saw one potential candidate after another being the subject of newspaper allegations and the party's poll ratings had slumped.

It was against this unlikely backcloth that the then leaderless Liberal Democrats pulled off their only by-election victory of the parliament. A Labour general election majority of 11,562 became a Liberal Democrat seat by 1,800 votes. Cameron's Conservatives came in fourth place with a reduced vote share.

The party, then led by Ming Campbell, almost pulled off a sensational victory four and a half months later in June 2006, in the rock solid Conservative outer London seat of **Bromley & Chislehurst**, where the late Eric Forth had secured a Conservative majority of 13,342 just over a year earlier. At the time the several polls were showing the Conservatives with double-digit leads yet the party only scraped home by 633 votes.

That outcome raised questions about whether the Conservative poll leads were illusory and also put Cameron, the leader who had only been in place for six months, under some pressure. The result simply reinforced the fact that in the previous twenty-four years fighting by-elections had become a form of political campaigning that were a nightmare for the Conservatives. These were electoral contests where, defending or trying to take a seat, whether in government or opposition, they simply seemed unable to compete. For not only did they fail to take any seats from other parties they were very vulnerable when trying to hold onto what had been won at the previous general election.

How could it be that a party that was claiming to be seriously challenging to win back power in a general election could have such a poor by-election record? Indeed there were many pundits who were saying that improving at by-elections might be a prerequisite for a general election victory for the Conservatives.

On the same day as Bromley & Chislehurst there was **Blaenau Gwent**, in what had been one of the safest Labour strongholds in Wales until a row over all-women short lists had prompted a local Labour activist, Peter Law, to fight and win as an Independent at the 2005 general election. Labour threw everything into the battle to retake the seat and the only opinion poll of the campaign had them well ahead. In the end they failed by 2,488 votes. The Conservatives ended up in fifth place, adding to the party's gloom of that day.

It was more than a year later in July 2007, exactly three weeks after Gordon Brown had become Prime Minister, that David Cameron's Conservatives had their next chance to end their by-election nightmare. The contests were to replace Tony Blair in **Sedgefield** and **Ealing, Southall** – both very safe Labour seats.

The big battle was in the west London constituency, where the Conservatives selected Surinderpal Singh Lit – commonly known as Tony Lit – as its candidate. He is the former managing director of Sunrise Radio and the son of Avtar Lit, who had contested the seat as an Independent in the 2001 general election, coming third. Lit only joined the Conservative party a few days before nominations and on the ballot paper he was described as belonging to 'David Cameron's Conservatives'. On the weekend before the election there were newspaper reports of how Lit had reportedly attended a Labour Party fund-raising event and Sunrise Radio had donated £4,800 to Labour the previous month. Labour held on easily, with the Liberal Democrats taking second place.

In Sedgefield Labour was returned with a reduced majority, with the Liberal Democrats pipping the Conservatives for second place, and so the Tory by-election nightmare continued. That day proved to be a high point for the Liberal Democrats and a low point for the Conservatives: David Cameron's party was determined not to be humiliated again.

Their chance came in **Crewe & Nantwich** in May 2008 following the death of the long-serving member of the House of Commons, Gwyneth Dunwoody. Her daughter, Tamsin Dunwoody, was selected as the Labour candidate, facing Edward Timpson, whose family fortune was based on the national shoe repair and key-cutting business. His apparent wealth and alleged privileged background became the key issue of what was the highest-profile by-election campaign for decades.

Labour supporters put on top hats in an effort to mock Timpson, who was described by Labour as being 'Lord Snooty' and a 'Tory Toff', in common with criticisms laid at the feet of his party leadership. In the end the Labour campaign flopped horribly, with the Conservatives breaking their prolonged by-election famine. This was the first seat to be taken by the Tories off another party since June 1982, during the supercharged political atmosphere created by the Falklands War.

It was not just the fact of victory that made Crewe & Nantwich so significant but the detailed numbers themselves. For on a turnout that was almost at general election levels the party's 2005 total of 14,162 rose to 20,539 votes. This followed the Conservative victories in the London and local elections three weeks earlier and record poll leads. From that moment the Conservative general election victory looked like the more probable outcome. Conversely, for the Liberal Democrats the by-election proved to be a turning point. Their vote went down 4 per cent and signalled that it was no longer going to be as easy again.

The next contest was a month later in the true-blue Oxfordshire seat of **Henley**, which had been vacated by Boris Johnson following his election as mayor of London. The Liberal Democrats mounted a high-powered campaign using what had become their standard approach but it was all to no avail. On a turnout down 17 points at 50.5 per cent, what was by then Nick Clegg's party failed to make any inroads. Their vote went up by nearly 2 per cent but the Conservative candidate saw his share rise 3.4 per cent. Perhaps the most significant aspect of the election was the decline of Labour, which finished behind the Greens and the BNP in fifth place. The party's share of just 3.1 per cent meant that it lost its deposit.

Labour, along with the Liberal Democrats, did not fight in the next instalment of the 2008 'Summer of By-elections' at **Haltemprice & Howden**. The seat had been made vacant by the Conservative shadow Home Secretary, David Davis, resigning in order to set off a debate on the erosion of civil liberties. He won easily with 73 per cent of the vote but there was no immediate return to the shadow Cabinet.

This was followed a fortnight later on 24 July 2008 by **Glasgow East**, where the sitting MP, David Marshall, had resigned on grounds of ill-health. This had been a rock-solid Labour seat, held by the party at the general election with a massive majority. Marshall secured more than 60 per cent of the vote with the SNP in second place on just 17 per cent – a massive margin.

Opinion polls during the campaign pointed to Labour hanging on with a double-digit majority but that is not what happened on the day. The SNP just squeezed in with a majority of 365 votes – an outcome that added to the problems faced by the Prime Minister, Gordon Brown.

Labour was very keen to hang on in the final by-election of 2008, which was also in Scotland at the Fife constituency of **Glenrothes**. An added dimension was that the seat is adjacent to Gordon Brown's and the candidate that Labour chose was the head of the school where the young Gordon had been taught.

Party organisers from throughout the country, together with dozens of MPs and other officials, were drafted into the area to boost the Labour effort and prevent another SNP victory. As polling day got closer, party officials felt confident enough to allow Brown and his wife Sarah to make visits.

The political background had changed dramatically since the summer. The failure of Lehman Brothers in September 2008, triggering off the global financial crisis, had given Labour a significant boost in the polls. Gordon Brown himself was credited with having played a decisive role – not just in the UK, but internationally as well.

The result, in the context of what had gone on earlier in 2008, was a sensation. Labour not only held on but increased its actual number of votes – something that is very rare for a governing party.

It was a very different story eight months later on 23 July 2009 at **Norwich North**. The sitting MP, Ian Gibson, resigned after Labour had taken action against him following the MP expenses farrago. There was a view that he had been unfairly singled out and that in revenge he decided to resign the seat so as to trigger the by-election. Within the constituency he appeared to be receiving considerable backing and there was talk of him standing as an Independent, though he ultimately decided not to do so.

When the votes were counted Labour saw a massive reduction in its vote from 44.9 per cent at the general election to a meagre 18.2 per cent. There was some relief that they had held onto second place. The Conservative candidate, Chloe Smith, swept in on 39.5 per cent of the vote, so chalking up the party's second by-election gain from Labour in the parliament. The Liberal Democrats came in third with a reduced vote share while UKIP got into fourth place ahead of the Green Party, who had had hopes at one stage of possibly winning the seat.

At time of writing, Labour and the SNP are planning to slog it out in yet another Scottish seat, **Glasgow North East**, a by-election caused by the resignation of the sitting MP, Michael Martin, following his decision to step down as Speaker of the House of Commons.

Mike Smithson is the founder and editor of PoliticalBetting.com.

Change we can believe in?
How electoral law has altered since 2005

Donal Blaney

After myriad changes to election law between 1997 and 2005, the third term of the Labour government has seen comparatively fewer changes than some had predicted (and others had hoped or feared).

Following the upheavals wrought on the political system by the Political Parties, Elections and Referendums Act 2000, further modifications had been anticipated – not least in an effort to make voting more appealing to younger voters, who, in contrast to the United States, have been voting in smaller and smaller numbers. Indeed one prominent Conservative MEP, Daniel Hannan, frequently cites the fact that in June 2004 more people voted to evict a housemate on *Big Brother* than had voted in the European elections the previous day as evidence of the disconnect between the governed and those they elect.

The principal statute of relevance – the Electoral Administration Act 2006 – contains a number of provisions designed to address the various frauds perpetrated in the 2005 general election, in particular as relate to absentee voting, and various offences as to false registration. The intention to impede or prevent the free exercise of the franchise is now a criminal offence – not merely succeeding in doing so.

Those intent on passing themselves off as deceased or non-existent electors will find it harder to do so in 2010 than in 2005 because of the need to provide a signature and date of birth (although those voting in person at a polling station may still do so without providing any proof of identity whatsoever – a situation that continues to cause concern when tales of personation are rife). Whether this will change if voting at supermarkets or online becomes commonplace will have to be seen.

The 2006 act also brought in detailed provisions concerning so-called CORE schemes (CORE standing for Co-ordinated On-line Records of Electors), not least as concerns access to electoral registration records. Such a step, in an era when privacy concerns have been heightened by the losses of personal data by a number of departmental and non-governmental bodies, is controversial. In an effort to address some voters' fears, anonymous registration is permitted under the 2006 act (although again this does make one wonder whether all voters are equal while some voters are more equal than others).

The 2006 act also saw the minimum age for a Member of Parliament reduced from twenty-one to eighteen – a change designed, again, to appeal to younger voters (along with the mooted plans for widespread text and online voting). This was expected to herald a change in the voting age to sixteen but although that reform has been the subject of speculation, it has not yet been forthcoming (albeit the government continues to make warm noises about votes at sixteen and members of the UK Youth Parliament were given the right to sit in the chamber of the House of Commons this past summer). The most prominent teenage candidate in 2010 will be Emily Benn, the granddaughter of Labour veteran Tony, who was selected as a seveteen-year-old candidate in 2007 to fight East Worthing & Shoreham.

The 2006 act also provides for Irish and certain Commonwealth citizens to be permitted to stand as candidates in parliamentary elections, thereby amending the Act of Settlement 1700 (confirming quite how marvellously arcane English law truly is).

After the death of the Liberal Democrat candidate for South Staffordshire in 2005, following the close of nominations, the returning officer was compelled to abandon the poll. The 2006 act changed the procedures to be followed in the event of a candidate's death.

A theme that has run through much of the government's legislation on elections is the perceived need to regulate donations – and, since the Labour Party loans scandal, loans – to political parties. The 2006 act tightens up the law in this regard (part of a series of changes that have brought into the public domain the names of hitherto unknown donors such as Michael Brown and David Abrahams). The government has announced its intention to focus next on the support provided to the Conservative Party by the likes of Lord Ashcroft, suggesting that further changes to party financing laws will be enacted before the general election.

A minor statute that might be of passing interest to local councillors was the Local Government and Public Involvement in Health Act 2007, which allowed for the change in electoral cycles in district and parish council elections (but which is of little direct interest for the 2010 general election). Likewise certain changes were made to the National Assembly of Wales by the Government of Wales Act 2006, which, again, while of interest to Welsh politicians and voters in 2011, are not relevant when it comes to the general election itself in 2010.

Turning to non-statutory measures, political candidates and their agents will want to ensure that they are fully conversant with the many circulars and memoranda issued since the 2005 general election. It is remarkable when reading these circulars and memoranda, which run to over 400 pages in the election lawyer's bible (*Schofield's Election Law*), that so much attention is paid to the perceived increased risk of electoral fraud. Agents must ensure that candidates and party campaigners alike know what is and is not permissible lest (through inadvertence) defeat through disqualification is snatched from the jaws of election victory on (or soon after) polling day. Training is essential because ignorance of the law is no defence.

The majority of statutory instruments passed since 2005 do not relate directly to the general election – instead concentrating on local elections, elections to the Welsh Assembly, the London Assembly and the European Parliament. Those engaged in politics at local, devolved or EU level will need to be familiar with the many important changes brought about by these reforms, many of which are technical and, from the perspective of a political operative, convoluted and easy to fall foul of if care is lacking.

Candidates and agents will, of course, be aware (one hopes!) of the changes to boundaries brought in by the Parliamentary Constituencies (England) Order 2007, as it is under those boundaries, and not existing ones, that the 2010 general election will be fought. These boundary changes, the Conservatives believe, will give them a notional advantage of two dozen seats or so when compared to the 2005 general election result.

What does or does not constitute a valid vote, and the methods for challenging an election, remain largely unaltered and it is the procedure by which to challenge an election which, after all, is what will most concern disgruntled (and indeed successful) candidates. Those wishing to challenge a result must continue to do so by way of the arcane election petition procedure and, as was recently discovered by one party's own election law expert, failure to follow the rather rudimentary and straightforward requirements of the Election Petition Rules 1960 renders an election petition struck out. For whereas the courts have discretion on how to proceed when it comes to minor or technical breaches of court rules, that discretion does not extend to breaches of key aspects of the election petition rules – sometimes with very harsh results indeed.

In the recent case of *McMurtrie v. Fernandes*, the petitioner's petition was compelled to be withdrawn because it was not served, as required under the election petition rules, on the Director of Public Prosecutions. The divisional court concurred with the sorrowful submissions of the petitioner's counsel that nothing could be done to save an incompetent petition that, through the admitted negligence of the petitioner's solicitors, had not been properly served, thus resulting not only in the withdrawal of the petition but an order being made for the petitioner to pay the respondent's costs on the punitive indemnity basis.

Thus it can be seen that while election law is a niche area of practice, even the most seasoned of practitioners – in this instance a solicitor with some twenty-five years' experience as an election lawyer, and retained by the Labour Party itself – is not immune from mistakes.

The lesson for candidates and agents is clear: election law is an area of practice where it does not make sense to cut corners, because the consequences are potentially disastrous if it all goes wrong. Forewarned is forearmed. Ensure that you are trained in how to comply with the law or face the consequences.

Donal Blaney is principal of the niche litigation firm Griffin Law, Solicitors and Commissioners for Oaths (www.griffinlaw.co.uk).

Fear and loathing on the campaign trail 2010?
How the media will cover the next general election

Jon Craig

We could be, as my Sky News colleague Adam Boulton has declared in his blog, 'close to a historic breakthrough' in general election coverage by the media. Lord Mandelson, no less, has suggested that at this election the Prime Minister and the Leader of the Opposition could go head to head in a TV debate during the campaign. If it does happen, it will shape the entire media coverage of the election campaign: by newspapers, broadcasters, websites, bloggers and every other news and opinion provider. Even in an election campaign in which many MPs' chief concern will be questions locally about their expenses, a TV debate between the party leaders would dominate coverage.

I know... we've been here before. It has been suggested, proposed and even discussed by party leaders, their spin doctors and broadcasters previously, but this is different.

If it was any Cabinet minister other than Lord Mandelson suggesting a TV debate between Gordon Brown and David Cameron, I'd be more sceptical. But the idea comes from the man who has masterminded political and media strategy for the PM since his elevation to the role of unofficial Deputy Prime Minister. His master's voice, you might say.

Usually, the call for a TV debate in an election campaign comes from an opposition leader: Neil Kinnock challenged Margaret Thatcher in 1987 and John Major in 1992 and Tony Blair was challenged by William Hague in 2001 and Michael Howard in 2005. In 1997 there were discussions, but they broke down with all sides blaming each other and accusing their opponents of running scared.

I can confirm that this time the idea is being seriously considered inside 10 Downing Street. There are no plans for a debate as yet, but it's not being ruled out either. As one of the PM's inner circle put it to me: 'The door is open.'

The door may, of course, be slammed firmly shut nearer polling day, and any debate would be unlikely to happen without Nick Clegg being included too. It may not get the ratings of *Britain's Got Talent* or *The X Factor*, and Dimbleby, Boulton, Paxman or Humphrys may not have quite the box office appeal of Simon Cowell (or Amanda Holden, or even, dare I say it, the former *Daily Mirror* editor Piers Morgan).

That said, a prime-time TV debate between Brown and Cameron wouldn't just be replayed endlessly on the news channels and on news bulletins on the terrestrial channels, it would also be given acres of column inches in the newspapers. I can imagine sketchwriters like Quentin Letts, Ann Treneman, Simon Hoggart and Simon Carr salivating at the prospect already. There would also be the inevitable psycho-babble from the body language experts. Gordon's bitten fingernails would be analysed forensically and the lady newspaper columnists would no doubt question whether David dyes his hair.

At every general election the TV coverage of the campaign gets more slick and more sophisticated than in the previous one. New technical graphics, gizmos and other tricks are shown off by the broadcasters in the run-up to polling day and – especially – on election night.

If, like me, you watch those re-runs of old election nights on BBC Parliament on Bank Holidays you'll have seen just how crude and haphazard TV reporting of politics was not that many years ago, not to mention the sight of Robin Day smoking his cigar in the studio! This time, as well as the satellite trucks and other resources and expertise that bring live coverage to the TV screen, Sky News and other broadcasters will be using more U-pods – the one-man band of TV news – bringing more news than ever before to viewers as it happens, not after it has happened.

There is, inevitably, some pooling of resources by broadcasters during election campaigns. That means that at times one camera will cover an event for BBC, ITV, Sky News and Channel Four and the material will be pooled. The broadcasters, as a rule, take it in turns to provide the pool camera. The system has its disadvantages. There's little scope for gaining exclusive material, obviously, but it means we can all get access to more material because we're sharing it.

Sky News will send a political correspondent on the road – and in the air, no doubt – with the party leaders, and Adam Boulton will mastermind my channel's coverage and present twice-nightly special election programmes. Adam not only covered the 2008 US presidential election, but also witnessed Barack Obama's first 100 days in the Oval Office. We broadcasters, like the political parties, will have learned the lessons of the Obama campaign.

I had dinner with Labour's general secretary, Ray Collins, after he returned from studying the Obama campaign. He's enthusiastic about Labour adopting some of the Obama team's modern campaign methods, using the latest web technology, though I suspect Gordon Brown may take some persuading to go too far after his 'You Tube if you want to' embarrassment over MPs' expenses.

We will, however, see a lot of WebCameron during the election campaign. We're likely to see a lot of the Cameron family, too, giving another contrast between the party leaders. Who can forget Gordon Brown declaring in his 2008 party conference speech: 'My children aren't props, they're people'?

The parties always make these webcasts available to broadcasters and they can often be useful in TV news packages, adding to their appeal.

This election will also be the first bloggers' and twitterers' election. We'll see it from MPs like Tom Watson and Tom Harris from Labour and from Tories like Nadine

Dorries, and Lib Dems like Lynne Featherstone. These blogs or Twitter feeds often provide news lines for broadcasters and newspapers, and breaking news at that. We're also likely to see prolific blogging and twittering from political journalists whose day job is writing for newspapers or TV reporting. Critics of lobby journalists who say Westminster should be opened up to bloggers forget that many lobby correspondents are bloggers and twitterers too. Fraser Nelson of the *Spectator*, Paul Waugh of London's *Evening Standard*, Benedict Brogan of the *Daily Telegraph*, George Parker of the *Financial Times* and Sam Coates of *The Times* are but a few of the regulars among print journalists. Among broadcasting bloggers, besides Sky News' own Boulton and Co., there's the BBC's Nick Robinson and – for aficionados north of the border – the 'Blether with Brian' blog, by BBC Scotland's political editor Brian Taylor.

Blogging gets an audience way beyond the internet. Many newspaper diary columns these days are stuffed full of items lifted from political blogs. The *Daily Mail*'s Ephraim Hardcastle and Hickey in the *Daily Express* are probably the worst offenders, though I suppose we should regard it as a form of compliment. And some political correspondents are truly multimedia journalists these days. At the Norwich North by-election, the *Guardian*'s Andrew Sparrow wrote day-long blogs as well as filing for the paper, earning him the tag 'increasingly indispensable' from the doyen of political bloggers, Iain Dale.

Let's not forget, too, the role of radio. I'm a big fan of radio phone-ins during election campaigns. I enjoy hearing normally sure-footed party leaders trip up when asked unexpected questions by stroppy voters, who often trap politicians better than even the most accomplished presenter. Nor should we forget – even though they're going through a tough time – the role of local newspapers in general election campaigns. During the expenses scandal, many MPs were savaged by their local paper and some incumbents will struggle to survive if local coverage of their claims for moats, silk cushions, chandeliers and fancy gardening remains unrelentingly hostile until polling day.

In the national press, the big fascination in the run-up to polling day will be the speculation about which party papers like the *Sun* and other News International titles will support. I always thought the 'It's the *Sun* wot won it' slogan after John Major defeated Neil Kinnock in 1992 was rather an exaggerated boast, but the politicians are desperate for the endorsement of Britain's biggest-selling daily tabloid. An interview with David Cameron under the headline 'I'm ready to govern' was a hint, perhaps, that the *Sun* may switch back to the Tories after backing Tony Blair at the last three general elections.

More influential than leader columns in newspapers, however, are opinion polls. 'The only poll that matters', Margaret Thatcher used to say, 'is the poll on election day.' Well, up to a point, Maggie. Opinion polls reveal which party has momentum and sharp changes in poll ratings can bring about U-turns in policy or tactics during a campaign. A dramatic opinion poll, therefore, can shape the media coverage of an election campaign. Just like a TV debate between the party leaders. If the historic breakthrough happens.

Jon Craig is the chief political correspondent for Sky News.

Things can only get beta:
will this be the first 'internet election'?

Matt McGregor

In late 2007, before the Iowa caucuses and long before Super Tuesday, Barack Obama was 20 points down in the polls, and was being written off by the pundits. But by the time he addressed a New York rally that autumn, using a powerful email list, staff and citizen bloggers, and harnessing the enthusiasm of volunteers, the junior US senator from Illinois capped a fundraising quarter to bring in $20 million. The haul amazed those same pundits – not least because it was raised in small donations from over 300,000 different people, nearly 100,000 of them new donors.

The role of the internet in that achievement, and the use of new media to build the strongest, most effective grassroots campaign in US political history, poses a question to British political parties and others seeking to influence elections. How will the internet change the way that our campaigns are fought?

Obama's online effort in 2008 is a model that everyone wants to emulate – but there are different views of what that model is and even more divergent opinions on it means for British politics. Does an 'internet election' mean that the internet will become a medium through which gaffes, rows, stunts and the other typical election fare will happen? Or is there a more fundamental shift happening, where online organising allows the parties to renew more traditional forms of voter contact and grassroots organising?

Online campaigning pops into public consciousness most readily when politicians make mistakes. George Allen's infamous YouTube moment came in 2006. Standing for re-election as a Virginia senator, Allen used a racial term to describe a campaign worker from his opponent's staff who was filming his event – and the footage became an instant YouTube sensation that helped destroy Allen's seemingly impregnable lead in the polls. Closer to home in the 2008 London mayoral race, Boris Johnson endured an evening of bad headlines after footage of him apparently accepting Labour figures on the cost of his bus plan appeared on YouTube. The ease with which campaign volunteers, members of the public and perhaps most crucially supporters of independent activist groups can now video and upload footage of candidates means that it is almost inevitable that some poor MP or candidate will find themselves at the centre of a media storm.

YouTube also offers the parties a route around the patronising ban on even well-regulated political advertising in the UK. While parties are not allowed to communicate effectively through TV or radio with voters, except through 1950s-style public information films, YouTube offers an alternative route to deliver quality video on very up-to-date issues. As in the 2008 presidential elections, parties can influence voters with quality online videos and advertising – but they can also influence the media cycle with a well-timed 'contrast' advert. The overall online advertising offering from both main parties has been poor to date, especially when it comes to video, but the party that really invests in both time and money could reap real rewards.

Blogs too will play a bigger role than ever before. The media have had a monopoly on what constitutes news and how it is reported. The politicians have learned to manage relations with the media. All this has been undermined by the opportunity for anyone with a laptop and the nous for a story to raise issues that, grudgingly, the media often follow, and which the politicians must react to. Guido Fawkes and Iain Dale are almost household names and will play a big role in the coming election. But the more research-focused blogs such as Dizzy Thinks (on the right) and Tory Troll (on the left) are the ones to watch for the future, and others will emerge.

The ease with which research and information can be disseminated direct to voters via the internet will also have an impact. Independent initiatives such as FactCheck.org in the US are starting to be mirrored here, and parties of all stripes will begin to find their assertions under increasing scrutiny. Scrutiny has taken place before – but the Clinton War Room's slogan of 'Speed Kills' matters more when information can go to 100,000 people on an email list within an hour of a gaffe taking place. Even quicker are 'real-time' applications like Twitter, which can spread news within minutes of something happening. It is perfect for sharing content through links and covering events 'live'.

Like other recent developments in the traditional media, the internet will likely shorten the news cycle, quicken the pace of the campaign and widen the number of sources reporting it. Citizen journalists and bloggers will supplement, but not supplant, the traditional media.

Party machines have long been concerned with controlling their own 'amateurs' – the activists who make up the grassroots. These are the knockers on doors, the leaflet deliverers, the people who represent the party in their own local communities. And it is at this level that the internet can really change the way elections are fought.

The awe with which Barack Obama's campaign is held because of its online success is often misdirected. Obama's background as a community organiser was what made his online campaign tick – not wizardry with new internet gimmicks. The American right has started to realise this and responded by seeking to organise its own grassroots campaigns to oppose Obama's agenda.

Political activists are engaged people. Eager and enthusiastic – more so than people in party HQs sometimes credit – they want to be engaged and put to work.

Volunteers, in their own communities and workplaces, are better advocates than the politicians can ever be. The party that better adapts to use the internet as a real organising tool will reap the rewards.

Email is the area where this is illustrated best. Supporters want to get timely, action-orientated messages from the party, not telling them what to think, but giving them an opportunity to do something concrete to help. Email is only the first step, though – putting supporters to work, as in traditional campaigning, is what will deliver concrete results. Labour's online phone bank, inspired by Obama's, is one sign of life in this area. Putting tools in the hands of local organisers to get more people going door to door more often and more easily would go a long way towards reintroducing the main parties to many local communities.

The parties will be able to utilise the social networks of their members and supporters. By providing key facts online, and the tools for supporters to spread the information, people will talk to each other, bypassing the media filter. The Ken Livingstone campaign circulated information about Boris Johnson's vote against mandatory prison sentences for possession of guns in this way – thousands of people sent tailored emails to friends, work colleagues and family members. The best advocates for a policy or idea are not politicians, but ordinary people talking to people in their own social circles.

Supporters have their own stories too, often very inspiring. Labour have recently utilised this by telling the stories of people benefiting from improved cancer care. The Conservatives have created a 'supporter wall' where their voters can explain in their own words why they're backing the Tories.

The same principle applies to facilitating people reaching out to local news outlets. Local paper letters pages can be a useful avenue for advocating a vote in the run-up to an election, and with strong online relationships, parties can encourage and facilitate members to speak out in their own words. These stories may not be as slick as the products of focus groups and spin doctors, but they have the added benefit of authenticity, which cannot be created. The Obama campaign, and campaign groups like the anti-BNP 'Hope Not Hate' campaign in the UK, have used technology to lower the barrier to people telling their stories, and have benefited from it.

The myth is that the internet 'changes everything'. But nothing here fundamentally changes the rules of the game – it just changes the way the game is played. The 'news cycle' will become even more compressed as events happen even faster. Parties will need to develop a proactive approach to giving bloggers information, and responding to inaccuracies online.

Parties and politicians are not the only potential beneficiaries of online campaigning. If anything there is even greater potential for independent campaign groups to use online tactics to influence the direction of the campaign. Groups such as the Taxpayers' Alliance on the right or trade unions on the left have access to a wide base of active supporters online. If utilised correctly, they now have the ability to inject themselves aggressively into the election campaign, and have an impact beyond their traditional roles like surveying party candidates. The current wave of demos at 'town hall' meetings in America gives us a glimpse of what could happen at hustings across the country if pressure groups can organise their supporters online to take action offline.

Previous advances in political methods have been used to help parties position themselves around the 'centre' and target swing voters in marginal seats with their message. But organising online is better suited to motivating and organising 'the base' – core supporters across the country. It also needs long-term investment in the organisational and technical infrastructure required, as well as a more open attitude. This suited the Democrats' 50 State Strategy in the US, but may yet be a step beyond the British parties.

That brings us to the other myth – that the internet can or will mean the end of traditional street politics. If anything, the opposite is true. The Obama campaign's success in building an online movement meant that they had also built a big offline movement. The bigger the email list of enthusiastic supporters, the more people will want to join in and knock on the doors of their neighbours.

Nothing can change the maxim that all politics is local. The best way to win elections is to have the best platform, messages that resonate with the electorate and people representing the party in their own local communities – speaking to people, working for them. No email, tweet or Facebook message will change a person's vote. The next election will not be won or lost online. Nonetheless, new technology will change the way the campaign is fought. In that sense, we may be about to see the first internet election. But who that benefits most remains an open question.

Matthew McGregor is the director of Blue State Digital's London office (www. bluestatedigital.com) and has worked for Jon Cruddas, Ken Livingstone and TULO, the trade union–Labour liaison organisation.

'Meet the new boss, same as the old boss': do manifestos really matter?

Greg Callus

It is a regular complaint by those with apathetic leanings that there is little point in voting because 'all the parties are just the same'. Learned tomes could be written about the death of ideology in British politics at the end of the twentieth century, and certainly it is fair to say that the next general election will not be as titanic an intellectual clash as seen in the 1970s and 1980s, but it would be fairly cynical to claim that policy no longer has any role in determining which party will take power.

In this chapter, I hope to give a brief overview of expectations of the major party manifestos, and to try and discern which policy areas will really be affected by the result of the next election, and which are unlikely to see significant change whatever the result. This obviously comes with multiple caveats – the manifestos have not yet been published, so we rely on existing policy statements from the parties at time of writing. Those policies may change, become more focused, or see a shift in prominence within the party platform between now and the election – that is perhaps inevitable, but nonetheless the general sketching of battle lines might, I hope, be somewhat useful.

Clearly there are some areas where the differences between the parties are fairly insignificant. David Cameron's first year as leader is still remembered for the emphasis placed on the new Tory commitment to environmentalism as part of the grand detoxification strategy. Labour responded by touting their green credentials from the rafters, and an area of policy usually left to the Liberal Democrats became a claimed trophy of all three main parties. Whilst there remain differences between the parties in terms of measures to take (such as eco-towns, micro-generation, or the extent of carbon reduction) the policy statements are essentially interchangeable. Similarly, differences in the field of international development are difficult to discern: all parties recognise that whilst the emphasis should be on trade reform (liberalisation with an eye to sustainability), both Labour and the Conservatives explicitly cite their plans to meet the UN target of 0.7 per cent GDP in foreign aid.

Indeed, the entire realm of foreign affairs (with the notable exception of Europe) seems to elicit little disagreement between the parties. All acknowledge the importance of Britain working within NATO and the UN, hat-tip the Special Relationship with the US, state allegiance to the importance of international law but emphasise the need for reform of international institutions. Unlike other countries, where the foreign policy is a defining feature of the character of a political party or its leader, British politics seems determined to keep its foreign policy free of ideology except when discussing the European Union.

Europe is a clear dividing line for the parties. The Liberal Democrats are unashamedly pro-European, as demonstrated by Nick Clegg's first three-line whip being to force his MPs' abstention rather than derail the ratification of the Lisbon Treaty. Labour is similarly in favour of expanding the EU, using the union to implement trade and climate change policy, and potentially joining the single currency. The Conservatives stand out as the only major party to be broadly Eurosceptic – they state that they would never take Britain into the euro, and have promised a referendum on the Lisbon Treaty if it is not ratified by all member states when they take office. If it has been ratified, they plan to attempt the repatriation of powers, especially those related to the European Social Chapter, in a fundamental renegotiation.

There are some areas where the general language of the parties is indistinguishable, but closer inspection allows nuggets of independent thought to be discovered. Communities and local government is one such area: decentralisation, power to local people, and devolution of budgetary freedoms are the ubiquitous themes, replete with the usual buzzwords about community cohesion. But there are differences of shade. Labour remains keen on regeneration, especially through regional development agencies, meaning central government investment in public spaces. The Conservatives emphasise the need for limiting quangos and allowing residents to block council tax rises to ensure efficiency. The Lib Dems' preference for local income tax is well known, but their focus on increasing social housing under the purview of local government is also significant.

The language of defence is also telling: Labour's focus is on investment, the Conservatives discuss commitment and the Military Covenant, and the Lib Dems fold in their policy with foreign affairs, climate change and a focus on disarmament. Perhaps the most stark commitment is that from the third largest party, that they will renounce full-scale renewal of Trident and begin a major reduction of Britain's nuclear arsenal. More detail from the other parties will likely emerge after the next Strategic Defence Review in early 2010.

Like defence, transport is characterised by marked differences in approach and tone, but ending up at similar positions with a single important difference. Traditionally, Conservatives have been seen as the ally of the motorist, Labour of the railways, and the Lib Dems the enemy of the airline. All this is softened to moderation, though the latter acknowledge their support for road pricing, whilst the Tories are unequivocal that Heathrow will not have its third runway and that BAA will not retain its monopoly in the South East. The talk of investment in national high-speed rail is common to the opposition parties, whereas Labour boast increases in rail capacity whilst supporting the sustainable expansion of air travel.

In years gone by, health and education were the major battlegrounds at election time, and these were not areas of policy innovation: the debate only ever centred around the public/private divide and funding levels. Labour secured three terms based on their promises to invest in public services, but both issues are now less important than at any juncture since 1997. Ipsos MORI have run a Monthly Issues Tracker for many years, and whilst health and education were top in Labour's early terms, they now rank well below crime, immigration and the economy. Other changes also mean that this debate will likely mature at the next election, not least the commitment by the Conservatives to ring-fence the National Health Service budget from cuts, and David Cameron's dismissal of Tory MPs' calls for a return to advocating grammar schools.

So although not the burning issue it has been in recent elections, the issue of public services is likely to loom large over the next election. If the Conservatives can persuade voters that the NHS is safe in their hands, it will be the ultimate proof that Cameron's 'detoxification' of the brand is complete – though some felt that project suffered for this summer's intervention by Daniel Hannan MEP, who critiqued the NHS (he supports a move to a Singapore-style system) whilst appearing on US television talking about American healthcare reform. His views were disavowed by David Cameron, after a trend on Twitter called #welovetheNHS admonished the Tory MEP.

More in spite of that episode than because of it, the Tories seem keen to talk about health and education if simply to show that they have fresh policy ideas, rather than feeling locked into support either for significant cuts or unfettered investment. For the Labour Party, investment in health and education has been the centrepiece of their twelve years in government, and there are senior Labour figures who still believe that whilst the country might be leaning towards Cameron, the notion of entrusting the NHS to the Conservatives might still be alien to the voters Labour won in the last three elections.

So what are the major parties likely to suggest is the tonic required for the National Health Service? Well, Labour holds to the line that has been so successful since 1997 – expanding schemes such as cancer screening, longer opening hours, choice of surgery and hospital, and public health (with a focus on obesity). It is a given that this will require additional money, although the long-stated Labour aim of having Britain meet the European 13 per cent average for proportion of GDP spent on healthcare (currently at 9 per cent of UK GDP) is not immediately evident.

The Conservatives will, they say, match Labour's spending plans for the NHS, even including the real terms increases in the Budget. Many of their specific proposals focus on non-fundamental reorganisation (for the purposes of decentralising power and removing ministerial responsibility for allocating budgets) or on specific bugbears: the prohibition of mixed private/NHS care, or the unavailability of cancer drugs that are commonly prescribed throughout the EU. In the speech discussing quangos, Cameron singled out NICE (the National Institute for Health and Clinical Excellence) for some criticism on this issue, and treatment choice is one of the more likely flashpoints should Healthcare become an electoral battle over the coming year.

There are also some quite radical proposals which will make for an interesting debate between the parties. The Conservatives are calling for an NHS Constitution (in common with the Liberal Democrats) enshrining the 'core values' in legislation, the creation of an independent NHS Board to oversee funding allocation between strategic health authorities and trusts, and the institution of HealthWatch, which will act as the body representing patients' interests. As well as the governance debate, there is likely to be attention given to IT capabilities in the NHS. The National Programme for IT (NPfIT) is likely to come under renewed scrutiny, although all parties acknowledge the need for improved and harmonised IT infrastructure as a means of saving money and improving services. The Conservatives have challenged Labour's means of delivering this, and are recommending that competing private sector solutions, even free open-source modules as offered by companies like Google, should be investigated as potential solutions.

Education policy elucidates some interesting differences. Both Labour and the Liberal Democrats make commitments concerning early years education, though with a focus on providing families with access to childcare – the Lib Dems would guarantee twenty hours a week of free childcare as well as aim to cut class sizes to fifteen or fewer for children aged below seven years of age. Labour's pledges are for guaranteed study/apprenticeships/training for all those under eighteen years of age, and a massive expansion in one-to-one tuition in English and maths. The continuation of academies and specialist and trust schools is promised.

The Conservative manifesto on education is perhaps their best known policy area. Adopting what is known as the Swedish Free School model, the Conservatives would support the institution of new schools within the state sector, to cater for the specific local and specialist demands of parents as part of a general decentralisation and reassignment of power to parents. They would significantly reform central government tests and encourage smaller schools, as well ensuring more teaching by ability.

In further and higher education, the Conservatives do not go so far as to match Labour on their apprenticeships pledge, but do set out how they would focus resources on NEETs (those Not in Employment, Education, or Training) through a specialist NEETs Fund. They eschew the Labour target to have 50 per cent of the population attend university, and welcome the impact that higher fees have had on university funding. They would restrict rises for part-time and mature students, but would allow universities greater autonomy from government, which presumably would include the possibility of removing the cap on tuition fees. By contrast, the Liberal Democrat 2009 spring conference renewed that party's pledge to scrap tuition fees altogether. This policy cannot be overturned by the leadership, though news reports have indicated that it may not feature (or at least not prominently) in the Lib Dem general election manifesto. The Labour Party, which first introduced tuition fees and top-up fees, has pledged to increase grants for the least well-off.

The final two areas of manifesto comparison are those which have, in the last 18 months, become the two runaway leading issues in the MORI Monthly Issues Tracker: the economy and the criminal justice system.

Criminal justice is no longer divided strictly along party lines – the days of hardline social Liberals and hang-'em-and-flog-'em Tories are no longer, but rather there is a mixture of all sentiments within each of the parties. All parties agree on the need for more police officers. Conservatives would increase stop-and-search powers and make it easier for police to use surveillance by reforming the Regulation of Investigatory Powers Act, whilst stopping abuse by councils. With the extension of the period of detention without charge for terror suspects, it is often said that Labour has become the most audibly authoritarian of the parties – perhaps partly the burden of government in a time of terror – and the opposition parties seem to want to play to the civil liberties advocates without committing to being any softer or less rigorous in treating people's main priority which is street crime. Knife-related crimes will see attention from all the parties, and whilst liberalisation of drugs is unlikely, the building of new prisons is almost certain.

The major differences that we will see from the government's programme if the Conservatives are elected will be the scrapping of the ID card and database in its entirety, the election of police commissioners and other ways of democratising law enforcement, and a re-examination of parole and early release. Many of their reforms are also part of the Liberal Democrat platform, and that party claims to favour a non-ideological debate about crime, with evidence-based criminal justice policy.

The financial crisis has recast the economic debate, and whilst the last three elections have operated as though spending were a good in itself and cuts were an intrinsic evil, both Labour and the Conservatives have retreated to ideological positions in the face of economic catastrophe. Labour's economic competence was the bedrock of its deal with the electorate, and proving that its social democratic model was affordable and supported healthy growth underpinned everything else that they have done since 1997. Capitalising on Black Wednesday, and giving independence to the Bank of England in their first week in power allowed Labour to dispel the idea that the Conservatives were the natural party of government.

Now, having weathered what we hope are the worst of the storms, Labour's economic mettle will be put to the test. The cost of bailing out the banking system, the 'quantitative easing' and recapitalisation, might have ensured that the UK financial sector avoided a complete meltdown, but it did so at great cost. The budget deficit is forecast to be around £170 billion for the next four years. Labour's renewed love of Keynes is going to produce historically staggering public debt, and it is this debt which will be at the crux of whether the Labour Keynesians or the Conservative deficit hawks sound more convincing in the eyes of the electorate.

Many of the proposals put forward by the Conservatives are tax cuts, or reductions and freezes in levies: freezing council tax for two years, a six-month temporary 1 per cent cut in national insurance, the pledges on stamp duty and inheritance tax, and a reduction in corporation tax. Without yet further deficit spending, there will inevitably be cuts across all government departments except Health and International Development. How deep these cuts go, and to what extent the public trusts that they can come from efficiencies rather than reductions in frontline services, will be the point upon which the next election will likely hinge.

It is impossible to predict what measures will and will not be in the party manifestos, but based on public policy statements to date, this concise account hopefully has framed the likely points of ideological difference (where they exist at all) and suggest what changes we might see depending on the election result. The parties might not be as ideologically far-flung as once they were, but there is still plenty of variety even in the centre ground of British politics.

Greg Callus, writing as 'Morus', is the deputy editor of PoliticalBetting.com.

Preface to the party campaigns chapters

Greg Callus

The following three chapters are the result of our wanting to extend the book in a slightly different direction. Whilst the polling and constituency information and the party manifestos are largely available to the general public (should they be sufficiently interested to find them), much of the work of a general election campaign remains behind closed doors, available only to the professional campaign managers. We wanted to give our readers a view into that world – where political strategising, message management and operational brilliance are the most prized political assets. The back rooms of national political campaigns are where the shape of the general election campaign (and results) are largely determined, and we have asked three people who are most at home in that environment to give us the benefit of their insight.

We asked James McGrath (Conservative), Mark Pack (Liberal Democrat) and Paul Richards (Labour) to take a look at their respective party's campaign: what would be its strengths and weaknesses? What should be the strategy adopted by the national campaign management, and what messages would prove most effective? What would be their advice to the campaigns (or rather, what would they do if they were in charge)? We also asked them to highlight some of the key personnel on the campaigns – the men and women of the stuffy back rooms who will wield such influence, and yet who might not be recognisable names, even to political enthusiasts.

Each of them has responded with their own insight and emphasis – we hope that this short collection of chapters sheds some light onto a world that few of us will ever get to see first hand.

Going fourth into that good night?
Labour's general election campaign

Paul Richards

A range of obstacles stands between Gordon Brown and a popular mandate to serve in No. 10. His advisers and ministers will be assessing the hostile terrain: a resurgent Conservative Party which has had significant poll leads for over a year; a cash-strapped Labour Party, with the lowest membership for decades; a record of defeats since 2007 in elections for councils, the London mayor, the European Parliament, and in by-elections in Glasgow, Norwich and Crewe; and a growing list of sitting Labour MPs walking away from their seats.

The backdrop to the election is the expenses scandal, which has ruined careers and reputations, and dragged politics into the quicksand. Hanging like black clouds over all of our heads are the recession, mass unemployment and looming public spending cuts. Even the most optimistic of Labour loyalists recognises that Labour will need to defy political gravity to win a fourth term in office. This election outcome will likely be decided by some tens of thousands of voters in a couple of dozen seats in outer London, Kent, around the coast, and in English towns, so Labour must cast aside dreams of landslide victories and flag-waving crowds, and play for a narrow win.

Two previous elections weigh heavily on the election planning at No. 10. One is Labour's landslide victory in 1945; the other is the Conservatives' surprise success in 1992.

In 1945, Churchill was ejected from office because voters felt that, although he had done a good job as a war leader, it was time for a change to something different in peacetime. The 1945 election is the best evidence that voters don't cast their votes to thank their politicians. They vote based on what parties will do for them in the future, not what they've done in the past. The anxiety in No. 10 is that whilst voters may recognise Gordon Brown's actions in stabilising the banks as having saved the economy from a much worse fate, it won't count in the polling stations. Labour can win the argument, but lose the election.

The precedent of 1992 provides a little more comfort to Labour. The country was in recession, with widespread business failures, home repossessions and economic uncertainty. The opinion polls pointed to a hung parliament, or even a narrow Labour majority. The governing party looked tired after three terms in office, and its unelected leader (who had struggled to find his feet after replacing a three-times election winner) was untested in a general election. Many commentators said that failing to call an early election in 1990 was a mistake. Waiting in the wings was an opposition party which was energised, hungry and slick. A Conservative defeat was widely predicted, by the media, pundits and politicians. But voters, especially in the south of England, felt that Labour was too much of a risk, and clung to the Conservatives for fear of something worse. The hope in No. 10 is that for all the Conservatives' repositioning and detoxification, voters will consider David Cameron too much of a risk in uncertain economic times.

Labour might not have the multi-million pound budgets of years past to fight a high-resource campaign. They will need to rely on innovation and local initiatives, especially online. Billboards are an expensive luxury, of limited use other than making politicians feel good; Labour should make a virtue of banishing them from its campaign playbook. More than ever, the quality and commitment of Labour's candidates will be decisive in a series of contests fought on local issues.

What should Labour's national campaign strategy be? It should be built on four pillars of strength, as set out below.

1. Labour is right, the others are wrong

The economy will be the dominant issue. Throughout the banking crisis, Labour has led world opinion on what to do, and has taken action which has saved the banks, and with them our pensions, savings, and national prosperity. At the G20, Gordon Brown showed global leadership on the economy. Labour will argue that the Tories made the wrong calls throughout the crisis, because they remain ideologically wedded to deregulation.

Labour will drop the 'cuts v. investment' slogan. It hasn't worked, because the electorate knows cuts must be made. They see profligacy in public expenditure and understand that cuts will come whoever wins the election. Labour needs to redraw the battle lines: it will cut wherever necessary, whilst protecting front-line services; the Tories will cut wherever possible, because they believe in a smaller state. The argument will be about not whether to cut, but what to cut, and who has the steadiest hand when wielding the scalpel.

2. This is a general election, not *The X Factor*

Labour needs to make the election a choice between competing approaches to global recession, not a referendum on the personality of Gordon Brown. The party has lost the battle over who voters would most like to go for a drink with: David Cameron has the X Factor on chat shows and phone-ins. Labour must change the terms of a debate: not a vote for who you want to be your friend, but who you trust to look after your job, business and pension. The choice should be as stark as serious/trivial, substance/spin, strong/weak.

This means a focus on Labour's practical ways to help people through the recession. It also means a relentless and merciless attack on the threat to jobs, homes and businesses posed by a Conservative win. Negative campaigning doesn't always work, but it does if it goes with the grain of what people already think and feel. In 1997, the Tories' 'New Labour, New Danger' campaign was met with derision, because it did not play to genuine fears. It made the Tories look desperate and nasty. In 1992, the Tories' 'tax bombshell' campaign chilled the blood of the floating voters who saw the billboard posters, because it resonated with their heartfelt fears about Labour's economic competence. The Tories placed a tax bombshell billboard on the Walworth Road, near Labour's HQ, and when I first saw it, my heart sank – such was its potency.

Labour must go on the attack, but in ways which chime with people's own anxieties about the Tories' record on jobs and public services, and which play to the rational fear of what the Americans would call 'changing horses mid-stream'.

3. Labour's team has strength in depth

Labour must avoid a presidential-style election, Brown versus Cameron. DVDs of *The West Wing* should be banned from No. 10. The election should be about Labour's team (steeled by experience) versus the Conservative team (untried and untested). Ministers such as Peter Mandelson, Alan Johnson, David Miliband, Andy Burnham, Tessa Jowell and Ed Miliband need to dominate the campaign, to demonstrate strength in depth and unity at the top of the government.

The Tories' campaign is built around Cameron, which only works for as long as Cameron is seen as an asset. If Cameron falters, so does the Conservatives' campaign. Much of the shadow Cabinet (for example Greg Clark, Jeremy Hunt, Owen Patterson, Andrew Mitchell, David Mundell) is composed of people who are not necessarily household names even in their own households. Tony Blair fought the 1997 election with a shadow Cabinet which included known figures such as Gordon Brown, Robin Cook, Jack Straw, Mo Mowlam, Donald Dewar, David Blunkett and John Prescott. Cameron is surrounded by lesser-known characters, and Labour should point this out. It might feed into the sense of risk, though it might also backfire if the voters want a fresh start.

4. The election is about the future, not a chance to say thanks

If Labour accepts the lessons from 1945, it needs to build a campaign based on its forward offerings, not on the long lists of achievements which characterise ministerial speeches. No-one is in the mood for expressing gratitude. Voters are making a hard-nosed assessment on 'what's in it for them' at a time when belts are tightened. Cameron's most potent argument in this election is that 'it's time for a change'. Experience around the world shows that 'time for a change' can shift people's votes, but it is not a magic formula. Labour's slogan in 1992 was also 'time for a change' but it didn't open the door to No. 10 for Neil Kinnock. The Conservatives, by replacing Margaret Thatcher with John Major, had given the electorate enough of a sense of change.

Labour needs to be the party of change in 2010. It is a hard trick to pull off after thirteen years in office, but one Major ably managed on his soap-box in 1992. This can be done with a political programme which addresses people's concerns about their services, jobs, homes, businesses, crime and anti-social behaviour. The 2010 election will be one fought on domestic issues. In a recession, with mounting unemployment, people's minds are focused on their own wallets and purses. Labour's manifesto has to be fizzing with energy and practical new ideas. It can't be lists of departmental initiatives and schemes which make little sense to the voters.

Its theme should be passing power to the people, and away from central government. Devolution of power meets the twin challenges of the times: it helps cut budgets without slashing services; and it rebuilds trust in politics by bringing decision-making down to the neighbourhood level. It can also outflank, or at least neutralise, the Tories' attempts to be the party of devolution and local control.

These four pillars – taking the right decisions on the economy, being serious not trivial, having strength in depth, and having an attractive forward offer – should be the foundations of Labour's campaign.

Labour knows it faces an uphill struggle; the challenge is hard, but it is not insurmountable.

Paul Richards is a former special adviser and Labour parliamentary candidate, and author of How to Win an Election. *He writes a weekly column for* Progress.

Great expectations:
the Conservatives' general election campaign

James McGrath

I suppose the first thing I would do is have a small but discreetly controlled panic. Centre-right parties across the world, being the proud adherents of tradition, have a remarkable history of losing unloseable elections. With the Conservatives odds-on favourites to win the next election, with clear poll leads over Brown and his cronies, the next election is ours to lose.

I am also mindful that the last thing David Cameron and Conservative Campaign Headquarters (CCHQ) need is someone offering up additional gratuitous advice.

The campaign has already started

The 2010 general election campaign started some time ago. Does it matter when the Conservative campaign started? Of course it does – you can't fatten a pig on market day and you can't win an election by starting the campaign when the Commons is dissolved.

But when? Some readers would suggest the election of David Cameron in 2005. Others may argue that it was the phoney campaign of October 2007. Wiser heads will point to the 'election' of Michael Howard in 2003. Those muttering down in the back rows may say while Michael Howard's election was significant, more important were his decisions to bring in Lynton Crosby in late 2004 and then appoint Francis Maude as chairman in May 2005.

However, my view is that the 2010 campaign commenced when Maggie Throup was selected as the candidate for Solihull in July 2005. Why? Any election campaign, whether in the Maldives or Solihull, centres on two key areas – organisation and message. I would also add a third element – hunger. The hunger for the fight, hunger to win and hunger for power. It was the selection of Maggie Throup only two months after the general election in Solihull, a seat that we should never have lost, that (to me) sent the signal 'enough is enough – we have our hunger back'.

The structure needs to be nailed down

For a campaign director the first issue concerns power, namely the director's. The most important question to be asked about any campaign, indeed any organisation, is 'Who's in charge?' Sometimes you probably don't want to know the answer – especially if it is Peter Mandelson. Sometimes you will be surprised by the answer – especially if it is Peter Mandelson.

In running the campaign, all decisions should emanate from the campaign director's desk or from people suitably empowered. A serious issue in any campaign, unless the structure is settled early (and communicated widely), is authority creep. Everyone becomes a strategist and suddenly you have swarms of mini-West Wingers walking briskly while impaling their ears upon BlackBerrys and offering gratuitous advice. We all know how annoying unsolicited gratuitous advice can be.

Before the campaign proper begins, you need to have confirmed meeting schedules with the attendees and the meeting's remit of responsibilities clearly outlined. Meetings that are well run are an important tool in maintaining control while achieving outcomes. The meetings will range from the small and strategic with the party/campaign leadership to the large and bonhomous with the entire CCHQ staff.

At the risk of coming across as some form of paper-clip Nazi, I emphasise that campaigns and politics are process driven. I raise this because one subject for the Tories remains George Osborne's continuing role as shadow Chancellor and general election campaign co-ordinator and how that ties in with Eric Pickles's role as chairman, Andy Coulson's as chief communicator, and the Ashcroft target seats operation. While everything may be working smoothly now in peacetime, this structure requires resolution during the actual formal campaign.

The message is king

After reorganising the roles and reporting structures I would find known message offenders and remove their phones and BlackBerrys while locking them in a darkened room under Millbank Tower. I would then double-lock the room. To be really safe I would then melt the keys. We cannot afford habitual shadow ministerial message recalcitrants to be allowed anywhere near the media – otherwise our message is destroyed. Think of Howard Flight's efforts during the 2005 campaign or Oliver Letwin's contribution to the 2001 campaign.

This is a serious point – the message is king. The Tories need a small team of shadow ministers to act as the 'rent-a-quotes' with the message discipline tenacity of Daleks to inhabit the rolling news channels. Key media performers like Grant Shapps, Chris Grayling, Sayeeda Warsi and Michael Gove would be key sales staff for our message. But the message has to be based on something other than George Osborne's finely tuned political nose. And that is where Lord Ashcroft's polling operations come into their own and their research must lie behind all our messaging.

It must not only be key MPs who push the message; every staffer and every campaign volunteer must be briefed on the message and the message hammered into them. Too many campaigns keep the research secret without diluting the narrative to the campaign.

I would use as many channels of communication as possible, although I remain sceptical about the use of billboards. If I had a choice between spending money on a billboard or a direct mail piece, I would choose the latter every time. The 2005 election barely saw the internet used by parties as a campaign tool so 2010 will be the first real internet campaign. While the UK's Victorian-era restrictions limit TV and radio usage, the internet is wide open for the Tories to continue their domination.

The strategy is clear – Labour

The strategy is quite clear and is on two political fronts, Labour and Liberal Democrat. Against Labour, we must compress their vote by crowning Gordon Brown and every Labour MP with a crown of thorns reflecting the poor state of public finances and the economy.

One thing the Tories need to prepare for are Labour's dirty tricks. Labour will fight dirty and will use every stunt possible from the Peter Mandelson textbook.

The strategy is clear – Liberal Democrat

For our friends in the Liberal Democrats, we must continue the 'love bombing' with the aim to sideline them as irrelevant and unable to win. Liberal Democrat voters must feel angry about Labour, doubtful about their party's competence and reassured the Conservatives will make changes. George Osborne's speech back in August to Demos about the progressive Conservatives is part of this continual outreach to certain sections of the Liberal Democrat vote.

At the same time the Conservative campaign must encourage our core vote (the 33 per cent who stuck by us through the bad days) and our new vote (anywhere between 5 per cent and 12 per cent) to come out and support their local Tory PPC. This means we must continuously push our message of holding Labour to account while clearly and constantly demonstrating

1. that we know there is a serious crisis facing Britain;
2. that we have a serious plan for the problem;
3. that we will have to make tough and unpopular decisions.

The machine is working – Getting out the Vote (GOTV)

The Conservative Party machine, when it works, is a frighteningly productive vote-grabbing and election-winning device. It is the machine that has shown in the Boris campaign and numerous by-elections since that it is focused on targeting resources to maximise GOTV.

This has come about because the machine has slowly been rebuilt. The appointment of Lynton Crosby reminded the Conservatives of the importance of well-trained professional staff. Equally important, the target seat operation under the direction of Stephen Gilbert and Lord Ashcroft – where all target seats are ruthlessly assessed and candidates expected to reach key performance criteria to maintain eligibility for support – is an outfit that keeps Labour MPs awake at night.

Winning the war and winning the peace

The Tories must not only win the war, they must win the peace. There are four points to be made on us winning the peace:

1. We cannot take the election for granted and assume that we will win. We must fight for every last vote.
2. We must be ready to govern. We must not only have a manifesto ready for implementation but a communications plan for the manifesto.
3. We must govern well.
4. We cannot let the campaign machine or the party organisation rest or slow down after the election.

And should the voters trust us with their future, it will not be a time for celebration or chinking of glasses. There will be no space for rock bands nor crowds cheering with flittering Union Flags; in troubled times, the Tories will win with sobriety and empathy. They will have to make tough decisions. They will govern for all of us instead of playing Labour's sectarian parlour games. And the victory should echo this mood.

David Cameron should pause at the entrance to No. 10 and reflect on the challenge while giving thanks. The next image should be of the Cameron Economic War Cabinet meeting to action the mandate, and then the changes will start. The next election campaign will have begun...

Key backroom people

Other publications have covered the usual suspects behind the campaign and Team Cameron but all have missed one key member of the Cameron decision-making matrix: Samantha, his wife. While not a formal campaigner nor a politico, of all the people behind the scenes, Samantha is the most influential.

When you look at the key people behind the Conservative campaign machine it is reassuring that many have been involved with the party for some time. While there are numerous new and fresh (and experienced) faces in the media and research departments in CCHQ, in the campaign team you see more old hands – Conservative Party true believers who stayed or joined when we were at the nadir of opposition, and that is a good thing. A true strength.

Lord Ashcroft is one of the heroes of the Conservative Party. Ever wonder why Labour target him so much? It is because he is such a threat, but that comes not from his money, rather from his understanding of what drives a campaign and his ability to surround himself with the best staff. He also has a healthy disrespect for authority.

Speaking of staff, Stephen Gilbert, Lord Ashcroft's chief of staff, in reality should be the campaign director. Experienced. Tough. Respected. Good at managing some of the crazier ideas coming from other areas within CCHQ. Working with him at CCHQ are Gavin Barwell, Stephen Phillips and Stephen Parkinson, who are helping with the campaign staff out in the field. The target seats are clustered into 'battlegrounds', and each one has a battleground director delivering and overseeing the campaign – working around the country with local candidates, agents and campaign directors. The battleground directors are the most important campaign staff but are folks you rarely hear about, names such as Chris Scott, Stuart Hands, Robert Ashman, Mike Dolley, Hayward Burt, Darren Mott and Marion Little. They are the 'unsung heroes'.

Fighting the campaign through digital communications are Rishi Saha, Craig Elder and Samuel Coates. Sam has experience and temperament beyond his relative youth. Backed up by Anne Nunan, who built and held together conservatives.com, along with Rishi, the Conservative internet operations are streets ahead of the other political parties.

Liz Sugg directs the tours and events. And that is a hell of a job. Liz and her scarily efficient team are responsible for ensuring that every David Cameron and campaign event runs smoothly.

I will end with the chairman, Eric Pickles, a wily operator with a superb understanding of the absurd. He is one of the few shadow Cabinet members to have serious organisational and campaign experience.

There is an old saying that 'failure is an orphan while success has many parents' and should the Conservative Party win the next election, it's not just those named above but the hundreds of former (think David Canzini) and current staff (think Richard Murphy or Diane Clarke) and thousands of volunteers who can claim credit.

James McGrath is an Australian political strategist who has worked on elections ranging from Boris Johnson's London mayoral race to the presidential election in the Maldives.

Follow the yellow brick road?
The Liberal Democrats' general election campaign

Mark Pack

The 1997 general election turned out to be a once-in-a-generation opportunity for many local Liberal Democrat campaign teams to gain a parliamentary seat from the Conservatives. At the tail end of a by then deeply unpopular Conservative government, the election saw unprecedented numbers of seats falling to the party. A few seats that were not quite gained from the Conservatives in 1997 did subsequently fall in 2001 and 2005, but it was the 1997 election with the Conservatives in government that was the main opportunity. Nearly every campaign that missed then did not subsequently win.

The next general election looks most likely to present the Liberal Democrats with a similar opportunity for seats to be gained from the party in government, this time Labour. The crucial difference, however, is the battle between the Liberal Democrats and the main opposition party. In 1997, with Tony Blair's Labour Party in opposition, there were very few Liberal Democrat MPs who had to hold onto their seat against a major challenge from the opposition party. Next time, with David Cameron's Conservative Party as the opposition, there are many Liberal Democrat MPs who will have to hold their seats against a Conservative challenge. Whilst 1997 was therefore mainly a contest for the Liberal Democrats against one other major party, the next general election will be a contest against two.

That is the double-pronged challenge facing the Liberal Democrats – gaining large numbers of seats from Labour whilst making small progress or holding their own against the Conservatives. (In Scotland and Wales there are few seats where there is a direct Liberal Democrat–nationalist battle, though the SNP's ability to take votes off Labour may actually assist the Liberal Democrats in making gains.)

But it is not only individual local campaign teams who face a make-or-break opportunity. So does Nick Clegg. For the leader of the third party, his first general election offers the prospect of enhancing or ruining his reputation on the national stage. Both media habits and media regulations see the third party leader given significantly more coverage in a general election campaign than at other times. For most of the public, it is the first time they really get a chance to form deeply rooted views of the person. Paddy Ashdown and Charles Kennedy both prospered in this limelight. Ming Campbell never got the chance to find out, and now Clegg has the opportunity ahead of him.

There are some promising signs that Clegg will make good use of this opportunity. Off the back of the recession and MPs' expenses scandal, he has steadily improved his personal standings with the electorate, and indeed for three consecutive months prior to the writing of this piece had higher net ratings with MORI than Cameron. Moreover, he communicates best when he is in conversation rather than soundbite mode. Being on TV or radio and being able to talk (and be reported) at length plays to his strengths, and a general election campaign will give him many more opportunities to do both. It will not just be a case of more coverage but coverage which suits his natural communication style.

The campaign will be unusual in that the party will have two major national figures, with Vince Cable being as well known amongst the public as Nick Clegg. Moreover, the popularity and high level of tabloid newspaper coverage garnered by Norman Baker, combined with continuing affection for both Charles Kennedy and Paddy Ashdown, mean the party will not be short of figures with national media profiles and popular support. The challenge will be as much about presenting Clegg as about working out how to turn a team of popular individuals into votes for the party.

Even turning the popularity of one person into votes has always been tricky for the Liberal Democrats, with detailed academic analysis of the link between the popularity of the party's leaders and the its poll ratings only showing a very weak correlation. Having a handful of such figures is a different – but very welcome – communications challenge for the party to crack.

Of course, popular senior figures and the party more generally also need to have a message and policies to underpin it. There was widespread agreement in the party that its 2005 manifesto was rather like a collection of nice ingredients but without a recipe. The individual policies were popular ones, but they did not add up to an overall compelling story and so the party's message was rather less than the sum of its parts.

The leadership contest between Nick Clegg and Chris Huhne featured at times acerbic exchanges on policy, but in the end the differences did not amount to very much. Moreover, whilst the period of settling in for a new party leader often makes their approach to policy clearer, in Clegg's case the rapidly changing economic situation has made much of the discussions of only a couple of years ago already feel like they were from a different world.

On individual issues, such as the rights of Gurkhas and the future of Trident, Clegg has carved out some distinctive stances but these do not add up to a clear overall theme on their own. This search for an effective theme is made harder by David Cameron's revitalisation of the Conservatives and his clear intention to present his party – despite its name – as being the choice for people who want change.

So far, the Liberal Democrat response has been to offer a different, better, more radical version of change, as shown in the titles of various major policy initiatives in 2008 and 2009: 'Make it happen', 'Take back power' and 'A fresh start for Britain', to name but three. That theme which pays more attention to the environment, changes the political system substantially, and gives more power to individuals is likely to be played out repeatedly during Nick Clegg's first general election as leader – with the added thread of Vince Cable's economic credibility.

It will not just be with a new leader that the Liberal Democrats approach the next general election. It will also be the first since 1992 in which Chris Rennard, in one post or another, is not the key person in the party's campaigning. The campaign will be heavily reliant on his successful work to improve the party's organisation and finances from their previous precarious position – and also on the extensive work that took place to prepare the party for a general election as early as 2007 (an election after which Rennard was planning to retire). Part of that progress has been avoiding a repeat of the various one-off financial debacles that occurred earlier – the sort of work which does not attract much attention but brings significant benefits.

The team running the next general election campaign is heavily based on the key staff appointments and structural changes that Rennard made. It comprises individuals who have myriad sorts of experience but will be new to some of the challenges of organising a national campaign whilst also successfully marshalling scores of target constituencies and their individual campaigns.

It will be Hilary Stephenson's first general election as director of campaigns. She has an impressive track record in her patch in the north, where she both was a key member of the winning team in Hazel Grove and then had wider responsibilities as one of the deputy directors. As one former colleague puts it, 'Success has a habit of following her around.'

In as interim chief executive is Chris Fox, another person with a long track-record of party involvement but new to the role. In addition to his experience as a Liberal Democrat parliamentary candidate in 1997 (for Windsor) and a very successful career in PR and communications, he has also in the past been involved with a ginger group (Liberal Future) that was seen as being on the right of the party and at times quite hostile to party activists. Since becoming director of policy and communications, he has impressed many with his decisive action and the extra edge he has added to the party's media work. The election campaign will be his chance to prove those doubters wrong.

Playing another key role in the general election campaign will be John Sharkey – former chief executive of Saatchi and Saatchi and one of the advisers closest to Nick Clegg. Sharkey, unusually, has detailed experience of working on a general election campaign – but for the Conservatives, as he was a senior figure at Saatchis in 1987. He also played a significant role behind the scenes in helping the Liberal Democrat 1997 general election campaign, advising on advertising and election broadcasts.

Meanwhile, in the target seats the Liberal Democrats will have two main organisational challenges. First, the party will be fighting to win in double the number of seats it fought a decade ago. That is a massive (and largely unheralded) step forward – and will stretch the party's money and volunteers thin. Second, in many of those seats the party will be trying to run a winning campaign with a much weaker local campaign organisation than was traditionally seen as necessary. It is a cliché with much truth that northern seats being fought against Labour have a less wealthy electorate less interested in joining and helping organisations than those seats previously won from the Conservatives in southern England.

The party's 'textbook' campaign plans have steadily evolved to reflect these new challenges – and the changing tactics of other parties. With a greater emphasis on casework, the internet, canvassing, direct mail and the smart use of data, the target seat campaigns put to the test at the next election will be different in many important respects from those of 1997.

The next election will also put to the test the party's approach to getting better gender and ethnic balance amongst its MPs. That approach has been two-fold: individual encouragement and mentoring alongside giving extra help to campaigns with a female or ethnic minority candidate that show a spark of potential.

In 2001 and 2005 half the gains made by Liberal Democrat candidates were in seats with women candidates – and this was not a coincidence. The party has also had a high proportion of female candidates in winnable or possibly winnable by-elections. But overall these efforts only increased the proportion of women Lib Dem MPs from 6 per cent to 16 per cent between 1997 and 2005, with a major limiting factor on that growth being the pattern of retiring male MPs being succeeded by male candidates. The signs for 2010 are more promising, with at least three retiring male Liberal Democrat MPs being replaced by female candidates.

The party is yet to win a seat in a general election with a black or minority ethnic candidate after Parmjit Singh Gill's failure to retain Leicester South, won in a 2004 by-election. There are some prospects of rectifying this at the next general election, though the party is less confident of success in this area than improving the gender balance in Parliament.

The party therefore faces challenges and opportunities on a range of fronts. Whilst many commentators have taken it as a nearly foregone conclusion that 2005 was the Liberal Democrats' high-water mark, there are many in the party who remember similar comments after 1997 – which were wrong. Given the huge variations from the national average which are often seen in seats that host an intensive Liberal Democrat campaign, who is right may well not be clear until all the votes are counted. My own prediction? That's between me and the bookmakers!

Mark Pack, formerly the Liberal Democrats' director of innovation, is now an associate director at Mandate Communications.

Outside the mainstream:
where might the major parties be beaten?

Greg Callus

The big political story of 2009 has been the revelation of the misuse of expenses and allowances by Members of Parliament. The serialisation of the unredacted claims in the *Daily Telegraph* has caused mandatory deselections, encouraged premature retirements, and cast a shadow over the work of many otherwise well-thought-of public servants.

One particularly striking feature of the scandal was the extent to which minor parties benefited in the opinion polls. Combined support for the three main parties fell as low as 70 per cent in Westminster voting intention polls (ComRes, 31 May 2009), suggesting that minor parties were garnering support simply for being outside mainstream politics and therefore less guilty in the court of public opinion.

But if collectively reaching 30 per cent in opinion polls was a good result, few could have predicted that differential turnout in the 2009 European elections (whereby supporters of the major parties simply abstained) could have not only seen the 'Others' reach the heady heights of 42.9 per cent (of which only 2.9 per cent was the Scottish and Welsh nationalist parties). The tumultuous impact of 'Expensesgate', combined with a botched Cabinet reshuffle which fell apart before polling day, meant that UKIP managed to come second only to the Conservatives in the popular vote, and drew level with the Labour Party with thirteen MEPs elected. Where the Labour vote collapsed particularly badly, the BNP prospered, allowing the party to win seats in both the North West and Yorkshire & Humberside regions. But perhaps the most surprising result of the weekend came in the local elections held on the same day: in Doncaster, Labour lost the mayoralty of the city to a member of the English Democrats.

The European elections, of course, are distinguished by being the only UK-wide elections which use a version of proportional representation (PR), with seats allocated using the D'Hondt method. This allows minor parties to win seats much more easily, because the greatest impediment non-mainstream parties face in attracting voters is persuading them that they are not a wasted vote, and there are no wasted votes under pure PR. It would be foolish to assume that the gains made by parties such as UKIP or the Green Party could be remotely mirrored by similar successes at a general election to the Westminster Parliament. The 'first past the post' (FPTP) system used for Westminster constituencies rarely allows the election of MPs from outside the three major parties in England, and the crowded political scene in Wales, Scotland and Northern Ireland has never been fertile ground for minor party support.

This chapter will try to discern where the minor parties stand the best chance of staging a breakthrough and winning a seat at Westminster. This is not a prediction of success – the likelihood is that there will be no new MPs from outside of the Big Five in Great Britain (Labour, Conservative, Lib Dem, SNP, Plaid Cymru) – however, there are hotspots of localised support for minor parties, and looking at where they should be focusing their efforts will, I hope, be insightful. For the purposes of brevity, we will include within this chapter UKIP, the Green Party, the BNP and the English Democrats as well as the prospective fortunes of Independent candidates.

UKIP are easily the best-performing 'minor' party in the UK, based on the number of candidates they manage to field, the money they spend on campaigns, and their success in garnering vote share from the larger parties. In beating Labour in the European elections, they benefited from the focus on Britain's membership of the EU, the ill feeling over the refusal of the government to hold a referendum on the Lisbon Treaty, and (ironically, some felt) the fallout of the expenses scandal.

UKIP's strongest performances, at a regional level, were in the South West, the South East , the East of England, and the West Midlands – in each of those regions it won enough vote share to get two MEPs. However, the party enjoyed localised support in other regions that allowed it to come first or second in several local authorities which overlap considerably with Parliamentary constituencies.

But UKIP have never enjoyed similar success in FPTP elections. Its vote share at UK general elections has increased steadily since its inception (0.3 per cent in 1997, 1.5 per cent in 2001, 2.2 per cent in 2005) but it has yet to win a Westminster constituency, and its only parliamentary representation has come through the defection of existing members (Lords Pearson and Willoughby de Broke are members, and the Parliament website temporarily referred to Bob Spink, MP for Castle Point, as having defected to UKIP from the Conservatives before he realigned as an Independent). The party has a handful of councillors, but neither controls nor is the main opposition in any local authority (a arguable exception being Staffordshire County Council, which has 49 Conservatives, 4 Lib Dems, 4 UKIP, 3 Labour and 2 Independents). Its best results in constituencies at the 2005 general election were to finish third on 9.5 per cent in Boston & Skegness, and fourth on 10.4 per cent in South Staffordshire.

Looking at the European election results by local authority (and in some cases at a ward level) we can build up a picture of the localised support that UKIP enjoy. As expected, there are a number of local authorities where UKIP were actually the 'winner' of the popular vote. Where there is significant overlap between the local authority boundaries and a parliamentary constituency, it would suggest that UKIP have at least some chance of winning a FPTP election in that area.

The South West region is the most fruitful area for UKIP, where 2009 saw them 'win' North Devon, Plymouth City, Torbay and Torridge, as well as coming a very close second to the Conservatives in places such as Weymouth & Portland. However, in none of these constituencies at the 2005 election did UKIP come better than fourth place. In the West Midlands region, UKIP came first in Dudley, Newcastle-under-Lyme and Stoke-on-Trent, but in all but Newcastle-under-Lyme the 2005 general election saw UKIP manage only fifth place behind the three major parties and the BNP.

The other area in which perhaps UKIP have rather more potential to win a seat at Westminster is in the north-east of England (the North East region, the East Riding of Yorkshire and the north of the East Midlands region). In the 2009 European elections, UKIP came second in North Lincolnshire, North East Lincolnshire and the East Riding of Yorkshire. But their best results were in areas in which Labour, rather than the Conservatives, have been traditionally strong. UKIP came first in the popular vote in both Hartlepool and Kingston upon Hull. They had managed a weak fourth in the Hartlepool constituency in 2005, and did not even compete the three Hull seats at the last general election. Where popular wisdom holds that UKIP are disgruntled Eurosceptic former Tories, they actually take a significant number of votes from Old Labour voters in some areas, and where the Conservatives are not a realistic force (as in Hull), UKIP flourish more than could be expected when the Labour vote collapses.

The Green Party will also be hoping to put up a significant challenge to the major parties at the next election – disaffected voters of the left have been known to be split between the Greens and the Liberal Democrats before now, but the rise in popular support for the ecologically minded minor party indicated to some that not only were the Lib Dems being tarred with the expenses scandal brush, but also that Nick Clegg's party was so large in Parliament as to no longer represent rebellion against the mainstream.

The Greens have seen a resurgence in popular vote in recent years. In the 2004 European elections they won 6.1 per cent of the vote, which rose to 8.7 per cent in 2009, though still only giving the party two MEPs under the reapportionment. Whilst the party has two members of the London Assembly, and is the largest party on several councils, it no longer has any representatives in Parliament, since the death of Lord Beaumont of Whitley in April 2008.

Using the same methods as for UKIP, we can see the Westminster seats where the Greens could pose a challenge based on the local authorities where they came first in the 2009 European elections, places where they have a significant presence in local government, and their best performances at the 2005 general election. Though Leeds West and four seats in London saw vote share above 7 per cent in 2005, there are three cities where it is almost unanimously agreed that the Green Party stands its greatest chance of winning a seat under FPTP: Oxford, Norwich and Brighton & Hove.

Of the 125 Green councillors currently in office, 13 are from Norwich City Council (with another 19 from the East of England region), 13 from Brighton &

Hove Council, 9 from Oxford and Oxfordshire councils, 13 from London councils, and another 13 from Lancaster and Lancashire councils. Brighton, Pavilion saw the Greens win a record 21.9 per cent at the 2005 general election, with a respectable 7 per cent reached in Brighton, Kemptown. Norwich South, a constituency covered by a council on which the Greens are now the main opposition, only saw them take 7.4 per cent in 2005, and they will be hoping to improve upon that performance at the next election.

At the 2009 European elections, the Greens won Brighton & Hove (31.4 per cent), Norwich (24.9 per cent), and Oxford (26.1 per cent) – even allowing for lower turnout, that is a significant number of people in those cities who have demonstrated that they are prepared to vote for the party. They are fielding strong candidates in each of their target seats: party leader Caroline Lucas will fancy her chances in Brighton, Pavilion, especially since the withdrawal of the Conservative candidate, TV doctor David Bull, from that contest. Veteran campaigner Peter Tatchell is contesting Oxford East for the party, whilst author Chris Goodall contests Oxford West & Abingdon. Labour's Charles Clarke MP will face a tough fight in Norwich South from the Green's youthful deputy leader, Cllr Adrian Ramsay.

However, there is an element whereby the Greens might fail to reach expectations in the FPTP format. By-elections often provide the perfect chance for smaller parties to break into the House of Commons, and the 2009 Norwich North by-election was the ideal opportunity (coming so soon after the European elections) for the Greens to prove that localised campaigning could win them the seat vacated by Dr Ian Gibson. The party had a strong local candidate in Cllr Rupert Read, who had only just lost out on winning a seat in the European Parliament in June. Labour's vote was clearly collapsing and their campaign cursed (the Labour candidate, Chris Ostrowski, actually missed the count as he was in hospital with swine flu), and the stars seemed aligned. But in spite of these factors, the Greens only won 9.74 per cent (up from 2.7 per cent in 2005), coming fifth behind the Liberal Democrats.

The big impediment to the Greens making more ground in this by-election seems to have been largely financial. The party in the Eastern region put out an article on their website indicating that they had spent only £12,000 on the by-election versus an estimated £100,000 spent by the Conservative campaign that proved victorious by a considerable margin. Fundraising is not easy even for larger parties, who can provide access to frontbench politicians and the trappings of power. Raising money for parties who stand such a slim chance of electoral success is comparatively impossible, and this impediment seems to be what will stop the majority of minor parties from managing to win a seat at Westminster in 2010. Even UKIP, who spent an estimated seven-figure sum on their European campaign in 2009, will struggle to be effective standing in more than a handful of seats when facing party machines capable of outspending them ten to one.

Of course, some seats don't require much money to tip the balance, and there is little doubt that willing volunteers for canvassing and campaigning are worth more than you would ever be prohibited from paying them under electoral law. As was evident during the 2008 London mayoral race, parties such as the BNP and the Christian People's Alliance did not have large advertising budgets, but the sheer numbers of activists on the ground allowed them to take fifth and sixth place respectively, with Richard Barnbrook becoming the BNP's sole representative on the London Assembly.

The BNP has never performed well at general elections – its 119 candidates in 2005 won 0.7 per cent of the national vote share, although this was more than three times its vote share in 2001. The party has just over fifty councillors across the UK, with the major breakthroughs coming in 2006. The party's success has centred around former Labour strongholds – Barking & Dagenham in London, areas such as the Black Country in the West Midlands, Oldham and Burnley in the North West, and sporadic parts of Yorkshire.

Somewhat surprisingly, although the party managed to elect two Members of the European Parliament in June 2009, off a national vote share of 6.2 per cent (up from 4.9 in 2004), the number of votes cast rose by only around 150,000 and the party did not win any local authority outright, unlike UKIP and the Greens. Their best results were in Barking & Dagenham (second with 19.4 per cent) and Stoke-on-Trent and Thurrock (in both cases coming fourth with about 17.5 per cent). Comparing these results to the constituencies at the 2005 general election, there is a mixed picture. The BNP was stymied in the 2009 local elections in Burnley by the Lib Dems, but they increased their vote share in a seat where they won over 10 per cent in 2005. Conversely, Dewsbury was their second best seat at the last general election, where they managed 13.1 per cent – the seat falls in Kirklees Council, where the BNP managed only 11.4 per cent at the recent European elections.

Certainly, Barking & Dagenham remains the best bet for the British National Party to win representation at Westminster, but in a sign of confidence that has expanded to places such as Rotherham and Dudley, the party's leader, Nick Griffin MEP, will be standing in the Thurrock constituency, where Andrew MacKinlay MP (Lab) has recently announced his retirement. The BNP will almost certainly not win a seat at the general election – if not least for higher turnout and tactical voting by mainstream party members to keep them out. If the BNP can reach the heady heights of more than 20 per cent of constituency vote share in Barking, they should consider that a success.

Beyond UKIP, the Greens and the BNP, the only seats in Great Britain that will not be won by the Big Five are likely to be where the MP is incumbent. Bob Spink (Castle Point) and Bob Wareing (Liverpool, West Derby) will both, we believe, be running as Independents against new candidates selected by their parties (Conservatives and Labour respectively). Dr Richard Taylor is believed to be standing for what would be an historic third term as the Independent MP for Wyre Forest (under the rubric 'Independent Kidderminster Hospital and Health Concern'). Similarly, Dai Davies will be standing again as an Independent (under the banner 'People's Voice') in Blaenau Gwent, in the seat that as an agent he had helped win for the Independent Peter Law, who died in 2006 (the first time an Independent had followed another Independent MP in a seat since the 1920s in The Wrekin).

George Galloway, former Labour MP, and now party leader of the far-left Respect, is not running again in Bethnal Green & Bow, the seat he took from Labour's Oona King in 2005. He has decided to focus on the new seat called Poplar & Limehouse (against Labour MP Jim Fitzpatrick), which is based on the old Poplar & Canning Town with some wards from Bethnal Green & Bow. To hold one seat would be a wonderful result for Respect – to increase to two seats would be nothing short of remarkable.

There is no shortage of other political parties who might have merited a mention in this chapter, but for reasons of space: the new Pirate Party, the Christian People's Alliance, various socialist parties and so on. The one party that might manage more of a breakthrough than expected is the English Democrats in Doncaster. The previous mayor of Doncaster was Independent Martin Winter – he was replaced in 2009, not by another Independent (Michael Thomas Maye), who came second, but rather by Peter Davies, the candidate for the English Democrats. Mayoral challenges can provide a good basis for the many Independent mayors and councillors to make the challenge for Westminster. There are around 2,100 Independent councillors across the UK (about 10 per cent of the total number), and they are the largest grouping in the Local Government Association (LGA) in Wales. The mayor of Mansfield, Tony Egginton, won re-election having beaten the sitting Labour MP to take office. It would be interesting to see whether a well-liked local mayor could make the transition to Westminster elections with a swing result larger than might be otherwise expected.

The prospects for Independents are rarely good elsewhere – Kitty Ussher in Burnley faced a stiff challenge from Independents in 2005, but in no other seats did the Independent make the top three places in any constituency on the British mainland. Ironically, one of the few places where an Independent candidate might flourish is in one of the formerly safest seats in the country: Buckingham. The incumbent, John Bercow MP, enjoyed one of the largest Conservative majorities in recent times, but was elected Speaker of the House of Commons on 22 June 2009.

Bercow has the unenviable task of defending his seat as Speaker. Under normal circumstances this would be unproblematic, as major parties traditionally do not run against the Speaker, yet in a perverse way, he may be more vulnerable to a minor party/Independent challenge than ever. As well as the issue of a clear run for an Independent (without main parties taking vote share), there are also the questions of the Speaker's expenses and ongoing transparency, and the fact that the lie of the land has changed. In elections past, Bercow would have been able to take significant money from his Conservative Constituency Association in Buckingham, but now he is officially non-partisan, this is now an unlikely solution. The other problem for Bercow is that Buckingham voters seem more than content to vote for the Conservatives' nominated candidate – however, his election highlighted the general dislike that CCHQ and Conservative MPs often have for the new Speaker. Might the seat be a little more unpredictable now that Conservative voters know that John Bercow is not one of them at all? A strong Independent, or rather 'Condependent', suggests itself – and a decent candidate who has a handle on media politics could make it happen.

Independents and minor parties flourish where the opposition in that seat is far too weak to challenge, and yet for specific reasons the dominant party is unlikely to offer the same support again. The classic example is the rebellion of Labour voters in Blaenau Gwent over the party's insistence on all-women shortlists. The seat was as deep red as they come, with no meaningful opposition, yet an Independent who sounded very much like the perfect candidate for that political geography was able to snatch victory. And as Martin Bell's famous 1997 victory over Tory Neil Hamilton in Tatton showed, it is almost impossible for Independents to win unless other opposition parties step aside. Esther Rantzen has said she will contest a seat in Luton as an Independent, although the MP she was targeting (Margaret Moran) has decided to retire anyway.

None of the minor parties or Independent candidates are likely to win representation in the House of Commons next time around, but there are certain areas where it will be worth looking out for results of parties like the Greens or the BNP. I hope this chapter has given an overview of the targets of these smaller parties, and why those targets have been chosen.

Minor parties and Independents will always struggle with a lack of funds, a lack of manpower, or a lack of political influence. All gains and losses take time, and if the tribalist politics of smaller groupings has been anything to go by, without a move towards a system of PR, it seems implausible that minor parties and Independents will manage to break through at the next general election.

Greg Callus, writing as 'Morus', is the deputy editor of PoliticalBetting.com.

The bookies' favourites:
what the betting markets say

Robin Hutchison

It was the morning of 10 October 1963 and with an hour to go until racing all was quiet in the Betting Room at Ganton House, a horseshoe's throw from London's Carnaby Street. Well-thumbed copies of the *Sporting Life* and the *Greyhound Express* sat among the ashtrays as the Ladbrokes traders weighed up another afternoon of profit and loss.

The spell was broken by news that Conservative Prime Minister Harold Macmillan had told his party conference that he was stepping down owing to ill health. Surprise was swiftly followed by speculation as to who might succeed him.

Never one to turn down an opportunity, Ladbrokes' managing director, Cyril Stein, agreed with his eager young PR man Ron Pollard that the firm should open a book on the contest. Ron duly made Rab Butler the odds-on favourite at 4/6, quoted Lord Hailsham at 7/4 and Reggie Maudling at 6/1, and dismissed Sir Alec Douglas-Home as the 16/1 rank outsider. As Macmillan's Blackpool sickbed became the centre of the vortex, the firm took £16,000 on his replacement in the first forty-eight hours alone.

Within days Butler was drifting like a barge in the betting as Douglas-Home made a late surge up the rails. By the morning of 18 October the tortoise had beaten the hares.

The ink was yet to dry on the evening papers when the first requests for a book on the general election began to arrive, including a bet of £700 to win £400 on Labour from one wealthy supporter. In the next year more than 10,000 wagers flooded in. Some were for amounts as small as five shillings whilst one struck by the hotelier Maxwell Joseph came in at a cool £50,000, at the time the record single bet taken by a British bookie.

By polling day, 15 October 1964, Ladbrokes had taken £603,000. A Conservative victory would have cost the firm £1.5 million and all but bankrupted them in the process, but the Tories failed to hold on, with Labour winning a majority of just four seats. Refuge was taken in the words of a Conservative, Stanley Baldwin, who once said you should never complain and never explain.

Well, a whole media industry has grown up around the first of those, with newspapers and readers alike delighting in the bookies' every squeak and squeal. But, as the two examples of the industry's early forays into politics may suggest, there isn't always a great deal of science behind proceedings. Pollsters may be the all-knowing sages at election time, but our job has never been to correctly guess the winner. We make our money out of others trying to do so, and rest assured we'll be attempting that again as we gallop headlong towards the latest round of ballot box-borne soul-searching.

On the surface things look a lot less exciting than they did back in 1964. There is much more a sense of the inevitable than back then, as there was in 1997, when 'things could only get better'. All the data and the gulf in the odds between the Big Two parties would suggest that David Cameron and his supporters will win with several furlongs to spare.

Yet there is much more to betting on a general election than which party will be first past the post. Much, for instance, is assumed but little is actually known as to how the expenses scandal will play out. Ladbrokes already have well over a hundred of the more closely contested constituencies priced up, and more than one incumbent MP is looking nervously over his or her shoulder.

Much of the shrewd money has already been laid down in the areas where the more venal are expecting to be tipped into their moats. But our odds compilers are deliberately short about many of their challengers, independent or otherwise, in a strategic bid to staunch the flow. They are also on the skinny side about many of those taking on sitting Labour MPs in areas in which the blue tide is expected to wash over. It would only take a small swing back to Gordon Brown – or indeed a new Labour leader – to ensure they stayed red for another four years. And there is much to be said for the school of thought that argues that not all of those hard-working Liberal Democrat MPs will succumb to that same tide in the marginals of southern and south-western England.

If it's the bigger picture that floats your boat rather than the individual constituencies then you could always have a bet on the number of seats (various ranges offered) each party will win. At the time of writing we were unable to decide between 175–199 and 200–224 for Labour and made these options joint 3/1 favourites. The 350–374 range was the 10/3 favourite for the Tories, with 50–59 at 11/4 for the Lib Dems and 16–20 at 15/8 for the SNP.

You can also bet on the chances of the fringe parties winning a seat (including the Tories in Scotland!) and whole host of special bets which will pop into the heads of the traders nearer the time. We'll even be betting 'in running' on the night as each constituency pins its colours to the mast and the dust is blown off the swingometers.

Whilst gambling on politics or anything else for that matter may not be to everyone's taste, I'd argue that it will always be one of the truest measures of public opinion. Some voters have long picked the party they think will win in a bid to share the love and they've told the pollsters what they think they want them to hear, but nobody has ever given money to a bookie because it seemed like the right thing to do.

Of course we too have opinions on the outcomes of everything we bet on. But the hand that guides the tiller is the weight of money. The truth is everyone has an opinion on politics and come polling day anything up to £10 million will have been placed by those prepared to match their money to their mouths. If nothing else it will be a tremendous distraction from the newspapers and the horseracing, not to mention the dirty ashtrays.

Robin Hutchison is the PR manager for the high-street bookmaker Ladbrokes, responsible for their sports and political markets.

All change? The expected demographics of the next House of Commons

Greg Callus

In the last ten years, membership of the British Parliament has changed quite radically. The House of Lords (for example) was stripped of 758 hereditary peers, with only 92 permitted to sit under the 1999 House of Lords Act. There are 746 current members of that chamber, of whom more than 400 have been appointed since New Labour came to power in 1997. The number of female peers has gone up by over 50 per cent, and the proportion of peers who are black or minority ethnic (BME) stands at around 4 per cent. There cannot have been such large-scale changes of membership in the upper chamber since the Life Peerages Act of 1958.

The House of Commons, by comparison, seems a fairly stable institution with respect to its membership – turnover of MPs tends to be around 20 per cent at a general election, and with the exception of the 49th parliament (1983–7), with its fifteen resignations by Northern Irish Unionists in protest at the Anglo-Irish Agreement, there are rarely more than twenty-five by-elections between dissolutions.

Yet every once in a while, there is an election where the political geography changes so significantly as to see a much greater turnover of MPs and the character of the House of Commons is itself changed. The Labour landslide of 1997 would be one example, where 'turnover' (new MPs replacing those defeated or retiring) reached an impressive 39.3 per cent (259 new MPs out of 659 in the 52nd parliament). Could the next election be as significant?

Possibly so. We have seen some astonishing opinion poll leads for the Conservatives since the-election-that-never-was, with David Cameron's party regularly polling twenty points ahead of the Government (the highest being a 28-point lead from Ipsos MORI back in September 2008). Whilst not expecting the general election to be quite that disastrous for Labour, it does seem likely that the Conservative lead will be in the mid-teens, and that a swing of around 12 per cent from Labour to Conservative is not unthinkable. The spread-betting markets, usually excellent indicators of electoral prospects, have suggested a Conservative majority of around 50–60 seats, giving them perhaps 354 seats or so out of a possible 650.

Using this as our premise, we should compare them to the notional 2005 general election results (votes from 2005 counted on the basis of boundaries in use at the next general election), which would have seen Labour win 343 seats, the Conservatives 214, the Liberal Democrats 63 and other parties 30 seats. Thus our understanding of 'turnover' will be based on the presumption of approximately 140 gains for the Conservative Party, plus the replacement of MPs in otherwise 'safe' seats who are retiring. There have been more than eighty announced retirements so far, though where those are members of the Labour and Liberal Democrats the respective seats are often within the scope of the 140 constituencies expected to be ceded to the Conservatives. However, there are around thirty Tory MPs also expected to retire, meaning that there could be in excess of 170 new MPs under the leadership of David Cameron in the next parliament. Because the Conservatives start from a lower base of seats than did Labour in 1997, it would be a little surprising if there were as many new MPs as there were more almost thirteen years ago, even allowing for forty changes of MP outwith the Tory Party.

So given that the bulk of the new intake will be Conservative freshmen, how will Parliament be different? This chapter will seek to suggest the headline changes that can be expected, though with the caveat that any such predictions can be blighted by false precision, and that all trends must be qualified with the assumptions of the result given above.

There will, of course, be key demographic shifts largely driven by the so-called A-list: a measure instituted by David Cameron back in 2006 to increase the numbers of female and BME Conservative MPs. Labour has in the past taken a lead on diversity of its parliamentary party, usually through all-women or all-BME shortlists, though this has backfired in a number of traditional stronghold seats such as Blaenau Gwent, where the late Peter Law ran as an Independent and defeated the woman Labour had chosen to replace him.

There are currently 128 female MPs: 96 Labour (28 per cent of the party), 18 Conservative (9 per cent), 9 Lib Dem (14 per cent), and 3 'others'. Women account for just over 19 per cent of the House of Commons, but this proportion is a somewhat recent development. The number of women in the Commons doubled from 60 to 120 at the 1997 general election. The bulk of these were the sixty-four 'Blair Babes', who represented 35 per cent of the new intake. No-one expects the next election to see such a significant increase in female MPs, but in victory the Conservatives will not be as male dominated as they have been in the past.

Even with four prominent female Conservatives retiring (and perhaps more to follow), David Cameron should see the numbers of women on the government benches more than treble if he wins the keys to No. 10. There are just over forty female Conservative PPCs who would expect to be elected if the Conservatives win a majority of fifty. Women account for 28 per cent of all Conservative candidates, and around a quarter of those in winnable seats – not quite the same level as that managed by Tony Blair, but a clear indication of the success of having a quarter of all target seats pick candidates from the A-list.

Women candidates & MPs elected at each election since 1970

	MPS	% OF ALL MPS	CANDIDATES	% OF ALL CANDIDATES
1970	26	4.1	99	5.4
1974 Feb	23	3.6	143	6.7
1974 Oct	27	4.3	161	7.1
1979	19	3.0	216	8.4
1983	23	3.5	280	10.9
1987	41	6.3	329	14.2
1992	60	9.2	571	19.3
1997	120	18.2	672	18.0
2001	126	17.9	636	19.2
2005	128	19.8	720	20.3

Source: *Rallings and Thrasher,* British Electoral Facts, *2006*

The proportion of MPs from BME backgrounds will still not come that close to proportionality with the population as a whole. Though the number has likely risen since last counted at the 2001 census, the Office for National Statistics suggests that just under 8 per cent of the population selected an ethnicity other than 'white'. At present there are only fifteen BME MPs, or 2.3 per cent of the total Commons chamber. This is unlikely to change significantly at the next election – although there are maybe eight or nine BME Conservatives who stand a good chance of election, Labour could well lose at least two or three BME MPs, as well as one retirement that has already been announced. It is possible that BME representation will reach 3.5 per cent, but 4 per cent seems highly implausible.

BME MPs elected at elections since 1979

	CON	LAB	LIB DEM	TOTAL
1979	0	0	0	0
1983	0	0	0	0
1987	0	4	0	4
1992	1	5	0	6
1997	0	9	0	9
2001	0	12	0	12
2005	2	13	0	15

Source: *Rallings and Thrasher,* British Electoral Facts, *2006*

BME candidates at elections since 1979

	CON	LAB	LIB DEM	TOTAL
1979	2	1	2	5
1983	4	6	8	18
1987	6	14	9	29
1992	8	9	5	22
1997	9	13	17	39
2001	16	21	29	66
2005	41	32	40	113

Source: *Rallings and Thrasher,* British Electoral Facts, *2006*

So the story, when we look at female and BME representation at least, is of little change, though that is no mean feat given that a similar Conservative victory five or ten years ago would have seen a significant drop in those numbers. The status quo across the House will only be achieved by the expected trebling of female Tory MPs, and a massive percentage increase of BME MPs within the Conservative Party. Until 2005, when Michael Howard saw two BME Conservatives elected, there had only ever been one Asian Conservative elected, Sir Mancherjee Bhownagree, who left office in 1906. It is not inconceivable that there would be more black and Asian MPs on the Conservative benches in the next House of Commons than in the Labour and Liberal Democrat ranks combined.

One area where there has been an expectation of significant change is in the age profile of the House of Commons. Elections with high turnover usually have notable numbers of retirees (who are usually the older MPs) and thus new blood can significantly affect the average age of the Commons. However, somewhat counter-intuitively, the last five or so general elections have been striking in that each has returned a House of Commons generally more advanced in years than its predecessor.

After the 1987 general election, 116 MPs were under the age of 40, with 368 in total under the age of 50. The Parliament elected in 2005 saw only 92 under the age of 40 (of whom only three were in their twenties), with only 283 in total under the age of 40.

After the election, 197 MPs were in their 50s, 79 in their 60s, and 6 in their 70s. By the 2005 general election, 249 were in their 50s, 100 were in their 60s, and 14 were in their 70s. Clearly general increased life expectancy and a particularly good standard of living had contributed to a much older House than had sat eighteen years earlier.

The Conservative Party currently in Parliament has an average age of just under fifty years old, almost three years younger than the Labour figure, but 3.5 years above that for the Lib Dems. This will not change radically, although the proportion of under-forties in the new intake could be almost as high as a third, whereas only 17 per cent of the current group of Conservative MPs have yet to see their fortieth birthday. The number of retirements should bring down the mean age of the House somewhat, but the median age is unlikely to change significantly, with any drop in the Conservative figure offset by rises in the Labour and Lib Dem numbers, as their younger MPs (many elected in the heady landslides of 1997 and 2001) are some of the first to fall to the opposition.

Although three MPs were elected in 2005 whilst still in their twenties (Jo Swinson, Sarah Teather and David Lammy), this number has shrunk to just two – Teather and Lammy have celebrated their thirtieth birthdays, whilst 29-year-old Swinson has recently been replaced as Baby of the House by 27-year-old Chloe Smith, winner of the 2009 Norwich North by-election. There are, at time of writing, no more than eight PPCs in their twenties who stand even a reasonable chance of winning at the next election, so the record of ten MPs under thirty (set in 1983 and 1997) seems unlikely to be emulated, even though the age of eligibility for standing as an MP has dropped from twenty-one to just eighteen.

Age of MPs elected at the 2005 election

	CON	LAB	LIB DEM
20–29	0	1	2
30–39	36	39	17
40–49	75	91	18
50–59	56	158	18
60–69	2	8	0
70–79	0	1	0

Source: Butler & Kavanagh, The British General Election of 2005, *Macmillan, 2005*

Average age of MPs at general elections since 1979

1979	49.6
1983	48.8
1987	49.0
1992	50.0
1997	49.3
2001	50.3
2005	51.2

Source: House of Commons research paper 09/31

So if gender balance, the age profile and the ethnicity of MPs is likely to remain insignificantly changed, what will be different about the next intake of members of the House of Commons? Well, their realms of experience would seem to be notably different, and their political views might be considered a little unorthodox even within their own parties.

Two major surveys have been conducted this year to assess the changing demographic of the expected 2010 intake. One was conducted by the Madano Partnership, a business communications consultancy, the other by ConservativeHome, which is the activist website for Conservative Party grass roots and one of the UK's most influential blogs. A trend noted by Madano confirmed anecdotal expectations of 'the class of 2010': looking at 242 PPCs in target seats (predominantly Conservatives), they found that almost half the Tory PPCs had been privately educated, but that the total across the parties was almost a third (as against only 13 per cent of the new intake after the 1997 general election). The proportion of Labour MPs educated at private schools has risen from the 7 per cent scored in 1997 – a level which was in line with the country at large – to around 18 per cent now, and the new intake of Labour MPs will be closer to the latter than the former.

Interestingly, the increase in numbers attending university has clearly happened a little late for the expected 2010 intake – the numbers are unlikely to be much changed from the present, where around 80 per cent of Conservatives and Lib Dems have at least a bachelor's degree, versus just under two thirds of Labour MPs.

Not only will the new intake be more likely to have been privately educated, but their career history is also more likely to have been in the private sector than the current crop of MPs. Whilst it has been said that David Cameron is appealing to 'Holby City woman', there seems no chance of him recruiting the 8 per cent of his new MPs from the NHS as Labour managed in 1997 – maybe only one or two of his new intake will have worked within Britain's largest employer. Labour's 1997 intake was dominated by teachers/lecturers

(22 per cent) and trade unionists/political activists. The latter are a growing profession within Parliament generally, but the significant groups within the Conservative Party are likely to be lawyers (around 20 per cent of the party at present) and the growing number of former management consultants who are Tory PPCs in winnable seats.

The survey conducted by ConservativeHome (under the brand name Conservative Intelligence) looked more closely at the political views of its party's candidates in the 220 target seats. They received 144 responses, which suggested that on certain issues, this intake of MPs are likely to be classic Conservatives. They overwhelmingly support nuclear power, teaching British history in all schools, devolution of power to councils (many of them are former councillors), and freedom of choice for parents considering private education. There are, however, some interesting surprises.

The class of 2010 seems to be significantly more Eurosceptic than the Conservative Party of years past – 85 per cent would support the repatriation of powers or a fundamental renegotiation of Britain's relationship with the EU (5 per cent would withdraw, 10 per cent accept the status quo). Again, 85 per cent want a lower limit for abortions, and they would overwhelmingly support recognising marriage through the tax system. Yet this social conservatism also renders some eye-catching results.

The recognition of marriage in all aspects should be afforded to same-sex civil partners, agreed the sample group by a margin of two to one, with almost as many supporting this as the repeal of inheritance tax. The NHS is clearly favoured – it runs the first-placed Ministry of Defence close for the department that should be protected from cuts, and almost three quarters will use the NHS once elected, rather than use private healthcare. Support for the Union (versus discomfort at the idea of an independent Scotland) is a mere 54 per cent as against 46 per cent who would not be uncomfortable with dissolving the Union in principle. They are evenly split on the question of whether they would have voted for Barack Obama or John McCain had they been American citizens.

There is clearly a new and strange breed of Conservative MP about to be unleashed on the House of Commons, and this group will be almost as totemic of the expected Conservative victory as the Blair Babes were in 1997. They are likely to play a pivotal role, unlike their New Labour forerunners, because the expected majority is likely to be much smaller, and with the level of retirements so high, David Cameron will likely lead a government of the neophytes. Our estimates suggest that half the government benches will be filled with brand new MPs, with a further seventh of Cameron's party only having been elected since 2005. It is difficult to foresee how (if he wins an overall majority) more than a third of the Conservative parliamentary party will have more than five years' experience of the Commons under their belts, which could make for a fascinating first-term dynamic.

Parliament is changing, but we will probably not see quite the scale of change witnessed in 1997. The preservation of the status quo is itself attributable to significant changes within the Conservative Party, but it will be the magnitude of the victory that will determine quite how different the House of Commons will look when the new intake make their maiden speeches.

Greg Callus, writing as 'Morus', is the deputy editor of PoliticalBetting.com.

Lists

Iain Dale

15 little-known facts about general election results

- At the 2005 election, 1,385 candidates lost their deposits, including five Conservatives and one Liberal Democrat.
- At the last election there were 18,975 overseas voters.
- The largest majority ever received by a successful candidate was when the Conservative Sir A. C. Lawson won Brighton in 1931 with a stunning majority of 62,253. He also holds the record for the most votes ever received in a general election, with a massive 75,205 in the same election.
- The smallest general election majority was two votes, achieved by Mark Oaten in Winchester in 1997 and A. J. Flint in Ilkeston North in 1931.
- The smallest number of votes ever cast for a candidate in a general election was one – for Ms C. Taylor-Dawson, who stood in Cardiff North in 2005.
- The highest turnout in an individual seat in a general election was 93.4 per cent in Fermanagh & South Tyrone in 1951.
- The lowest turnout was in Lambeth in 1918, when only 29.7 per cent of the electorate bothered to vote.
- The highest number of candidates to stand in a seat at a general election is fifteen, in Sedgefield, Tony Blair's former seat, in 2005.
- The average size of a constituency is 60,000–70,000 voters. But in 1935 in the constituency of Romford there were 167,939 voters on the electoral register.
- Southwark North holds the record for the smallest number of voters on the register in a single-member seat, with 14,108 in 1945.
- In 1992 the Lib Dems won Inverness, Nairn & Lochaber with only 26 per cent of the vote. A mere 1,741 votes separated the winner from the fourth-placed candidate.
- When the Conservatives won the Crewe & Nantwich by election in May 2008, it was their first by-election gain from Labour since 1978.
- The highest number of recounts at a general election count is seven, held at Brighton, Kemptown in 1964 (Labour's D. H. Hobden won with a majority of seven) and Peterborough in 1966, where Sir Harmer Nicholls was returned with a majority of three votes.

- The record for the longest count is held by Derbyshire North East. At the 1922 election the count took 18¼ hours.
- In Harlow in 2005 the result was not announced until 11.40 a.m. on the Saturday following the election. There had been three recounts and the counting agents were exhausted.

All statistics listed are taken from British Electoral Facts *or* The Media Guide to the New Parliamentary Constituencies, *by kind permission of Professors Colin Rallings and Michael Thrasher.*

Votes for parties 1983–2005

	2005	2001	1997	1992	1987	1983
Con	8,784,915	8,357,615	9,600,943	14,093,007	13,760,583	13,012,316
Lab	9,552,436	10,724,953	13,518,167	11,560,484	10,029,807	8,456,934
Lib	5,985,454	4,814,321	5,242,947	5,999,606	7,341,633	7,780,949
SNP	412,267	464,314	621,550	629,564	416,473	331,975
PC	174,838	195,893	161,030	154,947	123,599	125,309
UKIP	605,973	390,563	105,722	0	0	0
Green	283,414	166,477	63,991	171,927	89,753	53,848
BNP	192,745	47,129	35,832	7,005	0	0
UUP	127,414	216,839	258,349	271,049	276,230	259,952
DUP	241,856	181,999	107,348	103,039	85,642	152,749
SDLP	125,726	169,865	190,814	184,445	154,087	137,012
SF	174,530	175,933	126,921	78,291	83,389	102,701

Seats won 1983–2005

	2005	2001	1997	1992	1987	1983
Con	198	166	165	336	376	397
Lab	355	412	418	271	229	209
Lib	62	52	46	20	22	23
SNP	6	5	6	3	3	2
PC	3	4	4	4	3	2
UUP	1	6	10	9	9	11
DUP	9	5	2	3	3	3
SDLP	3	3	3	4	3	1
SF	5	4	2	0	1	1
Others	4	2	3	1	1	1
Total	646	659	659	651	650	650

% vote share per party 1983–2005 (excl. Northern Ireland)

	2005	2001	1997	1992	1987	1983
Con	33.2	32.7	31.5	42.8	43.3	43.5
Lab	36.1	42.0	44.3	34.4	31.5	28.3
Lib	22.6	18.8	17.2	17.8	23.1	26.0
SNP	1.6	1.8	2.0	1.9	1.3	1.1
PC	0.7	0.8	0.5	0.5	0.4	0.4
UKIP	2.3	1.5	0.3	0	0	0
Green	1.1	0.7	0.2	0.5	0.3	0.2
Others	2.4	1.7	4.0	3.0	0.1	0.4

Votes per seat won 1983–2005

	2005	2001	1997	1992	1987	1983
Con	44,335	50,332	58,128	41,811	36,597	32,777
Lab	26,908	26,031	32,340	42,659	43,798	40,464
Lib	96,539	92,583	113,977	299,980	333,711	338,302

Voter turnout

1970	72.0%
1974 Feb	78.8%
1974 Oct	72.8%
1979	76.0%
1983	72.7%
1987	75.3%
1992	77.7%
1997	71.4%
2001	59.4%
2005	61.4%

Number of postal voters at each election since 1979

1979	846,335
1983	757,604
1987	947,948
1992	835,074
1997	937,205
2001	1,758,055
2005	5,362,501

Number of spoilt ballot papers at each election since 1974

1974 Feb	42,252
1974 Oct	37,706
1979	117,848
1983	51,104
1987	36,945
1992	39,726
1997	93,408
2001	100,005
2005	85,038

Average number of candidates per seat at each election since 1970

1970	2.9
1974 Feb	3.4
1974 Oct	3.5
1979	4.1
1983	4.0
1987	3.6
1992	4.5
1997	5.7
2001	5.0
2005	5.5

Quickest results 1959–2005

1959	Billericay	9.57 p.m.
1964	Cheltenham	10.00 p.m.
1966	Cheltenham	10.04 p.m.
1970	Guildford	11.10 p.m.
1974 Feb	Guildford	11.10 p.m.
1974 Oct	Guildford	11.10 p.m.
1979	Glasgow Central	11.34 p.m.
1983	Torbay	11.10 p.m.
1987	Torbay	11.02 p.m.
1992	Sunderland South	11.06 p.m.
1997	Sunderland South	10.46 p.m.
2001	Sunderland South	10.41 p.m.
2005	Sunderland South	10.43 p.m.

Top 200 Conservative targets (seat, % swing required, incumbent party)

1	Gillingham & Rainham	0.02	Lab
2	Crawley	0.02	Lab
3	York Outer	0.22	Lib
4	Romsey & Waterside	0.23	Lib
5	Harlow	0.29	Lab
6	Cheltenham	0.33	Lib
7	Croydon Central	0.36	Lab
8	Portsmouth North	0.38	Lib
9	Battersea	0.41	Lab
10	Hove	0.50	Lab
11	Somerton & Frome	0.56	Lib
12	Eastleigh	0.56	Lib
13	Westmorland & Lonsdale	0.85	Lib
14	Milton Keynes North	0.86	Lab
15	Stroud	0.93	Lab
16	Dartford	0.95	Lab
17	South Basildon & East Thurrock	1.07	Lab
18	Ealing Central & Acton	1.08	Lab
19	City of Chester	1.10	Lab
20	Hereford & South Herefordshire	1.19	Lib
21	Colne Valley	1.26	Lab
22	Cardiff North	1.26	Lab
23	Hastings & Rye	1.27	Lab
24	Calder Valley	1.37	Lab
25	Stourbridge	1.46	Lab
26	Carshalton & Wallington	1.47	Lib
27	Milton Keynes South	1.52	Lib
28	Corby	1.56	Lab
29	Taunton Deane	1.65	Lib
30	Perth & North Perthshire	1.66	SNP
31	Vale of Glamorgan	1.68	Lab
32	South Swindon	1.75	Lab
33	South Dorset	1.86	Lab
34	Northampton South	1.89	Lab
35	High Peak	1.90	Lab
36	Loughborough	1.94	Lab
37	Aberconwy	1.96	Lab
38	Watford	1.97	Lab

39	Birmingham, Edgbaston	2.00	Lab
40	Stafford	2.00	Lab
41	Angus	2.10	SNP
42	Broxtowe	2.22	Lab
43	Chippenham	2.35	Lib
44	Burton	2.40	Lab
45	Brighton, Kemptown	2.42	Lab
46	Bury North	2.52	Lab
47	Redditch	2.60	Lab
48	Rugby	2.60	Lab
49	Pendle	2.65	Lab
50	Wolverhampton South West	2.66	Lab
51	Carmarthen West & South Pembrokeshire	2.66	Lab
52	South Ribble	2.71	Lab
53	South Derbyshire	2.73	Lab
54	Bristol North West	2.85	Lab
55	Dumfries & Galloway	2.87	Lab
56	Tamworth	2.94	Lab
57	Torbay	3.01	Lib
58	Cleethorpes	3.03	Lab
59	Sutton & Cheam	3.11	Lib
60	South Swindon	3.12	Lab
61	Westminster North	3.30	Lab
62	Worcester	3.39	Lab
63	North Cornwall	3.43	Lib
64	Harrow East	3.44	Lab
65	Richmond Park	3.55	Lib
66	Great Yarmouth	3.69	Lab
67	Cheadle	3.70	Lib
68	Eltham	3.80	Lab
69	Brigg & Goole	3.92	Lab
70	Portsmouth South	4.00	Lib
71	Bedford	4.02	Lab
72	Stevenage	4.03	Lab
73	Hendon	4.03	Lab
74	Chatham & Aylesford	4.13	Lab
75	Brentford & Isleworth	4.14	Lab
76	Bradford West	4.17	Lab
77	Rossendale & Darwen	4.18	Lab
78	Hammersmith	4.22	Lab
79	Blackpool North & Cleveleys	4.24	Lab
80	Halifax	4.38	Lab
81	Lancaster & Fleetwood	4.41	Lab
82	Dewsbury	4.44	Lab
83	Dudley South	4.45	Lab
84	Northampton North	4.50	Lab
85	Warrington South	4.58	Lab
86	Truro & Falmouth	4.63	Lib
87	Wirral South	4.65	Lab
88	Southport	4.66	Lib
89	Lincoln	4.74	Lab
90	North West Leicestershire	4.75	Lab
91	Wyre Forest	4.76	Ind
92	Gedling	4.82	Lab
93	Halesowen & Rowley Regis	4.83	Lab

94	Nuneaton	4.87	Lab
95	Leeds North West	5.08	Lab
96	Brecon & Radnorshire	5.09	Lib
97	Camborne & Redruth	5.13	Lib
98	Warwick & Leamington	5.17	Lab
99	Dover	5.20	Lab
100	Keighley	5.24	Lab
101	Newton Abbott	5.25	Lib
102	North Devon	5.35	Lib
103	Poplar & Limehouse	5.42	Lab
104	Bury North	5.52	Lab
105	Stirling	5.46	Lab
106	Plymouth, Sutton & Devonport	5.56	Lab
107	Dudley North	5.57	Lab
108	Elmet & Rothwell	5.71	Lab
109	Reading West	5.74	Lab
110	Tynemouth	5.83	Lab
111	Morecambe & Lunesdale	5.87	Lab
112	Pudsey	5.87	Lab
113	South East Cornwall	5.89	Lib
114	Ipswich	5.91	Lab
115	Bolton West	5.98	Lab
116	Bolton North East	5.99	Lab
117	Waveney	6.00	Lab
118	Sefton Central	6.01	Lab
119	Tooting	6.09	Lab
120	St Austell & Newquay	6.22	Lab
121	Amber Valley	6.27	Lab
122	Barrow & Furness	6.27	Lab
123	Winchester	6.37	Lib
124	Gloucester	6.47	Lab
125	Berwickshire, Roxburgh & Selkirk	6.50	Lib
126	Thurrock	6.51	Lab
127	Argyll & Bute	6.52	Lib
128	Brighton, Pavilion	6.56	Lab
129	Mid Dorset & North Poole	6.56	Lab
130	Copeland	6.62	Lab
131	Oxford West & Abingdon	6.71	Lib
132	Stockton South	6.72	Lab
133	Carlisle	6.73	Lab
134	Batley & Spen	6.77	Lab
135	Bath	6.78	Lib
136	Kingswood	6.88	Lab
137	Hyndburn	6.90	Lab
138	Weaver Vale	7.01	Lab
139	East Renfrewshire	7.02	Lab
140	West Lancashire	7.05	Lab
141	Vale of Clwyd	7.09	Lab
142	Moray	7.32	SNP
143	Luton South	7.35	Lab
144	Telford	7.51	Lab
145	Coventry South	7.59	Lab
146	North Warwickshire	7.63	Lab
147	Newport West	7.64	Lab
148	Crewe & Nantwich	7.75	Lab

149	Leeds North East	7.75	Lab
150	Colchester	7.80	Lib
151	Erewash	7.83	Lab
152	Dagenham & Rainham	7.85	Lab
153	Sherwood	7.95	Lab
154	Ellesmere Port & Neston	7.99	Lab
155	Derby North	8.07	Lab
156	Sheffield, Hallam	8.09	Lib
157	Harrogate & Knaresborough	8.11	Lib
158	Norwich South	8.17	Lab
159	Edinburgh South	8.18	Lab
160	Luton North	8.19	Lab
161	Chorley	8.21	Lab
162	Edinburgh South West	8.24	Lab
163	Norwich North	8.30	Lab
164	Ochil & South Perthshire	8.43	Lab
165	Lewes	8.44	Lib
166	Gower	8.48	Lab
167	Birmingham, Selly Oak	8.57	Lab
168	Exeter	8.63	Lab
169	North Norfolk	8.64	Lib
170	Yeovil	8.66	Lab
171	Bristol East	8.68	Lab
172	Wakefield	8.75	Lab
173	Blackpool South	8.84	Lab
174	Bridgend	8.93	Lab
175	Bassetlaw	8.96	Lab
176	West Aberdeenshire & Kincardine	8.97	Lib
177	Kingston & Surbiton	9.05	Lib
178	Harrow West	9.13	Lab
179	Middlesbrough South & East Cleveland	9.26	Lab
180	Ealing North	9.31	Lab
181	Southampton, Test	9.59	Lab
182	Nottingham South	9.60	Lab
183	Feltham & Heston	9.63	Lab
184	Twickenham	9.64	Lib
185	Plymouth, Moor View	9.68	Lab
186	Blackburn	9.72	Lab
187	Delyn	9.77	Lab
188	Dulwich & West Norwood	9.88	Lab
189	Clwyd South	9.92	Lab
190	Slough	9.93	Lab
191	Hazel Grove	9.96	Lib
192	Birmingham, Northfield	9.96	Lab
193	Brent North	10.02	Lab
194	Newcastle-under-Lyme	10.19	Lab
195	Walsall South	10.38	Lab
196	Walsall North	10.39	Lab
197	Morley & Outwood	10.47	Lab
198	Edinburgh North & Leith	10.49	Lab
199	Cannock Chase	10.50	Lab
200	Southampton, Itchen	10.50	Lab

Top 50 Labour targets (seat, % swing required, incumbent party)

1	Sittingbourne & Sheppey	0.03	Con
2	Clwyd West	0.07	Con
3	Hemel Hempstead	0.18	Con
4	Kettering	0.20	Con
5	North East Somerset	0.23	Con
6	Finchley & Golders Green	0.35	Con
7	Shipley	0.48	Con
8	Dundee East	0.48	SNP
9	Rochester & Strood	0.57	Con
10	Wellingborough	0.62	Con
11	Manchester, Withington	0.69	Lib
12	Gravesham	0.72	Con
13	Wirral West	0.76	Con
14	Preseli Pembrokeshire	0.77	Con
15	Filton & Bradley Stoke	0.79	Con
16	Reading East	0.86	Con
17	South Thanet	0.88	Con
18	Bethnal Green & Bow	1.05	Res
19	Enfield North	1.18	Con
20	Bristol West	1.27	Lib
21	Scarborough & Whitby	1.33	Con
22	Enfield, Southgate	1.36	Con
23	The Wrekin	1.43	Con
24	St Albans	1.47	Con
25	Shrewsbury & Atcham	1.80	Con
26	Staffordshire Moorlands	1.93	Con
27	Dumfriesshire, Clydesdale & Tweeddale	1.95	Con
28	Ilford North	2.07	Con
29	Forest of Dean	2.15	Con
30	Selby & Ainsty	2.15	Con
31	Putney	2.40	Con
32	Leeds North West	2.48	Lib
33	Hornsey & Wood Green	2.53	Lib
34	Wimbledon	2.85	Con
35	Beverley & Holderness	3.12	Con
36	Basingstoke	3.14	Con
37	Chesterfield	3.18	Lib
38	Camborne & Redruth	3.54	Lib
39	Birmingham, Yardley	3.65	Lib
40	Clacton	4.25	Con
41	East Dunbartonshire	4.35	Lib
42	Peterborough	4.47	Con
43	Inverness, Nairn, Badenoch & Strathspey	4.69	Lib
44	Monmouth	4.96	Con
45	Na h-Eileanan an Iar	5.21	SNP
46	Bosworth	5.36	Con
47	Basildon & Billericay	5.61	Con
48	Harwich & North Essex	5.86	Con
49	Chipping Barnet	6.01	Con
50	Hexham	6.14	Con

Top 30 Liberal Democrat targets (seat, % swing required, incumbent party)

1	Guildford	0.09	Con
2	Solihull	0.12	Con
3	Rochdale	0.17	Lab
4	Oxford East	0.37	Lab
5	Edinburgh South	0.47	Lab
6	Hampstead & Kilburn	0.57	Lab
7	Eastbourne	0.70	Con
8	Islington South & Finsbury	0.78	Lab
9	Watford	1.17	Lab
10	Ealing Central & Acton	1.37	Lab
11	Aberdeen South	1.62	Lab
12	Weston-super-Mare	2.13	Con
13	Ludlow	2.18	Con
14	West Dorset	2.31	Con
15	Meon Valley	2.45	Con
16	Central Devon	2.49	Con
17	Edinburgh North & Leith	2.52	Con
18	Torridge & West Devon	2.68	Con
19	Wells	2.87	Con
20	Totnes	2.88	Con
21	West Worcestershire	3.02	Con
22	Newbury	3.21	Con
23	City of Durham	3.69	Lab
24	Norwich South	3.70	Lab
25	Leicester South	3.78	Lab
26	Liverpool, Wavertree	4.45	Lab
27	Chelmsford	4.60	Con
28	Oldham East & Saddleworth	5.19	Lab
29	Haltemprice & Howden	5.26	Con
30	Orpington	5.39	Con

Top 20 SNP targets (seat, % swing required, incumbent party)

1	Ochil & South Perthshire	0.74	Lab
2	Dundee West	7.28	Lab
3	Kilmarnock & Loudoun	9.80	Lab
4	Aberdeen North	10.08	Lab
5	Argyll & Bute	10.49	Lib
6	Edinburgh East	11.51	Lab
7	Linlithgow & East Falkirk	12.07	Lab
8	Stirling	12.49	Lab
9	North Ayrshire & Arran	12.98	Lab
10	Paisley & Renfrewshire North	13.45	Lab
11	Lanark & Hamilton East	14.14	Lab
12	East Lothian	14.19	Lab
13	Dunfermline & West Fife	14.25	Lab
14	Midlothian	14.26	Lab
15	Glenrothes	14.27	Lab
16	Glasgow North	14.50	Lab
17	Gordon	14.53	Lab
18	Edinburgh South West	14.60	Lab
19	Falkirk	14.73	Lab
20	Livingston	14.77	Lab

Top 10 Plaid Cymru targets (seat, % swing required, incumbent party)

1	Ceredigion	0.31	Lib
2	Arfon	0.91	Lab
3	Ynys Môn	1.75	Lab
4	Llanelli	10.23	Lab
5	Aberconwy	15.06	Lab
6	Carmarthen West & South Pembrokeshire	15.84	Lab
7	Cardiff West	15.97	Lab
8	Gower	17.69	Lab
9	Neath	17.74	Lab
10	Clwyd South	17.89	Lab

Ten seats with the highest % turnout at the 2005 election

1	West Dorset	76.4
2	Thornbury & Yate	73.6
3	Monmouth	73.4
4	Richmond Park	73.2
5	East Dunbartonshire	73.1
6	North Norfolk	72.7
7	Newbury	72.6
8	Orpington	72.4
9	Twickenham	72.3
10	East Renfrewshire	72.1

Ten seats with the lowest % turnout at the 2005 election

1	South Staffordshire	37.6
2	Manchester Central	41.8
3	Liverpool, Riverside	42.6
4	Glasgow Central	43.9
5	Leeds Central	44.3
6	Kingston upon Hull West & Hessle	44.8
7	West Ham	44.9
8	Birmingham, Ladywood	45.1
9	Salford & Eccles	45.5
10	Liverpool, West Derby	45.7

Swings at post-war elections (%)

1950	2.9 Con
1951	1.1 Con
1955	1.8 Con
1959	1.2 Con
1964	3.1 Lab
1966	2.8 Lab
1970	4.9 Con
1974 Feb	0.8 Lab
1974 Oct	2.2 Lab
1979	5.3 Con
1983	4.1 Con
1987	1.7 Lab
1992	2.1 Lab
1997	10.2 Lab
2001	1.8 Con
2005	3.1 Con

Entrants & leavers at general elections 1979–2005

	NEW MPS	DEFEATED MPS	RETIRING MPS	TOTAL MPS	% TURNOVER
1979	128	65	61	635	20.2
1983	156	64	71	650	24.0
1987	130	40	86	650	20.0
1992	138	59	79	651	21.2
1997	259	132	116	659	39.3
2001	99	22	78	659	15.0
2005	123	50	86	646	19.0

Source: House of Commons Library

Ten best Conservative results in 2005 (% change)

1	Brentwood	15.5
2	Dumfries & Galloway	11.6
3	Wyre Forest	9.7
4	Isle of Wight	9.2
5	Welwyn Hatfield	9.2
6	Folkestone	8.9
7	Henley	7.4
8	Berwickshire, Roxburgh & Selkirk	6.9
9	Crawley	6.8
10	North Tyneside	6.7

Ten best Labour results in 2005 (% change)

1	Dumfries & Galloway	8.8
2	Ryedale	6.0
3	Torbay	5.3
4	St Helens South	4.8
5	Kingston & Surbiton	4.4
6	Oldham East & Saddleworth	2.6
7	Brentwood	2.2
8	Islwyn	2.2
9	North Cornwall	2.1
10	Ribble Valley	2.1

Ten best Lib Dem results in 2005 (% change)

1	Brent East	36.9
2	Birmingham, Ladywood	23.2
3	Birmingham, Hodge Hill	21.4
4	Manchester, Withington	20.4
5	Cambridge	18.9
6	Hornsey	17.6
7	City of Durham	17.1
8	Hartlepool	15.4
9	East Dunbartonshire	14.8
10	Ealing, Southall	14.4

Ten largest Green votes in 2005 (%)

1	Brighton, Pavilion	21.9
2	Lewisham, Deptford	11.1
3	Hackney North	9.9
4	Holborn & St Pancras	8.1
5	Leeds West	7.5
6	Norwich South	7.4
7	Islington North	7.1
8	Brighton, Kemptown	7.0
9	Dulwich & West Norwood	6.5
10	Sheffield Central	6.0

Ten largest UKIP votes in 2005 (%)

1	South Staffordshire	10.4
2	Boston & Skegness	9.6
3	Bognor Regis	8.0
4	Staffordshire Moorlands	7.9
5	Plymouth, Devonport	7.9
6	Torbay	7.8
7	Totnes	7.7
8	Louth	7.7
9	South West Devon	7.5
10	Castle Point	7.5

Ten largest BNP votes in 2005 (%)

1	Barking	16.9
2	Dewsbury	13.1
3	Burnley	10.3
4	West Bromwich West	9.9
5	Dudley North	9.7
6	Dagenham	9.3
7	Keighley	9.2
8	Stoke-on-Trent South	8.7
9	Bradford South	7.8
10	Stoke-on-Trent Central	7.8

Five largest Respect votes in 2005 (%)

1	Bethnal Green & Bow	35.9
2	Birmingham, Small Heath	27.5
3	East Ham	20.7
4	West Ham	19.5
5	Poplar & Canning Town	16.5

Retiring MPs at the next election

List courtesy of Anthony Wells's UK Polling Report, as of 17 August 2009

Labour

Hilary Armstrong – North West Durham

John Austin – Erith & Thamesmead

John Battle – Leeds West

Colin Burgon – Elmet

Richard Caborn – Sheffield Central

Colin Challon – Morley & Outwood

Ben Chapman – Wirral South

David Chaytor – Bury North

Michael Clapham – Barnsley West & Penistone (abolished)

Harry Cohen – Leyton & Wanstead

Frank Cook – Stockton North

Jim Cousins – Newcastle upon Tyne Central

Ann Cryer – Keighley

John Cummings – Easington

Janet Dean – Burton

Jim Devine – Livingston

Bill Etherington – Sunderland North

Neil Gerrard – Walthamstow

John Grogan – Selby

Doug Henderson – Newcastle upon Tyne North

Keith Hill – Streatham

Patricia Hewitt – Leicester West

Beverley Hughes – Stretford & Urmston

John Hutton – Barrow & Furness

Brian Iddon – Bolton South East

Adam Ingram – East Kilbride, Strathaven & Lesmahagow

Lynne Jones – Birmingham, Selly Oak

Martyn Jones – Clwyd South

Ruth Kelly – Bolton West

Fraser Kemp – Houghton & Washington East

David Lepper – Brighton, Pavilion

Christine McCafferty – Calder Valley
Ian McCartney – Makerfield
Rosemary McKenna – Cumbernauld, Kilsyth & Kirkintilloch East
Andrew MacKinlay – Thurrock
Bob Marshall-Andrews – Medway
Eric Martlew – Carlisle
Alan Milburn – Darlington
Margaret Moran – Luton South
Elliot Morley – Scunthorpe
Kali Mountford – Colne Valley
Chris Mullin – Sunderland South
Doug Naysmith – Bristol North West
Bill Olner – Nuneaton
Greg Pope – Hyndburn
Bridget Prentice – Lewisham East
John Prescott – Kingston upon Hull East
Ken Purchase – Wolverhampton North East
John Reid – Airdrie & Shotts
Martin Salter – Reading West
Mohammed Sarwar – Glasgow Central
Clare Short[1] – Birmingham, Ladywood
Alan Simpson – Nottingham South
John Smith – Vale of Glamorgan
Helen Southworth – Warrington South
Howard Stoate – Dartford
Gavin Strang – Edinburgh East
David Taylor – North West Leicestershire
Mark Todd – South Derbyshire
Paul Truswell – Pudsey
Des Turner – Brighton, Kemptown
Kitty Ussher – Burnley
Rudi Vis – Finchley & Golders Green
Alan Williams – Swansea West
Betty Williams – Conwy
Tony Wright – Cannock Chase
Derek Wyatt – Sittingbourne & Sheppey

Conservative

Michael Ancram – Devizes
Peter Atkinson – Hexham
Tim Boswell – Daventry
Angela Browning – Tiverton & Honiton
John Butterfill – Bournemouth West
Derek Conway[2] – Old Bexley & Sidcup
David Curry – Skipton & Ripon
Christopher Fraser – South West Norfolk

Paul Goodman – Wycombe
John Greenway – Ryedale
Douglas Hogg – Sleaford & North Hykeham
Michael Howard – Folkestone & Hythe
Michael Jack – Fylde
Julie Kirkbride – Bromsgrove
Andrew Mackay – Bracknell
David Maclean – Penrith & the Border
Humfrey Malins – Woking
Michael Mates – East Hampshire
Malcolm Moss – North East Cambridgeshire
Andrew Pelling – Croydon Central
Michael Spicer – West Worcestershire
Anthony Steen – Totnes
Ian Taylor – Esher & Walton
Peter Viggers – Gosport
Ann Widdecombe – Maidstone & the Weald
Ann Winterton – Congleton
Nicholas Winterton – Macclesfield

Liberal Democrat
John Barrett – Edinburgh West
Colin Breed – South East Cornwall
Paul Keetch – Hereford
Mark Oaten – Winchester
Matthew Taylor – Truro
Phil Willis – Harrogate & Knaresborough

SNP
Alex Salmond – Banff & Buchan

Bruce George announced in 2007 that, have previously said he would stand down, he would stand again if an early election was held during 2007. He subsequently announced his intention to stand after all.

The following sitting MPs do not currently have a seat at the next election, either through boundary changes or through losing selection battles, though they may yet be selected for alternate seats: Ian Stewart, Eddie O'Hara, John Greenway, Frank Cook, Quentin Davies. Bob Wareing was deselected as Labour MP for Liverpool, West Derby, but has indicated he will stand as an Independent Labour candidate.

1 *Clare Short was elected as a Labour MP but resigned the Labour whip on 20 October 2006. She had previously ruled out standing again as a Labour candidate, but has not ruled out standing under another label.*

2 *Derek Conway was elected as a Conservative MP but had the whip withdrawn on 30 January 2008 following revelations that he had been paying a researcher's salary to his sons from his allowances while they were at university.*

Preface to the regional and constituency profiles

Greg Callus

No guide to the next general election could neglect to provide an in-depth view of the electoral map, both at a regional and at a constituency level. This section of the book is therefore composed of three significant contributions.

Each region of the United Kingdom is introduced by an essay from the estimable Robert Waller – each of these either has been, or soon will be, published in *Total Politics* magazine. For those who are not satisfied, I can only recommend his book *The Almanac of British Politics*, which no student of elections and psephology should be without.

Within each regional sub-chapter, we have provided a table of (what we felt was) the most useful information for each of the 650 constituencies in operation at the next election. Of these 650, a full 200 have been chosen for a closer look, and these detailed seat profiles have been written for us by Daniel Hamilton of ComRes.

All numerical data in this section is courtesy of Professors Colin Rallings and Michael Thrasher at the Election Centre at the University of Plymouth. Their notional results from the 2005 general election, as found in The Media Guide to the New Parliamentary Constituencies, are considered the definitive authority by BBC, ITN, PA News and Sky News, and we are very grateful for their kind permission in allowing us to republish them here.

Notes on the data tables
The regions into which this section is divided are not the same as the regional constituencies for the European Parliament. Those twelve regions are huge and diverse, and do not best lend themselves to regional analysis. We have been guided by Robert Waller's work, and the definition of each region (which counties and metropolises are contained within it) can be found in his essays.

All 2005 general election results (votes received and vote share, both by party) given for constituencies in the United Kingdom are 'notional'. Notional results are not a prediction, or a counterfactual history of boundary changes. They are the real

2005 votes counted according to the new boundaries that will be in place at the next election. Similarly, notional majority and notional turnout has been provided for comparative purposes, based on the changes made by the Boundary Commissions of England, Wales and Scotland. Constituencies in Northern Ireland have not undergone boundary changes, so the Northern Irish results given for 2005 are the actual votes and vote shares by party, and the actual turnout and majority.

All constituency names are the official names (down to hyphens and apostrophes) as provided to us by the various Boundary Commissions. Other variants can occasionally be found in other sources, but we hope that our ordering by region will help alleviate confusion as well as providing an authoritative guide.

The listing of prospective parliamentary candidates (PPCs) for the next general election is, we believe, correct at the time of going to press (September 2009). Obviously many constituencies have not yet selected candidates (none of the Northern Irish parties have any confirmed candidate in place at this time), but based on our including only the top three parties in each constituency, around three quarters of the candidate names in 2010 are to be found here.

We have adopted a policy of assuming that sitting Members of Parliament will stand again, unless there has been a public announcement that they will not contest the next election. For this reason, sitting MPs from Northern Ireland have been included, even though each must face re-selection.

The names of candidates from 2005 have been included to show where perennial challengers, and/or former MPs for that seat, are challenging again. Seats where no 2005 candidate names are provided have been considered 'new seats', and thus were not 'fought by candidate' last time around. Our definition of a 'new seat' is one where the percentage boundary change from the old seat is greater than 75 per cent, according to notional figures from Profs Rallings & Thrasher. This figure was itself the topic of some internal debate, but we felt that it was the best available compromise between providing as much information as possible (such as candidate names from 2005) whilst not failing to recognise where a seat was effectively unrecognisable from its previous boundaries.

Honorifics, pre- and post-nominals (with the exception of 'MP') have been avoided for purposes of clarity and ease of reading. We apologise to the various Knights, Ladies, Councillors, Mayors, recipients of the MBE/OBE/CBE, or other PPCs who are affected, and hope they understand our reasoning.

Sitting Members of Parliament are denoted, but they are only afforded the post-nominal 'MP' if they were a Member of Parliament when standing for election (though, of course, technically once dissolution has been granted by the monarch, they are not strictly MPs). We wanted to show where an incumbent MP was running once again, and so whilst all non-retiring MPs are given the post-nominal in the column denoting candidates for the next election, those MPs elected for the first time at the 2005 election will not have the letters after their name in the column giving candidates from the election in 2005, as they were not MPs at the time.

We have taken the non-controversial decision (for reasons of space) to give details by party only for those parties/candidates who came notionally first, second or third in 2005, and to group all other parties/candidates into 'others' on a seat-by-seat basis. Only once (Plaid Cymru in Ceredigion, 1992 general election) has a party come from fourth to win the seat at a general election, though this remarkable feat did also happen once in a by-election (Glasgow Govan, 1988, as SNP supporters will never forget). Rank outsiders can win from time to time – Martin Bell in Tatton for instance – but such exceptions garner enough coverage that I'm sure we may be forgiven for our exclusion.

There may be a handful of errors of exclusions, for which I take full responsibility, but I hope that (given the parameters we have chosen to set, and the scale of the task) this will meet the satisfaction of the most information-hungry political observer.

South West England

The far south-western corner of England, the peninsula which takes in Cornwall, Devon and Somerset, displays a different pattern of contest in parliamentary elections from any other region. Here alone the two-party battle is between the Liberal Democrats and the Conservatives, with Labour, the national governing party, lagging in third place. Nevertheless this will still be a key area of targets which will help to decide who wins the next general election. This is because the Conservatives, in order to secure enough MPs to form a government, and perhaps even an overall majority, will find it much easier to do so if they advance on two fronts rather than one, against both their main rivals. The South West is critical in this, as there are at least eleven vulnerable Liberal Democrat targets in these three counties alone – which accounts for nearly half of the twenty-five seats the Tories are most likely to gain from them.

In the 2005 general election in the three south-westernmost counties (including those parts of the former Avon historically in Somerset), the Conservatives returned nine MPs, Labour just four – and the Liberal Democrats no fewer than twelve. There is no doubt about who, uniquely, the 'major' parties are here. The strongest county of all for the Lib Dems is Cornwall, where they won all five seats for the first time in living memory, taking Falmouth & Camborne to add to previous gains from the Conservatives. The reasons for this local hegemony go way back to a much older, nineteenth-century, cleavage in political choice: as in other parts of the 'Celtic fringe', there is an ancestral link between religious (and hence political) Nonconformism and Liberal support. The association of the 'chapel' community vote with the Liberals contrasted with the Church of England, or 'Tory Party at prayer', was noted decades ago by historians such as Henry Pelling and Kenneth Wald, whose study of constituency voting around the turn of the last century was aptly entitled *Crosses on the Ballot*. There is a feeling here that the parties of national government are based a long way away, in metropolitan centres, and have little regard for the particular problems of what is, in parts, a relatively poor area of Britain. Indeed, until the recent expansion of the EU, Cornwall met its criteria under the regional aid policy.

Nevertheless, Cornwall's population has expanded recently after a long period of stability, or stagnation, and it has been granted a sixth and additional constituency in the boundary review which comes into effect at the next election. This has reinvigorated hopes among Conservatives that they may win a seat in the county for the first time since 1992. Perhaps this is because it means that they would have at least one contest where the Liberal Democrats would not have an incumbent MP, for there is a proven personal vote bonus in such cases, and much more for the Lib Dems than for any other party. Indeed with the announced retirements of Matthew Taylor (Truro & St Austell) and Colin Breed (South East Cornwall) there will now be three 'open' seats, in American parlance.

However, the Tories should be wary of assuming gains based on application of uniform swings from national opinion polls in the mid-term period. The Liberal Democrat percentage tends to rise during the campaign, given some greater equalisation of publicity, and also their strength tends not to slip away so much in their own power bases. In such circumstances, the Conservatives will be doing very well if they win any of the six Cornish divisions. Technically the easiest to gain in the county would be North Cornwall, where Sian Flynn needs a 3.5 per cent swing, but it should be borne in mind that there is an incumbent here, and a first-term one too, who should be beginning to reap the rewards of personal constituency service. This is Dan Rogerson, the youngest male MP when elected at twenty-nine last time. Indeed, the only younger member elected in England was Julia Goldsworthy in Falmouth & Camborne, to whom much the same applies. She is now to fight a cut-down seat of Camborne & Redruth, the only three-way marginal in the whole of this region (see *One to Watch* below).

If the Tories are to break their duck in Cornwall, it may be better to look at the new constituencies without incumbents. Truro will now be paired with Falmouth, taking just over half (51 per cent) of Matthew Taylor's current seat together with that part of Julia Goldsworthy's which looks to the Channel rather than the Atlantic. The new Lib Dem candidate, Terrye Teverson, has been calculated to start with a notional majority of just under 4,000 in an all-female contest with the Tories' Sarah Newton, though there is a substantial working-class and Labour vote, especially in the port of Falmouth, to be squeezed. The other 'new' seat, St Austell & Newquay, crosses the whole of Cornwall from coast to coast across the massive china clay workings (such as the site of the Eden Project): Stephen Gilbert will be defending a notional majority of nearly 6,000 against Caroline Righton. This will require a swing of around 6 per cent, which is similar to the task facing the Conservative Sheryl Murray against the new Lib Dem Karen Gillard in South East Cornwall, over towards the Devon border. It is noteworthy that should the Tories gain up to four seats in Cornwall, they would all be women.

The Lib Dem–Conservative battle continues in Devon and Somerset. Perhaps the best chance the Tories have in the whole region is in the urban seat of Torbay, where Marcus Wood cut Adrian Sanders's majority to 2,000 in 2005 with a 5 per cent swing, and is having another go. Since then, in May 2007 the Tories swept to control of Torbay Council, making fourteen gains, including twelve from the Lib Dems. Devon also has undergone boundary changes. The renamed Newton About should be slightly safer for the Liberal Democrat MP Richard Younger-Ross than its predecessor, Teignbridge, but the new and extra seat in the county, Central

Devon (something of a mish-mash gathered from five previous constituencies), has a notional majority of 2,338 for the Conservatives. This should be an opportunity for Mel Stride to enter Parliament, though it must be remembered that notionals are not predictions, but attempted recalculations of last time's results on the new boundaries. It is locally expected that Nick Harvey, the Liberal Democrat MP in North Devon, around Barnstaple and Ilfracombe, will hold on for a fifth term in Jeremy Thorpe's old seat. On the other hand, Totnes may move in the reverse direction. Although Anthony Steen held on against well-publicised Lib Dem challenges in 2001 and 2005, it was he who hit the (expenses) headlines before being ordered not to stand again by his leader David Cameron in the early summer of 2009.

In Somerset the name to conjure with is – Rees-Mogg. Jacob of that dynasty, headed by the former *Daily Telegraph* editor William, appears to have benefited from boundary changes which have transformed the former Wansdyke into the new North East Somerset, and a small Labour majority for Dan Norris MP into a tiny notional Conservative lead. Moreover, the closest Conservative chance of a gain from the Liberal Democrats in Somerset falls to Jacob's sister Annunziata, who needs only a swing of 0.6 per cent in Somerton & Frome to overturn the notional majority of 595 of the bearded optician David Heath. Elsewhere in the county, Taunton has twice seen a see-saw between Conservative and Liberal Democrat, but Jeremy Browne has been helped by boundary changes which see two Exmoor wards removed from the seat, now to be named Taunton Deane.

The Labour government should not be totally forgotten in the South West, of course. Of their four existing seats, as mentioned above they have technically lost one (Wansdyke) even before the election due to boundary changes. They should hold one safe seat in the working-class northern parts of the region's big city, now to be known as Plymouth, Moor View; and Exeter's Ben Bradshaw has been favourably helped by the boundary changes which remove some of the edges of that cathedral city to the new Devon Central. However, there is one critical Labour–Conservative marginal. Two famous constituency names are now to be linked in the central Plymouth division, Sutton and Devonport – which between them have been the base of a variety of characters such as Alan Clark, David Owen, Dame Joan Vickers and Michael Foot in his first parliamentary incarnation. One suspects that whoever wins this, Linda Gilroy MP for Labour or Oliver Colville for the Conservatives, may join a plurality for their own party after the next election.

Target seats

SEAT	SWING REQUIRED %	MP	CHALLENGER
Conservative from Labour			
Plymouth, Sutton & Devonport	5.6	Linda Gilroy	Oliver Colville
Exeter	8.7	Ben Bradshaw	Hannah Foster
Labour from Conservatives			
North East Somerset	0.3	(Jacob Rees-Mogg)	Dan Norris MP
Conservative from Lib Dem			
Somerton & Frome	0.6	David Heath	Annunziata Rees-Mogg
Taunton Deane	1.7	Jeremy Browne	Mark Formosa
Torbay	3.1	Adrian Sanders	Marcus Wood
North Cornwall	3.5	Dan Rogerson	Sian Flynn
Truro & Falmouth	4.7	(Terrye Teverson)	Sarah Newton
Camborne & Redruth (3rd place)	5.2	Julia Goldsworthy	George Eustice
Newton Abbot	5.3	Richard Younger-Ross	Anne-Marie Morris
North Devon	5.4	Nick Harvey	Philip Milton
South East Cornwall	5.9	(Karen Gillard)	Sheryl Murray
St Austell & Newquay	6.3	(Stephen Gilbert)	Caroline Righton
Bath	6.8	Don Foster	Fabian Richter
Lib Dem from Conservatives			
Weston-super-Mare	2.3	John Penrose	Mike Bell
Central Devon	2.5	(Mel Stride)	Sally Morgan
Torridge & West Devon	2.7	Geoffrey Cox	Adam Symons
Wells	2.9	David Heathcoat-Amory	Tessa Hunt
Totnes	2.9	Anthony Steen*	Julian Brazil

One to watch: Camborne & Redruth

Actual majority 2005 (Falmouth & Camborne): LD 1,886 (3.9%) – Julia Goldsworthy MP
Notional majority 2005 (Camborne & Redruth): LD 2,733 (7.1%)
Labour candidate: Jude Robinson
Conservative candidate: George Eustice

In days when the county's economy is largely driven by tourism, it may come as a surprise to some to find that there was once a thriving mining industry in Cornwall, though based on tin rather than coal. The gritty working-class towns of Camborne and Redruth lay at the centre of this, although the last mine, South Crofty, closed about ten years ago; but this is still an area with a tradition of Labour support, electing Candy Atherton for Falmouth & Camborne from 1997 to 2005. Since then, major boundary changes have taken a third of the voters into the new Truro & Falmouth, leaving a three-way marginal. In the notional results for Camborne & Redruth for 2005, Julia Goldsworthy's Liberal Democrats stand on 13,830 votes, Labour on 11,097 and the Conservatives on 9,874, requiring a swing of only 5.2 per cent to take the seat themselves. Perhaps the most likely result if for the youthful Goldsworthy to squeeze Labour as they perhaps drop to second place, but if George Eustice could advance from third to first it would surely betoken a national Tory government. It might be remembered that Falmouth & Camborne was held by his party from 1970 to 1997, including by Sebastian Coe long before the successful Olympic bid. His predecessor as Tory MP for twenty-two years, David Mudd, actually stood as an Independent in 2005, though he only secured 2 per cent of the vote; and with the ructions concerning the official candidate that year, Ashley Crossley, openly gay and threatened with deselection, it could be argued that the Tories crippled themselves and underperformed. United, could they spring a huge surprise, leaping from bronze to gold medal position?

Bath

Lib Dem notional majority of 5,624; notional turnout: 69.1%

PARTY	2005 CANDIDATE	NOTIONAL 2005 VOTES	NOTIONAL 2005 % VOTE	PPC FOR NEXT GE
Lib Dem	Don Foster MP	18,845	45.4	Don Foster MP
Conservative	Sian Dawson	13,221	31.9	Fabian Richter
Labour	Harriet Ajderian	5,974	14.4	Hattie Ajderian
Others		3,426	8.3	

Almost every general election has an 'Enfield, Southgate' moment – the humiliating and all-too-public slaying by a political neophyte of a long-serving parliamentarian. Don Foster's graceless ousting of Conservative Chairman Chris Patten at the 1992 election thrilled Liberal Democrats and provided the foundations for the party's dramatic advances in the South West at the following general election. A pretty part of the world, Bath's Regency terraces have long been home to a very moderate breed of educated voter – many of them employed in the town's large education sector. The Liberal Democrats have maintained their narrow advantage over the Conservatives in recent years, leading in the 2007 borough council and 2009 European elections. Fabian Richter will fight the seat for the Tories.

Bridgwater & West Somerset

Conservative notional majority of 10,081; notional turnout: 64.0%

PARTY	2005 CANDIDATE	NOTIONAL 2005 VOTES	NOTIONAL 2005 % VOTE	PPC FOR NEXT GE
Conservative	Ian Liddell-Grainger MP	23,140	45.4	Ian Liddell-Grainger MP
Labour	Matthew Burchell	13,059	25.6	Kathy Pearce
Lib Dem	James Main	11,545	22.6	Theo Butt Philip
Others		3,244	6.4	

Camborne & Redruth

Lib Dem notional majority of 2,733; notional turnout: 63.2%

PARTY	2005 CANDIDATE	NOTIONAL 2005 VOTES	NOTIONAL 2005 % VOTE	PPC FOR NEXT GE
Lib Dem	Julia Goldsworthy	13,830	35.9	Julia Goldsworthy MP
Labour	Candy Atherton MP	11,097	28.8	Jude Robinson
Conservative	Ashley Crossley	9,874	25.6	George Eustice
Others		3,776	9.8	

Located 250 miles from central London and formed from parts of the existing Falmouth & Camborne and Truro & St Austell constituencies, Camborne & Redruth is one of Britain's most westerly constituencies. It is also a closely fought three-way marginal with Labour, the Conservatives and Liberal Democrats all in sight of victory. Labour's support is greatest in the former tin- and copper-mining town of Redruth, the Liberal Democrats dominate in Cornwall's largest town, Camborne, and the Conservatives are strongest in the rural areas surrounding both towns. Sitting Falmouth & Camborne MP Julia Goldsworthy has announced she will fight this seat for the Liberal Democrats. Seeking to oust her will be former Labour councillor Jude Robinson and David Cameron's former press secretary George Eustice.

North Cornwall

Lib Dem notional majority of 2,892; notional turnout: 64.5%

PARTY	2005 CANDIDATE	NOTIONAL 2005 VOTES	NOTIONAL 2005 % VOTE	PPC FOR NEXT GE
Lib Dem	Dan Rogerson	17,812	42.3	Dan Rogerson MP
Conservative	Mark Formosa	14,920	35.4	Sian Flynn
Labour	David Acton	5,272	12.5	Peter Watson
Others		4,094	9.7	

One of the most remote and picturesque constituencies in the United Kingdom, the North Cornwall constituency is set at the heart of Bodmin Moor, taking in the attractive towns of Launceston, Bude and Boscastle. The constituency's attractive scenery and beaches bring hundreds of thousands of tourists to the area each year, providing significant local employment. At 27%, the proportion of pensioners living in this seat is well above average. Liberal Democrat prospects here are boosted slightly by the transfer of Conservative-inclined wards around the towns of Newquay and Edgcumbe to the new St Austell & Newquay constituency. In a seat where the power of personal votes matters more than most, incumbent Liberal Democrat MP Dan Rogerson will hope to defeat Conservative Sian Flynn in order to secure a second term.

South East Cornwall

Lib Dem notional majority of 5,485; notional turnout: 67.6%

PARTY	2005 CANDIDATE	NOTIONAL 2005 VOTES	NOTIONAL 2005 % VOTE	PPC FOR NEXT GE
Lib Dem	Colin Breed MP	21,795	46.8	Karen Gillard
Conservative	Ashley Gray	16,310	35.0	Sheryll Murray
Labour	Colin Binley	4,873	10.5	Bill Stevens
Others		3,608	7.7	

Held by Liberal Democrat MP Colin Breed since 1997, the South East Cornwall constituency is demographically divided between largely unskilled agricultural workers and middle-class professionals who commute in their thousands to nearby Plymouth each day. Despite being represented by the pro-European Liberal Democrats, this is a deeply Eurosceptic constituency where anger at damage to the fishing sector by the Common Fisheries Policy runs deep. UKIP placed a strong second at the 2009 European elections. As with many other South West constituencies, the constituency is almost exclusively white (99.3%) and enjoys high levels of owner occupation (74%). Tory-defector Karen Gillard, a Plymouth city councillor until 2007, will fight the seat for the Liberal Democrats while high-profile local campaigner Sheryll Murray will do battle for the Conservatives.

Central Devon

Conservative notional majority of 2,338; notional turnout: 69.8%

PARTY	2005 CANDIDATE	NOTIONAL 2005 VOTES	NOTIONAL 2005 % VOTE	PPC FOR NEXT GE
Conservative	n/a	20,517	43.8	Mel Stride
Lib Dem	n/a	18,179	38.8	Sally Morgan
Labour	n/a	5,429	11.6	Digby Trout
Others		2,755	5.9	

East Devon

Conservative notional majority of 9,168; notional turnout: 68.0%

PARTY	2005 CANDIDATE	NOTIONAL 2005 VOTES	NOTIONAL 2005 % VOTE	PPC FOR NEXT GE
Conservative	Hugo Swire MP	22,535	47.3	Hugo Swire MP
Lib Dem	Tim Dumper	13,367	28.0	Paul Buchanan
Labour	James Court	8,691	18.2	Gareth Manson
Others		3,079	6.5	

North Devon

Lib Dem notional majority of 5,276; notional turnout: 68.2%

PARTY	2005 CANDIDATE	NOTIONAL 2005 VOTES	NOTIONAL 2005 % VOTE	PPC FOR NEXT GE
Lib Dem	Nicholas Harvey MP	22,869	46.4	Nicholas Harvey MP
Conservative	Orlando Fraser	17,593	35.7	Philip Milton
Labour	Mark Cann	4,379	8.9	Mark Cann
Others		4,427	9.0	

Once held by former Liberal Party leader Jeremy Thorpe, this seat was regained by Nick Harvey for the Lib Dems from Conservative Tony Speller at the 1992 general election. Unlike many of their long-standing constituencies, the Liberal Democrats have never been able to establish a firm stranglehold on this seat. Barnstaple and Ilfracombe, the largest population centres in the constituency, have suffered considerably over the past decades with the decline of their tourist industries and experience considerable social problems. Both towns are overwhelmingly favourable towards the Liberal Democrats. The Conservatives remain strong across most of the constituency, their support hardening the further away from the coast and into the Devon countryside one travels. The incumbent's opponent comes in the form of Philip Milton, a local bookshop owner and restaurateur.

South West Devon

Conservative notional majority of 9,442; notional turnout: 68.2%

PARTY	2005 CANDIDATE	NOTIONAL 2005 VOTES	NOTIONAL 2005 % VOTE	PPC FOR NEXT GE
Conservative	Gary Streeter MP	20,831	44.4	Gary Streeter MP
Labour	Christopher Mavin	11,389	24.3	Luke Pollard
Lib Dem	Judy Evans	11,179	23.8	n/a
Others		3,532	7.5	

Torridge & West Devon

Conservative notional majority of 2,732; notional turnout: 71.2%

PARTY	2005 CANDIDATE	NOTIONAL 2005 VOTES	NOTIONAL 2005 % VOTE	PPC FOR NEXT GE
Conservative	Geoffrey Cox	21,520	42.3	Geoffrey Cox MP
Lib Dem	David Walter	18,788	36.9	Adam Symons
Labour	Rebecca Richards	5,363	10.5	Darren Jones
Others		5,235	10.3	

Exeter

Labour notional majority of 8,559; notional turnout: 64.3%

PARTY	2005 CANDIDATE	NOTIONAL 2005 VOTES	NOTIONAL 2005 % VOTE	PPC FOR NEXT GE
Labour	Ben Bradshaw MP	20,887	42.1	Ben Bradshaw MP
Conservative	Peter Cox	12,328	24.9	Hannah Foster
Lib Dem	Jon Underwood	10,376	20.9	Graham Oakes
Others		5,983	12.1	

Seized in 1997 by openly gay Culture, Media and Sport Secretary Ben Bradshaw after an unpleasant campaign in which allegations of homophobia were made against the Conservatives, Exeter is one of Labour's safest seats in the South West. Tightly drawn to include the town's urban wards, boundary changes which transfer the rural St Loyes and Topsham wards to East Devon will frustrate Tory prospects. Levels of owner occupation are, at 64.9%, low for a South West constituency. The University of Exeter is located here, resulting in a considerable proportion of middle-class Labour voters. Charity fundraiser Hannah Foster, a former chairman of her party's youth wing, is energetically challenging for the Conservatives. UKIP MEP the Earl of Dartmouth will also contest the seat.

Newton Abbot

Lib Dem notional majority of 4,830; notional turnout: 68.9%

PARTY	2005 CANDIDATE	NOTIONAL 2005 VOTES	NOTIONAL 2005 % VOTE	PPC FOR NEXT GE
Lib Dem	Richard Younger-Ross MP	20,967	45.6	Richard Younger-Ross MP
Conservative	Stanley Johnson	16,137	35.1	Anne-Marie Morris
Labour	Chris Sherwood	5,233	11.4	Jermaine Atiya-Alla
Others		3,675	8.0	

The new name for the current Teignbridge constituency, this seat includes the Devon towns of Teignmouth, Kingsteignton and Dawlish and substantial parts of the Dartmoor National Park. This constituency is generally middle-class in nature with a high number of second-home owners. At 77.3% levels of owner occupation here are extremely high, as is the proportion of those over the age of sixty (28.1%). Agriculture and tourism are the constituency's two largest employers. While the Liberal Democrats continue to dominate at a local government level, Conservative chances in this redrawn constituency are boosted by the loss of several wards to Devon Central. Richard Younger-Ross has held this seat for the Liberal Democrats since the 2001 general election and will be challenged by Conservative Anne-Marie Morris.

Plymouth, Moor View

Labour notional majority of 7,740; notional turnout: 58.2%

PARTY	2005 CANDIDATE	NOTIONAL 2005 VOTES	NOTIONAL 2005 % VOTE	PPC FOR NEXT GE
Labour	Alison Seabeck	17,739	44.4	Alison Seabeck MP
Conservative	Richard Cuming	9,999	25.0	Matthew Groves
Lib Dem	Judith Jolly	7,583	19.0	n/a
Others		4,639	11.6	

A new and rather ornate name for a constituency which would be better described as Plymouth North, this constituency delivered Labour a majority of just a shade under 20,000 at the 1997 general election. Moor View is a tough, working-class constituency which enjoys little of the historical prestige of the neighbouring Sutton & Devonport seat: almost four in five residents have no qualifications, a third of properties are council owned and unemployment is considerably higher than the national average. There are no particularly strong areas for the Conservatives in this constituency, yet the party is broadly tied with Labour in the Budshead, Eggbuckland and Southway areas in the north of the seat. Labour dominates, with insurmountable leads in Honicknowle and St Budeaux – home to large council estates with considerable crime and social problems. Sitting Labour MP and former government whip Alison Seabeck will face competition from Conservative Matthew Groves.

Plymouth, Sutton & Devonport

Labour notional majority of 4,472; notional turnout: 55.5%

PARTY	2005 CANDIDATE	NOTIONAL 2005 VOTES	NOTIONAL 2005 % VOTE	PPC FOR NEXT GE
Labour	Linda Gilroy MP	16,370	40.7	Linda Gilroy MP
Conservative	Oliver Colvile	11,898	29.6	Oliver Colvile
Lib Dem	Karen Gillard	9,102	22.6	n/a
Others		2,875	7.1	

No other constituency is so steeped in Britain's maritime tradition in quite the same way as Plymouth, Sutton & Devonport; the staging point of Francis Drake's victories, home of the world's largest naval base and haven for small manufacturing industries serving the shipping industry. Despite having the same name as the constituency once represented by Tory diarist Alan Clark, the present make-up of the constituency shares little real resemblance to it and is largely urban in composition. Owner occupation levels in the constituency stand at 54.8%, with 20.4% of homes privately rented – perhaps unsurprising given the transitory residence status of many of the military families who move to the area. Oliver Colvile, who fought the seat the 2001 and 2005 general elections, will hope to make it third time lucky and unseat sitting MP Linda Gilroy, who has held the seat since 1997.

St Austell & Newquay

Lib Dem notional majority of 5,723; notional turnout: 64.9%

PARTY	2005 CANDIDATE	NOTIONAL 2005 VOTES	NOTIONAL 2005 % VOTE	PPC FOR NEXT GE
Lib Dem	n/a	21,747	47.3	Stephen Gilbert
Conservative	n/a	16,024	34.8	Caroline Right
Labour	n/a	6,335	13.8	Lee Jameson
Others		1,895	4.1	

A newly created constituency, St Austell & Newquay comprises roughly half of the current Truro & St Austell seat, plus a quarter of Cornwall North and a tenth of the Cornwall South East constituencies. With around 20,000 residents apiece, both St Austell and Newquay are vibrant towns whose populations can grow dramatically during the summer months as thousands of tourists visit the area's attractive beach resorts. Unsurprisingly, tourism is the largest local employer here although agriculture dominates when one travels inland. The Conservatives were the largest party here in the inaugural Cornwall unitary council elections in 2009. The Liberal Democrat candidate will be Stephen Gilbert while the Conservatives are fielding former TV-am television presenter Caroline Righton. Local councillor Dick Cole, the leader of the Cornish nationalist Mebyon Kernow party, will also stand.

St Ives

Lib Dem notional majority of 10,711; notional turnout: 67.7%

PARTY	2005 CANDIDATE	NOTIONAL 2005 VOTES	NOTIONAL 2005 % VOTE	PPC FOR NEXT GE
Lib Dem	Andrew George MP	22,651	51.8	Andrew George MP
Conservative	Christian Mitchell	11,940	27.3	Derek Thomas
Labour	Michael Dooley	5,473	12.5	Phillippa Latimer
Others		3,627	8.3	

North Somerset

Conservative notional majority of 10,364; notional turnout: 71.7%

PARTY	2005 CANDIDATE	NOTIONAL 2005 VOTES	NOTIONAL 2005 % VOTE	PPC FOR NEXT GE
Conservative	Liam Fox MP	21,631	41.8	Liam Fox MP
Lib Dem	Mike Bell	15,624	30.2	Brian Matthew
Labour	Chanel Stevens	11,267	21.8	n/a
Others		3,214	6.2	

North East Somerset

Conservative notional majority of 212; notional turnout: 71.4%

PARTY	2005 CANDIDATE	NOTIONAL 2005 VOTES	NOTIONAL 2005 % VOTE	PPC FOR NEXT GE
Conservative	Chris Watt	18,149	39.1	Jacob Rees-Mogg
Labour	Dan Norris MP	17,937	38.6	Dan Norris MP
Lib Dem	Gail Coleshill	9,096	19.6	Gail Coleshill
Others		1,234	2.7	

Somerton & Frome

Lib Dem notional majority of 595; notional turnout: 69.2%

PARTY	2005 CANDIDATE	NOTIONAL 2005 VOTES	NOTIONAL 2005 % VOTE	PPC FOR NEXT GE
Lib Dem	David Heath MP	23,341	43.8	David Heath MP
Conservative	Clive Allen	22,746	42.6	Annunziata Rees-Mogg
Labour	Joseph Pestell	5,775	10.8	David Oakensen
Others		1,488	2.8	

Taunton Deane

Lib Dem notional majority of 1,868; notional turnout: 69.2%

PARTY	2005 CANDIDATE	NOTIONAL 2005 VOTES	NOTIONAL 2005 % VOTE	PPC FOR NEXT GE
Lib Dem	Jeremy Browne	25,159	44.4	Jeremy Browne MP
Conservative	Adrian Flook	23,291	41.1	Mark Formosa
Labour	Andrew Govier	6,844	12.1	n/a
Others		1,355	2.4	

One of only three Liberal Democrat seats to be lost to the Conservatives in 2001, sitting MP Jeremy Browne turned the tables on one-term Tory Adrian Flook to snatch the seat back by 537 votes at the last election. The constituency is centred on the towns of Taunton and Wellington – both Liberal Democrat strongholds – and scores of attractive Tory-inclined villages. Minor boundary changes boost the Liberal Democrat majority to 1,700 votes, the constituency losing the heavily Tory rural wards of Dulverton & Brushford, Quarme, Brompton Ralph and Haddon to Bridgwater & West Somerset. Support for the Tories and Liberal Democrats on Taunton Deane Borough Council is evenly divided, the parties holding 25 and 26 seats respectively. Mark Formosa, a former Restormel councillor, will contest the seat for the Conservatives.

Tiverton & Honiton

Conservative notional majority of 9,007; notional turnout: 70.4%

PARTY	2005 CANDIDATE	NOTIONAL 2005 VOTES	NOTIONAL 2005 % VOTE	PPC FOR NEXT GE
Conservative	Angela Browning MP	23,961	46.7	Neil Parish
Lib Dem	David Nation	14,954	29.1	Jon Underwood
Labour	Fiona Bentley	6,851	13.3	Vernon Whitlock
Others		5,566	10.8	

Torbay

Lib Dem notional majority of 2,727; notional turnout: 60.2%

PARTY	2005 CANDIDATE	NOTIONAL 2005 VOTES	NOTIONAL 2005 % VOTE	PPC FOR NEXT GE
Lib Dem	Adrian Sanders MP	18,943	41.8	Adrian Sanders MP
Conservative	Marcus Wood	16,216	35.8	Marcus Wood
Labour	David Pedrick-Friend	6,555	14.5	David Pedrick-Friend
Others		3,634	8.0	

The former constituency of spy writer Rupert Allason ('Nigel West'), Torbay was lost to Liberal Democrat Adrian Sanders by 12 votes at the 1997 general election. The 'English Riviera', whose council has alternated violently between the Conservatives and Liberal Democrats in recent years, is one of only a handful of areas to have a directly elected mayor, with Conservative Nick Bye in post since 2005. A major tourist destination, the town of Torquay attracts more than a million tourists each year. Support for the Labour Party is limited, council housing is scarce and almost a third of residents are over retirement age. UKIP, who saved their deposit last time, will put up a strong fight. Restaurateur-turned-headhunter Marcus Wood, who fought the seat in 2005, will again challenge for the Conservatives.

Totnes

Conservative notional majority of 2,693; notional turnout: 69.7%

PARTY	2005 CANDIDATE	NOTIONAL 2005 VOTES	NOTIONAL 2005 % VOTE	PPC FOR NEXT GE
Conservative	Anthony Steen MP	20,009	42.8	Sarah Wollaston
Lib Dem	Julian Brazil	17,316	37.1	Julian Brazil
Labour	Valerie Burns	5,674	12.1	Carol Whitty
Others		3,736	8.0	

Truro & Falmouth

PARTY	2005 CANDIDATE	NOTIONAL 2005 VOTES	NOTIONAL 2005 % VOTE	PPC FOR NEXT GE
Lib Dem	n/a	17,406	41.0	Terrye Teverson
Conservative	n/a	13,475	31.7	Sarah Newton
Labour	n/a	8,090	19.0	Charlotte MacKenzie
Others		3,509	8.3	

Lib Dem notional majority of 3,931; notional turnout: 65.0%

A newly formed constituency, Truro & Falmouth is formed of half of the current Truro & St Austell seat and a third of Falmouth & Camborne – both of which are currently held by the Liberal Democrats. Employment in both towns has traditionally revolved around industry – mining in Truro and docks in Falmouth – but the tourist-driven service sector now dominates. At 27.1%, the proportion of pensioners here is well above average. Historically weak on a local government level, the Conservatives secured their best local performance in decades at the 2009 Cornwall unitary council elections. Terrye Teverson will defend the seat for the Liberal Democrats against a challenge from Conservative Sarah Newton. UKIP, who were close to topping the poll here at the 2009 European elections, are fielding Glen Corcoran.

Wells

PARTY	2005 CANDIDATE	NOTIONAL 2005 VOTES	NOTIONAL 2005 % VOTE	PPC FOR NEXT GE
Conservative	David Heathcoat-Amory MP	23,071	43.6	David Heathcoat-Amory MP
Lib Dem	Tessa Munt	20,031	37.8	Tessa Munt
Labour	Dan Whittle	8,288	15.6	Andy Merryfield
Others		1,575	3.0	

Conservative notional majority of 3,040; notional turnout: 67.7%

Weston-super-Mare

PARTY	2005 CANDIDATE	NOTIONAL 2005 VOTES	NOTIONAL 2005 % VOTE	PPC FOR NEXT GE
Conservative	John Penrose	19,760	40.3	John Penrose MP
Lib Dem	Brian Cotter MP	17,672	36.1	Mike Bell
Labour	Damien Egan	9,151	18.7	David Bradley
Others		2,394	4.9	

Conservative notional majority of 2,088; notional turnout: 65.6%

Yeovil

PARTY	2005 CANDIDATE	NOTIONAL 2005 VOTES	NOTIONAL 2005 % VOTE	PPC FOR NEXT GE
Lib Dem	David Laws MP	26,076	51.5	David Laws MP
Conservative	Ian Jenkins	17,297	34.1	Kevin Davis
Labour	Colin Rolfe	5,346	10.6	Lee Skevington
Others		1,946	3.8	

Lib Dem notional majority of 8,779; notional turnout: 63.8%

Formerly held by Paddy Ashdown, the Yeovil constituency has elected a Liberal Democrat member of Parliament since 1983. Yeovil, which is well known for aircraft-manufacturing and defence logistics industries, is by far the largest town in the constituency and delivers the Liberal Democrats near-slavish loyalty. The Conservatives are far more competitive in the rest of this rural constituency, yet only hold substantial majorities over the Liberal Democrats in South Petherton and Blackdown. Aside from small pockets of support in Yeovil and Chard, the Labour Party is an irrelevance here. South Somerset District Council has been under outright Liberal Democrat control since 1987. Incumbent MP David Laws will face a challenge from former Kingston Conservative councillor Kevin Davis.

Wessex

Wessex may evoke images of Thomas Hardy's *Far from the Madding Crowd*, but in electoral politics nothing could be further from the truth given the vibrant three-party competition to be expected at the next general election. The counties of Dorset, Gloucestershire, Hampshire and Wiltshire are bristling with key marginal constituencies, on which the fortunes of Labour, Conservative and Liberal Democrat alike depend, with throngs of candidates and activists generating an atmosphere of anything but peace and quiet.

Gloucestershire has been defined to include Bristol, where the pattern has been further complicated by boundary changes. With the quadrants making up the seats having been reorientated, Bristol North West gains the strongly Conservative wards of Westbury-on-Trym and Stoke Bishop from Bristol West, which leaves that seat as safer for first-term Liberal Democrat Stephen Williams while making Labour's chances of holding North West against the Tories even more perilous. They will further not be helped by Doug Naysmith's decision to retire, and the Conservative candidate Charlotte Leslie will be a strong favourite to pull off the 3 per cent swing required. However, in order to be sure of forming a government, the electoral arithmetic requires the Tories to gain a much harder target in the city, Bristol East, where Adeela Shafi needs a swing of nearly 9 per cent against Kerry McCarthy.

There is plenty of further interest just beyond the city boundaries. Some 32,000 voters from the old Bristol North West have been placed with 16,500 from Liberal Democrat Northavon and 13,750 from Labour Kingswood in an entirely new seat, to be named Filton & Bradley Stoke. Filton is well known as the site of the Rolls-Royce engine factory and airport, but Bradley Stoke is an entirely new town, only built since 1987 (and known by some as 'Sadly Broke' due to negative housing equity in its early years). The first result here will be more difficult to predict than almost any other in Britain, with no sitting candidates and three-way marginal status. The tentative notional figures for a hypothetical 2005 contest have the Conservatives ahead, which is good news for Jack LoPresti, but there is enough doubt for the seat to figure as both a Labour and a Lib Dem target in the tables below. Kingswood is definitely a Tory target from Labour, but also without doubt a tough one – as with Bristol East they need a large swing (7 per cent) and the ability to repeat their wins in their 1980s heyday.

There are three other key Conservative targets in Gloucestershire. Two are currently held by Labour and one by the Liberal Democrats. Stroud has seemed since 1997 to be an unlikely Labour seat, being one of the most rural constituencies they hold, and it would take only a 1 per cent swing for Neil Carmichael to oust David Drew MP. A more significant gain, though, would be the county town itself, for if the Tories can take Gloucester they should at least be the largest party in the Commons. Meanwhile, Cheltenham is one of the Lib Dems' most vulnerable seats on paper, for with the retirement of Nigel Jones in 2005 Martin Horwood held on with a majority more than halved to 2,300 – and the addition of 5,000 rural voters reduces that in notional terms to just 316. However, the Liberal Democrats were only a couple of per cent behind in the May 2008 borough elections, and the power of a first-term incumbency effect should never be underestimated.

Moving down to Dorset, there are no significant boundary changes, but South Dorset, based on Weymouth and Portland, must be one of Labour's most vulnerable seats. The current Education Minister, Jim Knight, did very well to increase his majority from a perilous 153 to nearly 2,000 in 2005, more perhaps as a result of incumbency than because the Tory candidate was caught doctoring a campaign photograph, but he remains the only Labour candidate ever to win a seat in Dorset in a general election, and even this tenure looks very impermanent. The Liberal Democrats still entertain hopes of gains in Bournemouth West, North Dorset and West Dorset (against Oliver Letwin), but one feels their best opportunity may have passed. Annette Brooke remains very popular in Mid Dorset & North Poole, though, and is a narrow favourite to hold on for a third term.

In Wiltshire, there certainly have been boundary changes, with the creation of a new and seventh seat. This is Chippenham, and it should provide one of the most interesting contests anywhere in Britain (see *One to Watch* below). Elsewhere in Wiltshire, the Conservatives will expect to take both Swindon seats, and indeed must, in order even to be the largest party nationally.

The largest county in this survey is Hampshire, and it has been getting even more populous, which explains why yet again it is granted an extra seat by the Boundary Commission, making eighteen in all, equal with Essex the most of any shire county. The new seat is in the south-east of the county, and is to be called Meon Valley, and it reflects the predominant pattern of marginality in Hampshire – between Conservative and Liberal Democrat. The notional figures suggest that the Conservatives are starting with a lead of just 2,378 – but it should be remembered that 42 per cent of the new Meon Valley seat is taken from Winchester, where Mark Oaten won by a comfortable 7,500 in 2005, and with there now being no incumbent Lib Dem MP, his opponent then, George Hollingbery, should be able to take a place in the Commons next time. Oaten's retirement in embarrassing circumstances also means that Martin Tod will find it harder than the figures suggest to defend the 6.4 per cent swing needed in the rump of Winchester. All the other three Liberal Democrat seats in Hampshire are on the Conservative target list as well. The most vulnerable is Romsey, now renamed with the addition of 'Southampton North' to reflect the presence of two wards from that city instead of just one. Sandra Gidley holds a notional lead of just 204 against the Tory challenge of Caroline Nokes. Just to the north-east of Southampton rather than the north-west, Eastleigh may be harder to win than the 0.6 per cent swing indicates, as Chris Huhne has raised his profile markedly with two second place finishes in his party's leadership contests since the last election – in 2006 and 2007, the latter being very close. In the tight grid of streets in Portsmouth South, the most densely populated seat outside London, another figure with an SDP background, Mike Hancock, seems to have a large personal base as long as he keeps standing.

However, the Tories will be most disappointed if they don't achieve the minimal advance needed to take Portsmouth North, while if they can gain either of Labour's other seats in Hampshire, the Southampton divisions of Test and Itchen (named after the two rivers, but effectively West and East respectively), they will be certainly be on target for a working overall majority – and the Conservatives gained control of Southampton City Council in May 2008 by making eight gains, sweeping across the city. This shows that the elimination of Labour in Hampshire, and indeed Wessex as a whole (apart from Bristol South), is not completely out of the question, and if this were to happen, in Hardyesque terms the Conservatives would return to their native office, and Labour would head for a Jude-like obscurity.

Target seats

SEAT	SWING REQUIRED %	MP	CHALLENGER
Conservative from Labour			
Portsmouth North	0.4	Sarah McCarthy-Fry	Penny Mordaunt
Stroud	1.0	David Drew	Neil Carmichael
South Swindon	1.8	Anne Snelgrove	Robert Buckland
South Dorset	1.9	Jim Knight	Richard Drax
Bristol North West	2.9	Doug Naysmith*	Charlotte Leslie
North Swindon	3.2	Michael Wills	Justin Tomlinson
Gloucester	6.5	Parmjit Dhanda	Richard Graham
Kingswood	6.9	Roger Berry	Owen Inskip
Bristol East	8.7	Kerry McCarthy	Adeela Shafi
Southampton, Test	9.6	Alan Whitehead	Jeremy Moulton
Southampton, Itchen	10.5	John Denham	Royston Smith
Labour from Conservatives			
Filton & Bradley Stoke	0.8	(Jack LoPresti)	Ian Boulton
Conservative from Lib Dems			
Romsey & Southampton North	0.3	Sandra Gidley	Caroline Nokes
Cheltenham	0.4	Martin Horwood	Mark Coote
Eastleigh	0.6	Chris Huhne	Maria Hutchings
Chippenham	2.4	(Duncan Hames)	Wilfred Emmanuel-Jones
Portsmouth South	4.0	Mike Hancock	Flick Drummond
Winchester	6.4	(Martin Tod)	Steve Brine
Mid Dorset & North Poole	6.6	Annette Brooke	Nick King
Lib Dem from Conservatives			
West Dorset	2.4	Oliver Letwin	Mike Bell
Meon Valley	2.5	(George Hollingbery)	Liz Leffman
Filton & Bradley Stoke	3.6	(Jack LoPresti)	John Kiely
Bournemouth West	3.8	(Conor Burns)	Sally Morgan
North Dorset	4.3	Robert Walter	Adam Symons

One to watch: Chippenham

Notional majority 2005: LD 2,183 (4.7%)
Liberal Democrat candidate: Duncan Hames
Conservative candidate: Wilfred Enmanuel-Jones

Carved out of North Wiltshire, Westbury and Devizes, the brand new division is a rather compact urban core based on the towns of Melksham, Trowbridge, Bradford-on-Avon and Chippenham itself, and seems almost to be designed to bring together Liberal Democrat voters, giving them a notional extra seat with a hypothetical majority of 2,183 had it been in existence in 2005. The Conservatives have selected an unusual candidate – the black farmer Wilfred Emmanuel-Jones. It will be fascinating to see how he does against the Lib Dem Duncan Hames, in the context of an untried seat with no sitting MP and a likely national Tory surge.

Aldershot

Conservative notional majority of 6,345; notional turnout: 63.6%

PARTY	2005 CANDIDATE	NOTIONAL 2005 VOTES	NOTIONAL 2005 % VOTE	PPC FOR NEXT GE
Conservative	Gerald Howarth MP	18,474	44.0	Gerald Howarth MP
Lib Dem	Adrian Collett	12,129	28.9	n/a
Labour	Howard Linsley	9,113	21.7	Jonathan Slater
Others		2,246	5.4	

Basingstoke

Conservative notional majority of 2,651; notional turnout: 61.0%

PARTY	2005 CANDIDATE	NOTIONAL 2005 VOTES	NOTIONAL 2005 % VOTE	PPC FOR NEXT GE
Conservative	Maria Miller	16,409	38.8	Maria Miller MP
Labour	Paul Harvey	13,758	32.6	Funda Pepperell
Lib Dem	Jen Smith	9,261	21.9	n/a
Others		2,839	6.7	

Bournemouth East

Conservative notional majority of 5,874; notional turnout: 58.9%

PARTY	2005 CANDIDATE	NOTIONAL 2005 VOTES	NOTIONAL 2005 % VOTE	PPC FOR NEXT GE
Conservative	Tobias Ellwood	18,949	45.3	Tobias Ellwood MP
Lib Dem	Andrew Garratt	13,075	31.3	n/a
Labour	David Stokes	7,761	18.6	David Stokes
Others		2,050	4.9	

Bournemouth West

Conservative notional majority of 2,766; notional turnout: 53.8%

PARTY	2005 CANDIDATE	NOTIONAL 2005 VOTES	NOTIONAL 2005 % VOTE	PPC FOR NEXT GE
Conservative	John Butterfill MP	14,476	39.5	Conor Burns
Lib Dem	Richard Renaut	11,710	32.0	Alasdair Murray
Labour	Dafydd Williams	8,384	22.9	Sharon Carr-Brown
Others		2,043	5.6	

Bristol East

Labour notional majority of 7,335; notional turnout: 63.0%

PARTY	2005 CANDIDATE	NOTIONAL 2005 VOTES	NOTIONAL 2005 % VOTE	PPC FOR NEXT GE
Labour	Kerry McCarthy	19,236	45.5	Kerry McCarthy MP
Conservative	Julia Manning	11,901	28.2	Adeela Shafi
Lib Dem	Philip James	8,318	19.7	Michael Popham
Others		2,811	6.7	

The site of Tony Benn's humiliating defeat at the 1983 general election, Bristol East has been held by Labour since their ousting of Tory Jonathan Sayeed in 1992. This constituency contains some of the Bristol's poorer communities, including the Eastville and St George areas, where the Labour Party has long dominated. No area of this seat can be described as 'safe' for the Conservatives but the party performs well in leafy Stockwood on the city's outer reaches. The Conservatives will be disappointed not to have advanced further on a local government level in recent years, holding four seats (level pegging with Labour) to the six of the Liberal Democrats. The party's chances are, however, slightly improved by the transfer of a safe Labour ward to Bristol South. Conservative Adeela Shafi will fight incumbent Labour MP Kerry McCarthy for her seat.

Bristol North West

Labour notional majority of 2,781; notional turnout: 68.7%

PARTY	2005 CANDIDATE	NOTIONAL 2005 VOTES	NOTIONAL 2005 % VOTE	PPC FOR NEXT GE
Labour	n/a	18,649	38.2	Sam Townend
Conservative	n/a	15,868	32.5	Charlotte Leslie
Lib Dem	n/a	12,138	24.8	Paul Harrod
Others		2,196	4.5	

While technically already in existence, the Boundary Commission has radically altered the composition of this seat – and substantially boosted Conservative chances of victory here. Most notably, the sprawling private housing estate Bradley Stoke – a Liberal Democrat stronghold – will leave the constituency at the general election while Tory-inclined Westbury-on-Trym and Stoke Bishop will be transferred in from Bristol West. The constituency remains a diverse social mix, encompassing wealthy commuter suburbs which favour the Conservatives and areas of genuine deprivation around the industrial Avonmouth Docks. Levels of owner occupation here are, at 65.5%, significantly below average with one in five homes council owned. While this is undoubtedly a Labour and Conservative marginal, the Liberal Democrats retain a strong local government base in the constituency. Sitting MP Doug Naysmith has opted for retirement and is replaced as Labour candidate by Sam Townend. He will face Conservative columnist for the *Daily Mail* newspaper Charlotte Leslie.

Bristol South

Labour notional majority of 10,928; notional turnout: 59.0%

PARTY	2005 CANDIDATE	NOTIONAL 2005 VOTES	NOTIONAL 2005 % VOTE	PPC FOR NEXT GE
Labour	Dawn Primarolo MP	21,364	48.6	Dawn Primarolo MP
Lib Dem	Kay Bernard	10,436	23.7	Mark Wright
Conservative	Graham Hill	8,623	19.6	Mark Lloyd Davies
Others		3,544	8.1	

Bristol West

Lib Dem notional majority of 1,147; notional turnout: 63.6%

PARTY	2005 CANDIDATE	NOTIONAL 2005 VOTES	NOTIONAL 2005 % VOTE	PPC FOR NEXT GE
Lib Dem	Stephen Williams	17,599	39.1	Stephen Williams MP
Labour	Valerie Davey	16,452	36.5	Paul Smith
Conservative	David Martin	7,373	16.4	Nick Yarker
Others		3,632	8.1	

Cheltenham

PARTY	2005 CANDIDATE	NOTIONAL 2005 VOTES	NOTIONAL 2005 % VOTE	PPC FOR NEXT GE
Lib Dem notional majority of 316; notional turnout: 62.4%				
Lib Dem	Martin Horwood	18,877	39.4	Martin Horwood MP
Conservative	Vanessa Gearson	18,561	38.7	Mark Coote
Labour	Christopher Evans	5,652	11.8	James Green
Others		4,814	10.0	

The Liberal Democrat Nigel Jones captured Cheltenham in 1992 after a bitter campaign in which allegations of racism against black Tory candidate John Taylor were levelled. The Conservatives are desperate to return the opulent spa town and its regency terraces to their column. Slight boundary changes bring the notional Liberal Democrat majority down to 515 votes, a figure almost identical to the 538-vote lead the Conservatives had over the Liberal Democrats in the 2009 county council elections. Cheltenham is a rare battle between two genuinely home-grown candidates: the sitting MP since 2005, Martin Horwood, and Conservative teacher Mark Coote. With the borough council having seesawed between Conservative and Liberal Democrat control for years, neither candidate starts as favourite.

Chippenham

PARTY	2005 CANDIDATE	NOTIONAL 2005 VOTES	NOTIONAL 2005 % VOTE	PPC FOR NEXT GE
Lib Dem notional majority of 2,183; notional turnout: 66.9%				
Lib Dem	n/a	19,704	42.4	Duncan Hames
Conservative	n/a	17,521	37.7	Wilfred Emmanuel-Jones
Labour	n/a	7,801	16.8	Nick Thomas-Symonds
Others		1,419	3.1	

A new creation of the Boundary Commission, Chippenham is formed of roughly two fifths of the current North Wiltshire seat, a quarter of Westbury and a fifth of Devizes. Taking in the town of Chippenham itself as well as Melksham and Bradford-on-Avon, the Liberal Democrats hold a slender notional majority of just over 1,000 votes. A relatively compact urban constituency by South West standards, many residents commute to nearby Swindon, Bath and Bristol. The Liberal Democrats narrowly outpaced the Conservatives in the 2009 unitary council elections. Jamaican-born Conservative Wilfred Emmanuel-Jones, the founder of the 'Black Farmer' sausage range, will face Liberal Democrat Duncan Hames, a former West Wiltshire councillor.

Christchurch

PARTY	2005 CANDIDATE	NOTIONAL 2005 VOTES	NOTIONAL 2005 % VOTE	PPC FOR NEXT GE
Conservative notional majority of 14,640; notional turnout: 70.3%				
Conservative	Christopher Chope MP	25,886	55.3	Christopher Chope MP
Lib Dem	Leslie Coman	11,246	24.0	n/a
Labour	Jim King	7,297	15.6	Robert Deeks
Others		2,378	5.1	

The Cotswolds

PARTY	2005 CANDIDATE	NOTIONAL 2005 VOTES	NOTIONAL 2005 % VOTE	PPC FOR NEXT GE
Conservative notional majority of 10,742; notional turnout: 67.2%				
Conservative	Geoffrey Clifton-Brown MP	24,907	49.4	Geoffrey Clifton-Brown MP
Lib Dem	Philip Beckerlegge	14,165	28.1	Roger Brown
Labour	Mark Dempsey	9,392	18.6	Mark Dempsey
Others		1,987	3.9	

Devizes

Conservative notional majority of 12,259; notional turnout: 65.3%

PARTY	2005 CANDIDATE	NOTIONAL 2005 VOTES	NOTIONAL 2005 % VOTE	PPC FOR NEXT GE
Conservative	Michael Ancram MP	21,849	51.0	n/a
Labour	Sharon Charity	9,590	22.4	Sharon Charity
Lib Dem	Fiona Hornby	9,549	22.3	Nic Coome
Others		1,825	4.3	

Mid Dorset & North Poole

Lib Dem notional majority of 5,931; notional turnout: 72.0%

PARTY	2005 CANDIDATE	NOTIONAL 2005 VOTES	NOTIONAL 2005 % VOTE	PPC FOR NEXT GE
Lib Dem	Annette Brooke MP	22,596	50.0	Annette Brooke MP
Conservative	Simon Hayes	16,665	36.9	Nick King
Labour	Philip Murray	4,547	10.1	Chris Thompson
Others		1,412	3.1	

A cumbersomely, yet precisely, named seat, Mid Dorset & North Poole was gained from the Conservatives by Liberal Democrat Annette Brooke at the 2001 general election after years of domination on a local government level. This is an attractive part of the world with extremely high levels of owner occupation, low unemployment and a substantial elderly population. There are no particularly large towns in the seat, the largest settlements being Corfe Mullen and Upton with less than 10,000 residents. The Liberal Democrats will be disappointed to lose their stronghold of Alderney to Bournemouth West while at the same time gaining the Tory-inclined Wimborne Minster and Colehill wards from North Dorset. In her bid for a third term, Annette Brooke will face Bournemouth Conservative councillor Nick King.

North Dorset

Conservative notional majority of 4,200; notional turnout: 69.3%

PARTY	2005 CANDIDATE	NOTIONAL 2005 VOTES	NOTIONAL 2005 % VOTE	PPC FOR NEXT GE
Conservative	Robert Walter MP	22,721	46.4	Robert Walter MP
Lib Dem	Emily Gasson	18,521	37.8	Emily Gasson
Labour	John Yarwood	4,709	9.6	Mike Bunney
Others		3,005	6.1	

South Dorset

Labour notional majority of 1,812; notional turnout: 69.4%

PARTY	2005 CANDIDATE	NOTIONAL 2005 VOTES	NOTIONAL 2005 % VOTE	PPC FOR NEXT GE
Labour	Jim Knight MP	20,231	41.6	Jim Knight MP
Conservative	Ed Matts	18,419	37.9	Richard Drax
Lib Dem	Graham Oakes	7,647	15.7	Ros Kayes
Others		2,287	4.7	

The only Conservative seat won in 1997 to fall to the Labour Party at the 2001 general election, locally popular Cabinet minister Jim Knight is defending an 1,800-vote majority. The fortunes of Weymouth, the constituency's largest town, have closely mirrored the decline of British coastal tourism. Tourism does, however, remain a substantial local employer in Weymouth itself and along the stunning Jurassic Coast. Almost entirely white, a fifth of residents have no qualifications although rates of home ownership are high at 72.7%. Labour lost all of its county council seats in 2009, the Conservatives winning five to the Liberal Democrats' three. The Conservative challenge comes in the form of Richard Drax, a high-profile former television reporter and local farmer.

West Dorset

Conservative notional majority of 2,461; notional turnout: 76.4%

PARTY	2005 CANDIDATE	NOTIONAL 2005 VOTES	NOTIONAL 2005 % VOTE	PPC FOR NEXT GE
Conservative	Oliver Letwin MP	24,763	46.5	Oliver Letwin MP
Lib Dem	Justine McGuinness	22,302	41.9	Sue Farrant
Labour	Dave Roberts	4,124	7.7	Steve Bick
Others		2,036	3.8	

Eastleigh

Lib Dem notional majority of 534; notional turnout: 64.4%

PARTY	2005 CANDIDATE	NOTIONAL 2005 VOTES	NOTIONAL 2005 % VOTE	PPC FOR NEXT GE
Lib Dem	Chris Huhne	18,313	38.3	Chris Huhne MP
Conservative	Conor Burns	17,779	37.2	Maria Hutchings
Labour	Chris Watt	10,069	21.1	n/a
Others		1,615	3.4	

Formed from the railway town of Eastleigh and the eastern suburbs of Southampton, the constituency was first won by the Liberal Democrats in a 1994 by-election caused by the untimely death of Tory Stephen Milligan. Aside from two Labour councillors in the working-class Eastleigh South ward, the Liberal Democrats hold every local government seat in the constituency – unusual for a seat that the Conservatives failed to win by less than 600 votes in 2005. Feisty campaigner Maria Hutchings, recruited by the Conservatives after her public 'handbagging' of Tony Blair at the last election, will contest the seat against incumbent Liberal Democrat Chris Huhne.

Fareham

Conservative notional majority of 11,702; notional turnout: 66.9%

PARTY	2005 CANDIDATE	NOTIONAL 2005 VOTES	NOTIONAL 2005 % VOTE	PPC FOR NEXT GE
Conservative	Mark Hoban MP	24,151	49.7	Mark Hoban MP
Labour	James Carr	12,449	25.6	James Carr
Lib Dem	Richard de Ste-Croix	10,551	21.7	n/a
Others		1,425	2.9	

Filton & Bradley Stoke

Conservative notional majority of 653; notional turnout: 62.4%

PARTY	2005 CANDIDATE	NOTIONAL 2005 VOTES	NOTIONAL 2005 % VOTE	PPC FOR NEXT GE
Conservative	n/a	14,629	35.5	Jack Lopresti
Labour	n/a	13,976	33.9	Ian Boulton
Lib Dem	n/a	11,703	28.4	John Kiely
Others		935	2.3	

Forest of Dean

Conservative notional majority of 2,049; notional turnout: 70.8%

PARTY	2005 CANDIDATE	NOTIONAL 2005 VOTES	NOTIONAL 2005 % VOTE	PPC FOR NEXT GE
Conservative	Mark Harper	19,474	40.9	Mark Harper MP
Labour	Isabel Owen	17,425	36.6	Bruce Hogan
Lib Dem	Christopher Coleman	8,185	17.2	Christopher Coleman
Others		2,556	5.4	

Gloucester

Labour notional majority of 6,063; notional turnout: 62.4%

PARTY	2005 CANDIDATE	NOTIONAL 2005 VOTES	NOTIONAL 2005 % VOTE	PPC FOR NEXT GE
Labour	Parmjit Dhanda MP	22,289	47.6	Parmjit Dhanda MP
Conservative	Paul James	16,226	34.7	Richard Graham
Lib Dem	Jeremy Hilton	6,409	13.7	Jeremy Hilton
Others		1,897	4.1	

Situated on the banks of the river Severn some 90 miles from London, Gloucester was gained for Labour from Conservative Douglas French at the 1997 general election. Gloucester is a key regional business centre with many people travelling from miles around to the city shopping facilities. Aside from the large service sector, the town's largest employer is the former building society Cheltenham and Gloucester, which is headquartered here. A relatively compact constituency, Labour is strongest in the central wards of Gloucester city while the Conservatives perform strongly in the southerly Quedgeley wards. The seat is home to a small yet growing Asian population and has an owner occupation rate of around 75%. Sitting Labour MP Parmjit Dhanda, who contested the recent Commons Speaker election on a modernising platform, will be opposed by Conservative banker Richard Graham.

Gosport

Conservative notional majority of 5,730; notional turnout: 61.2%

PARTY	2005 CANDIDATE	NOTIONAL 2005 VOTES	NOTIONAL 2005 % VOTE	PPC FOR NEXT GE
Conservative	Peter Viggers MP	19,268	44.8	n/a
Labour	Richard Williams	13,538	31.5	Graham Giles
Lib Dem	Roger Roberts	7,145	16.6	n/a
Others		3,083	7.2	

East Hampshire

Conservative notional majority of 5,968; notional turnout: 64.6%

PARTY	2005 CANDIDATE	NOTIONAL 2005 VOTES	NOTIONAL 2005 % VOTE	PPC FOR NEXT GE
Conservative	n/a	21,441	47.0	Damian Hinds
Lib Dem	n/a	15,473	33.9	Adam Carew
Labour	n/a	7,499	16.4	Jane Edbrooke
Others		1,176	2.6	

North East Hampshire

Conservative notional majority of 11,189; notional turnout: 62.6%

PARTY	2005 CANDIDATE	NOTIONAL 2005 VOTES	NOTIONAL 2005 % VOTE	PPC FOR NEXT GE
Conservative	James Arbuthnot MP	22,784	53.1	James Arbuthnot MP
Lib Dem	Adam Carew	11,595	27.0	n/a
Labour	Kevin McGrath	7,102	16.6	n/a
Others		1,397	3.3	

North West Hampshire

Conservative notional majority of 12,683; notional turnout: 66.0%

PARTY	2005 CANDIDATE	NOTIONAL 2005 VOTES	NOTIONAL 2005 % VOTE	PPC FOR NEXT GE
Conservative	George Young MP	25,079	50.5	George Young MP
Lib Dem	Martin Tod	12,396	25.0	Tom McCann
Labour	Mick Mumford	10,357	20.8	n/a
Others		1,851	3.7	

Havant

Conservative notional majority of 6,395; notional turnout: 60.4%

PARTY	2005 CANDIDATE	NOTIONAL 2005 VOTES	NOTIONAL 2005 % VOTE	PPC FOR NEXT GE
Conservative	David Willetts MP	18,192	44.3	David Willetts MP
Labour	Sarah Bogle	11,797	28.7	Robert Smith
Lib Dem	Alex Bentley	8,293	20.2	n/a
Others		2,754	6.7	

Isle of Wight

Conservative notional majority of 12,978; notional turnout: 62.0%

PARTY	2005 CANDIDATE	NOTIONAL 2005 VOTES	NOTIONAL 2005 % VOTE	PPC FOR NEXT GE
Conservative	Andrew Turner MP	32,717	48.9	Andrew Turner MP
Lib Dem	Anthony Rowlands	19,739	29.5	Jill Wareham
Labour	Mark Chiverton	11,484	17.2	Mark Chiverton
Others		2,903	4.3	

Kingswood

Labour notional majority of 6,145; notional turnout: 69.1%

PARTY	2005 CANDIDATE	NOTIONAL 2005 VOTES	NOTIONAL 2005 % VOTE	PPC FOR NEXT GE
Labour	Roger Berry MP	20,498	45.9	Roger Berry MP
Conservative	Owen Inskip	14,353	32.1	Chris Skidmore
Lib Dem	Geoff Brewer	8,054	18.0	n/a
Others		1,742	3.9	

Four miles east of Bristol city centre, and fashioned out of the former Bristol South East constituency represented until 1983 by Tony Benn, Kingswood has been held by Labour backbencher Roger Berry since 1992. The bulk of the constituency is heavily inclined towards the Labour Party with Kingswood having once been a coal-mining and shoe-manufacturing town. Industry remains important in the town with its excellent transport links and proximity to pleasant countryside making it an attractive place for businesses to locate. There is a considerable amount of residual Conservative support here with the party holding strong leads in the commuter suburbs of Longwell Green, Bitton and Stoke Gifford. Chris Skidmore will challenge for the Conservatives.

Meon Valley

Conservative notional majority of 2,378; notional turnout: 71.1%

PARTY	2005 CANDIDATE	NOTIONAL 2005 VOTES	NOTIONAL 2005 % VOTE	PPC FOR NEXT GE
Conservative	n/a	22,228	45.9	George Hollingbery
Lib Dem	n/a	19,850	41.0	Liz Leffman
Labour	n/a	5,141	10.6	Howard Linsley
Others		1,225	2.5	

New Forest East

Conservative notional majority of 7,653; notional turnout: 66.0%

PARTY	2005 CANDIDATE	NOTIONAL 2005 VOTES	NOTIONAL 2005 % VOTE	PPC FOR NEXT GE
Conservative	Julian Lewis MP	23,333	49.4	Julian Lweis MP
Lib Dem	Brian Dash	15,680	33.2	Terry Scriven
Labour	Stephen Roberts	5,787	12.3	Peter Sopowski
Others		2,422	5.1	

New Forest West

Conservative notional majority of 16,183; notional turnout: 66.0%

PARTY	2005 CANDIDATE	NOTIONAL 2005 VOTES	NOTIONAL 2005 % VOTE	PPC FOR NEXT GE
Conservative	Desmond Swayne MP	24,646	55.9	Desmond Swayne MP
Lib Dem	Mike Bignell	8,463	19.2	n/a
Labour	Crada Onuegbu	7,295	16.5	Janice Hurne
Others		3,676	8.3	

Poole

Conservative notional majority of 6,035; notional turnout: 63.9%

PARTY	2005 CANDIDATE	NOTIONAL 2005 VOTES	NOTIONAL 2005 % VOTE	PPC FOR NEXT GE
Conservative	Robert Syms MP	18,296	43.4	Robert Syms MP
Lib Dem	Mike Plummer	12,261	29.1	n/a
Labour	Darren Brown	9,561	22.7	Jason Sanderson
Others		2,026	4.8	

Portsmouth North

Labour notional majority of 315; notional turnout: 60.1%

PARTY	2005 CANDIDATE	NOTIONAL 2005 VOTES	NOTIONAL 2005 % VOTE	PPC FOR NEXT GE
Labour	Sarah McCarthy-Fry	15,858	38.5	Sarah McCarthy-Fry MP
Conservative	Penny Mordaunt	15,543	37.8	Penny Mordaunt
Lib Dem	Gary Lawson	8,361	20.3	Darren Sanders
Others		1,407	3.4	

Portsmouth South

Lib Dem notional majority of 2,955; notional turnout: 57.4%

PARTY	2005 CANDIDATE	NOTIONAL 2005 VOTES	NOTIONAL 2005 % VOTE	PPC FOR NEXT GE
Lib Dem	Mike Hancock MP	15,370	41.6	Mike Hancock MP
Conservative	Caroline Dinenage	12,415	33.6	Flick Drummond
Labour	Mark Button	8,268	22.4	John Ferrett
Others		869	2.4	

The 1997 general election marked a return to the House of Commons for Liberal Democrat Mike Hancock, who, having been elected for the seat in a 1984 by-election, missed out on victory by about 250 votes in the 1987 and 1992 elections. Portsmouth South includes the city's best-known areas, including the city centre, historic harbour and dockyards. While the Conservatives have made gains in the constituency in recent years, the Liberal Democrats hold significant leads in the Charles Dickens, Fratton and Milton wards. As with many seats in the south coast, this not a wealthy area: fewer than three in five homes are owner occupied (56.4%), almost a quarter have no central heating or private bathroom and unemployment is well above the national average. Flick Drummond will hope to gain this constituency for the Conservatives.

Romsey & Southampton North

Lib Dem notional majority of 204; notional turnout: 66.4%

PARTY	2005 CANDIDATE	NOTIONAL 2005 VOTES	NOTIONAL 2005 % VOTE	PPC FOR NEXT GE
Lib Dem	Sandra Gidley MP	19,217	43.6	Sandra Gidley MP
Conservative	Caroline Nokes	19,013	43.1	Caroline Nokes
Labour	Matthew Stevens	4,816	10.9	Aktar Beg
Others		1,025	2.3	

Conservative challenger Caroline Nokes, defeated by 125 votes at the 2005 general election, is again seeking to avenge her party's 2000 by-election loss to the Liberal Democrat Sandra Gidley, after the sad death of veteran Tory Sir Michael Colvin. The diverse constituency stretches from the closely contested northern Southampton wards of Bassett and Swaythling, home to the largest university hall of residence in Europe, to the suburban bliss of Chilworth, Nursling and Rownhams, where Conservative votes are weighed rather than counted. The close parliamentary contest is mirrored on a local government level with the Conservatives holding 19 seats to the Liberal Democrats' 13.

Salisbury

PARTY	2005 CANDIDATE	NOTIONAL 2005 VOTES	NOTIONAL 2005 % VOTE	PPC FOR NEXT GE
Conservative	Robert Key MP	21,085	46.4	Robert Key MP
Lib Dem	Richard Denton-White	12,225	26.9	Nick Radford
Labour	Calre Moody	8,455	18.6	Andrew Roberts
Others		3,679	8.1	

Conservative notional majority of 8,860; notional turnout: 68.5%

Southampton, Itchen

Labour notional majority of 8,479; notional turnout: 54.7%

PARTY	2005 CANDIDATE	NOTIONAL 2005 VOTES	NOTIONAL 2005 % VOTE	PPC FOR NEXT GE
Labour	John Denham MP	19,493	48.3	John Denham MP
Conservative	Flick Drummond	11,014	27.3	Royston Smith
Lib Dem	David Goodall	8,373	20.7	David Goodall
Others		1,495	3.7	

The safer of the two Southampton constituencies for Labour, Communities Secretary John Denham has held this seat since ousting Conservative minister Christopher Chope in 1992. This constituency includes the majority of Southampton's recognisable areas, including city centre, docks and new shopping developments at Banana Wharf. Despite strong Conservative advances at a local government level (they took outright control of the council in 2008), the residents of this seat are generally predisposed towards Labour, with many large council estate and higher than average levels of unemployment. At a mere one in ten, the proportion of residents in full-time education is lower here than in neighbouring Test. The Conservatives are fielding Royston Smith, the high-profile deputy leader of Southampton City Council.

Southampton, Test

Labour notional majority of 7,817; notional turnout: 55.9%

PARTY	2005 CANDIDATE	NOTIONAL 2005 VOTES	NOTIONAL 2005 % VOTE	PPC FOR NEXT GE
Labour	Alan Whitehead MP	18,022	44.2	Alan Whitehead MP
Conservative	Stephen MacLoughlin	10,205	25.0	Jeremy Moulton
Lib Dem	Steve Sollitt	9,826	24.1	Dave Callaghan
Others		2,714	6.7	

In this historically more marginal of the two Southampton city constituencies, veteran Conservative MP James Hill was ousted by local councillor Alan Whitehead by almost 14,000 votes at the 1997 general election. This constituency includes some strong areas for the Conservatives, particularly in Ocean Village and Shirley, yet the sizeable amount of social housing in the Millbrook and Redbridge wards gives Southampton, Test a decidedly Labour tilt. The constituency has experienced vast immigration from European Union accession states in the past half-decade and houses many students from the University of Southampton, leading to significant housing overcrowding problems. The Conservatives triumphed at the 2008 local elections, taking outright control of the council. Jeremy Moulton, the cabinet member for finance on Southampton City Council, will fight the constituency for the Conservatives.

Stroud

	Labour notional majority of 996; notional turnout: 70.1%			
PARTY	**2005 CANDIDATE**	**NOTIONAL 2005 VOTES**	**NOTIONAL 2005 % VOTE**	**PPC FOR NEXT GE**
Labour	David Drew MP	21,592	40.2	David Drew MP
Conservative	Neil Carmichael	20,596	38.3	Neil Carmichael
Lib Dem	Peter Hirst	7,499	13.9	n/a
Others		4,088	7.6	

Even the most optimistic of Labour strategists could never have predicted Stroud, nestled at the foot of the Cotswold Hills in the attractive Gloucestershire countryside, would ever fall to the party of Keir Hardie. Stroud is an attractive market town originally built around the cloth trade which has in recent years become a centre for light industry and manufacturing. Stroud has marketed itself as a 'book town' and is home to a substantial left-leaning literary community, evident in the success of the Green Party in capturing council seats locally. Three quarters of homes here are owner occupied and an above-average number of residents hold university degrees. The Conservatives dominate Stroud Borough Council, holding 31 seats to Labour's seven. Conservative Neil Carmichael will face incumbent Labour MP David Drew in their third consecutive match-up.

North Swindon

	Labour notional majority of 2,675; notional turnout: 60.7%			
PARTY	**2005 CANDIDATE**	**NOTIONAL 2005 VOTES**	**NOTIONAL 2005 % VOTE**	**PPC FOR NEXT GE**
Labour	Michael Wills MP	19,311	45.1	Michael Wills MP
Conservative	Justin Tomlinson	16,636	38.9	Justin Tomlinson
Lib Dem	Mike Evemy	5,502	12.9	n/a
Others		1,362	3.2	

Located in central Wiltshire, Swindon enjoys excellent railway and road links to London, the Midlands and the West Country. North Swindon is the more working-class of the town's two seats yet enjoys low unemployment as a result of significant investment from service industries in the past two decades. The Conservatives now dominate Swindon Borough Council, and in the long term, the demographics of this seat favour them. While some of Swindon's poorest wards are found within the boundaries of this seat, the proportion of middle-class professionals making their homes here can only be expected to grow in the coming years as the construction of upscale private estates on the cusp of the Wiltshire countryside continues at fever pitch. Justice Minister Michael Wills faces a challenge from Swindon councillor and former Conservative Future chairman Justin Tomlinson.

South Swindon

	Labour notional majority of 1,493; notional turnout: 58.9%			
PARTY	**2005 CANDIDATE**	**NOTIONAL 2005 VOTES**	**NOTIONAL 2005 % VOTE**	**PPC FOR NEXT GE**
Labour	Anne Snelgrove	17,227	40.4	Anne Snelgrove MP
Conservative	Robert Buckland	15,734	36.9	Robert Buckland
Lib Dem	Sue Stebbing	7,244	17.0	n/a
Others		2,421	5.7	

Thought by many to be a safe Conservative seat following the addition of several rural wards from neighbouring Devizes, Labour surprised many by ousting veteran Tory Simon Coombs at the 1997 general election. Stretching from the centre of the former railway town to the wilds of rural Wiltshire, both major parties have areas of considerable residual strength here. Labour dominate in the Central and Parks wards, home to much of the town's decaying council housing stock, while the Conservatives lead convincingly in the rural Wroughton and Chiseldon areas. With a number of large technology and service sector firms based here, unemployment is not a problem. There are few areas which represent the scale of the Conservative Party's comeback from the near-obliteration on a local government level they suffered than Swindon, where the party now holds the council with a 27-seat majority. Welsh-born barrister Robert Buckland will fight incumbent Labour MP Anne Snelgrove for her seat.

Tewkesbury

Conservative notional majority of 9,130; notional turnout: 62.2%

PARTY	2005 CANDIDATE	NOTIONAL 2005 VOTES	NOTIONAL 2005 % VOTE	PPC FOR NEXT GE
Conservative	Laurence Robertson MP	22,238	48.2	Laurence Robertson MP
Lib Dem	Alistair Cameron	13,108	28.4	Alistair Cameron
Labour	Charles Mannan	9,364	20.3	Stuart Emmerson
Others		1,442	3.1	

Thornbury & Yate

Lib Dem notional majority of 11,060; notional turnout: 73.6%

PARTY	2005 CANDIDATE	NOTIONAL 2005 VOTES	NOTIONAL 2005 % VOTE	PPC FOR NEXT GE
Lib Dem	Steve Webb MP	25,622	54.3	Steve Webb MP
Conservative	Chris Butt	14,562	30.9	Matthew Riddle
Labour	Patricia Gardener	5,122	10.9	Roxanne Egan
Others		1,854	3.9	

North Wiltshire

Conservative notional majority of 6,888; notional turnout: 69.5%

PARTY	2005 CANDIDATE	NOTIONAL 2005 VOTES	NOTIONAL 2005 % VOTE	PPC FOR NEXT GE
Conservative	James Gray MP	22,321	49.7	James Gray MP
Lib Dem	Paul Fox	15,433	34.4	Mike Evemy
Labour	David Nash	5,365	11.9	Jason Hughes
Others		1,778	4.0	

South West Wiltshire

Conservative notional majority of 8,568; notional turnout: 64.6%

PARTY	2005 CANDIDATE	NOTIONAL 2005 VOTES	NOTIONAL 2005 % VOTE	PPC FOR NEXT GE
Conservative	Andrew Murrison MP	22,321	49.1	Andrew Murrison MP
Lib Dem	Duncan Hames	13,753	30.3	Trevor Carbin
Labour	Phil Gibby	7,807	17.2	Rebecca Rennison
Others		1,573	3.5	

Winchester

Lib Dem notional majority of 6,524; notional turnout: 71.8%

PARTY	2005 CANDIDATE	NOTIONAL 2005 VOTES	NOTIONAL 2005 % VOTE	PPC FOR NEXT GE
Lib Dem	Mark Oaten MP	25,621	50.0	Martin Tod
Conservative	George Hollingbery	19,097	37.3	Steve Brine
Labour	Patrick Davies	4,774	9.3	Patrick Davis
Others		1,714	3.3	

Of all the constituencies lost by the Conservatives in 1997 no loss can have been more frustrating than Gerry Malone's defeat by just two votes at the hands of Liberal Democrat Mark Oaten. An idyllic town in south Hampshire, famous for its public school, Winchester is in easy commuting distance of both London and Southampton. Boundary changes make this seat slightly more urban and Liberal Democrat-leaning in nature, transferring several Conservative-inclined wards to the new Meon Valley constituency. While the Conservatives narrowly control the city council, the Liberal Democrats won six of the seven seats and close to half of the votes in the constituency in the 2009 county council elections. After being hit by a high-profile sex scandal, Oaten has opted to retire and is replaced as Liberal Democrat candidate by Martin Tod. Marketing professional Steve Brine will fight the seat for the Conservatives.

South East England

The south-eastern corner of England, the counties of Kent, Surrey and Sussex, will be a truly crucial battleground in the next general election, for symbolic as well as practical reasons. This is because the South East has been an essential and also a typical element in the success of 'New Labour' over the past decade or so, proving that they can win the key marginal constituencies in a predominantly white, owner-occupied and largely middle-class region where previously the party had struggled to make any significant impact. Indeed in the four elections from 1979 to 1992 'old' Labour had not won a single seat in these counties – and the Conservatives had been returned each time to power, a phalanx of south-eastern English seats as the cornerstone of Margaret Thatcher's governments.

Then in 1997 Tony Blair's party made no fewer than thirteen gains, demonstrating an ability to break out far from their traditional heartlands, conveying an appeal to the ever-growing number of floating voters exercising their choice on the basis of a renewed image of competence and moderation. None of the thirteen Labour constituencies were regained by the Tories in 2001, and only one, Gravesham, in 2005. Thus the South East continued both to contribute to and embody Blairite success in office. The Conservatives had nurtured high hopes of kick-starting their recovery in traditionally their strongest region, but signally failed.

Why did Labour hold a dozen of their seats in Kent and Sussex? As ever, individual constituencies do vary in nature and response, but perhaps the key was the continued boom in the economy. A BBC *Newsnight* survey after the 2005 election found that voters in Kent, in particular, were motivated especially on instrumental grounds, that is, by they judged what was best for the pockets of themselves and their immediate families. They were less concerned than those in university seats, for example, and those employed in the public sector, by doubts over the war in Iraq. Continued relatively low unemployment and inflation, and – in a region with an above average rate of owner occupation – interest rates, had kept the South East loyal to the party of the Blair–Brown government. If this is so, then the very different economic prospects for an election in 2009 or even 2010 suggest that next time the Conservatives' hopes might be much better founded.

It will not take a huge swing to make the electoral landscape of the far South East undergo another sea-change. While Labour still held twelve of the forty-three constituencies in 2005, they are all vulnerable and some had the thinnest of majorities – literally, in the case of Crawley, which was held by Laura Moffatt by just thirty-seven votes, the smallest lead anywhere in Britain. It was even announced on television that Medway had fallen to the Tories, though in the end Bob Marshall-Andrews held on by 213 to stimulate (or irritate) his own party as well as others for one more term. In Sittingbourne & Sheppey the majority was seventy-nine. It seemed that Labour had benefited from the luck that was going, but a platform for real change next time had been set.

Indeed, although the boundary changes which come into force at the next election are not major, with no new or additional seats being created this time, even modest redrawing of ward allocations has already technically tipped three Labour divisions in Kent over to the Conservatives on 'notional' 2005 results. This means that if the sitting MPs Derek Wyatt (Sittingbourne & Sheppey) and Stephen Ladyman (South Thanet) win again, or the retiring Bob Marshall-Andrews's replacement, Teresa Murray, takes Rochester & Strood (the former Medway), they would count as Labour gains. The three Conservatives who are, in this virtual reality, 'defending' these seats are, respectively, Gordon Henderson, Laura Sandys and Mark Reckless.

In fact the 'science' of notional 2005 results, even as practised by Professors Rallings and Thrasher of Plymouth University, though it will be accepted as the benchmark for the next general election by all the news media, is not perfect, especially when it gets down to majorities such as a mere twenty-two in Sittingbourne & Sheppey. What we can say with certainty is that many seats in the region were very close indeed, with three notionals under fifty votes, and ten under 1,000 (see tables).

Aside from the three already 'gained', the Conservatives will make all the other Labour seats key targets. The most likely to fall of all are Gillingham & Rainham (notional majority for Paul Clark MP – 15 votes!), the unchanged Crawley in West Sussex (37, as mentioned above), Hove (448) and Dartford (860). The Tories have 'great expectations' in all three of the Medway town seats, renamed so that each title includes a pair of towns, while Hove, despite having undergone some social change in recent decades, must still sound one of the most unlikely names in the Labour list – the openly gay Conservative candidate last time, Nick Boles, has now found a safe seat at Grantham & Stamford in Lincolnshire, and has passed the standard to Mike Weatherly. Howard Stoate, one of the few medical doctors in the House, faced an uphill task on the Thames riverfront at Dartford against the same Tory opponent as in 2005, Gareth Johnson – but in late July 2009 Stoate announced his retirement on the grounds that new rules regarding second jobs would prevent him from working as a GP. He would probably have experienced no such conflict of loyalties: all these four constituencies will require a swing of less than 1 per cent and should change hands if the national party shares are even level.

Almost as likely to change hands from Labour to Conservative are the coastal Hastings & Rye (1.3 per cent) and Brighton's east end, Kemptown (2.5 per cent), both in East Sussex, and another Medway seat, Chatham & Aylesford, would fall if the Conservatives should become the largest party nationally, with a 4.3 per cent swing. Finally, the Tories need to complete a clean sweep by taking the two 'safest' Labour seats in the region if they are to win an overall majority: these are Dover in

Kent, which would need a swing of 5.3 per cent to overturn Gwyn Prosser's notional majority of 5,005 in a little changed seat, and Brighton, Pavilion in East Sussex (6.6 per cent), where the sitting member since 1997, David Lepper, is retiring.

The Liberal Democrats and other parties also have interest in the region, of course. The Lib Dems have one seat at present, Lewes in East Sussex, which should remain safe for one of the most active of all MPs, Norman Baker, who has regularly asked more questions per session than anyone in the Commons. Surrey, at least as presently constituted outside the bounds of Greater London, has never elected a Labour member, but there are Liberal Democrat possibilities among its eleven seats. Sue Doughty held the Guildford seat for one term between 2001 and 2005, but then lost a titanic battle to the Conservative Anne Milton by just 347 on one of the country's highest turnouts, over 68 per cent; the boundary changes reduce this lead notionally to just eighty-nine, yet another two-figure majority in the South East. The Lib Dems also have much less likely targets in South West Surrey and Woking. However, these require swings of 6 per cent and 8 per cent respectively and the Tories have come back strongly in local elections in these districts in recent years, gaining control of both Woking and Waverley councils in 2007, the latter (which is very similar to the South West Surrey constituency) with no fewer than twenty-four gains from the Liberal Democrats. A much better prospect on paper for the Lib Dems is Eastbourne in East Sussex, where they were only 672 behind notionally in 2005, especially as it was they who made nine council gains to take control in 2007. This seat, which they held briefly after a by-election following Ian Gow's murder by the IRA in 1990, must be seen as their only realistic chance of a parliamentary gain. Stephen Lloyd again stands against the sitting Tory, Nigel Waterson, who recaptured it in 1992.

Nor should we forget the Greens. Their very best performance in the UK in 2005 was in Brighton, Pavilion, where they more than doubled their share from 9 per cent to 22 per cent, and their representation on Brighton and Hove Council doubled from six to twelve councillors in 2007. This means that their first ever sole party leader, Caroline Lucas, may stand a chance of becoming their first elected representative in the Westminster Parliament, in what must be seen as a unique three-way Labour–Conservative–Green marginal. Finally, while it may be thought that the part of the British Isles nearest to Europe may be less hostile to the EU, in fact it is one of the stronger areas for UKIP, and their leader Nigel Farage opted to stand defiantly in South Thanet in 2005, achieving 5.0 per cent of the vote.

Overall, though, the south-easternmost counties constitute a key major party battle that will strongly influence the identity of the next government. This time the Conservatives must do much better than in 1997, 2001 and 2005, if David Cameron is to become Prime Minister, and the New Labour era of success to be ended decisively. It is likely that it will again depend in this region on economics – will Gordon Brown and his party be punished for a severe recession, or will his experience and stewardship be valued, as financial storms rage around the Sussex and Kentish coast, the white cliffs of 'Albion', against which so many threats have been launched, and some repelled, from the Romans and Saxons through to Napoleon and Hitler?

Target seats

SEAT	SWING REQUIRED %	MP	CHALLENGER
Conservative from Labour			
Gillingham & Rainham	0.02	Paul Clark	Rehman Chishti
Crawley	0.05	Laura Moffatt	Henry Smith
Hove	0.6	Celia Barlow	Mike Weatherly
Dartford	1.0	Howard Stoate*	Gareth Johnson
Hastings & Rye	1.3	Michael Jabez Foster	Amber Rudd
Brighton, Kemptown	2.5	Des Turner*	Simon Kirby
Chatham & Aylesford	4.2	Jonathan Shaw	Tracey Crouch
Dover	5.3	Gwyn Prosser	Charlie Elphicke
Brighton, Pavilion	6.6	David Lepper*	
Lib Dem from Conservatives			
Guildford	0.2	Anne Milton	Sue Doughty
Eastbourne	0.8	Nigel Waterson	Stephen Lloyd
Green from Labour			
Brighton, Pavilion	7.8	David Lepper*	Caroline Lucas

One to watch: Dover

Actual majority 2005: Labour 4,941 (10.3%) – Gwyn Prosser MP
Notional majority 2005: Labour 5,005 (10.4%)
Conservative candidate: Charlie Elphicke

Dover is one of only three British towns that the French dignify with their own version of the name (Douvres, Londres, Edimbourg), and this measure of its importance is in some ways true in parliamentary terms. The safest of Labour's seven seats in Kent in 2005 (but not safe), the Channel port amid the white cliffs at the closest point to the Continent has often swung to the party which wins power at a general election – to Labour in 1945, 1964 and 1997, to the Conservatives in 1970. It now lies in that vital band of constituencies which the Conservatives would need to become the largest party (around a 5 per cent swing) to an overall majority (8 per cent) – in either case, if they win Dover it is almost certain that David Cameron would be Prime Minister. Labour have had at least an even chance for decades though. Besides the gritty port beneath the mighty castle, they have done very well in that most unlikely of coalfields, developed in the 1920s but now entirely defunct, around Aylesham and the inland part of Deal. Although miners came from all over Britain to work there, the current MP is still a rare Welshman sitting for an English seat. The Tory candidate, Charlie Elphicke, a tax solicitor and research fellow of the Centre for Policy Studies, will be hoping to make it one fewer.

Arundel & South Downs

Conservative notional majority of 12,291; notional turnout: 70.8%

PARTY	2005 CANDIDATE	NOTIONAL 2005 VOTES	NOTIONAL 2005 % VOTE	PPC FOR NEXT GE
Conservative	Nick Herbert	25,968	50.3	Nick Herbert MP
Lib Dem	Derek Deedman	13,677	26.5	Derek Deedman
Labour	Sharon Whitlam	8,947	17.3	James Field
Others		3,016	5.9	

Ashford

Conservative notional majority of 12,268; notional turnout: 65.4%

PARTY	2005 CANDIDATE	NOTIONAL 2005 VOTES	NOTIONAL 2005 % VOTE	PPC FOR NEXT GE
Conservative	Damian Green MP	25,225	51.4	Damian Green MP
Labour	Valerie Whitaker	12,957	26.4	Chris Clark
Lib Dem	Chris Took	7,648	15.6	Chris Took
Others		3,205	6.5	

Bexhill & Battle

Conservative notional majority of 15,893; notional turnout: 66.8%

PARTY	2005 CANDIDATE	NOTIONAL 2005 VOTES	NOTIONAL 2005 % VOTE	PPC FOR NEXT GE
Conservative	Gregory Barker MP	27,316	54.2	Gregory Barker MP
Lib Dem	Mary Varrall	11,423	22.7	Mary Varrall
Labour	Michael Jones	9,016	17.9	James Royston
Others		2,659	5.3	

Bognor Regis & Littlehampton

Conservative notional majority of 8,617; notional turnout: 63.1%

PARTY	2005 CANDIDATE	NOTIONAL 2005 VOTES	NOTIONAL 2005 % VOTE	PPC FOR NEXT GE
Conservative	Nick Gibb MP	19,309	45.2	Nick Gibb MP
Labour	George O'Neill	10,692	25.0	Michael Jones
Lib Dem	Simon McDougall	9,357	21.9	Simon McDougall
Others		3,408	8.0	

Brighton, Kemptown

Labour notional majority of 1,853; notional turnout: 58.7%

PARTY	2005 CANDIDATE	NOTIONAL 2005 VOTES	NOTIONAL 2005 % VOTE	PPC FOR NEXT GE
Labour	Des Turner MP	14,939	39.0	Simon Burgess
Conservative	Judith Symes	13,086	34.1	Simon Kirby
Lib Dem	Marina Pepper	6,482	16.9	Juliet Williams
Others		3,831	10.0	

Arguably the less bohemian of the two Brighton city constituencies, Kemptown is considerably more residential in composition than neighbouring Pavilion. Taking in wards in the east of the city, the constituency also includes the Conservative strongholds of Peacehaven and Telscombe Cliffs, which are every bit the sleepy Sussex stereotype. Labour support is strongest in the Brighton city wards with the tough Moulsecoomb and Whitehawk estates resulting in more than a fifth of the constituency's residents living in social housing. The Green Party, whilst weaker here than in neighbouring Pavilion, holds council seats in Queen's Park. With sitting MP Dr Des Turner opting for retirement, former city council leader Simon Burgess will hope to hold the seat for Labour. Local entrepreneur and former nightclub operator Simon Kirby will fight the seat for the Conservatives.

Brighton, Pavilion

Labour notional majority of 5,867; notional turnout: 62.3%

PARTY	2005 CANDIDATE	NOTIONAL 2005 VOTES	NOTIONAL 2005 % VOTE	PPC FOR NEXT GE
Labour	David Lepper MP	16,283	36.4	Nancy Platts
Conservative	Mike Weatherley	10,416	23.3	n/a
Green Party	Keith Taylor	9,804	21.9	Caroline Lucas
Others		8,238	18.4	

A rare three-way marginal, Brighton, Pavilion is set to be an exciting battle between Labour, the Conservatives and the Green Party. The city's famous Marine Parade, the University of Sussex and quirky shopping areas are all found within the constituency's boundaries. For years a Conservative stronghold, the changing demographics and social outlook of the seat saw Labour win by more than 13,000 votes in 1997. The Greens, who have steadily built up their local government base in the past years and topped the poll at the 2009 European elections, are fielding high-profile MEP and party leader Caroline Lucas. With sitting MP David Lepper retiring, Nancy Platts will hope to hold the seat for Labour. The Conservatives will select a candidate later this year, with TV doctor David Bull having recently withdrawn as the PPC to work on health policy for the party.

Canterbury

Conservative notional majority of 7,579; notional turnout: 66.4%

PARTY	2005 CANDIDATE	NOTIONAL 2005 VOTES	NOTIONAL 2005 % VOTE	PPC FOR NEXT GE
Conservative	Julian Brazier MP	20,590	44.5	Julian Brazier MP
Labour	Alex Hilton	13,011	28.1	Jean Samuel
Lib Dem	Jenny Barnard-Langston	9,935	21.5	Guy Voizey
Others		2,749	5.9	

Chatham & Aylesford

Labour notional majority of 3,289; notional turnout: 60.6%

PARTY	2005 CANDIDATE	NOTIONAL 2005 VOTES	NOTIONAL 2005 % VOTE	PPC FOR NEXT GE
Labour	Jonathan Shaw MP	17,960	45.1	Jonathan Shaw MP
Conservative	Anne Jobson	14,671	36.8	Tracey Crouch
Lib Dem	Debbie Enever	5,388	13.5	n/a
Others		1,846	4.6	

Forty minutes by train from central London, the Chatham & Aylesford constituency is quite literally split down the middle — by both the M2 motorway and its diverse social mix. The former naval dockyard town of Chatham, which has struggled for years with high unemployment and urban decay, provides the base of Labour's support, while Walderslade and Aylesford towards the south of the seat are firmly part of the Conservative-inclined commuter belt. Being so close to London, the population of the area is predicted to grow significantly in the coming years as new housing developments continue to spring up at a frantic pace. Work and Pensions Minister Jonathan Shaw, who has held the seat for Labour since 1997, will face a challenge from Conservative Tracey Crouch.

Chichester

Conservative notional majority of 10,457; notional turnout: 65.1%

PARTY	2005 CANDIDATE	NOTIONAL 2005 VOTES	NOTIONAL 2005 % VOTE	PPC FOR NEXT GE
Conservative	Andrew Tyrie MP	24,693	48.0	Andrew Tyrie MP
Lib Dem	Alan Hilliar	14,236	27.7	Martin Lury
Labour	Jonathan Austin	9,553	18.6	Simon Holland
Others		2,973	5.8	

Crawley

PARTY	2005 CANDIDATE	NOTIONAL 2005 VOTES	NOTIONAL 2005 % VOTE	PPC FOR NEXT GE
Labour notional majority of 37; notional turnout: 58.3%				
Labour	Laura Moffatt MP	16,411	39.1	Laura Moffatt MP
Conservative	Henry Smith	16,374	39.0	Henry Smith
Lib Dem	Rupert Sheard	6,503	15.5	n/a
Others		2,685	6.4	

After holding her seat by a nail-biting 37 votes in 2005, former nurse and Crawley mayor Laura Moffatt had her slim margin of victory tattooed on her feet. Given dramatic Conservative advances in the constituency on a local government level since then, she may well live to regret that decision. Previously represented by Nicholas Soames, the constituency encompasses concrete-dominated Crawley town, Gatwick airport and the Conservative bastions of Maidenbower, Pound Hill and Worth. It has amongst the highest ethnic minority populations of any southern seat. Henry Smith, who has led West Sussex County Council since 2003 and fought the seat at the last two elections, will hope to make it third time lucky.

Dartford

PARTY	2005 CANDIDATE	NOTIONAL 2005 VOTES	NOTIONAL 2005 % VOTE	PPC FOR NEXT GE
Labour notional majority of 860; notional turnout: 63.2%				
Labour	Howard Stoate MP	19,518	43.0	n/a
Conservative	Gareth Johnson	18,658	41.1	Gareth Johnson
Lib Dem	Peter Bucklitsch	4,581	10.1	James Willis
Others		2,585	5.7	

Located on the banks of the Thames estuary just 15 miles south-east of central London, Dartford has voted for the winning party in each general election since 1951. Dartford grew rapidly in the post-war years and is now firmly commuter territory with the newly opened Eurostar terminal at Ebbsfleet set to link the area to London St Pancras in eight minutes by 2012. Dartford, with its sprawling business parks, has a distinctly industrial feel while the surrounding villages form the basis of Conservative support. The deprived Swanscombe area has been regenerated in recent years by the opening of the Bluewater shopping complex yet has resulted in Dartford town's rapid decline as a retail centre. With sitting Labour MP, Dr Howard Stoate, returning to general practice at the next election, solicitor Gareth Johnson will hope to take the seat for the Conservatives.

Dover

PARTY	2005 CANDIDATE	NOTIONAL 2005 VOTES	NOTIONAL 2005 % VOTE	PPC FOR NEXT GE
Labour notional majority of 5,005; notional turnout: 67.3%				
Labour	Gwyn Prosser MP	21,833	45.3	Gwyn Prosser MP
Conservative	Paul Watkins	16,828	35.0	Charlie Elphicke
Lib Dem	Antony Hook	7,605	15.8	n/a
Others		1,879	3.9	

The centre of the British cross-channel ferry industry, the Dover constituency has been held by Labour MP Gwyn Prosser since 1997. As one might expect, support for Labour is robust in Dover town, a mix of elegant Regency properties and rapidly decaying tenement blocks which were thrown up in the aftermath of World War Two bomb damage. Labour is also strong in rural Aylesham, home to the former Betteshanger colliery, which closed in 1989. While the coastal town of Deal is fairly evenly politically divided, the rest of the constituency is far more favourable to the Conservatives with villages such as River, Kearsney and Temple Ewell backing the party by landslide margins. Solicitor Charlie Elphicke will fight the constituency for the Conservatives.

Eastbourne

PARTY	2005 CANDIDATE	NOTIONAL 2005 VOTES	NOTIONAL 2005 % VOTE	PPC FOR NEXT GE
Conservative notional majority of 672; notional turnout: 63.1%				
Conservative	Nigel Waterson MP	20,594	43.1	Nigel Waterson MP
Lib Dem	Stephen Lloyd	19,922	41.7	Stephen Lloyd
Labour	Andrew Jones	5,142	10.8	Dave Brinson
Others		2,164	4.5	

Epsom & Ewell

Conservative notional majority of 16,342; notional turnout: 66.2%

PARTY	2005 CANDIDATE	NOTIONAL 2005 VOTES	NOTIONAL 2005 % VOTE	PPC FOR NEXT GE
Conservative	Chris Grayling MP	26,832	54.9	Chris Grayling MP
Lib Dem	Jonathan Lees	10,490	21.5	Jonathan Lees
Labour	Charlie Mansell	9,773	20.0	Craig Montgomery
Others		1,738	3.6	

Esher & Walton

Conservative notional majority of 7,727; notional turnout: 62.2%

PARTY	2005 CANDIDATE	NOTIONAL 2005 VOTES	NOTIONAL 2005 % VOTE	PPC FOR NEXT GE
Conservative	Ian Taylor MP	21,882	45.7	n/a
Lib Dem	Mark Marsh	14,155	29.6	n/a
Labour	Richard Taylor	9,309	19.4	Francis Eldergill
Others		2,532	5.3	

Faversham & Mid Kent

Conservative notional majority of 8,927; notional turnout: 65.2%

PARTY	2005 CANDIDATE	NOTIONAL 2005 VOTES	NOTIONAL 2005 % VOTE	PPC FOR NEXT GE
Conservative	Hugh Robertson MP	21,295	50.1	Hugh Robertson MP
Labour	Andrew Bradstock	12,368	29.1	Ashok Rehal
Lib Dem	David Naghi	7,119	16.7	n/a
Others		1,734	4.1	

Folkestone & Hythe

Conservative notional majority of 12,446; notional turnout: 68.7%

PARTY	2005 CANDIDATE	NOTIONAL 2005 VOTES	NOTIONAL 2005 % VOTE	PPC FOR NEXT GE
Conservative	Michael Howard MP	27,587	53.9	Damian Collins
Lib Dem	Peter Carroll	15,141	29.6	Neil Matthews
Labour	Maureen Tomison	6,449	12.6	Donald Worsley
Others		1,976	3.9	

Gillingham & Rainham

Labour notional majority of 15; notional turnout: 64.0%

PARTY	2005 CANDIDATE	NOTIONAL 2005 VOTES	NOTIONAL 2005 % VOTE	PPC FOR NEXT GE
Labour	Paul Clark MP	18,009	40.7	Paul Clark MP
Conservative	Tim Butcher	17,994	40.7	Rehman Chisti
Lib Dem	Andrew Stamp	6,774	15.3	Andrew Stamp
Others		1,434	3.2	

Gravesham

Conservative notional majority of 654; notional turnout: 65.7%

PARTY	2005 CANDIDATE	NOTIONAL 2005 VOTES	NOTIONAL 2005 % VOTE	PPC FOR NEXT GE
Conservative	Adam Holloway	19,739	43.7	Adam Holloway MP
Labour	Chris Pond MP	19,085	42.2	Kathryn Smith
Lib Dem	Bruce Parmenter	4,851	10.7	Bruce Parmenter
Others		1,504	3.3	

Guildford

Conservative notional majority of 89; notional turnout: 67.0%

PARTY	2005 CANDIDATE	NOTIONAL 2005 VOTES	NOTIONAL 2005 % VOTE	PPC FOR NEXT GE
Conservative	Anne Milton	22,112	43.4	Anne Milton MP
Lib Dem	Sue Doughty MP	22,023	43.3	Sue Doughty
Labour	Karen Landles	5,033	9.9	Tim Shand
Others		1,725	3.4	

Hastings & Rye

Labour notional majority of 1,156; notional turnout: 58.9%

PARTY	2005 CANDIDATE	NOTIONAL 2005 VOTES	NOTIONAL 2005 % VOTE	PPC FOR NEXT GE
Labour	Michael Foster MP	18,519	40.6	Michael Foster MP
Conservative	Mark Coote	17,363	38.1	Amber Rudd
Lib Dem	Richard Stevens	7,228	15.9	Nick Perry
Others		2,472	5.4	

Gained from the Conservatives in 1997 by local solicitor Michael Foster on an 18.5% swing, this is a seat the Labour Party never expected to win. The town of Hastings, located just over 60 miles from London and home to the bulk of the constituency's population, has long suffered from a lack of inward investment partly caused by its woeful road and rail links. The town has long been a Labour bastion, with low owner occupation rates (65.8%) and a third of residents having no qualifications. At the other end of the social spectrum, the genteel town of Rye with its cobbled streets, ornate churches and medieval lanes is similarly loyal to the Conservatives. Businesswoman Amber Rudd will fight the seat for the Conservatives.

Horsham

Conservative notional majority of 10,780; notional turnout: 67.1%

PARTY	2005 CANDIDATE	NOTIONAL 2005 VOTES	NOTIONAL 2005 % VOTE	PPC FOR NEXT GE
Conservative	Francis Maude MP	24,557	49.3	Francis Maude MP
Lib Dem	Rosie Sharpley	13,777	27.7	n/a
Labour	Rehman Chishti	8,316	16.7	Andrew Skudder
Others		3,120	6.3	

Hove

Labour notional majority of 448; notional turnout: 62.7%

PARTY	2005 CANDIDATE	NOTIONAL 2005 VOTES	NOTIONAL 2005 % VOTE	PPC FOR NEXT GE
Labour	Celia Barlow	16,829	37.4	Celia Barlow MP
Conservative	Nicholas Boles	16,381	36.4	Mike Weatherley
Lib Dem	Paul Elgood	8,077	18.0	n/a
Others		3,665	8.2	

Despite this seat being almost entirely contiguous with Brighton, Hove residents go to very great lengths to assert its asymmetry from the remainder of the city's urban sprawl. Hove, with its beautifully manicured gardens and large elderly population, is much closer to the stereotype of a sleepy Sussex seaside town than the remainder of the city. The constituency is, however, still home to a large transient population with more than a fifth of residents living in privately rented accommodation and some areas of real poverty. Labour support is strongest in the Portslade area in the west of the constituency while the Conservatives dominate in Stanford and Westbourne, home to one of the country's largest Jewish communities. Conservative businessman Mike Weatherley will fight Labour MP Celia Barlow for her seat.

Lewes

Lib Dem notional majority of 7,889; notional turnout: 69.7%

PARTY	2005 CANDIDATE	NOTIONAL 2005 VOTES	NOTIONAL 2005 % VOTE	PPC FOR NEXT GE
Lib Dem	Norman Baker MP	24,071	51.5	Rory Baker MP
Conservative	Rory Love	16,182	34.6	Jason Sugarman
Labour	Richard Black	4,370	9.4	Hratche Koundarjian
Others		2,096	4.5	

Located around 10 miles north of Brighton, the Lewes constituency was gained from the Conservatives by the Liberal Democrats in 1997. Lewes, the wealthy and well-educated county town of East Sussex, comprises only a small part of this predominantly rural and middle-class seat. Given the attractive nature of the land, the constituency is home to large numbers of commuters to nearby Brighton and central London. Four in five properties are owner occupied while only one in ten are council owned. Tactical voting for the Liberal Democrats has consigned Labour to a distant third place in this constituency during the past two elections, although the party does find some support in the port of Newhaven. Sitting MP Norman Baker, whose party continues to dominate on a local government level, will face Conservative barrister Jason Sugarman.

Maidstone & The Weald

Conservative notional majority of 12,922; notional turnout: 65.1%

PARTY	2005 CANDIDATE	NOTIONAL 2005 VOTES	NOTIONAL 2005 % VOTE	PPC FOR NEXT GE
Conservative	Ann Widdecombe Mp	23,088	51.8	Helen Grant
Lib Dem	Mark Corney	10,166	22.8	Peter Carroll
Labour	Beth Breeze	9,983	22.4	Rav Seeruthun
Others		1,343	3.0	

Mole Valley

Conservative notional majority of 11,997; notional turnout: 71.4%

PARTY	2005 CANDIDATE	NOTIONAL 2005 VOTES	NOTIONAL 2005 % VOTE	PPC FOR NEXT GE
Conservative	Paul Beresford MP	27,060	54.8	Paul Beresford MP
Lib Dem	Nasser Butt	15,063	30.5	Alice Humphreys
Labour	Farmida Bi	5,310	10.7	n/a
Others		1,982	4.0	

Reigate

Conservative notional majority of 11,093; notional turnout: 65.1%

PARTY	2005 CANDIDATE	NOTIONAL 2005 VOTES	NOTIONAL 2005 % VOTE	PPC FOR NEXT GE
Conservative	Crispin Blunt MP	21,198	48.6	Crispin Blunt MP
Lib Dem	Jane Kulka	10,105	23.1	Jane Kulka
Labour	Samual Townend	9,388	21.5	Robert Hull
Others		2,960	6.8	

Rochester & Strood

Conservative notional majority of 503; notional turnout: 62.4%

PARTY	2005 CANDIDATE	NOTIONAL 2005 VOTES	NOTIONAL 2005 % VOTE	PPC FOR NEXT GE
Conservative	Mark Reckless	18,877	42.6	Mark Reckless
Labour	Bob Marshall-Andrews MP	18,374	41.5	Teresa Murray
Lib Dem	Geoffrey Juby	5,468	12.4	Geoff Juby
Others		1,547	3.5	

Runnymede & Weybridge

Conservative notional majority of 12,349; notional turnout: 58.3%

PARTY	2005 CANDIDATE	NOTIONAL 2005 VOTES	NOTIONAL 2005 % VOTE	PPC FOR NEXT GE
Conservative	Phillip Hammond MP	22,366	51.4	Phillip Hammond MP
Labour	Paul Greenwood	10,017	23.0	Paul Greenwood
Lib Dem	Henry Bolton	7,771	17.9	n/a
Others		3,370	7.7	

Sevenoaks

Conservative notional majority of 13,060; notional turnout: 66.0%

PARTY	2005 CANDIDATE	NOTIONAL 2005 VOTES	NOTIONAL 2005 % VOTE	PPC FOR NEXT GE
Conservative	Michael Fallon MP	22,982	51.4	Michael Fallon MP
Lib Dem	Ben Abbotts	9,922	22.2	Alan Bullion
Labour	Tim Stanley	9,492	21.2	n/a
Others		2,339	5.2	

Sittingbourne & Sheppey

Conservative notional majority of 22; notional turnout: 65.1%

PARTY	2005 CANDIDATE	NOTIONAL 2005 VOTES	NOTIONAL 2005 % VOTE	PPC FOR NEXT GE
Conservative	Gordon Henderson	17,933	41.7	Gordon Henderson
Labour	Derek Wyatt MP	17,911	41.7	n/a
Lib Dem	Jane Nelson	5,478	12.7	n/a
Others		1,660	3.9	

Spelthorne

Conservative notional majority of 9,936; notional turnout: 62.7%

PARTY	2005 CANDIDATE	NOTIONAL 2005 VOTES	NOTIONAL 2005 % VOTE	PPC FOR NEXT GE
Conservative	David Wilshire MP	21,620	50.5	David Wilshire MP
Labour	Keith Dibble	11,684	27.3	Robert Ferguson
Lib Dem	Simon James	7,318	17.1	Mark Chapman
Others		2,207	5.2	

East Surrey

Conservative notional majority of 15,921; notional turnout: 65.8%

PARTY	2005 CANDIDATE	NOTIONAL 2005 VOTES	NOTIONAL 2005 % VOTE	PPC FOR NEXT GE
Conservative	Peter Ainsworth MP	27,659	56.2	Peter Ainsworth MP
Lib Dem	Jeremy Pursehouse	11,738	23.8	n/a
Labour	James Bridge	7,288	14.8	Matthew Rodda
Others		2,568	5.2	

Surrey Heath

Conservative notional majority of 10,845; notional turnout: 64.3%

PARTY	2005 CANDIDATE	NOTIONAL 2005 VOTES	NOTIONAL 2005 % VOTE	PPC FOR NEXT GE
Conservative	Michael Gove	24,642	51.5	Michael Gove MP
Lib Dem	Rosalyn Harper	13,797	28.8	Duncan Clark
Labour	Chris Lowe	7,989	16.7	Neeraj Patil
Others		1,430	3.0	

South West Surrey

Conservative notional majority of 5,969; notional turnout: 69.9%

PARTY	2005 CANDIDATE	NOTIONAL 2005 VOTES	NOTIONAL 2005 % VOTE	PPC FOR NEXT GE
Conservative	Jeremy Hunt	26,903	50.6	Jeremy Hunt MP
Lib Dem	Simon Cordon	20,934	39.4	n/a
Labour	Tom Sleigh	4,171	7.8	Richard Mollet
Others		1,139	2.1	

Mid Sussex

Conservative notional majority of 6,462; notional turnout: 68.8%

PARTY	2005 CANDIDATE	NOTIONAL 2005 VOTES	NOTIONAL 2005 % VOTE	PPC FOR NEXT GE
Conservative	Nicholas Soames MP	24,715	48.3	Nicholas Soames MP
Lib Dem	Serena Tierney	18,253	35.6	n/a
Labour	Robert Fromant	6,567	12.8	n/a
Others		1,683	3.3	

North Thanet

Conservative notional majority of 6,118; notional turnout: 59.1%

PARTY	2005 CANDIDATE	NOTIONAL 2005 VOTES	NOTIONAL 2005 % VOTE	PPC FOR NEXT GE
Conservative	Roger Gale MP	19,126	47.9	Roger Gale MP
Labour	Iris Johnston	13,008	32.6	Michael Britton
Lib Dem	Mark Barnard	6,205	15.5	n/a
Others		1,566	3.9	

South Thanet

Conservative notional majority of 810; notional turnout: 65.0%

PARTY	2005 CANDIDATE	NOTIONAL 2005 VOTES	NOTIONAL 2005 % VOTE	PPC FOR NEXT GE
Conservative	Mark MacGregor	19,003	41.2	Laura Sandys
Labour	Stephen Ladyman MP	18,193	39.5	Stephen Ladyman MP
Lib Dem	Guy Voizey	5,631	12.2	n/a
Others		3,281	7.1	

Tonbridge & Malling

Conservative notional majority of 13,352; notional turnout: 68.3%

PARTY	2005 CANDIDATE	NOTIONAL 2005 VOTES	NOTIONAL 2005 % VOTE	PPC FOR NEXT GE
Conservative	John Stanley MP	24,357	52.8	John Stanley MP
Labour	Victoria Hayman	11,005	23.8	n/a
Lib Dem	John Barstow	8,980	19.5	Liz Simpson
Others		1,806	3.9	

Tunbridge Wells

Conservative notional majority of 11,572; notional turnout: 65.9%

PARTY	2005 CANDIDATE	NOTIONAL 2005 VOTES	NOTIONAL 2005 % VOTE	PPC FOR NEXT GE
Conservative	Greg Clarke	23,099	50.8	Greg Clarke MP
Lib Dem	Laura Murphy	11,527	25.3	n/a
Labour	Jacqui Jedrzejewski	9,309	20.5	Gary Heather
Others		1,568	3.4	

Wealden

Conservative notional majority of 12,812; notional turnout: 66.3%

PARTY	2005 CANDIDATE	NOTIONAL 2005 VOTES	NOTIONAL 2005 % VOTE	PPC FOR NEXT GE
Conservative	Charles Hendry MP	25,166	50.4	Charles Hendry MP
Lib Dem	Christopher Wigley	12,354	24.7	Chris Bowers
Labour	Dudley Rose	8,334	16.7	Lorna Blackmore
Others		4,067	8.1	

Woking

Conservative notional majority of 6,612; notional turnout: 63.3%

PARTY	2005 CANDIDATE	NOTIONAL 2005 VOTES	NOTIONAL 2005 % VOTE	PPC FOR NEXT GE
Conservative	Humfrey Malins MP	21,838	47.4	n/a
Lib Dem	Anne Lee	15,226	33.1	Rosie Sharpley
Labour	Ellie Blagbrough	7,507	16.3	Tom Miller
Others		1,474	3.2	

East Worthing & Shoreham

Conservative notional majority of 8,180; notional turnout: 61.8%

PARTY	2005 CANDIDATE	NOTIONAL 2005 VOTES	NOTIONAL 2005 % VOTE	PPC FOR NEXT GE
Conservative	Tim Loughton MP	19,540	43.9	Tim Loughton MP
Labour	Damiel Yates	11,360	25.5	Emily Benn
Lib Dem	James Doyle	10,840	24.3	n/a
Others		2,785	6.3	

Worthing West

Conservative notional majority of 9,383; notional turnout: 61.9%

PARTY	2005 CANDIDATE	NOTIONAL 2005 VOTES	NOTIONAL 2005 % VOTE	PPC FOR NEXT GE
Conservative	Peter Bottomly MP	21,391	47.6	Peter Bottomly MP
Lib Dem	Claire Potter	12,008	26.7	Hazel Thorpe
Labour	Antony Bignell	8,635	19.2	Ian Ross
Others		2,890	6.4	

South London

Unlike in North London, the eleven boroughs south of the Thames (plus the only one divided by the river, Richmond) treated here have not lost a seat overall in the boundary changes that come into force at the next general election. However, the Commission's review has made an impact on the notional results of constituencies should they have existed on the new lines in 2005, which technically means a net loss of one for the Conservatives and a gain for Labour that would seem to have gone against the national trend.

This is due to the divided nature of the borough of Croydon, which in recent decades has increasingly become a classic example of the variation found within the capital as one travels out from its centre. Croydon North is now effectively an inner city seat. By 2005 Malcolm Wicks had built up a majority for Labour of 14,000, as neighbourhoods like Thornton Heath have become more and more dominated by ethnic minority residents; on the latest boundaries North will be just 50.7 per cent white, with 24 per cent black and 19 per cent Asian. With non-white voters showing by far the greatest loyalty to Labour in recent elections, including those since 2005, Croydon North is now a safe seat. Croydon South, on the other hand, is one of the twenty-five strongest Conservative constituencies in the whole country, spreading out into the ex-Surrey North Downs around Purley, Sanderstead and Selsdon (where Edward Heath's famous conference took place in 1970, which made it a by-word for a commitment to free market economics, enshrined both in an eponymous pressure group and Harold Wilson's less admiring coinage of the term 'Selsdon man'). This leaves Croydon Central as a critical marginal battleground.

Even though only 6,000 votes have been moved between the three seats in the borough, this is sufficient to have just tipped Central from a real Tory majority in 2005 of just 75 to a notional Labour lead of 328. The situation was made even more interesting when Andrew Pelling MP, who had gained it that year, was first suspended by the Conservative Party after being arrested on charges of assaulting his pregnant second wife (though it should be stressed that no prosecution was ever brought), then announced his retirement. Now the new candidate Gavin Barwell will have to gain it all over again, as Central counts as very high on the Conservative target list, while Gerry Ryan finds himself as a notional defender. If he holds the seat, Labour are likely to win a fourth term in office.

More generally speaking, Croydon is a microcosm of South London, the metropolis as a whole, and indeed of the political geography of England, as the Conservatives have struggled to make an impact in the inner city, while Labour must hold at least some of their 1997 gains in the outer suburbs in order to stay in government. Another knife-edge defender for Labour is Martin Linton in the former category, by the Thames in Battersea. He has already done well to hold on so long in a borough, Wandsworth, controlled at local level since 1978 by the Conservatives (with their popular ultra-low council tax policy) – but it looks as if the Tories are about to extend their success to parliamentary level here, having already gained Putney in 2005. In the London Assembly election of May 2008 (when Labour were performing better than in most of 2009 in the polls) the Conservatives were 4,000 ahead in the party list vote within Battersea, and they were 20 per cent ahead in Wandsworth as a whole in the June 2009 European elections. Indeed they have a chance of a clean sweep in the borough at the next general election by taking the third seat, Tooting, as well. They were over 1,000 votes ahead here in May 2008, and Sadiq Khan must fight Mark Clarke's attempt to gain on a 6 per cent swing as if it were a true marginal.

The other constituency in the critical range which the Tories must win is in south-east London: Eltham, where David Gold needs a 4 per cent swing to oust the ex-cab driver Clive Efford. The likelihood of this happening is indicated by the fact that the Conservatives were ahead in 2008 in five of the seven wards which comprise a seat with a 20 per cent changed electorate next time. However the fifth and final seat on the Tory target list from Labour is a much less likely prospect: Tessa Jowell's Dulwich & West Norwood, at the outer end of the borough of Southwark. Labour retained a 3,500 lead in the Assembly elections, and the seat, which includes Coldharbour near the heart of Brixton as well as the atypical leafy Dulwich Village, is overall now one third non-white and has over a third social housing.

Three or four likely Conservative gains seem a rather thin reward between twelve boroughs, but critically for their chances of winning an overall majority, this is only half the story in South London. They also entertain high hopes of making gains from the Liberal Democrats, who have built up a swathe of five seats in the highly affluent outer south-west sector of the capital. Figures from the 2008 Assembly and 2009 Euro elections are even more favourable for the Tories on this battlefront, though it must be said that neither of these are likely to show the Liberal Democrat vote in a favourable light, especially as they cannot take into account the incumbency of the highly active and well-publicised MPs. In order of likelihood of gain, first is Carshalton & Wallington, where 64 year old Ken Andrew (the second oldest Tory in the country in a target seat, after the septuagenarian Brenda Porter in Southport) is trying for a third time to beat Tom Brake. Next door in the other Sutton borough seat, Philippa Stroud needs a swing that is twice as large, 3 per cent, but still very winnable on all election figures since 2005, including the 2006 borough contests. Third is the high-profile battle in Richmond Park (see *One to Watch* below). Fourth, but not out of the question, is Kingston & Surbiton, which Ed Davey gained by 56 votes in 1997 then won by 15,676 in 2001 (and 9,084 last time). The one which definitely won't be gained is

Twickenham, where the MP is the saintly and sainted Vince Cable, who must now hold one of the safest seats in the country for any party.

The Liberal Democrats only real hope of a gain from the Conservatives is in their historic totem of Orpington, where the 1962 by-election victory has never quite been forgotten; but all other election results since 2005, and boundary changes which lose 12,000 voters, suggest this is highly unlikely. There is a considerable shift of voters in outer south-east (or Kentish) London. For example, Lewisham West will now cross the boundary into Bromley and takes 42 per cent of its voters from Beckenham, which would suggest vulnerability for Labour there (especially with Green and Liberal Democrat local strength), except that the part of Bromley included around Penge (added to the name for the first time) is its innermost and most working class part. The Lib Dems still need a swing of nearly 10 per cent, though Bridget Prentice is retiring as MP.

Overall, the Tories will be pleased if they gain half a dozen of the twenty-seven seats in Greater London south of the river, a proportion which would see them just win a narrow overall majority if repeated across England as a whole. However, Labour's vote held up better in London than anywhere else in the 2009 Euro elections, and the power of Liberal Democrat incumbency in their south-western arc should not be underestimated. London is atypical of the nation – far more cosmopolitan, urban, and racially mixed, while also more professional, public sector, and middle class in its employment patterns. For perhaps the first time, the relative absence of the now disaffected white working class may mean that the Conservatives find South London one of the harder regions in which to advance.

Target seats

SEAT	SWING REQUIRED %	MP	CHALLENGER
Conservative from Labour			
Croydon Central	0.4	(Gerry Ryan)	Gavin Barwell
Battersea	0.5	Martin Linton	Jane Ellison
Eltham	3.8	Clive Efford	David Gold
Tooting	6.1	Sadiq Khan	Mark Clarke
Dulwich & West Norwood	9.9	Tessa Jowell	Kemi Adegoke
Conservative from Lib Dems			
Carshalton & Wallington	1.5	Tom Brake	Ken Andrew
Sutton & Cheam	3.2	Paul Burstow	Philippa Stroud
Richmond Park	3.6	Susan Kramer	Zac Goldsmith
Kingston & Surbiton	6.1	Ed Davey	Helen Whateley
Lib Dem from Conservatives			
Orpington	5.4	John Horam	David McBride
Lib Dem from Labour			
Streatham	8.8	Keith Hill*	Chris Nicholson
Lewisham West & Penge	9.6	Bridget Prentice*	Alex Feakes
Labour from Conservatives			
Putney	2.4	Justine Greening	Stuart King
Wimbledon	2.9	Stephen Hammond	Andrew Judge
Labour from Lib Dems			
Bermondsey & Old Southwark	8.0	Simon Hughes	Kirsty McNeill

One to watch: Richmond Park

Actual majority 2005: Lib Dem 3,731 (7.3%) – Susan Kramer MP
Notional majority 2005: Lib Dem 3,613 (7.1%)
Conservative candidate: Zac Goldsmith

There are very few voters in the royal park itself (deer have not been enfranchised) but this is still a very good name to unify the surrounding parts of Richmond and Kingston boroughs. Richmond Park is a very attractively placed seat, hence it has one of the most affluent, educated electorates: it lies second in the national list of professional and managerial workers, third in household disposable income, sixth in house prices. Yet it (including under previous names such as Richmond and Barnes) has also been a key and keenly fought Conservative–Liberal Democrat marginal for decades, with Jeremy Hanley holding on by hair-raising margins for the in the three elections between 1983 and 1992, and the Lib Dems winning the most recent three. Even more spice has been added by the selection of a photogenic 'celebrity' Conservative candidate in an 'open primary'. Zac Goldsmith is an environmentalist and the son of the late Sir James, whose Referendum Party intervened in the 1997 general election to the discomfiture of David Mellor in nearby Putney. It might be thought that Goldsmith *fils* must be the favourite to be the one to enter Parliament. The Conservatives were well ahead here in the 2008 Assembly and 2009 Euro elections, and although the Lib Dems regained Richmond borough council in May 2006, they were actually 3,000 votes behind within this seat, mainly due to the 28,000 voters from Kingston. Yet it may not be so simple. Susan Kramer is now completing her first term after taking over from Jenny Tonge, and will now have her own incumbency vote; and Goldsmith should note that fame and good looks have not traditionally won parliamentary seats in Britain. If he does win, it will be a very good sign that his party itself now has a wide and strong enough national appeal to form a new government.

Battersea

PARTY	2005 CANDIDATE	NOTIONAL 2005 VOTES	NOTIONAL 2005 % VOTE	PPC FOR NEXT GE
Labour notional majority of 332; notional turnout: 59.2%				
Labour	Martin Linton MP	16,615	40.7	Martin Linton MP
Conservative	Dominic Schofield	16,283	39.9	Jane Ellison
Lib Dem	Norsheen Bhatti	5,906	14.5	n/a
Others		2,054	5.0	

Home to the seemingly permanently derelict power station, parts of Clapham Common and Europe's busiest railway station at Clapham Junction, Battersea is near the top of the Tories' wish list. The Tories dominate at a local government level, holding 18 of the 21 seats in the constituency. In winning the seat in 1997, former *Guardian* journalist Martin Linton ousted Conservative Health Minister John Bowis on a swing of 10.2%, a relatively weak result for Labour given their average Greater London swing of 14.2% but indicative of the rapid transformation the constituency has undergone from working-class Labour bastion to closely fought marginal populated by first-time home owners and recently graduated young professionals. Pro-European Tory Jane Ellison will challenge for the Conservatives.

Beckenham

Conservative notional majority of 16,913; notional turnout: 65.3%

PARTY	2005 CANDIDATE	NOTIONAL 2005 VOTES	NOTIONAL 2005 % VOTE	PPC FOR NEXT GE
Conservative	Jacqui Lait MP	25,002	59.7	Jacqui Lait MP
Labour	Liam Curran	8,089	19.3	Damian Egan
Lib Dem	Jef Foulger	6,748	16.1	n/a
Others		2,025	4.8	

Bermondsey & Old Southwark

Lib Dem notional majority of 5,769; notional turnout: 48.8%

PARTY	2005 CANDIDATE	NOTIONAL 2005 VOTES	NOTIONAL 2005 % VOTE	PPC FOR NEXT GE
Lib Dem	Simon Hughes MP	17,177	47.6	Simon Hughes MP
Labour	Kirsty McNeill	11,408	31.6	Kirsty McNeill
Conservative	David Branch	4,671	13.0	Loanna Morrison
Other		2,796	7.7	

Bexleyheath & Crayford

Conservative notional majority of 5,167; notional turnout: 64.7%

PARTY	2005 CANDIDATE	NOTIONAL 2005 VOTES	NOTIONAL 2005 % VOTE	PPC FOR NEXT GE
Conservative	David Evennett	19,497	46.5	David Evennett MP
Labour	Nigel Beard	14,330	34.2	Howard Dawber
Lib Dem	David Raval	5,494	13.1	n/a
Others		2,579	6.2	

Bromley & Chislehurst

Conservative notional majority of 8,236; notional turnout: 62.6%

PARTY	2005 CANDIDATE	NOTIONAL 2005 VOTES	NOTIONAL 2005 % VOTE	PPC FOR NEXT GE
Conservative	Eric Forth MP	18,024	45.0	Bob Neill MP
Labour	Rachel Reeves	9,788	24.4	Chris Kirby
Lib Dem	Peter Brookes	9,494	23.7	Sam Webber
Others		2,739	6.8	

Camberwell & Peckham

Labour notional majority of 16,608; notional turnout: 51.9%

PARTY	2005 CANDIDATE	NOTIONAL 2005 VOTES	NOTIONAL 2005 % VOTE	PPC FOR NEXT GE
Labour	Harriet Harman MP	24,529	63.3	Harriet Harmen MP
Lib Dem	Richard Porter	7,921	20.4	n/a
Conservative	Jessica Lee	3,842	9.9	Andy Stranack
Others		2,481	6.4	

Carshalton & Wallington

Lib Dem notional majority of 1,225; notional turnout: 64.2%

PARTY	2005 CANDIDATE	NOTIONAL 2005 VOTES	NOTIONAL 2005 % VOTE	PPC FOR NEXT GE
Lib Dem	Tom Brake MP	16,870	40.4	Tom Brake MP
Conservative	Ken Andrew	15,645	37.5	Ken Andrew
Labour	Andrew Theobald	7,234	17.3	Shafiqul Khan
Others		2,019	4.8	

Historically a safe Conservative constituency in Westminster elections and a Liberal Democrat stronghold on a local level, the Liberal Democrats finally succeeded in wrestling this seat from centrist Conservative Nigel Forman at the 1997 general election and have held it ever since. Broadly speaking, it would be fair to describe the constituency, which is in easy commuting distance of central London, as middle-class suburbia. At 21% social housing is, however, more apparent here than in other Conservative–Liberal Democrat marginals. The Liberal Democrats continue to hold the upper hand at a local government level but there are patches of real affluence here which show near-absolute loyalty to the Tories, notably the Carshalton Beeches and Woodcote neighbourhoods. Conservative candidate Dr Ken Andrew will face incumbent MP Tom Brake – the third time the two men have battled for the seat.

Croydon Central

Labour notional majority of 328; notional turnout: 60.1%

PARTY	2005 CANDIDATE	NOTIONAL 2005 VOTES	NOTIONAL 2005 % VOTE	PPC FOR NEXT GE
Labour	Geraint Davies MP	18,745	41.1	Gerry Ryan
Conservative	Andrew Pelling	18,417	40.4	Gavin Barwell
Lib Dem	Jeremy Hargreaves	5,835	12.8	Stephen Dering
Others		2,595	5.7	

A relatively humdrum slice of suburbia, the Croydon Central constituency fell to Labour in 1997 on a dramatic 15.5% swing. Despite being gained by Conservative Andrew Pelling at the 2005 general election, small boundary changes have put this seat back in the Labour column – but only narrowly. The seat includes within its borders Croydon's thriving shopping areas, wealthy communities on the London and Surrey border, and the socially deprived New Addington council estate, which has seen a surge in BNP support in recent years. One in ten voters is black, many of who live in the Addiscombe and Woodside wards in the north of the constituency. With Pelling opting to retire after well-publicised marital problems, two high-profile councillors will battle it out for this seat: Conservative Gavin Barwell and Labour's Jerry Ryan.

Croydon North

Labour notional majority of 14,185; notional turnout: 52.6%

PARTY	2005 CANDIDATE	NOTIONAL 2005 VOTES	NOTIONAL 2005 % VOTE	PPC FOR NEXT GE
Labour	Malcolm Wicks MP	24,251	53.6	Malcolm Wicks MP
Conservative	Tariq Ahmad	10,066	22.3	Jason Hadden
Lib Dem	Adrian Gee-Turner	7,788	17.2	n/a
Others		3,120	6.9	

Croydon South

Conservative notional majority of 14,228; notional turnout: 63.4%

PARTY	2005 CANDIDATE	NOTIONAL 2005 VOTES	NOTIONAL 2005 % VOTE	PPC FOR NEXT GE
Conservative	Richard Ottaway MP	26,478	52.0	Richard Ottaway MP
Labour	Paul Smith	12,250	24.1	Jane Avis
Lib Dem	Sandra Lawman	10,400	20.4	n/a
Others		1,786	3.5	

Dulwich & West Norwood

Labour notional majority of 7,853; notional turnout: 56.8%

PARTY	2005 CANDIDATE	NOTIONAL 2005 VOTES	NOTIONAL 2005 % VOTE	PPC FOR NEXT GE
Labour	Tessa Jowell MP	17,590	44.2	Tessa Jowell MP
Conservative	Kim Humphreys	9,737	24.5	Kemi Adegoke
Lib Dem	Jonathan Mitchell	9,199	23.1	Jonathan Mitchell
Others		3,230	8.1	

Eltham

Labour notional majority of 2,904; notional turnout: 58.4%

PARTY	2005 CANDIDATE	NOTIONAL 2005 VOTES	NOTIONAL 2005 % VOTE	PPC FOR NEXT GE
Labour	Clive Efford MP	16,135	42.2	Clive Efford MP
Conservative	Spencer Drury	13,231	34.6	David Gold
Lib Dem	Ian Gerrard	6,636	17.4	n/a
Others		2,193	5.7	

The Conservatives are keen to reclaim this south-east London constituency, held by former London taxi driver Clive Efford since the 1997 general election. Located within the boundaries of the London Borough of Greenwich, this socially diverse constituency takes in the Ferrier Estate, described by many town planners as the country's worst social housing project, Kidbrooke and the more middle-class New Eltham and Oxleas Wood areas. A third of the housing in the constituency is council or housing association owned. As a rule, the north-west of the constituency favours Labour while the south-eastern areas closest to Bexley and Bromley are more Conservative inclined. Conservative prospects here are boosted by the number of affluent commuters who, attracted by the area's excellent transport links, opt to make their homes here. The Conservatives are fielding William Hague's former advisor David Gold.

Erith & Thamesmead

Labour notional majority of 9,870; notional turnout: 53.6%

PARTY	2005 CANDIDATE	NOTIONAL 2005 VOTES	NOTIONAL 2005 % VOTE	PPC FOR NEXT GE
Labour	John Austin MP	19,890	52.6	Teresa Pearce
Conservative	Chris Bromby	10,020	26.5	Colin Bloom
Lib Dem	Steven Toole	4,856	12.8	n/a
Others		3,039	8.0	

Greenwich & Woolwich

Labour notional majority of 11,638; notional turnout: 53.2%

PARTY	2005 CANDIDATE	NOTIONAL 2005 VOTES	NOTIONAL 2005 % VOTE	PPC FOR NEXT GE
Labour	Richard Raynsford MP	18,636	52.5	Richard Raynsford MP
Lib Dem	Christopher Le Breton	6,998	19.7	n/a
Conservative	Alistair Craig	6,244	17.6	Spencer Drury
Others		3,639	10.2	

Kingston & Surbiton

Lib Dem notional majority of 9,084; notional turnout: 67.7%

PARTY	2005 CANDIDATE	NOTIONAL 2005 VOTES	NOTIONAL 2005 % VOTE	PPC FOR NEXT GE
Lib Dem	Edward Davey MP	25,637	51.1	Edward Davey MP
Conservative	Kevin Davis	16,553	33.0	Helen Whately
Labour	Nick Parrott	6,610	13.2	Max Freedman
Others		1,373	2.7	

An archetypal slice of south-west London suburbia, Kingston & Surbiton produced one of the most shocking results of the 1997 general election in electing Liberal Democrat MP Ed Davey by 56 votes. Squeezing the sizeable Labour vote, Davey expanded his majority to in excess of 15,000 at the 2001 election, achieving a Tory to Lib Dem swing of 29.5% in two election cycles. Formed of Kingston's bustling town centre and the contiguous town of Surbiton, the constituency also includes leafy Chessington, Norbiton and New Malden. The seat, which enjoys speedy rail links to central London, is largely middle class in nature and is home to a large Sri Lankan community. The Conservatives, who have fought back hard at a local government level, are fielding Helen Whately.

Lewisham, Deptford

Labour notional majority of 13,012; notional turnout: 50.8%

PARTY	2005 CANDIDATE	NOTIONAL 2005 VOTES	NOTIONAL 2005 % VOTE	PPC FOR NEXT GE
Labour	Joan Ruddock MP	19,245	55.4	Joan Ruddock MP
Lib Dem	Columba Blango	6,233	17.9	n/a
Conservative	James Cartlidge	4,413	12.7	Gemma Townsend
Others		4,869	14.0	

Lewisham East

Labour notional majority of 8,758; notional turnout: 54.7%

PARTY	2005 CANDIDATE	NOTIONAL 2005 VOTES	NOTIONAL 2005 % VOTE	PPC FOR NEXT GE
Labour	Bridget Prentice MP	17,897	47.6	Bridget Prentice MP
Conservative	James Cleverly	9,139	24.3	Jonathan Clamp
Lib Dem	Richard Thomas	7,482	19.9	Pete Pattisson
Others		3,060	8.1	

Lewisham West & Penge

Labour notional majority of 7,779; notional turnout: 57.4%

PARTY	2005 CANDIDATE	NOTIONAL 2005 VOTES	NOTIONAL 2005 % VOTE	PPC FOR NEXT GE
Labour	n/a	18,801	46.3	Jim Dowd MP
Lib Dem	n/a	11,022	27.1	Alex Feakes
Conservative	n/a	8,787	21.6	Chris Phillips
Others		2,018	5.0	

Mitcham & Morden

Labour notional majority of 12,739; notional turnout: 60.7%

PARTY	2005 CANDIDATE	NOTIONAL 2005 VOTES	NOTIONAL 2005 % VOTE	PPC FOR NEXT GE
Labour	Siobhain McDonagh MP	22,526	56.7	Siobhain McDonagh MP
Conservative	Andre Shellhorn	9,787	24.6	Melanie Hampton
Lib Dem	Jo Christie-Smith	5,543	14.0	Diana Coman
Others		1,860	4.7	

Old Bexley & Sidcup

Conservative notional majority of 9,309; notional turnout: 65.2%

PARTY	2005 CANDIDATE	NOTIONAL 2005 VOTES	NOTIONAL 2005 % VOTE	PPC FOR NEXT GE
Conservative	Derek Conway MP	21,151	50.0	James Brokenshire
Labour	Gavin Moore	11,842	28.0	n/a
Lib Dem	Nick O'Hare	5,862	13.9	Duncan Borrowman
Others		3,451	8.2	

Orpington

Conservative notional majority of 5,221; notional turnout: 72.4%

PARTY	2005 CANDIDATE	NOTIONAL 2005 VOTES	NOTIONAL 2005 % VOTE	PPC FOR NEXT GE
Conservative	John Horam MP	24,800	51.2	John Horam MP
Lib Dem	Chris Maines	19,579	40.4	David McBride
Labour	Emily Bird	2,893	6.0	Stephen Morgan
Others		1,131	2.3	

Putney

Conservative notional majority of 1,723; notional turnout: 59.7%

PARTY	2005 CANDIDATE	NOTIONAL 2005 VOTES	NOTIONAL 2005 % VOTE	PPC FOR NEXT GE
Conservative	Justine Greening	15,193	42.3	Justine Greening MP
Labour	Tony Colman	13,470	37.5	Stuart King
Lib Dem	Jeremy Ambache	5,861	16.3	James Sandbach
Others		1,352	3.8	

Richmond Park

Lib Dem notional majority of 3,613; notional turnout: 73.2%

PARTY	2005 CANDIDATE	NOTIONAL 2005 VOTES	NOTIONAL 2005 % VOTE	PPC FOR NEXT GE
Lib Dem	Susan Kramer	23,771	46.7	Susan Kramer MP
Conservative	Marco Forgiona	20,158	39.6	Zac Goldsmith
Labour	James Butler	4,711	9.2	Eleanor Tunnicliffe
Others		2,311	4.5	

A Liberal Democrat seat since the 1997 general election, this charmingly named constituency takes the prosperous south-west London towns of Richmond and Barnes as well as the northern portion of Kingston upon Thames. While the constituency's numerous rail and Tube stations provide commuters with speedy links into central London, Richmond is an important business centre in its own right. At 48.7%, the proportion of residents holding university degrees is one of the highest in the country. Home to many young professionals, almost a fifth of homes are privately rented while two thirds are owner occupied. On a local government level, neither the Conservatives nor the Liberal Democrats have been able to establish themselves as the dominant force. Liberal Democrat MP Susan Kramer will seek to defend her seat from wealthy environmentalist Zac Goldsmith, one of the Conservative Party's highest-profile candidates.

Streatham

Labour notional majority of 6,584; notional turnout: 51.8%

PARTY	2005 CANDIDATE	NOTIONAL 2005 VOTES	NOTIONAL 2005 % VOTE	PPC FOR NEXT GE
Labour	Keith Hill MP	17,699	47.0	Chuka Umunna
Lib Dem	Darren Sanders	11,115	29.5	Chris Nicholson
Conservative	James Sproule	6,138	16.3	Rahoul Bhansali
Others		2,740	7.3	

Sutton & Cheam

Lib Dem notional majority of 2,689; notional turnout: 67.2%

PARTY	2005 CANDIDATE	NOTIONAL 2005 VOTES	NOTIONAL 2005 % VOTE	PPC FOR NEXT GE
Lib Dem	Paul Burstow MP	20,255	46.9	Paul Burstow MP
Conservative	Richard Willis	17,566	40.6	Philippa Stroud
Labour	Anand Shukla	5,116	11.8	n/a
Others		288	0.7	

Captured for the first time by the Liberal Democrats in a 1972 by-election, Sutton & Cheam returned to the party fold in 1997, following the ousting of Tory veteran Olga Maitland on 12.9% swing. This south-west London seat is comfortably middle class in nature, with four in five homes owner-occupied and extremely low rates of unemployment. Cheam, with its open parks and leafy lanes, provides the bedrock of Conservative support locally, while urban Sutton is more strongly inclined towards the Liberal Democrats. The Liberal Democrats have controlled Sutton Borough Council with healthy majorities since 1990. Paul Burstow will defend his seat for the Liberal Democrats while Philippa Stroud, the director of Iain Duncan Smith's Centre for Social Justice, will fight the seat for the Conservatives.

Tooting

Labour notional majority of 5,169; notional turnout: 59.3%

PARTY	2005 CANDIDATE	NOTIONAL 2005 VOTES	NOTIONAL 2005 % VOTE	PPC FOR NEXT GE
Labour	Sadiq Khan MP	18,129	42.7	Sadiq Khan MP
Conservative	James Bethell	12,960	30.5	Mark Clarke
Lib Dem	Stephanie Dearden	8,314	19.6	n/a
Others		3,054	7.2	

Held by Labour since the Second World War, Tooting has so far stubbornly refused to follow the rest of Wandsworth – the Thatcherite 'flagship borough' – by electing a Conservative MP. Less susceptible to the gentrification that has swept neighbouring Putney and Battersea in recent years, the Conservatives have firmly established themselves as the largest party of local government and hold 14 seats to Labour's seven. At 10% apiece, the proportion of black and Asian voters is above average, with a large Tamil community living in Tooting ward. Just over half of homes are owner occupied, yet a quarter are privately rented – many of them housing upwardly mobile young graduates. Currently held by Labour Transport Minister Sadiq Khan, management consultant and former Tory youth wing chairman Mark Clarke will contest the seat for the Conservatives.

Twickenham

Lib Dem notional majority of 9,965; notional turnout: 72.3%

PARTY	2005 CANDIDATE	NOTIONAL 2005 VOTES	NOTIONAL 2005 % VOTE	PPC FOR NEXT GE
Lib Dem	Vincent Cable MP	26,696	51.6	Vincent Cable MP
Conservative	Paul Maynard	16,731	32.4	Deborah Thomas
Labour	Brian Whitington	5,868	11.4	Brian Whitington
Others		2,392	4.6	

Located in south-west London, the Twickenham constituency has been held since 1997 by Liberal Democrat Treasury spokesman Vince Cable. Perhaps best known as the home of British rugby, Twickenham is a middle-class residential seat in easy commuting distance of central London. With the river Thames as its southern boundary, the constituency stretches from Twickenham town in the north of the seat southwards to the residential Hampton and Teddington areas. Two fifths of residents hold university degrees and around three quarters of homes are owner occupied. While the Conservatives have come back strongly in many other parts of London, the Liberal Democrats continue to dominate here in local government, holding 24 seats to the Tories' nine. Management consultant Deborah Thomas will fight the seat for the Conservatives.

Vauxhall

Labour notional majority of 8,503; notional turnout: 48.4%

PARTY	2005 CANDIDATE	NOTIONAL 2005 VOTES	NOTIONAL 2005 % VOTE	PPC FOR NEXT GE
Labour	Kate Hoey MP	17,928	51.7	Kate Hoey MP
Lib Dem	Charles Anglin	9,425	27.2	Caroline Pidgeon
Conservative	Edward Heckles	5,048	14.6	Glyn Chambers
Others		2,243	6.5	

Wimbledon

Conservative notional majority of 2,480; notional turnout: 67.8%

PARTY	2005 CANDIDATE	NOTIONAL 2005 VOTES	NOTIONAL 2005 % VOTE	PPC FOR NEXT GE
Conservative	Stephen Hammond MP	18,028	41.4	Stephen Hammond MP
Labour	Roger Casale	15,548	35.7	Andrew Judge
Lib Dem	Stephen Gee	7,908	18.2	Shas Sheehan
Others		2,072	4.8	

West London

Although not the largest of our regions, West London has seen proportionately some of the most dramatic boundary changes, which will have notable effects at the next general election. These involve the Boundary Commission changing its mind about which of the London boroughs should be split and paired in order to achieve more equal electorates. In the most recent review, it was decided to divide the borough of Hammersmith & Fulham (and the present seat of that name). Fulham is now to be linked with Chelsea (formerly joined with Kensington), in a very safe Conservative constituency. This is excellent news for first term Tory MP Greg Hands, who will now have one of the fifteen strongest seats for his party, having gained what was a marginal in 2005. Just over half of his old seat is now to form the core of the new Hammersmith, but that division will also take 27,000 voters within its borough from the current Ealing, Acton & Shepherds Bush, which is Labour held. This makes Hammersmith into a critical marginal, on which many eyes will focus (see *One to Watch* below).

In turn, these boundary changes mean that for the first time since 1992 the populous and heterogeneous west London local authority of Ealing will not be involved in any cross-borough constituencies, but will have three entirely of its own. Ealing, Southall was retained by Virendra Sharma in a by-election in July 2007 (during Gordon Brown's brief honeymoon as party leader and Prime Minister) with a fairly comfortable margin of 5,070 votes over the Liberal Democrats. Now it loses nearly 22,000 voters to other Ealing seats. This will make it far more clearly a 'majority ethnic minority' seat, with the non-white proportion according to the 2001 census rising from 52.7 per cent to 62.4 per cent. Ealing, Southall will now have a 23 per cent Sikh population, twice as high as the next constituency on that list (Feltham & Heston, also in West London), but there are also substantial Hindu, Muslim and Afro-Caribbean communities. Given the loyalty of these groups to Labour, Southall is likely to be the party's safest seat in this region.

The same cannot be said of the other two Ealing constituencies. The switching of wards means that Ealing North loses over 5,000 voters net, which increases the swing needed for the Conservatives to over 9 per cent, but according to recent national opinion polls it remains within their grasp. This would oust a well-known Labour figure: the friend of the media, the impish and ubiquitous Stephen Pound. Even more marginal is the entirely new Ealing Central & Acton. This rather clumsily named constituency takes the bulk of its electors (44,000) from the Ealing borough parts of Ealing, Acton & Shepherds Bush, but also 20,000 from Southall and 8,000 from Ealing North. For the Tories, these are rather helpfully some of the best Conservative wards in the three old seats that contain parts of Ealing. Not surprisingly, the Labour MP for the current Ealing, Acton & Shepherd's Bush, Andrew Slaughter, has decided to follow the Shepherd's Bush part into the new Hammersmith seat, leaving a newcomer (Bassam Mahfouz) with the unenviable task of defending Ealing Central & Acton against Angie Bray. The notional results calculated by Professors Michael Thrasher and Colin Rallings of Plymouth University (which will be used by the main media outlets that commissioned them) suggest that a swing of only 1.1 per cent is needed; though the alternative figures of Anthony Wells on UK Polling Report actually already put the Tories ahead, albeit by only eighty-four votes, in a hypothetical 2005 contest. We shall never find out whose notionals are closer, but in any case Ealing Central & Acton is a must-win for the Conservatives if they are at the very least to knock out Labour's overall majority. Both sets of calculations also suggest that the Liberal Democrats are in a strong third place, making this their only practical target in West London.

There are also major boundary changes affecting the borough of Harrow on the north-west edge of the metropolis. In 2005, Harrow East was the safer of two tight Labour marginals. Tony McNulty of East was a frequent media spokesman for the government, mainly as a Home Office Minister of State, until his return to the back benches in June 2009. In 2005 his majority was 4,730, or 9.3 per cent. Meanwhile Gareth Thomas of Harrow West won by only 2,028 (4.2 per cent). Now however, their respective safety is to be reversed. The Labour-inclined central wards of Harrow, Greenhill and Marlborough are switched from East to West. What is more, West loses 22,500 voters from the most Conservative parts of the whole borough, Pinner and Hatch End, to a new cross-borough seat – with Hillingdon – to be called Ruislip, Northwood & Pinner. As a consequence, West's notional majority is now nearly 8,000, and will need a pro-Tory swing of over 9 per cent. Tony McNulty, on the other hand, is vulnerable to a swing of just 3.5 per cent. The borough's best known institution is probably Harrow School, alma mater of many luminaries including Conservative Prime Ministers Winston Churchill, Stanley Baldwin and Robert Peel. However, it may not be widely known that both Harrow seats are now nearly 50 per cent non-white in population; the largest element consists of middle-class Hindus, which may also account for Harrow East sending more of its resident children to university than any other constituency in the United Kingdom. The ethnic makeup of the Harrow seats makes them harder to win for the Conservatives than their class structure implies, but there is a fair chance that both the former Brent council leader Bob Blackman (East) and Rachel Joyce (West) will pull off prestigious wins for their party.

Moving into Hillingdon, as well as the safe Tory Ruislip, Northwood & Pinner, there will be another new name. In exchange for the new electors from Harrow West, the present Ruislip-Northwood donates 24,000 voters (40 per cent of its total) to Uxbridge, which will now have '& South Ruislip' added to its name. This will remain safe for John Randall, who did well to hold the seat in the July 1997 by-election just after Labour's first Blairite landslide. In a knock-on effect, the Tory ward of West Drayton is in turn moved into Hayes & Harlington, the base of one of Labour's most persistent left-wing rebels, John McDonnell (who tried to gather enough nominations to stand against Gordon Brown in the 2007 non-leadership election). Although McDonnell's seat looked safe in 2005, with a majority of over 10,000, it should not be forgotten that Hayes & Harlington was won three times between 1983 and 1992 by a right-wing Tory, Terry Dicks (whose campaign posters entertainingly read 'I Love Dicks') – and West Drayton's arrival may just bring the seat within the outer range of their ambitions again.

Our final West London borough is Hounslow. Due perhaps to its proximity to Heathrow Airport, the two constituencies here also have a strong British Asian presence. There are only minor boundary changes in this geographically long thin borough. They are currently held by a husband-and-wife team, the only one with contiguous constituencies apart from the retiring Nicholas and Ann Winterton in Macclesfield and Congleton in Cheshire, but the chances of this lasting into the next parliament are not strong. Brentford & Isleworth in the eastern half of Hounslow borough extends to the affluent middle class areas around Chiswick such as Turnham Green and Ravenscourt Park, and Ann Keen would be defeated on a swing of just over 4 per cent to the Conservative candidate Mary Macleod. Feltham & Heston is 40 per cent non-white, and Alan Keen has a cushion against a swing of anything up to nearly 10 per cent. Its relative safety is also suggested by Labour's retention of a majority of councillors there even when they lost Hounslow in 2006 after thirty-five years of control. Labour were only 2.7 per cent behind the Tories across the whole of Hounslow in the May 2009 European elections. However, it should in summary be remembered that the only constituency in West London which was not won by the Conservatives in the 1980s was Southall – and should there be a landslide again in 2010, this could just happen again.

Target seats

SEAT	SWING REQUIRED %	MP	CHALLENGER
Conservative from Labour			
Ealing Central & Acton	1.1	(Bassam Mahfouz)	Angie Bray
Harrow East	3.5	Tony McNulty	Bob Blackman
Brentford & Isleworth	4.2	Ann Keen	Mary Macleod
Hammersmith	4.3	Andrew Slaughter	Shaun Bailey
Harrow West	9.2	Gareth Thomas	Rachel Joyce
Ealing North	9.4	Stephen Pound	Ian Gibb
Feltham & Heston	9.7	Alan Keen	Mark Bowen
Liberal Democrat from Labour			
Ealing Central & Acton	1.4	(Bassam Mahfouz)	Jon Ball

One to watch: Hammersmith

New constituency.
Notional majority 2005: Labour 3,673 (8.4%)
Labour candidate: Andrew Slaughter MP (Ealing, Acton and Shepherd's Bush)
Conservative candidate: Shaun Bailey

It is arguable that the constituency to watch in West London should be the new seat of Ealing Central & Acton, as it is notionally at least a close three way marginal, with Labour just 839 ahead of the Conservatives, and the Liberal Democrats only a further 222 votes behind. However, all recent opinion polls suggest that will be an easy Tory gain, and Labour could lose it without even their overall majority being threatened, so it is not really a key contest. On the other hand, if the Conservatives can win Hammersmith, they will be a least on target to be the largest party, which should be enough to form a government. Labour has realistic hopes of winning here, as is indicated by Andrew Slaughter's decision to contest this seat, rather than Ealing Central & Acton, where far more of his electors have gone. Another interesting feature is the identity of the Tory candidate. Shaun Bailey comes from a background which would scarcely have been conceivable for a prospective Conservative MP much less than a generation ago. A 38-year-old of Jamaican descent, he was raised by his mother in a North Kensington council estate, worked as a security guard to put himself through university, and co-founded a charity to address the problems of deprived young people. He won an open primary in 2007 to be selected as candidate for Hammersmith, and has already become established as a prominent spokesman on social issues. If Shaun Bailey should be elected in this vital swing seat, he will be one of the most visible symbols of the regeneration of his party – in more ways than one.

Brentford & Isleworth

Labour notional majority of 3,633; notional turnout: 52.8%				
PARTY	2005 CANDIDATE	NOTIONAL 2005 VOTES	NOTIONAL 2005 % VOTE	PPC FOR NEXT GE
Labour	Ann Keen MP	17,092	39.0	Ann Keen MP
Conservative	Alexander Northcote	13,459	30.7	Mary Macleod
Lib Dem	Andrew Dakers	10,068	23.0	Andrew Dakers
Others		3,220	7.3	

Based alongside the main arterial road out of west London, no seat embodied the scale of the 1997 rejection of the Conservatives in London as well as Brentford & Isleworth, with future Health Minister Ann Keen ousting jovial Tory Nirj Deva by a margin of over a little over 14,000 votes. Home to prosperous Chiswick and Osterley, which remained loyal to the Conservatives throughout their mid-1990s nadir, Labour has relied on overwhelming support in Brentford, Hounslow and Gunnersbury to deliver them healthy majorities at the past three general elections. Almost a third of the constituency's residents were born outside the United Kingdom, leading to sizeable Hindu, Muslim and Sikh communities. This time around, Keen faces a much tougher time in the form of Scots-born management consultant Mary Macleod.

Chelsea & Fulham

Conservative notional majority of 10,253; notional turnout: 52.5%

PARTY	2005 CANDIDATE	NOTIONAL 2005 VOTES	NOTIONAL 2005 % VOTE	PPC FOR NEXT GE
Labour	n/a	12,944	33.4	Bassam Mahfouz
Conservative	n/a	12,105	31.2	Angie Bray
Lib Dem	n/a	11,883	30.6	Jon Ball
Others		1,869	4.8	

Ealing Central & Acton

Labour notional majority of 839; notional turnout: 56.0%

PARTY	2005 CANDIDATE	NOTIONAL 2005 VOTES	NOTIONAL 2005 % VOTE	PPC FOR NEXT GE
Labour	n/a	12,944	33.4	Bassam Mahfouz
Conservative	n/a	12,105	31.2	Angie Bray
Lib Dem	n/a	11,883	30.6	Jon Ball
Others		1,869	4.8	

Ealing North

Labour notional majority of 8,126; notional turnout: 60.1%

PARTY	2005 CANDIDATE	NOTIONAL 2005 VOTES	NOTIONAL 2005 % VOTE	PPC FOR NEXT GE
Labour	Stephen Pound MP	20,483	46.9	Stephen Pound MP
Conservative	Roger Curtis	12,357	28.3	Ian Gibb
Lib Dem	Francesco Fruzza	8,390	19.2	Francesco Fruzza
Others		2,429	5.6	

Located in relatively peaceful north-west London, the Ealing North constituency fell to Labour at the 1997 general election. This is a largely middle-class and residential constituency comprising the suburban Northolt, Greenford and Perivale areas. The constituency enjoys excellent transport links which make it an appealing home for many commuters into central London. Some 67.1% of homes in this leafy constituency are owner occupied with 20.4% being drawn from social housing stock. A fifth of local residents are drawn from the Asian community, 9.7% being Muslim, 8.6% Hindu and 3% Sikh. Boundary changes which transfer part of the Labour-friendly Greenford ward into the seat from neighbouring Southall slightly boost the projected Labour majority here. Colourful Labour maverick Stephen Pound will face Conservative candidate Ian Gibb.

Ealing, Southall

Labour notional majority of 13,140; notional turnout: 54.9%

PARTY	2005 CANDIDATE	NOTIONAL 2005 VOTES	NOTIONAL 2005 % VOTE	PPC FOR NEXT GE
Labour	Piara Khabra MP	19,634	57.3	Virendra Sharma MP
Conservative	Mark Nicholson	6,494	18.9	Gurcharan Singh
Lib Dem	Nigel Bakhai	6,254	18.2	Nigel Bakhai
Others		1,901	5.5	

Feltham & Heston

PARTY	2005 CANDIDATE	NOTIONAL 2005 VOTES	NOTIONAL 2005 % VOTE	PPC FOR NEXT GE
Labour notional majority of 7,598; notional turnout: 47.8%				
Labour	Alan Keen MP	18,978	48.1	Alan Keen MP
Conservative	Mark Bowen	11,380	28.8	Mark Bowen
Lib Dem	Satnam Kaur Khalsa	6,586	16.7	Munira Wilson
Others		2,516	6.4	

A closely fought marginal constituency throughout the Thatcher years, sitting MP Alan Keen ousted Conservative Patrick Ground QC by little over 1,000 votes at the 1992 general election. Heathrow airport is of crucial political importance to residents of the constituency, both for providing a large number of jobs and for galvanising opposition towards night flights and a third runway. Sharing little of the middle-class character of nearby Twickenham, both Feltham and Heston are firmly working-class towns dominated by low-level manufacturing and the airline service sector. Sikhs, Hindus and Muslims make up around 10% of the local population apiece. Welsh-born Mark Bowen, a dogged local campaigner and deputy leader of Hounslow Borough Council since 2006, will fight the seat for the Conservatives.

Hammersmith

PARTY	2005 CANDIDATE	NOTIONAL 2005 VOTES	NOTIONAL 2005 % VOTE	PPC FOR NEXT GE
Labour notional majority of 3,673; notional turnout: 58.5%				
Labour	n/a	18,463	42.4	Andrew Slaughter MP
Conservative	n/a	14,790	34.0	Shaun Bailey
Lib Dem	n/a	8,267	19.0	Merlene Emerson
Others		2,021	4.6	

Formed out of the Conservatives' Hammersmith & Fulham and Labour's Ealing, Acton & Shepherd's Bush constituencies, this new constituency will be fought for the first time at the coming general election. This West London seat is incredibly diverse in nature, mixing the poverty of the predominantly Afro-Caribbean White City council estate with the opulence of well-heeled Ravenscourt Park. At a local government level, both major parties are evenly matched, the Conservatives holding 15 seats to Labour's 13. Only two in five homes here are owner occupied, a fifth are privately rented and more than a third are social housing. With the BBC Television Centre located at White City, this is a well-educated constituency in which 43.6% of residents hold university degrees. Transport links to central London are excellent, making this a popular area for young families and professionals. Sitting Labour MP Andrew Slaughter will hope to hold off a challenge from Conservative charity director Shaun Bailey.

Harrow East

PARTY	2005 CANDIDATE	NOTIONAL 2005 VOTES	NOTIONAL 2005 % VOTE	PPC FOR NEXT GE
Labour notional majority of 2,934; notional turnout: 61.2%				
Labour	Tony McNulty MP	19,366	45.5	Tony McNulty MP
Conservative	David Ashton	16,432	38.6	Bob Blackman
Lib Dem	Pash Nandhra	6,043	14.2	n/a
Others		757	1.8	

Bob Blackman, the Conservative leader on Brent Council and former London Assemblyman for Harrow, needs a swing of little over 3% to oust tough-talking former Home Office minister Tony McNulty MP in the redrawn Harrow East constituency. It was previously the safer (for Labour) of the two Harrow constituencies, but Conservative chances have been boosted significantly by the transfer of the Labour-inclined wards of Greenhill and Marlborough to Harrow West. A prosperous constituency characterised by long driveways and cedar-lined avenues, Harrow East is one of the most ethnically diverse seats in the country with large numbers of Hindu (23.9%), Jewish (10.3%) and Muslim (7.1%) residents.

Harrow West

	Labour notional majority of 7,742; notional turnout: 64.3%			
PARTY	2005 CANDIDATE	NOTIONAL 2005 VOTES	NOTIONAL 2005 % VOTE	PPC FOR NEXT GE
Labour	Gareth Thomas MP	20,622	48.6	Gareth Thomas MP
Conservative	Mike Freer	12,880	30.4	Rachel Joyce
Lib Dem	Christopher Noyce	7,919	18.7	n/a
Others		985	2.3	

Of all the constituencies the party gained in 1997, few could have ever predicted that on election night Harrow West would fall to Labour on an 18.1% swing. Located in the north-west corner of London and home to the famous Harrow public school, this is a broadly middle-class constituency with a sizeable and affluent ethnic population – a fifth (18.3%) of residents are Hindu, 8.3% are Muslim and 7.3% are black. One of its few successes in the recent round of boundary changes, Labour's notional majority in Harrow West has been boosted from 2,000 to 7,000 following the transfer of the safe Conservative wards of Hatch End and Pinner to the new Ruislip, Northwood & Pinner constituency. International Development Minister Gareth Thomas will defend his seat for Labour while NHS doctor Rachel Joyce will challenge for the Conservatives.

Hayes & Harlington

	Labour notional majority of 10,594; notional turnout: 55.3%			
PARTY	2005 CANDIDATE	NOTIONAL 2005 VOTES	NOTIONAL 2005 % VOTE	PPC FOR NEXT GE
Labour	John McDonnell MP	20,844	56.4	John McDonnell MP
Conservative	Richard Worrall	10,250	27.7	n/a
Lib Dem	Jon Ball	3,637	9.8	n/a
Others		2,208	6.0	

Kensington

	Conservative notional majority of 4,540; notional turnout: 51.8%			
PARTY	2005 CANDIDATE	NOTIONAL 2005 VOTES	NOTIONAL 2005 % VOTE	PPC FOR NEXT GE
Conservative	Malcolm Rifkind	14,078	43.8	Sir Malcolm Rifkind MP
Labour	Catherine Atkinson	9,538	29.7	Sam Gurney
Lib Dem	Jennifer Kingsley	6,467	20.1	Iarla Kilbane-Dawe
Others		2,139	6.4	

Ruislip, Northwood & Pinner

	Conservative notional majority of 13,274; notional turnout: 62.3%			
PARTY	2005 CANDIDATE	NOTIONAL 2005 VOTES	NOTIONAL 2005 % VOTE	PPC FOR NEXT GE
Conservative	n/a	23,652	54.7	Nick Hurd MP
Labour	n/a	10,378	24.0	n/a
Lib Dem	n/a	7,049	16.3	n/a
Others		2,139	4.9	

Uxbridge & South Ruislip

	Conservative notional majority of 7,178; notional turnout: 58.6%			
PARTY	2005 CANDIDATE	NOTIONAL 2005 VOTES	NOTIONAL 2005 % VOTE	PPC FOR NEXT GE
Conservative	John Randall MP	17,712	44.4	John Randall MP
Labour	Roderick Dubrow-Marshall	10,534	26.4	Sidharath Garg
Lib Dem	Tariq Mahmood	9,034	22.7	Mike Cox
Others		2,578	6.5	

North and East London

When Labour came to power in 1997, they benefited from their largest swings in the capital city, particularly in outer London, where that which accounted for Michael Portillo in Enfield, Southgate was only a typical example. In all they gained twenty-two seats, nearly half of them in north and east London. Because of the scale of this advance, and as London has a record of being one of the most volatile of regions, at the next election it offers the Conservatives the chance of reversing the pattern of dominance by achieving many vital gains of their own – especially as over the two subsequent contests they have only regained six of these seats. There is much to be said of the theory that the capture of the capital city will chop off the head of the opposing forces.

London only loses one constituency overall in the forthcoming boundary changes, and that is north of the river, in the borough of Havering on the Essex border, as Hornchurch and Upminster are in effect merged. These were both won by the Conservatives in 2005, so technically it is they who lose a seat. Of the two sitting MPs, it was Upminster's 67-year-old Angela Watkinson who came out on top in the selection process, leaving the much younger James Brokenshire of Hornchurch to take to the road. He did not have to move far, eventually being elected to replace the disgraced Derek Conway just across the river in Old Bexley & Sidcup.

There have also been extensive boundary modifications elsewhere, though, that have favoured the Tories much more. In fact, the notional figures for the revised seats, estimating how they would have voted if the new lines had been in place in 2005, have already awarded them two of their ostensible chief targets: Enfield North, where Joan Ryan is to fight to 'regain' her present seat, and Finchley & Golders Green, where Rudi Vis has taken the apparently sensible decision to retire. The new Conservative MPs for these seats are likely to be Nick de Bois and Mike Freer.

We may analyse five other Conservative targets from Labour in three categories. These are: those which could fall even without becoming the largest party; those which if taken would help the Tories secure the most seats in a hung parliament; and finally those that if taken, would suggest a Tory overall majority.

In the first category, we find two seats, Westminster North (a 3.3 per cent swing is required) and Hendon (4.1 per cent). Westminster North is nowhere near as favourable for Karen Buck as her present seat of Regent's Park & Kensington North, but she has nowhere to go. This is largely a recreation of the Westminster North seat which existed before the last boundary changes in 1997, which was held by the Conservative John Wheeler, and the likely winner is the barrister Joanne Cash (not related to the veteran Eurosceptic MP for Stone, Bill Cash). Hendon has been held since 1997 for Labour by Andrew Dismore. The May 2006 Barnet borough election results suggests that this is well within the Tories' reach, as they took four wards by large margins to Labour's three.

In the second group, seats needed to make the Conservatives the largest party in the Commons, is the newly drawn Hampstead & Kilburn, but there the task is made harder for the Conservatives by starting from third place in the notional figures, as described under Liberal Democrat chances below. It may seem a real surprise to see that the other seat in this category is in the heart of the traditionally working-class East End: Poplar & Limehouse (see *One to Watch* below).

It is a measure of the mountain that the Conservatives have to climb to secure an overall majority – and this is often underestimated by commentators – that they also need to go ahead to claim seats with swings of around 8 to 10 per cent, which in this region would oust a well known and heavyweight Labour figure: Jon Cruddas, thought by many to be a strong candidate for the Labour leadership, offering a new direction untainted by high office – should they lose under Gordon Brown. Cruddas will not be eligible if he loses his seat, though – and this is made possible by the boundary changes that see plain Dagenham become Dagenham & Rainham, taking 41 per cent of its voters from Havering borough, these forming actually a plurality of the current voters of the Tory Hornchurch seat. He must watch out too for his vote being split by the BNP, at their strongest anywhere in the borough of Barking & Dagenham. All in all, Dagenham & Rainham may be an outside tip for one of the shock gains of the 2009 – or more likely 2010 – election.

London is not a two-party state. In addition to Respect's chances in the East End, the Liberal Democrats will be looking to hold and even increase their tally of two seats in North and East London (out of eight in the capital as a whole). They have two good chances of gains from Labour, and one oddball situation. The former are Islington South & Finsbury and Hampstead & Kilburn, both of which require swings of less than 1 per cent against three-figure (notional) majorities. In fact Islington South is an unchanged seat, and Emily Thornberry will be defending a lead of just 484 votes in her first contest in 2005 after succeeding the poplar Chris Smith. Labour did return thirteen councillors to the Lib Dems' ten in the wards here in May 2006, though, and Ms Thornberry may still just be favourite after five years' incumbency.

Hampstead & Kilburn presents a different situation, though. This new seat, crossing the Camden–Brent borough boundary, takes a third of its voters from Sarah Teather's abolished Brent East, which reduces Glenda Jackson's notional majority to 474 votes over the Liberal Democrats (and 13 per cent from the Tories in third place). Yet bravely, Sarah Teather has not chosen to fight this very winnable opportunity but to stay with the bulk of her constituents to fight Labour's Dawn Butler (of Brent South) in a much harder prospect, the new Brent Central. This will take a technical swing of nearly 10 per cent and would seem to be one of the most bold and apparently selfless choices made for the next general election.

The other Lib Dem sitting MP faces much less of a challenge. Lynne Featherstone, with a personal vote built up since her first election last time, and with her principal opposition (Labour) in decline nationally, and nearly a full slate of her party cohorts again returned to Haringey council in 2006, seems a certain victor again. However, this can not be said of very many MPs and constituencies in North and East London. In these cosmopolitan and diverse parts of the capital, with their mix of classes and ethnic groups, many surprises are possible. Conservatives, Liberal Democrats, Labour, Respect and even the BNP have chances of gains: if the last named could repeat their 2006 local election performance in Barking, where they topped the poll in the six wards where they put up candidates, they will seriously worry Margaret Hodge MP (and a good many others besides). Six of the ten seats in Britain with a majority of non-white voters are in this sub-region: East Ham, Brent North, Brent Central, West Ham, Bethnal Green & Bow and Ilford South. This creates both a stimulating infusion of ethnic variety and reaction to it. There is no melting pot in the land like the nation's huge capital, and this makes its electoral contests volatile, stimulating, unpredictable – and exciting for watchers and participants alike, true features of democratic competition.

Target seats

SEAT	SWING REQUIRED %	MP	CHALLENGER
Conservative from Labour			
Westminster North	3.3	Karen Buck	Joanne Cash
Hendon	4.1	Andrew Dismore	Matthew Offord
Poplar & Limehouse	5.5	Jim Fitzpatrick	Tim Archer
Hampstead & Kilburn	6.7	Glenda Jackson	Chris Philp
Dagenham & Rainham	7.9	Jon Cruddas	Simon Jones
Lib Dem from Labour			
Hampstead & Kilburn	0.6	Glenda Jackson	Ed Fordham
Islington South & Finsbury	0.8	Emily Thornberry	Bridget Fox
Brent Central	9.6	Dawn Butler	Sarah Teather MP
Labour from Conservatives			
Finchley & Golders Green	0.4	(Mike Freer)	Alison Moore
Enfield North	1.2	(Nick de Bois)	Joan Ryan MP
Enfield, Southgate	1.4	David Burrowes	Bambos Charalambous
Labour from Lib Dems			
Hornsey & Wood Green	2.6	Lynne Featherstone	Karen Jennings
Labour from Respect			
Bethnal Green & Bow	1.2	(Abjol Miah)	Rushanara Ali
Respect from Labour			
Poplar & Limehouse	5.9	Jim Fitzpatrick	George Galloway MP
BNP from Labour			
Barking	11.5	Margaret Hodge	Richard Fullbrook

One to watch: Poplar & Limehouse

Actual majority 2005 (Poplar and Canning Town): Labour 7,129 (18.3%) –
Jim Fitzpatrick MP
Notional majority 2005: Labour 3,823 (10.8%)
Conservative candidate: Tim Archer
Respect candidate: George Galloway MP

Poplar and Limehouse: names reflecting the constituencies of two former Labour party leaders, George Lansbury and Clement Attlee. That the Conservatives technically need only a 5.5 per cent swing is due to two factors. One is the gentrification of Docklands, epitomised by the luxury flats in the Isle of Dogs near Canary Wharf, which enabled the Tories to top the poll in three wards of Tower Hamlets borough in 2006 – Millwall, Blackwall & Cubitt Town and St Katherine's & Wapping (who would have believe some of those names would fall a few decades ago?). Conversely, the other is that the notional figures for 2005 for this revised seat include several thousand votes for Respect, who seriously attacked the Labour vote in Tower Hamlets, including of course George Galloway's victory in Bethnal Green & Bow against Oona King (which Labour will strenuously be trying to reverse next time; Galloway announced he is not standing again and passed the far left baton to Abjol Miah, from the local Bangladeshi community). The Conservative notional share in Poplar and Limehouse was still only 24 per cent, and one feels that it would take an even split between Labour and Respect to let them in even with a further positive swing. This was made more likely, though, by Galloway's nomination as Respect candidate for Poplar & Limehouse in November 2007 – having said he would only seek one term in Bethnal Green, he has merely moved next door. A more colourful – and perhaps more vitriolic – three-way contest can scarcely be imagined, not just within London, but anywhere within Britain.

Barking

Labour notional majority of 12,183; notional turnout: 48.2%

PARTY	2005 CANDIDATE	NOTIONAL 2005 VOTES	NOTIONAL 2005 % VOTE	PPC FOR NEXT GE
Labour	Margaret Hodge MP	18,293	49.6	Margaret Hodge MP
Conservative	Keith Prince	6,110	16.6	Simon Marcus
BNP	Richard Barnbrook	5,997	16.3	n/a
Others		6,471	17.6	

Bethnal Green & Bow

Respect notional majority of 804; notional turnout: 51.5%

PARTY	2005 CANDIDATE	NOTIONAL 2005 VOTES	NOTIONAL 2005 % VOTE	PPC FOR NEXT GE
Respect	George Galloway MP	14,015	36.5	Abjol Miah
Labour	Oona King MP	13,211	34.4	Rushanara Ali
Lib Dem	Syed Nurul Islam Dulu	4,721	12.3	Ajmal Masroor
Others		6,419	16.7	

Brent Central

Labour notional majority of 7,469; notional turnout: 55.4%

PARTY	2005 CANDIDATE	NOTIONAL 2005 VOTES	NOTIONAL 2005 % VOTE	PPC FOR NEXT GE
Labour	n/a	19,684	50.1	Dawn Butler MP
Lib Dem	n/a	12,215	31.1	Sarah Teather MP
Conservative	n/a	5,142	13.1	Sachin Rajput
Others		2,226	5.7	

Brent North

Labour notional majority of 8,830; notional turnout: 58.4%

PARTY	2005 CANDIDATE	NOTIONAL 2005 VOTES	NOTIONAL 2005 % VOTE	PPC FOR NEXT GE
Labour	Barry Gardiner MP	21,751	49.4	Barry Gardiner MP
Conservative	Bob Blackman	12,921	29.3	n/a
Lib Dem	Havard Hughes	8,571	19.5	James Allie
Others		811	1.8	

Chingford & Woodford Green

Conservative notional majority of 10,641; notional turnout: 62.9%

PARTY	2005 CANDIDATE	NOTIONAL 2005 VOTES	NOTIONAL 2005 % VOTE	PPC FOR NEXT GE
Conservative	Iain Duncan Smith MP	20,555	53.2	Iain Duncan Smith MP
Labour	Simon Wright	9,914	25.7	Catharine Arakelian
Lib Dem	John Beanse	6,832	17.7	Geoff Sneef
Others		1,347	3.5	

Chipping Barnet

Conservative notional majority of 5,457; notional turnout: 62.7%

PARTY	2005 CANDIDATE	NOTIONAL 2005 VOTES	NOTIONAL 2005 % VOTE	PPC FOR NEXT GE
Conservative	Theresa Villiers	20,825	45.9	Theresa Villiers MP
Labour	Pauline Coakley-Webb	15,368	33.8	Damien Welfare
Lib Dem	Sean Hooker	6,941	15.3	n/a
Others		2,274	5.0	

Cities of London & Westminster

Conservative notional majority of 7,352; notional turnout: 51.1%

PARTY	2005 CANDIDATE	NOTIONAL 2005 VOTES	NOTIONAL 2005 % VOTE	PPC FOR NEXT GE
Conservative	Mark Field MP	15,449	48.2	Mark Field MP
Labour	Hywel Lloyd	8,097	25.3	Dave Rowntree
Lib Dem	Marie-Louise Rossi	5,934	18.5	Naomi Smith
Others		2,539	7.9	

Dagenham & Rainham

Labour notional majority of 6,372; notional turnout: 56.8%

PARTY	2005 CANDIDATE	NOTIONAL 2005 VOTES	NOTIONAL 2005 % VOTE	PPC FOR NEXT GE
Labour	n/a	19,964	49.2	Jon Cruddas MP
Conservative	n/a	13,592	33.5	Simon Jones
Lib Dem	n/a	3,676	9.1	n/a
Others		3,374	8.3	

Located on the banks of the river Thames in London's flinty north-eastern corner, this new seat is formed of two thirds of the existing Dagenham constituency and half of the Conservative seat of Hornchurch. On paper, it's easy to see why Labour holds this seat: two fifths of the population have no qualifications, less than one in ten hold university degrees and a quarter live in social housing. Labour dominate in the Dagenham portion of this constituency, winning by huge margins in the Heath, River and Village wards while the leafier Elm Park and South Hornchurch wards in Havering are more favourable towards the Tories. The BNP has made solid inroads here in recent years. Former Lord Ashcroft aide and Waveney councillor Simon Jones will fight the seat for the Conservatives.

East Ham

Labour notional majority of 13,649; notional turnout: 47.6%

PARTY	2005 CANDIDATE	NOTIONAL 2005 VOTES	NOTIONAL 2005 % VOTE	PPC FOR NEXT GE
Labour	Stephen Timms MP	22,109	53.6	Stephen Timms MP
Respect	Abdul Khaliq Mian	8,460	20.5	n/a
Conservative	Sarah Macken	5,675	13.8	Paul Shea
Others		5,022	12.2	

Edmonton

Labour notional majority of 10,312; notional turnout: 57.4%

PARTY	2005 CANDIDATE	NOTIONAL 2005 VOTES	NOTIONAL 2005 % VOTE	PPC FOR NEXT GE
Labour	Andy Love MP	20,357	55.9	Andy Love MP
Conservative	Lionel Zetter	10,045	27.6	n/a
Lib Dem	Iarla Kilbane-Dawe	4,369	12.0	n/a
Others		1,635	4.5	

Enfield North

Conservative notional majority of 937; notional turnout: 60.3%

PARTY	2005 CANDIDATE	NOTIONAL 2005 VOTES	NOTIONAL 2005 % VOTE	PPC FOR NEXT GE
Conservative	Nick de Bois	17,167	43.1	Nick de Bois
Labour	Joan Ryan MP	16,230	40.8	Joan Ryan MP
Lib Dem	Simon Radford	4,548	11.4	n/a
Others		1,878	4.7	

Enfield, Southgate

Conservative notional majority of 1,127; notional turnout: 63.4%

PARTY	2005 CANDIDATE	NOTIONAL 2005 VOTES	NOTIONAL 2005 % VOTE	PPC FOR NEXT GE
Conservative	David Burrowes	18,134	43.8	David Burrowes MP
Labour	Stephen Twigg MP	17,007	41.0	Bambos Charalambous
Lib Dem	Ziz Kakoulakis	4,611	11.1	n/a
Others		1,681	4.1	

Finchley & Golders Green

Conservative notional majority of 294; notional turnout: 62.7%

PARTY	2005 CANDIDATE	NOTIONAL 2005 VOTES	NOTIONAL 2005 % VOTE	PPC FOR NEXT GE
Conservative	Andrew Mennear	16,692	39.8	Mike Freer
Labour	Rudi Vis MP	16,398	39.1	Alison Moore
Lib Dem	Sue Garden	7,186	17.1	Laura Edge
Others		1,663	4.0	

Formed out of the majority of the territory represented by Margaret Thatcher for 33 years, this North London constituency is one of the country's most closely fought marginals. Despite unfavourable demographic trends for the Conservatives this seat is broadly middle class in nature, encompassing Finchley, Golders Green and well-heeled Hampstead Garden Suburb. At almost 20%, the seat has the largest Jewish community of any British constituency and is also home to a sizeable number of Muslim (6%) and Hindu (6.8%) residents. The Conservatives, who dominated in the 2008 Greater London Authority elections, need to overturn a notional Labour majority of only 31 votes to return the seat to the blue column. Conservative Mike Freer, the leader of Barnet Borough Council, will fight Labour's Alison Moore.

Hackney North & Stoke Newington

Labour notional majority of 8,002; notional turnout: 49.3%

PARTY	2005 CANDIDATE	NOTIONAL 2005 VOTES	NOTIONAL 2005 % VOTE	PPC FOR NEXT GE
Labour	Diane Abbott MP	15,138	49.0	Diane Abbott MP
Lib Dem	James Blanchard	7,136	23.1	Keith Angus
Conservative	Ertan Hurer	4,512	14.6	Darren Caplan
Others		4,134	13.4	

Hackney South & Shoreditch

Labour notional majority of 9,629; notional turnout: 51.3%

PARTY	2005 CANDIDATE	NOTIONAL 2005 VOTES	NOTIONAL 2005 % VOTE	PPC FOR NEXT GE
Labour	Meg Hillier	16,178	52.7	Meg Hillier MP
Lib Dem	Hugh Bayliss	6,549	21.3	Dave Raval
Conservative	John Moss	4,230	13.8	Simon Nayyar
Others		3,740	12.2	

Hampstead & Kilburn

Labour notional majority of 474; notional turnout: 55.8%

PARTY	2005 CANDIDATE	NOTIONAL 2005 VOTES	NOTIONAL 2005 % VOTE	PPC FOR NEXT GE
Labour	Glenda Jackson MP	15,138	36.3	Glenda Jackson MP
Lib Dem	Ed Fordham	14,664	35.2	Ed Fordham
Conservative	Piers Wauchope	9,559	22.9	Chris Philp
Others		2,314	5.6	

A newly drawn seat, the constituency is formed of three quarters of Oscar-winning former actress Glenda Jackson's current Hampstead & Highgate, two fifths of Liberal Democrat Sarah Teather's Brent East patch and a sliver of Brent South. Hampstead & Kilburn is markedly less middle-class than its predecessor with the opulence of Hampstead Heath lying in stark contrast to the poverty of Kilburn. Such is the strength of the Irish vote in the Kilburn portion of the seat, John Hume's endorsement was actively touted by Labour during the 2003 Brent East by-election. One in ten voters in this new constituency is black, while the Muslim and Jewish population stand at 8% apiece. Labour's Jackson will face a tough battle to retain the constituency with both Liberal Democrat Ed Fordham and Conservative Chris Philp mounting highly credible challenges.

Hendon

Labour notional majority of 3,231; notional turnout: 58.8%

PARTY	2005 CANDIDATE	NOTIONAL 2005 VOTES	NOTIONAL 2005 % VOTE	PPC FOR NEXT GE
Labour	Andrew Dismore MP	18,101	45.2	Andrew Dismore MP
Conservative	Richard Evans	14,870	37.1	Matthew Offord
Lib Dem	Nahid Boethe	5,657	14.1	n/a
Others		1,459	3.6	

Most famous for its large police training college, or the professional poker quartet ('the Hendon Mob'), this is a predominantly middle-class and ethnically mixed constituency located in north-west London. Between 1992 and 2001 the seat recorded a 19.1% swing to Labour, indicating the scale of the party's progress in this traditionally Conservative area. As with nearby Finchley & Golders Green, one in five of the seat's residents are Jewish (17.3%) while almost one in ten are Hindu (8.7%) or Muslim (7.9%). Labour support is strongest in the south of the constituency with the wards of Burnt Oak and Colindale home to the large Grahame Park and Watling housing estates. Conversely, the Conservatives have traditionally been strongest in the constituency's northern wards, with Edgware in particular delivering the party overwhelming support. Conservative Matthew Offord, the deputy leader of Barnet Borough Council, will fight the hard-headed Labour incumbent Andrew Dismore MP.

Holborn & St Pancras

Labour notional majority of 8,348; notional turnout: 53.2%

PARTY	2005 CANDIDATE	NOTIONAL 2005 VOTES	NOTIONAL 2005 % VOTE	PPC FOR NEXT GE
Labour	Frank Dobson MP	19,872	45.1	Frank Dobson MP
Lib Dem	Jo Shaw	11,524	26.2	Jo Shaw
Conservative	George Lee	9,203	20.9	George Lee
Others		3,451	7.8	

Hornchurch & Upminster

Conservative notional majority of 8,058; notional turnout: 63.2%

PARTY	2005 CANDIDATE	NOTIONAL 2005 VOTES	NOTIONAL 2005 % VOTE	PPC FOR NEXT GE
Conservative	Angela Watkinson MP	23,375	47.5	Angela Watkinson MP
Labour	Keith Darvill	15,317	31.1	Kath McGuirk
Lib Dem	Peter Truesdale	4,184	8.5	n/a
Others		6,332	12.9	

Hornsey & Wood Green

Lib Dem notional majority of 2,395; notional turnout: 61.7%

PARTY	2005 CANDIDATE	NOTIONAL 2005 VOTES	NOTIONAL 2005 % VOTE	PPC FOR NEXT GE
Lib Dem	Lynne Featherstone	20,512	43.3	Lynne Featherstone MP
Labour	Barbara Roche MP	18,117	38.3	Karen Jennings
Conservative	Peter Forrest	6,014	12.7	Richard Merrin
Others		2,687	5.7	

Ilford North

Conservative notional majority of 1,735; notional turnout: 61.1%

PARTY	2005 CANDIDATE	NOTIONAL 2005 VOTES	NOTIONAL 2005 % VOTE	PPC FOR NEXT GE
Conservative	Lee Scott	18,349	43.8	Lee Scott MP
Labour	Linda Perham MP	16,614	39.6	Sonia Klein
Lib Dem	Mark Gayler	5,778	13.8	n/a
Others		1,176	2.8	

Ilford South

Labour notional majority of 9,228; notional turnout: 53.6%

PARTY	2005 CANDIDATE	NOTIONAL 2005 VOTES	NOTIONAL 2005 % VOTE	PPC FOR NEXT GE
Labour	Mike Gapes MP	20,856	48.9	Mike Gapes MP
Conservative	Stephen Metcalfe	11,628	27.2	Toby Boutle
Lib Dem	Matthew Lake	8,761	20.5	
Others		1,448	3.4	

Islington North

Labour notional majority of 6,716; notional turnout: 53.9%

PARTY	2005 CANDIDATE	NOTIONAL 2005 VOTES	NOTIONAL 2005 % VOTE	PPC FOR NEXT GE
Labour	Jeremy Corbyn MP	16,118	51.2	Jeremy Corbyn MP
Lib Dem	Laura Willoughby	9,402	29.9	n/a
Conservative	Nicola Talbot	3,740	11.9	Adrian Berrill-Cox
Others		2,234	7.1	

Islington South & Finsbury

Labour notional majority of 484; notional turnout: 53.6%

PARTY	2005 CANDIDATE	NOTIONAL 2005 VOTES	NOTIONAL 2005 % VOTE	PPC FOR NEXT GE
Labour	Emily Thornberry	12,345	39.9	Emily Thornberry MP
Lib Dem	Bridget Fox	11,861	38.3	Bridget Fox
Conservative	Melanie McLean	4,594	14.8	Antonia Cox
Others		2,161	7.0	

Leyton & Wanstead

Labour notional majority of 7,253; notional turnout: 53.8%

PARTY	2005 CANDIDATE	NOTIONAL 2005 VOTES	NOTIONAL 2005 % VOTE	PPC FOR NEXT GE
Labour	Harry Cohen MP	15,748	45.8	n/a
Lib Dem	Meher Khan	8,495	24.7	Farooq Qureshi
Conservative	Julien Foster	7,825	22.8	Edwin Northover
Others		2,287	6.7	

Poplar & Limehouse

Labour notional majority of 3,823; notional turnout: 50.0%

PARTY	2005 CANDIDATE	NOTIONAL 2005 VOTES	NOTIONAL 2005 % VOTE	PPC FOR NEXT GE
Labour	Jim Fitzpatrick MP	12,463	35.3	Jim Fitzpatrick MP
Conservative	Tim Archer	8,640	24.5	Tim Archer
Respect	Oliur Rahman	8,329	23.6	George Galloway MP
Others		5,844	16.5	

Situated in the heart of east London, the redrawn Poplar & Limehouse constituency is set to see a feisty contest between Labour minister Jim Fitzpatrick, George Galloway and local Conservative councillor Tim Archer. More than a third of local residents are Muslims, the majority of them Bengalis, who strongly supported Galloway's anti-war Respect ticket in 2005. The constituency, with an owner occupation rate of less than 50%, is a curious prospect for the Conservatives, who would need to benefit from a dramatic split in the Labour and Respect vote in order to pull off a win. Long-term Conservative prospects are boosted by the increasing numbers of professionals moving into the area in order to take advantage of the proximity of the numerous stylish Thames-side apartments and loft-conversation developments to Canary Wharf.

Romford

PARTY	2005 CANDIDATE	NOTIONAL 2005 VOTES	NOTIONAL 2005 % VOTE	PPC FOR NEXT GE
Conservative notional majority of 12,120; notional turnout: 61.9%				
Conservative	Andrew Rosindell MP	24,442	57.7	Andrew Rosindell MP
Labour	Margaret Mullane	12,322	29.1	Rachel Voller
Lib Dem	Geoff Seeff	3,572	8.4	n/a
Others		2,053	4.8	

Tottenham

PARTY	2005 CANDIDATE	NOTIONAL 2005 VOTES	NOTIONAL 2005 % VOTE	PPC FOR NEXT GE
Labour notional majority of 13,034; notional turnout: 47.8%				
Labour	David Lammy MP	18,343	57.9	David Lammy MP
Lib Dem	Wayne Hoban	5,309	16.8	David Schmitz
Conservative	William MacDougall	4,278	13.5	Sean Sullivan
Others		3,734	11.8	

Walthamstow

PARTY	2005 CANDIDATE	NOTIONAL 2005 VOTES	NOTIONAL 2005 % VOTE	PPC FOR NEXT GE
Labour notional majority of 7,993; notional turnout: 54.6%				
Labour	Neil Gerrard MP	17,323	50.3	Stella Creasy
Lib Dem	Farid Ahmed	9,330	27.1	Farid Ahmed
Conservative	Jane Wright	6,254	18.2	Andy Hemsted
Others		1,537	4.5	

West Ham

PARTY	2005 CANDIDATE	NOTIONAL 2005 VOTES	NOTIONAL 2005 % VOTE	PPC FOR NEXT GE
Labour notional majority of 12,274; notional turnout: 44.8%				
Labour	Lyn Brown MP	19,989	51.7	Lyn Brown MP
Respect	Lindsay German	7,715	20.0	n/a
Conservative	Chris Whitbread	4,659	12.1	Virginia Morris
Others		6,281	16.4	

Westminster North

PARTY	2005 CANDIDATE	NOTIONAL 2005 VOTES	NOTIONAL 2005 % VOTE	PPC FOR NEXT GE
Labour notional majority of 2,120; notional turnout: 50.8%				
Labour	Karen Buck MP	12,823	39.9	Karen Buck MP
Conservative	Jeremy Bradshaw	10,703	33.3	Joanne Cash
Lib Dem	Rabi Martins	6,322	19.7	Mark Blackburn
Others		2,308	7.2	

Held by Conservative minister John Wheeler until its abolition by the Boundary Commission in 1997, Westminster North will be reconstituted at the next general election. While located in close reach of some of London's wealthiest areas, this constituency contains areas of real deprivation that are far removed from Westminster's opulent outward image. Labour support is strongest in the tough Paddington and Ladbroke Grove areas, home to London's oldest black community, while the Conservatives dominate in leafy Regent's Park and St John's Wood. With 45% of local residents having been born outside the United Kingdom there are large black (10.1%), Muslim (14.1%) and Jewish (5.1%) communities locally. Unusually, roughly a third of residents live in owner-occupied, privately rented and social housing apiece. Labour's Karen Buck, who represents most of the seat's current territory, will do battle with Conservative barrister Joanne Cash.

Home Counties North

The very name 'Home Counties' evokes the metaphor of the 'true heart' of England, comfortable – verging on affluent – even in hard times, and redolent of the Second World War propaganda films that attempted to encapsulate what the nation was fighting to preserve. Yet this picture was outdated even in the 1940s. Majoresque images of village greens and smithies were already far outweighed by the advance not only of suburbia but of the kind of industry which boomed in the inter-war years, such as motor car manufacture in Luton and Oxford, chemicals and electrical goods. A better symbol of the northern Home Counties might be that of the modern factories, and, dare one say it, offices, along the A4 around Slough.

The transformation and growth of the five counties we define as 'Home Counties North' – Bedfordshire, Berkshire, Buckinghamshire, Hertfordshire and Oxfordshire – continued after World War Two. Hertfordshire, for example, was the fastest-growing county in the United Kingdom in the 1950s and 1960s. It was the only county to gain as many as four official New Towns under the provisions of Lord Reith's (other) great achievement, the Act of 1946 (Stevenage, the very first in Britain, Hemel Hempstead, Welwyn Garden City and Hatfield). Then in Buckinghamshire came not merely a New Town but a New City, that hyper-modernist hymn of praise to the automobile, sometimes wrongly thought to be named after two great Britons: Milton Keynes.

Therefore, as may be expected, Labour are, and need to be, competitive in this region if they are to win a general election and form a government. In 2005 they held eight seats within the five counties, securing representation in each, though five of Labour's losses in that election were recorded here: at Hemel Hempstead, Milton Keynes North East, Reading East, St Albans and Welwyn Hatfield – almost all with much larger than average swings to the Conservatives. If this trend were to continue and accelerate, as most 2009 opinion polls suggest, it is possible that Labour might lose all of their remaining constituencies in the region.

The most unlikely is Slough, but even the home of Ricky Gervais's comic creation would fall on a swing of 10 per cent, ousting Fiona Mactaggart, a slightly disaffected former minister. This seems unlikely, especially given that the non-white population of the Slough seat had reached 37 per cent by the time of the 2001 census and that this largely minority is largely Muslim – which accounts for a drop of 11 per cent in the Labour vote in 2005 as a result of the Iraq War, which almost entirely went to the anti-war Liberal Democrats and Respect parties, and may not be replicated next time. However, with controversy caused by an influx of newer immigrants, for example from eastern Europe, few of whom will exercise a vote, Labour must treat Slough as a marginal for the first time since 1997. If Slough cannot be counted on, none of their other seats in these counties can either.

Taking the other Conservative targets first, the most vulnerable are in the ever-expanding metropolis of Milton Keynes. According to the notional calculations of Professors Colin Rallings and Michael Thrasher of Plymouth University, which will be used by all the national media for the next election, boundary changes technically mean that the Tories' Mark Lancaster will have to regain his seat. Milton Keynes North East moves round a compass point to become North, gaining the old railway town of Wolverton, traditionally Labour's strongest area in the whole of Buckinghamshire (it was the one county council ward they held at their previous low ebb of 1977), and would thus have had a notional Labour lead of 848 votes in 2005. This should be well within the Conservatives' capabilities, especially given Mark Lancaster's incumbency vote built up over four or five years. Further good news for the Tories: the same switches between the 'MK' seats make the South West division, now South, even more vulnerable, as Phyllis Starkey would lose with a swing of well under 2 per cent. It is hard not to say that Milton Keynes is a harbinger of the way the general election as a whole will go, though it should be pointed out that the newest developments, ever encroaching into the remaining countryside, tend to be of relatively upmarket detached housing, and their inhabitants appear to be voting strongly Conservative in local elections at least. This suggests that if the Tories do not take both Milton Keynes seats, they will be condemned to circle the roundabouts of opposition in Parliament for several more years.

The rest of Buckinghamshire contains some of the safest Tory constituencies in Britain, and that of the new Speaker, John Bercow, but Bedfordshire is a different matter. In order to become the largest party in the Commons, the Tories will need to gain Bedford itself with a swing of a little more than 4 per cent, but the picture here is muddied a little by the campaign to save Bedford Hospital. Although the Independent Barry Monk withdrew in February 2009, having threatened to attempt to do what Dr Richard Taylor did as a candidate in Wyre Forest in (and since) 2001, it remains a live issue which may possibly help the Liberal Democrats to build on local election success in the town of Bedford and a strong third place performance in 2005.

Elsewhere in the county, if the Conservatives can take one or both of the Luton seats they will be on track for a comfortable overall majority. Luton, like Slough, does have a very prominent Asian community centred on the wards around Bury Park, though it is split almost evenly between the North and South seats. Luton also continues to suffer from the economic depression which has hit the motor industry particularly hard, with the severe downscaling of the commitment by General Motors – a major presence in the town since the 1920s. The embattled American giant still have their British headquarters in the town, but car manufacture stopped in 2002 and commercial vehicle production is also threatened. The troubles of Luton seem to be epitomised by the 30-point deduction for their football team due to financial difficulties, leaving their position in the league an almost impossible one. The Tories have been able to win Luton seats in their better years, especially when these have included substantial chunks of rural Bedfordshire (which is no longer the case), and if Labour lose their seats here, their position in the political league will also be in a highly parlous state. Esther Rantzen's decision at the end of July 2009 to come forward as a 'celebrity candidate' in Luton South – despite the retirement of Margaret Moran, following her use of expenses to treat dry rot in a house not in London or Luton but in Southampton – may actually help Labour save that seat, by splitting the opposition.

In Berkshire, Labour are also struggling to keep their remaining seat – will Reading West join East in falling to the Tories? Their chances will almost certainly have been reduced in February 2009 by the announcement that Martin Salter, a highly active and individual MP, would stand down at the age of fifty-four. This good news for the Tory candidate Alok Sharma was accompanied by the statement that Mr Salter did not wish to remain an MP into his sixties and seventies (perhaps in opposition?). Reading is another microcosm of England, once known for its beer, biscuits and bulbs, but now, set in the high-tech M4 corridor, more for IT and corporate headquarters such as Microsoft, Compaq and Oracle. As a British version of the American 'Middletown' beloved of social surveys, it was also the setting for one of the very first 'reality TV' shows, the original version of *The Family*. Once again, whichever party can win both its seats is likely to form the next government.

Hertfordshire is as close as we can get to 'modern Britain'. New Towns traditionally undergo large swings and back the winning party nationally. Having lost the parliamentary seats covering three of the four in the county in 2005, Labour must desperately hope that their continued ability to retain control of the borough council in the one remaining, Stevenage, indicates that Barbara Follett (wife of the thriller writer Ken) can stave off the 4 per cent swing needed by Tory candidate Stephen McPartland. Hertfordshire is not all a twentieth-century creation. Labour lost the county's medieval city, St Albans, in 2005 after an unlikely two-term tenure, and now are involved in an extraordinary three-way struggle in the mainly Victorian industrial town of Watford (see *One to Watch* below) – but are currently third favourites there, according to the bookmakers.

The Liberal Democrats are key players in Watford, and should also take centre stage as we come to our fifth and final county in Home Counties North: Oxfordshire. Although none of these counties have major boundary changes such as gaining an extra seat, something interesting has happened in Oxford. To even out the electorates of the two seats in that city of town and gown, the city centre and most of the university area has now been shifted from Oxford West & Abingdon (like so many constituencies influenced by academia, now a Lib Dem stronghold, for Evan Harris MP) to Oxford East. This should not threaten Dr Harris's established position, but it does render that of the former Cabinet minister Andrew Smith even more shaky in Oxford East. He had a 16,000 majority in 1997, but notionally in 2005 on the new boundaries this is reduced to just 332. The Lib Dem challenger, Steve Goddard, will hope that Labour remain unfashionable among students, and also that recent further cuts at the BMW-owned Cowley car plant also work against the government.

It is appropriate to finish with so mixed a seat as Oxford East, which dispels a number of myths: about the idea that the Liberal Democrats can expect a sharp decline in their number of seats next time; that the Home Counties are not an important region for Labour; and that it is a swathe of gentle, wealthy, untroubled shires. The area is in fact a key part of Middle England, including in an electoral and political sense.

Target seats

SEAT	SWING REQUIRED %	MP	CHALLENGER
Conservative from Labour			
Milton Keynes North	0.9	(Andrew Pakes)	Mark Lancaster MP
Milton Keynes South	1.6	Phyllis Starkey	Iain Stewart
Watford	2.0	Claire Ward	Richard Harrington
Bedford	4.1	Patrick Hall	Richard Fuller
Stevenage	4.1	Barbara Follett	Stephen McPartland
Reading West	5.8	Martin Salter*	Alok Sharma
Luton South	7.4	Margaret Moran*	Nigel Huddleston
Luton North	8.3	Kelvin Hopkins	Jeremy Brier
Slough	10.0	Fiona MacTaggart	Diana Coad
Labour from Conservatives			
Hemel Hempstead	0.2	Mike Penning	Ayfer Orhan
Reading East	0.9	Rob Wilson	Annaliese Dodds
St Albans	1.5	Anne Main	Roma Mills
Lib Dem from Conservatives			
Newbury	3.3	Richard Benyon	David Rendel
Lib Dem from Labour			
Oxford East	0.4	Andrew Smith	Steve Goddard
Watford	1.2	Claire Ward	Sal Brinton

One to watch: Watford

Actual majority 2005: Labour 1,151 (2.3%) – Claire Ward MP
Notional majority 2005: Labour 1,148 (2.3%)
Liberal Democrat candidate: Sal Brinton
Conservative candidate: Richard Harrington

Claire Ward was the youngest woman MP at twenty-four when she was elected as part of the Labour landslide on 1997, but her three-term hold seems likely to come to an end; indeed third place beckons, as she is assailed on two fronts. The closest challengers, and favourites, just over 1,000 votes behind in 2005, are the Liberal Democrats. They have shown their confirmed ability to win across Watford by the easy victories of Dorothy Thornhill in the directly elected mayoral elections of 2002 and 2006, and have a formidable second-time candidate in Sal Brinton next time. However, the Tories were also less than 2,000 behind Ward in 2005, and with their national opinion poll share above 40 per cent must hope they can come from third place to regain a seat held by John Major's confidant Tristan Garel-Jones from 1979 to 1997. The Conservative hopes took a blow of uncertain effect, though, when their original candidate, Ian Oakley, was arrested in 2008 and later pleaded guilty to seventy-five offences of harassment, criminal damage and intimidation against the Lib Dems and their candidate. After a psychologist's report revealing 'a history of mental health problems', Oakley was sentenced to an 18-week suspended jail sentence. The new candidate, Richard Harrington, selected in December 2008, may have more ground to make up than the raw figures imply. However if the Conservatives can use their renewed strength north of Watford, and south of Watford, they may yet signal a return to national power through a victory on that legendary dividing line, in Watford itself.

Aylesbury

Conservative notional majority of 9,314; notional turnout: 62.4%

PARTY	2005 CANDIDATE	NOTIONAL 2005 VOTES	NOTIONAL 2005 % VOTE	PPC FOR NEXT GE
Conservative	David Lidington MP	23,103	48.3	David Lidington MP
Lib Dem	Peter Jones	13,789	28.9	n/a
Labour	Mohammed Khaliel	8,730	18.3	Kathryn White
Others		2,161	4.5	

Banbury

Conservative notional majority of 10,090; notional turnout: 64.4%

PARTY	2005 CANDIDATE	NOTIONAL 2005 VOTES	NOTIONAL 2005 % VOTE	PPC FOR NEXT GE
Conservative	Tony Baldry MP	25,170	46.9	Tony Baldry MP
Labour	Leslie Sibley	15,080	28.1	Leslie Sibley
Lib Dem	Zoe Patrick	9,395	17.5	David Rundle
Others		4,040	7.5	

Beaconsfield

Conservative notional majority of 14,794; notional turnout: 63.2%

PARTY	2005 CANDIDATE	NOTIONAL 2005 VOTES	NOTIONAL 2005 % VOTE	PPC FOR NEXT GE
Conservative	Dominic Grieve MP	24,934	54.1	Dominic Grieve MP
Lib Dem	Peter Chapman	10,140	22.0	n/a
Labour	Alex Sobel	8,963	19.4	Tom Copley
Others		2,063	4.5	

Bedford

Labour notional majority of 3,413; notional turnout: 62.0%

PARTY	2005 CANDIDATE	NOTIONAL 2005 VOTES	NOTIONAL 2005 % VOTE	PPC FOR NEXT GE
Labour	Patrick Hall MP	17,657	41.6	Patrick Hall MP
Conservative	Richard Fuller	14,244	33.5	Richard Fuller
Lib Dem	Michael Headley	9,263	21.8	Henry Vann
Others		1,294	3.1	

Located some 60 miles north of London, Bedford is home to one the country's most ethnically diverse populations outside of a major city, with a sizeable black and Asian community. An educated town, more than 100 languages are spoken locally and the majority of residents are employed in the service sector. The Conservatives are strongest in Kempston, a pleasant commuter town for Bedford and Milton Keynes. Labour showed some resilience here at inaugural elections for the new Bedford unitary authority, winning seven seats to the Conservatives' nine. One of the few areas to directly elect its mayor, the position is currently filled by newspaper publisher Frank Branston – the 'Berlusconi of Bedford'. The sitting Labour MP, Patrick Hall, will once again be challenge by Conservative businessman Richard Fuller.

Mid Bedfordshire

Conservative notional majority of 11,593; notional turnout: 68.7%

PARTY	2005 CANDIDATE	NOTIONAL 2005 VOTES	NOTIONAL 2005 % VOTE	PPC FOR NEXT GE
Conservative	Nadine Dorries	23,408	46.6	Nadine Dorries MP
Lib Dem	Mark Chapman	11,815	23.5	n/a
Labour	Martin Lindsay	11,261	22.4	David Reeves
Others		3,738	7.4	

North East Bedfordshire

Conservative notional majority of 12,128; notional turnout: 68.3%

PARTY	2005 CANDIDATE	NOTIONAL 2005 VOTES	NOTIONAL 2005 % VOTE	PPC FOR NEXT GE
Conservative	Alistair Burt MP	24,592	49.9	Alistair Burt MP
Labour	Keith White	12,464	25.3	Ed Brown
Lib Dem	Stephen Rutherford	10,295	20.9	n/a
Others		1,966	4.0	

South West Bedfordshire

Conservative notional majority of 8,277; notional turnout: 62.8%

PARTY	2005 CANDIDATE	NOTIONAL 2005 VOTES	NOTIONAL 2005 % VOTE	PPC FOR NEXT GE
Conservative	Andrew Selous MP	22,114	48.3	Andrew Selous MP
Labour	Joyce Still	13,837	30.2	Prem Pal Sharma
Lib Dem	Andy Strange	7,723	16.9	n/a
Others		2,140	4.7	

Bracknell

Conservative notional majority of 14,655; notional turnout: 62.6%

PARTY	2005 CANDIDATE	NOTIONAL 2005 VOTES	NOTIONAL 2005 % VOTE	PPC FOR NEXT GE
Conservative	Andrew MacKay MP	22,789	49.9	n/a
Labour	Janet Keene	12,752	27.9	John Piasecki
Lib Dem	Lee Glendon	8,134	17.8	Ray Earwicker
Others		2,029	4.4	

Broxbourne

Conservative notional majority of 11,509; notional turnout: 59.2%

PARTY	2005 CANDIDATE	NOTIONAL 2005 VOTES	NOTIONAL 2005 % VOTE	PPC FOR NEXT GE
Conservative	Charles Walker	21,878	53.8	Charles Walker MP
Labour	Jamie Bolden	10,369	25.5	Michael Watson
Lib Dem	Andrew Porrer	4,973	12.2	
Others		3,408	8.4	

Buckingham

Conservative notional majority of 18,716; notional turnout: 68.2%

PARTY	2005 CANDIDATE	NOTIONAL 2005 VOTES	NOTIONAL 2005 % VOTE	PPC FOR NEXT GE
Conservative	John Bercow MP	28,781	58.2	n/a
Speaker				John Bercow MP
Labour	David Greene	10,065	20.3	n/a
Lib Dem		8,922	18.0	n/a
Others		1,705	3.4	

Chesham & Amersham

Conservative notional majority of 12,974; notional turnout: 66.7%

PARTY	2005 CANDIDATE	NOTIONAL 2005 VOTES	NOTIONAL 2005 % VOTE	PPC FOR NEXT GE
Conservative	Cheryl Gillan MP	25,427	53.5	Cheryl Gillan MP
Lib Dem	John Ford	12,453	26.2	Tim Starkey
Labour	Rupa Huq	6,479	13.6	n/a
Others		3,152	6.6	

Hemel Hempstead

Conservative notional majority of 168; notional turnout: 64.2%

PARTY	2005 CANDIDATE	NOTIONAL 2005 VOTES	NOTIONAL 2005 % VOTE	PPC FOR NEXT GE
Conservative	Michael Penning	18,567	40.1	Michael Penning MP
Labour	Tony McWalter MP	18,399	39.8	Ayfer Orhan
Lib Dem	Richard Grayson	7,823	16.9	Richard Grayson
Others		1,492	3.2	

Henley

Conservative notional majority of 13,366; notional turnout: 67.7%

PARTY	2005 CANDIDATE	NOTIONAL 2005 VOTES	NOTIONAL 2005 % VOTE	PPC FOR NEXT GE
Conservative	Boris Johnson MP	26,208	53.2	John Howell MP
Lib Dem	David Turner	12,842	26.1	n/a
Labour	Kaleem Saeed	7,397	15.0	n/a
Others		2,816	5.7	

Hertford & Stortford

Conservative notional majority of 12,756; notional turnout: 66.5%

PARTY	2005 CANDIDATE	NOTIONAL 2005 VOTES	NOTIONAL 2005 % VOTE	PPC FOR NEXT GE
Conservative	Mark Prisk MP	24,673	50.2	Mark Prisk MP
Labour	Richard Henry	11,917	24.2	Steve Terry
Lib Dem	James Lucas	9,056	18.4	
Others		3,503	7.1	

North East Hertfordshire

Conservative notional majority of 9,510; notional turnout: 66.6%

PARTY	2005 CANDIDATE	NOTIONAL 2005 VOTES	NOTIONAL 2005 % VOTE	PPC FOR NEXT GE
Conservative	Oliver Heald MP	23,149	48.1	Oliver Heald MP
Labour	Andy Harrop	13,639	28.3	Richard Henry
Lib Dem	Iain Coleman	9,782	20.3	Hugh Annand
Others		1,587	3.3	

South West Hertfordshire

Conservative notional majority of 8,640; notional turnout: 68.7%

PARTY	2005 CANDIDATE	NOTIONAL 2005 VOTES	NOTIONAL 2005 % VOTE	PPC FOR NEXT GE
Conservative	David Gauke MP	23,927	47.0	David Gauke MP
Lib Dem	Edward Featherstone	15,287	30.0	n/a
Labour	Kerron Cross	10,568	20.8	Karen McIntosh
Others		1,133	2.2	

Hertsmere

Conservative notional majority of 11,093; notional turnout: 63.0%

PARTY	2005 CANDIDATE	NOTIONAL 2005 VOTES	NOTIONAL 2005 % VOTE	PPC FOR NEXT GE
Conservative	James Clappison MP	22,665	53.2	James Clappison MP
Labour	Kelly Tebb	11,572	27.2	Sam Russell
Lib Dem	Jonathan Davies	7,817	18.4	n/a
Others		518	1.2	

Hitchin & Harpenden

Conservative notional majority of 11,064; notional turnout: 68.6%

PARTY	2005 CANDIDATE	NOTIONAL 2005 VOTES	NOTIONAL 2005 % VOTE	PPC FOR NEXT GE
Conservative	Peter Lilley MP	23,866	49.4	Peter Lilley MP
Lib Dem	Hannah Hedges	12,802	26.5	Nigel Quinton
Labour	Paul Orrett	10,593	21.9	Oli de Botton
Others		1,044	2.2	

Luton North

Labour notional majority of 6,439; notional turnout: 56.8%

PARTY	2005 CANDIDATE	NOTIONAL 2005 VOTES	NOTIONAL 2005 % VOTE	PPC FOR NEXT GE
Labour	Kelvin Hopkins MP	19,095	48.6	Kelvin Hopkins MP
Conservative	Hannah Hall	12,656	32.2	Jeremy Brier
Lib Dem	Linda Jack	6,130	15.6	Rabi Martins
Others		1,411	3.6	

A Tory stronghold throughout the Thatcher and Major years, the Conservatives saw their five-figure majority obliterated at the 1997 election by union official Kelvin Hopkins on a dramatic 17.4% swing. Almost entirely urban in composition, Luton North is not an area in possession of a rich architectural history, with the majority of homes here having been constructed in the post-war years. As with Luton South, there is a significant Asian (15.7%) and black (6.8%) population here. Labour remain strong here, holding 13 seats on Luton Borough Council, as compared to six Liberal Democrats and five Conservatives. Hopkins, a relentless Labour rebel who commutes to London each day on the Thameslink railway service, will hope to defeat Conservative barrister Jeremy Brier to win a fourth term.

Luton South

Labour notional majority of 5,698; notional turnout: 53.7%

PARTY	2005 CANDIDATE	NOTIONAL 2005 VOTES	NOTIONAL 2005 % VOTE	PPC FOR NEXT GE
Labour	Margaret Moran MP	16,577	42.8	n/a
Conservative	Richard Stay	10,879	28.1	Nigel Huddleston
Lib Dem	Qurban Hussain	8,729	22.5	Qurban Hussain
Others		2,563	6.6	

Historically the safer of the two Luton constituencies for Labour, this seat is home to Luton's bustling shopping areas, the former Vauxhall car plant and rapidly expanding airport. With almost one in five residents being Muslim, the seat recorded a dramatic 12.5% fall in Labour's share of the vote at the last election against a backdrop of considerable anti-war sentiment. Nevertheless, Labour's support is robust in Luton's ethnically diverse town centre while the Conservatives are strongest in the suburban Caddington, Hyde and Slip End wards, which fall under the boundaries of South Bedfordshire District Council. Incumbent Labour MP Margaret Moran, one of the highest-profile casualties of the expenses scandal, had announced her retirement before she was barred from standing again by Labour's 'star chamber'. Nigel Huddleston will contest the seat for the Conservatives while Qurban Hussain will fight for the Liberal Democrats, and an Independent challenge can be expected from the TV presenter Esther Rantzen.

Maidenhead

Conservative notional majority of 7,650; notional turnout: 70.3%

PARTY	2005 CANDIDATE	NOTIONAL 2005 VOTES	NOTIONAL 2005 % VOTE	PPC FOR NEXT GE
Conservative	Theresa May MP	25,434	51.8	Theresa May MP
Lib Dem	Kathy Newbound	17,784	36.2	Tony Hill
Labour	Janet Pritchard	4,476	9.1	Pat McDonald
Others		1,396	2.8	

Milton Keynes North

Labour notional majority of 848; notional turnout: 63.3%

PARTY	2005 CANDIDATE	NOTIONAL 2005 VOTES	NOTIONAL 2005 % VOTE	PPC FOR NEXT GE
Labour	Brian White	18,767	37.9	Andrew Pakes
Conservative	Mark Lancaster	17,919	36.2	Mark Lancaster MP
Lib Dem	Jane Carr	10,215	20.6	Jill Hope
Others		2,632	5.3	

Narrowly elected in 2005 for the Milton Keynes North East constituency, sitting Conservative MP Mark Lancaster will have been disappointed by the Boundary Commission's decision to transfer the safely Tory wards of Danesborough and Walton Park to Milton Keynes South, while gaining part of the Labour-inclined ward of Wolverton from the same seat. Slightly more urban in nature than its predecessor, Milton Keynes North remains a closely fought battleground with Labour strongest in the urban southern portions of the seat while the Conservatives dominate in the villages of Linford and Hanslope Park. The Liberal Democrats are strong here on a local government level. Former NUS president Andrew Pakes will hope to retain this notionally Labour constituency for his party while Jill Hope will fight for the Liberal Democrats.

Milton Keynes South

Labour notional majority of 1,497; notional turnout: 61.4%

PARTY	2005 CANDIDATE	NOTIONAL 2005 VOTES	NOTIONAL 2005 % VOTE	PPC FOR NEXT GE
Labour	Phyllis Starkey MP	20,104	40.8	Phyllis Starkey MP
Conservative	Iain Stewart	18,607	37.8	Iain Stewart
Lib Dem	Neil Stuart	7,483	15.2	n/a
Others		3,086	6.3	

Since the division in 1992 of Milton Keynes into two parliamentary constituencies, the southern portion of the town has always been the more favourable seat for Labour. Boundary changes, however, which transfer the urban Labour wards of Campbell Park, Middleton and Wolverton to Milton Keynes North East, significantly improve the Conservative Party's chances here at the expense of the neighbouring seat. This seat remains a classic urban/rural split, with the town centre areas favouring Labour, and the southern villages feeling every bit the Buckinghamshire Tory stronghold. For a south-east constituency, the proportion of residents living in social housing is high (22.5%) yet the managerial and professional class is also large here. Labour incumbent Dr Phyllis Starkey will face Iain Stewart, a former director of the Parliamentary Resources Unit, who will fight this seat for the Conservatives.

Newbury

Conservative notional majority of 3,452; notional turnout: 72.6%

PARTY	2005 CANDIDATE	NOTIONAL 2005 VOTES	NOTIONAL 2005 % VOTE	PPC FOR NEXT GE
Conservative	Richard Benyon	26,343	49.0	Richard Benyon MP
Lib Dem	David Rendel MP	22,891	42.6	David Rendel
Labour	Oscar Van Nooijen	3,191	5.9	Hannah Cooper
Others		1,339	2.5	

Oxford East

PARTY	2005 CANDIDATE	NOTIONAL 2005 VOTES	NOTIONAL 2005 % VOTE	PPC FOR NEXT GE
Labour notional majority of 332; notional turnout: 57.5%				
Labour	Andrew Smith MP	16,294	35.9	Andrew Smith MP
Lib Dem	Steve Goddard	15,962	35.2	Steve Goodard
Conservative	Virginia Morris	7,863	17.3	Ed Argar
Others		5,238	11.5	

Held by former Work and Pensions Secretary Andrew Smith since vanquishing Conservative Steve Norris at the 1987 general election, this seat is now a closely fought battle between Labour and the Liberal Democrats. Oxford East is home to the majority of the University of Oxford's colleges and the Oxford Brookes University campus, as well as the tough council estates, which have elected 'Independent Working Class Association' councillors in recent years. The manufacturing sector is surprisingly large here with the BMW Mini plant located in the Cowley area. With a quarter of the population in full-time education, it is not surprising that the private rented sector is large here. The real battle here is between Smith and Liberal Democrat councillor Steve Goddard. Ed Argar will contest the seat for the Conservatives while high-profile human rights activist Peter Tatchell will be the Green candidate.

Oxford West & Abingdon

PARTY	2005 CANDIDATE	NOTIONAL 2005 VOTES	NOTIONAL 2005 % VOTE	PPC FOR NEXT GE
Lib Dem notional majority of 6,816; notional turnout: 67.0%				
Lib Dem	Evan Harris MP	23,418	46.1	Evan Harris MP
Conservative	Amanda McLean	16,602	32.7	Nicola Blackwood
Labour	Antonia Bance	8,056	15.9	Richard Stevens
Others		2,692	5.3	

A Tory seat since its inception, years of dominance on a local government level helped Liberal Democrat Dr Evan Harris snatch this seat from Conservatives at the 1997 general election. Located to the east of Conservative leader David Cameron's Witney constituency, the seat contains the bulk of Oxford's 'picture postcard' areas, including the university and city walls, and the attractive market town of Abingdon. While demographically this may appear to be a Tory seat, the city's urban-based academic community and large student population largely favour the Liberal Democrats, whereas Conservative support is greatest in the towns of Kidlington and Abingdon. The Conservatives, who are fielding Nicola Blackman at the next general election, outpaced the Liberal Democrats by little more than 500 votes at the 2009 county council poll. The Green Party, who hold council seats here, are likely to save their deposit.

Reading East

PARTY	2005 CANDIDATE	NOTIONAL 2005 VOTES	NOTIONAL 2005 % VOTE	PPC FOR NEXT GE
Conservative notional majority of 739; notional turnout: 58.4%				
Conservative	Rob Wilson	15,386	35.6	Rob Wilson MP
Labour	Tony Page	14,647	33.9	Anneliese Dodds
Lib Dem	Prof John Howson	10,517	24.4	Gareth Epps
Others		2,610	6.0	

Reading West

Labour notional majority of 4,931; notional turnout: 59.9%

PARTY	2005 CANDIDATE	NOTIONAL 2005 VOTES	NOTIONAL 2005 % VOTE	PPC FOR NEXT GE
Labour	Martin Salter MP	19,362	45.0	Naz Sarkar
Conservative	Ewan Cameron	14,431	33.6	Alok Sharma
Lib Dem	Denise Gaines	6,781	15.8	Patrick Murray
Others		2,413	5.6	

A middle-class seat which stretches from the urban wards of Battle, Norcot and Minister out to prosperous Pangbourne and Purley-on-Thames in rural west Berkshire, the Tories must never have expected to lose this constituency. The Conservatives have made steady yet unspectacular local government advances in the Reading Borough portion of the seat in recent years, yet Labour demonstrated unusual resilience in the 2008 local elections. Liberal Democrat strength is confined to Tilehurst and is negligible in general elections. Represented since 1997 by laddish political fixer Martin Salter, who has opted to retire 'to spend more time fishing', Labour has selected Waltham Forest councillor Naz Sarkar while the Conservatives are fielding high-profile local businessman Alok Sharma.

St Albans

Conservative notional majority of 1,334; notional turnout: 68.5%

PARTY	2005 CANDIDATE	NOTIONAL 2005 VOTES	NOTIONAL 2005 % VOTE	PPC FOR NEXT GE
Conservative	Anne Main	16,921	37.3	Anne Main MP
Labour	Kerry Pollard MP	15,587	34.3	Roma Mills
Lib Dem	Michael Green	11,547	25.4	Sandy Walkington
Others		1,355	3.0	

Slough

Labour notional majority of 7,924; notional turnout: 53.8%

PARTY	2005 CANDIDATE	NOTIONAL 2005 VOTES	NOTIONAL 2005 % VOTE	PPC FOR NEXT GE
Labour	Fiona Mactaggart MP	18,434	46.2	Fiona Mactaggart MP
Conservative	Sheila Gunn	10,510	26.3	Diana Coad
Lib Dem	Thomas McCann	6,681	16.7	Chris Tucker
Others		4,282	10.7	

A grey town lying close to Heathrow airport on the Buckinghamshire–Berkshire border, Slough has long been pilloried for its lack of aesthetic charm. Unemployment is the constituency is low, with the town's excellent transport links encouraging many multinational firms to locate here. Almost a quarter of local residents were born outside the United Kingdom with significant Muslim (13.8%), Sikh (9.2%) and Hindu (4.5%) communities. Held since 1997 by former Home Office minister Fiona MacTaggart, Labour support is strongest in Slough town and Cippenham, while the Conservatives perform strongly in the more rural Upton and Langley areas. Diana Coad, a former haute-couture model and local councillor who fell 407 votes short of victory in considerably more marginal Stourbridge in 2005, returns to contest the seat she fought in the 2001 election.

Stevenage

Labour notional majority of 3,288; notional turnout: 62.6%

PARTY	2005 CANDIDATE	NOTIONAL 2005 VOTES	NOTIONAL 2005 % VOTE	PPC FOR NEXT GE
Labour	Barbara Follett MP	17,602	43.1	Barbara Follett MP
Conservative	George Freeman	14,314	35.0	Stephen MacPartland
Lib Dem	Julia Davies	7,500	18.4	Julia Davies
Others		1,424	3.5	

The first place to be officially designated as a New Town following the Second World War, Stevenage handed Labour an almost 12,000-vote majority at the 1997 general election. Home to around 80,000 people, the town of Stevenage is the largest constituent part of this seat. With almost a third of residents living in social housing, the constituency suffers from considerable social problems, with one of the highest teenage pregnancy and family breakdown rates in Europe. The Conservatives continue to underperform here on a local level, with Labour retaining 30 of the 39 seats on the local borough council. While Labour holds a tight grip on Stevenage town, the Conservatives enjoy a similarly dominant position in the rural east Hertfordshire portions of the seat. Labour Culture, Media and Sport Minister Barbara Follett will be opposed by Conservative Stephen MacPartland.

Wantage

Conservative notional majority of 8,039; notional turnout: 68.1%

PARTY	2005 CANDIDATE	NOTIONAL 2005 VOTES	NOTIONAL 2005 % VOTE	PPC FOR NEXT GE
Conservative	Ed Vaizey	22,424	43.1	Ed Vaizey MP
Lib Dem	Andrew Crawford	14,385	27.6	Alan Armitage
Labour	Mark McDonald	12,467	24.0	Steven Mitchell
Others		2,776	5.3	

Watford

Labour notional majority of 1,151; notional turnout: 64.9%

PARTY	2005 CANDIDATE	NOTIONAL 2005 VOTES	NOTIONAL 2005 % VOTE	PPC FOR NEXT GE
Labour	Claire Ward MP	16,572	33.6	Claire Ward MP
Lib Dem	Sal Brinton	15,421	31.2	Sal Brinton
Conservative	Ali Miraj	14,631	29.6	Richard Harrington
Others		2,758	5.6	

Located on the Hertfordshire border just north of London, only 1,941 votes separated Labour's Claire Ward from the third-placed Conservatives at the last general election. Watford is home to many commuters who make the 15-minute train journey to Euston station each day, yet as a result of its excellent transport the town has come into its own in recent years as an important base for the service and distribution sector. While on a parliamentary level Watford is a closely contested three-way marginal, the Liberal Democrats dominate locally, holding the elected mayoralty and a large majority on the borough council. Sal Brinton will again fight the seat for the Liberal Democrats while businessman Richard Harrington will stand for the Conservatives.

Welwyn Hatfield

Conservative notional majority of 5,946; notional turnout: 68.1%

PARTY	2005 CANDIDATE	NOTIONAL 2005 VOTES	NOTIONAL 2005 % VOTE	PPC FOR NEXT GE
Conservative	Grant Shapps	22,172	49.6	Grant Shapps MP
Labour	Melanie Johnson MP	16,226	36.3	Mike Hobday
Lib Dem	Sara Bedford	6,318	14.1	Paul Zukowskyj
Others		0	0.0	

Windsor

Conservative notional majority of 9,605; notional turnout: 64.1%

PARTY	2005 CANDIDATE	NOTIONAL 2005 VOTES	NOTIONAL 2005 % VOTE	PPC FOR NEXT GE
Conservative	Adam Afriyie	21,284	49.5	Adam Afriyie MP
Lib Dem	Antony Wood	11,679	27.1	Julian Tisi
Labour	Mark Muller	7,722	17.9	n/a
Others		2,356	5.5	

Witney

Conservative notional majority of 13,874; notional turnout: 69.0%

PARTY	2005 CANDIDATE	NOTIONAL 2005 VOTES	NOTIONAL 2005 % VOTE	PPC FOR NEXT GE
Conservative	David Cameron MP	25,579	49.4	David Cameron MP
Lib Dem	Liz Leffman	11,705	22.6	n/a
Labour	Tony Gray	11,592	22.4	Joe Goldberg
Others		2,935	5.7	

Wokingham

Conservative notional majority of 7,257; notional turnout: 67.8%

PARTY	2005 CANDIDATE	NOTIONAL 2005 VOTES	NOTIONAL 2005 % VOTE	PPC FOR NEXT GE
Conservative	John Redwood MP	22,619	48.1	John Redwood MP
Lib Dem	Prue Bray	15,362	32.7	Prue Bray
Labour	David Black	7,044	15.0	George Davidson
Others		1,987	4.2	

Wycombe

Conservative notional majority of 7,597; notional turnout: 61.4%

PARTY	2005 CANDIDATE	NOTIONAL 2005 VOTES	NOTIONAL 2005 % VOTE	PPC FOR NEXT GE
Conservative	Paul Goodman MP	20,831	47.4	Paul Goodman MP
Labour	Julia Wassell	13,234	30.1	Andrew Lomas
Lib Dem	James Oates	7,865	17.9	Steve Guy
Others		2,015	4.6	

East Anglia

The flatlands of East Anglia, rather like the South of England, will offer an acid test of Labour's durability as a competitive governing party at the next general election. In their 'wilderness years' between 1979 and 1997 Labour could hold no more than a handful of seats in the counties of Norfolk, Suffolk, Cambridgeshire and Essex. Then in 1997 they made enough gains in this largely unfamiliar terrain to support a national landslide, and these have almost all been held subsequently, which means that the Conservatives will have to re-establish near complete mastery of the region if they are to return to power in 2009 or 2010. We should however be a little wary of applying uniform swing theory here, though. There is a saying that 'Norfolk do different', and in electoral terms East Anglia as a whole has often been the region which has seen counter-cyclical swings.

For example, if we start with Norfolk itself, this is probably the only county which at one time harboured a significant rural working-class Labour vote, because of an unusually active development of agricultural trade unionism. For this reason, in the 1950s Labour held the county seats of Norfolk South West and Norfolk North, and came within 1,000 votes in Norfolk South; however, against the national tide in 1964 they lost South West, and North followed in 1970. With increasing mechanisation meaning fewer agricultural labourers, Labour is no longer competitive in the countryside. On the other hand, Labour have won the last three elections in the depressed seaside resort and port of Great Yarmouth, which the Conservatives must win with a required swing of 3.8 per cent to be on track even to be the largest party in the next House of Commons. The other Tory target in Norfolk was in the county town. In 2005 Norwich North was actually Labour's safest seat in the whole of the Eastern region. However, in the by-election on 23 July 2009, following the sudden resignation of the active MP, Dr Ian Gibson, following his removal as candidate by the central party's post-expenses 'star chamber', the Conservatives achieved double the 8 per cent swing required to elect 27-year-old Chloe Smith, who became the new 'Baby of the House'. Given the scale of her victory, a majority of over 7,000 against very divided opposition, she has an excellent chance of holding Norwich North at the general election.

We should not move on from Norfolk yet. There are two other types of contest that hold the interest. Both involve the Liberal Democrats. This has traditionally been a weak county for them, but in 2001 Norman Lamb gained the seat of North

Norfolk from the Tory David Prior, himself the son of the East Anglia-based former Cabinet minister Jim Prior, by less than 500 votes. However, it is usual for MPs, especially Liberal Democrats, to build up a large personal vote based on active service, and so it was par for the course when Lamb increased his majority over Iain Dale, a new candidate with no incumbency vote of his own, to over 10,000 in 2005. Now, though, more interest lies in a new and extra seat that has been carved out in Norfolk. Broadland is made up largely from Mid Norfolk, and MP Keith Simpson will contest it, but does include 13,000 votes from Lamb's seat, which puts the Lib Dems into second place in the notional result for 2005. In a way the extra seat is actually that named Mid Norfolk, but the Conservatives' George Freeman should be a safe new entrant to the Commons.

Finally, one of the most interesting seats in the whole country should be Norwich South. This urban seat, including the heart of the city, which was the second largest and most important in medieval England, saw the Labour former Home Secretary, now maverick, Charles Clarke's majority cut to just 3,653 by the Liberal Democrats in 2005, based on both the discontent with the Iraq War common to university and intellectual seats, and local government success on the city council. With a new candidate, Simon Wright, the Lib Dems will make Norwich South their top priority in the region, and Clarke must fight his seat very much as a marginal. It is more than two-way, as the Greens regard this as one of their two strongest chances in the whole of Britain. In the June 2009 county council elections they polled more votes than anyone else in the wards within South: 9,558, compared with 6,181 for the Lib Dems, 5,734 for the Conservatives, and 5,185 for fourth-placed Labour. This reflects Green strength on Norwich council too, where they became the second largest party in 2008 and are likely to overtake Labour in 2010. It is true that the Green performance in the Norwich North by-election in July 2009 was disappointing, just under 10 per cent and fifth place, but South is by far their stronger seat, and their candidate, Councillor Adrian Ramsay, should be included in a four-way competition that Clarke may just hold with a low share against divided opposition.

The competition in Suffolk is somewhat simpler, and there are no major boundary changes or extra seats, but it is still of critical importance. The two Labour constituencies are both vulnerable to pro-Tory swings of between 6 and 7 per cent – which puts them in the heart of the key range needed to decide the government of the United Kingdom. Waveney is centred on Lowestoft, the most easterly point in the whole of Britain. For the fascinating situation and convoluted history of Ipswich, see *One to Watch* below.

There are no key marginals in Cambridgeshire, since Peterborough was gained by the Conservative Stewart Jackson from the eccentric Labour MP Helen Clark (formerly Brinton) in 2005, and Cambridge itself was easily won by the Liberal Democrat David Howarth, who should build on his position using a term of incumbency. Essex, however, is a different matter. Undeniably part of eastern England, even if some should argue about 'East Anglia', Essex is one of the largest shire counties, and has been granted an additional, eighteenth, seat in the forthcoming boundary changes.

Although the new seat, Witham, will be safely Conservative – and therefore send an Asian woman, Priti Patel, to Parliament – the knock-on effects reverberate across the county. For example, there will no longer be a single seat of Basildon, which has an iconic history. Just over a third of the old Basildon is dispersed to the new Basildon & Billericay, which already has a notional Tory majority of over 4,500. The Labour MP Angela E. Smith will therefore defend South Basildon & East Thurrock, which might sound as if it should be safe – except that contrary to the regular pattern dictated by the prevailing winds in Britain, the eastern wards of Thurrock are not the best for Labour. As a result, on notional figures the Conservative candidate Stephen Metcalfe only needs a swing of 1.1 per cent to oust Smith and make sure that both Basildons will be lost to Labour. Would this be an omen once again of the defeat of the government as a whole?

In fact the Conservatives would probably need to remove both the other Labour seats in Essex. Harlow is another super-marginal, with the Foreign Office minister Bill Rammell losing to Robert Halfon on a swing of just 0.3 per cent as his actual 2005 majority of 97 is only increased to 230. A much sterner task is posed by the rump of Thurrock, where Jackie Doyle-Price needs to engineer a swing of 6.6 per cent – quite possible in a county of traditionally volatile movements of opinion, especially with the retirement of the voluble Andrew MacKinlay, an independently minded and active Labour MP somewhat like Ian Gibson.

The Conservatives could therefore win seventeen of the eighteen Essex seats – probably not a clean sweep, as the popular Liberal Democrat Bob Russell is standing again in the compact Colchester, where he has a substantial Labour third-place vote of 9,000 to squeeze. On the other hand, the Lib Dems are unlikely to succeed in their own best target, the reunited Chelmsford, where they several times ran Norman St John Stevas close (including by 378 votes in 1983) before he gave way to Simon Burns in 1987.

If Labour do follow up their Norwich North disaster by losing all the rest of seats in East Anglia, the Conservatives will win the general election, and the Liberal Democrats will become the second party in terms of seats in the east of England. However, with the volatility of opinion polls reflecting that of the electorate, and the region's habit of springing surprises, anyone betting on such an outcome, right up to polling day itself, would be advised to pay cautious attention to the history of one of the most historically rich and unpredictable parts of Britain.

Target seats

SEAT	SWING REQUIRED %	MP	CHALLENGER
Conservative from Labour			
Harlow	0.3	Bill Rammell	Robert Halfon
South Basildon & East Thurrock	1.1	Angela E. Smith	Stephen Metcalfe
Great Yarmouth	3.7	Anthony Wright	Brandon Lewis
Ipswich	6.0	Chris Mole	Ben Gummer
Waveney	6.1	Bob Blizzard	Peter Aldous
Thurrock	6.6	Andrew MacKinlay*	Jackie Doyle-Price
Conservative from Lib Dems			
Colchester	6.9	Bob Russell	Will Quince
North Norfolk	8.7	Norman Lamb	Trevor Ivory
Lib Dem from Labour			
Norwich South	3.8	Charles Clarke	Simon Wright
Lib Dem from Conservatives			
Chelmsford	4.7	Simon Burns	Stephen Robinson
Labour from Conservatives			
Norwich North	11.2**	Chloe Smith	

**Since July 2009 by-election*

One to watch: Ipswich

Actual majority 2005: Labour 5,332 (12.7%) – Chris Mole MP
Notional majority 2005: Labour 5,235 (11.8%)
Conservative candidate: Ben Gummer

On the surface, the county town and largest area in Suffolk presents a crucial but conventional challenge to the Conservatives. They need a swing of 6 per cent to take Labour's 101st safest seat, their own 113th target (86th against Labour). If this were achieved, with uniform swing they would be the largest party but a little short of an overall majority. However, odd things happen in Ipswich.

After the Labour (and former Liberal) MP, Sir Dingle Foot (the elder brother of Michael), was defeated in 1970 by just thirteen votes by the Conservative Ernle Money (Ipswich MPs seem to go in for imaginative names), there were a series of swings against the national tide. First, Money held on with an increased majority when Labour won the general election of February 1974. Then after he was replaced by Labour's Ken Weetch in October of that year, there was another odd result as he in turn increased his lead in 1979, Labour's second best result anywhere in Britain. His personal popularity in the town led it to be branded 'Ips-weetch'. This did not save him in 1987, though, when yet again Ipswich swung the other way from 'normal', and elected the Tory Michael Irvine (son of Labour's Sir Arthur Irvine). The seat switched for the fourth time since the war in the landslide of 1997, and although Jamie Cann died just after the 2001 election, Chris Mole retained it for Labour on a day in which the turnout marginally exceeded that for Ipswich Town (the 'Tractor Boys') versus Inter Milan at Portman Road.

Yet another relation will try to gain this vital but eccentric constituency for the Tories: the son of Suffolk Coastal's John Gummer, who has not announced his retirement, will try to make a father–son combination in the same county – thirty-year-old Ben Gummer. He has recently published a book on the Black Death, entitled *The Scourging Angel*; will this be an omen for the future of the Labour party, should the author take Ipswich?

Basildon & Billericay

Conservative notional majority of 4,559; notional turnout: 62.3%

PARTY	2005 CANDIDATE	NOTIONAL 2005 VOTES	NOTIONAL 2005 % VOTE	PPC FOR NEXT GE
Conservative	n/a	18,699	46.0	John Baron MP
Labour	n/a	14,140	34.8	Allan Davies
Lib Dem	n/a	5,376	13.2	n/a
Others		2,428	5.9	

South Basildon & East Thurrock

Labour notional majority of 905; notional turnout: 59.3%

PARTY	2005 CANDIDATE	NOTIONAL 2005 VOTES	NOTIONAL 2005 % VOTE	PPC FOR NEXT GE
Labour	Angela E. Smith MP	17,195	40.7	Angela E. Smith MP
Conservative	Aaron Powell	16,290	38.5	Stephen Metcalfe
Lib Dem	Martin Thompson	4,469	10.6	n/a
Others		4,336	10.3	

With the Boundary Commission's decision to split the town of Basildon in two, the prospect of gaining this newly drawn constituency is the closest the Conservatives are going to get to reliving David Amess's surprise victory on election night 1992. This newly formed constituency is essentially composed of the southern portion of Basildon town, tracts of rural marshland stretching along the banks of the river Thames, and the tough dock town of East Tilbury. Both Labour and the Conservatives can call on substantial reserves of support here, the Conservatives holding wide leads in Orsett and Pitsea and Labour dominating in Tilbury. The BNP is likely to save its deposit here. Communities Minister Angela Smith will fight this seat for Labour and will hope to hold off a challenge from energetic Conservative businessman Stephen Metcalfe.

Braintree

Conservative notional majority of 8,658; notional turnout: 64.2%

PARTY	2005 CANDIDATE	NOTIONAL 2005 VOTES	NOTIONAL 2005 % VOTE	PPC FOR NEXT GE
Conservative	n/a	22,422	49.9	Brooks Newmark MP
Labour	n/a	13,764	30.7	Bill Edwards
Lib Dem	n/a	6,100	13.6	n/a
Others		2,612	5.8	

Brentwood & Ongar

Conservative notional majority of 12,522; notional turnout: 67.9%

PARTY	2005 CANDIDATE	NOTIONAL 2005 VOTES	NOTIONAL 2005 % VOTE	PPC FOR NEXT GE
Conservative	Eric Pickles MP	24,865	54.0	Eric Pickles MP
Lib Dem	Gavin Stollar	12,343	26.8	David Kendall
Labour	John Adams	6,817	14.8	Heidi Benzing
Others		1,991	4.3	

Broadland

Conservative notional majority of 6,573; notional turnout: 64.4%

PARTY	2005 CANDIDATE	NOTIONAL 2005 VOTES	NOTIONAL 2005 % VOTE	PPC FOR NEXT GE
Conservative	Keith Simpson MP	20,442	43.4	Keith Simpson MP
Lib Dem	Vivienne Clifford-Jackson	13,869	29.5	n/a
Labour	Daniel Zeichner	11,128	23.6	Allyson Barron
Others		1,627	3.5	

Bury St Edmunds

Conservative notional majority of 10,080; notional turnout: 66.8%

PARTY	2005 CANDIDATE	NOTIONAL 2005 VOTES	NOTIONAL 2005 % VOTE	PPC FOR NEXT GE
Conservative	David Ruffley MP	24,549	46.4	David Ruffley MP
Labour	David Monaghan	14,469	27.3	Kevin Hind
Lib Dem	David Chappell	10,461	19.8	David Chappell
Others		3,480	6.6	

Cambridge

Lib Dem notional majority of 5,834; notional turnout: 58.9%

PARTY	2005 CANDIDATE	NOTIONAL 2005 VOTES	NOTIONAL 2005 % VOTE	PPC FOR NEXT GE
Lib Dem	David Howarth	21,278	44.8	David Howarth MP
Labour	Anne Campbell MP	15,444	32.5	Daniel Zeichner
Conservative	Ian Lyon	8,200	17.3	Richard Normington
Others		2,612	5.5	

North East Cambridgeshire

Conservative notional majority of 7,726; notional turnout: 59.1%

PARTY	2005 CANDIDATE	NOTIONAL 2005 VOTES	NOTIONAL 2005 % VOTE	PPC FOR NEXT GE
Conservative	Malcolm Moss MP	22,249	46.9	Steve Barclay
Labour	Ffinlo Costain	14,523	30.6	Peter Roberts
Lib Dem	Alan Dean	8,096	17.1	n/a
Others		2,538	5.4	

North West Cambridgeshire

Conservative notional majority of 10,925; notional turnout: 63.3%

PARTY	2005 CANDIDATE	NOTIONAL 2005 VOTES	NOTIONAL 2005 % VOTE	PPC FOR NEXT GE
Conservative	Shailesh Vara	24,491	46.2	Shailesh Vara MP
Labour	Ayfer Orhan	13,566	25.6	Chris Gudgin
Lib Dem	John Souter	12,128	22.9	n/a
Others		2,805	5.3	

South Cambridgeshire

Conservative notional majority of 9,634; notional turnout: 68.1%

PARTY	2005 CANDIDATE	NOTIONAL 2005 VOTES	NOTIONAL 2005 % VOTE	PPC FOR NEXT GE
Conservative	Andrew Lansley MP	24,621	46.5	Andrew Lansley MP
Lib Dem	Andrew Dickson	14,987	28.3	Sebastian Kindersley
Labour	Sandra Wilson	10,429	19.7	Tariq Sadiq
Others		2,909	5.5	

South East Cambridgeshire

Conservative notional majority of 8,110; notional turnout: 64.2%

PARTY	2005 CANDIDATE	NOTIONAL 2005 VOTES	NOTIONAL 2005 % VOTE	PPC FOR NEXT GE
Conservative	James Paice MP	24,422	47.1	James Paice MP
Lib Dem	Jonathan Chatfield	16,312	31.5	Jonathan Chatfield
Labour	Fiona Ross	11,065	21.4	John Cowan
Others		0	0.0	

Castle Point

Conservative notional majority of 8,201; notional turnout: 66.6%

PARTY	2005 CANDIDATE	NOTIONAL 2005 VOTES	NOTIONAL 2005 % VOTE	PPC FOR NEXT GE
Conservative	Bob Spink MP	22,118	48.3	Rebecca Harris
Independent				Bob Spink MP
Labour	Luke Akehurst	13,917	30.4	Julian Ware-Lane
Lib Dem	James Sandbach	4,719	10.3	n/a
Others		5,048	11.0	

Chelmsford

Conservative notional majority of 4,358; notional turnout: 61.1%

PARTY	2005 CANDIDATE	NOTIONAL 2005 VOTES	NOTIONAL 2005 % VOTE	PPC FOR NEXT GE
Conservative	Simon Burns MP	18,686	39.5	Simon Burns MP
Lib Dem	Stephen Robinson	14,328	30.3	Stephen Robinson
Labour	Russell Kennedy	12,749	26.9	Peter Dixon
Others		1,590	3.4	

Clacton

Conservative notional majority of 3,629; notional turnout: 62.5%

PARTY	2005 CANDIDATE	NOTIONAL 2005 VOTES	NOTIONAL 2005 % VOTE	PPC FOR NEXT GE
Conservative	Douglas Carswell	18,971	44.5	Douglas Carswell MP
Labour	Ivan Henderson MP	15,342	35.9	Ivan Henderson
Lib Dem	Keith Tully	5,776	13.5	n/a
Others		2,588	6.1	

Colchester

Lib Dem notional majority of 6,388; notional turnout: 56.5%

PARTY	2005 CANDIDATE	NOTIONAL 2005 VOTES	NOTIONAL 2005 % VOTE	PPC FOR NEXT GE
Lib Dem	Bob Russell MP	19,517	47.7	Bob Russell MP
Conservative	Kevin Bentley	13,129	32.1	William Quince
Labour	Laura Bruni	8,291	20.3	Jordan Newell
Others		0	0.0	

Epping Forest

Conservative notional majority of 13,473; notional turnout: 61.6%

PARTY	2005 CANDIDATE	NOTIONAL 2005 VOTES	NOTIONAL 2005 % VOTE	PPC FOR NEXT GE
Conservative	Eleanor Laing MP	22,679	52.7	Eleanor Laing MP
Labour	Bambos Charalambous	9,206	21.4	Bill Turner
Lib Dem	Michael Heavens	7,787	18.1	Ann Haigh
Others		3,329	7.7	

Great Yarmouth

Labour notional majority of 3,055; notional turnout: 60.0%

PARTY	2005 CANDIDATE	NOTIONAL 2005 VOTES	NOTIONAL 2005 % VOTE	PPC FOR NEXT GE
Labour	Tony Wright MP	18,850	45.6	Tony Wright MP
Conservative	Mark Fox	15,795	38.2	Brandon Lewis
Lib Dem	Stephen Newton	4,585	11.1	n/a
Others		2,148	5.2	

Located 20 miles east of Norwich on the Norfolk coast, Great Yarmouth has a long history as a tourist destination and fishing port. Yarmouth's tourist sector, much like the town's once-thriving fishing industry, has now seen better days yet still provides a considerable number of jobs locally. The decline of the town's traditional industries and the highly seasonal nature of many jobs has resulted in one of the country's worst unemployment rates outside northern England. Social problems are particularly acute in Yarmouth town, particularly in the Nelson, Central and Northgate areas, which rank amongst the poorest wards in England. Labour performs strongest in Yarmouth itself while the Conservatives lead by wide margins in the rural Norfolk countryside west of the town. Brentford Borough council leader Brandon Lewis will fight the seat for the Conservatives.

Harlow

Labour notional majority of 230; notional turnout: 62.3%

PARTY	2005 CANDIDATE	NOTIONAL 2005 VOTES	NOTIONAL 2005 % VOTE	PPC FOR NEXT GE
Labour	Bill Rammell MP	16,434	41.4	Bill Rammell MP
Conservative	Robert Halfon	16,204	40.8	Robert Halfon
Lib Dem	Lorna Spenceley	5,148	13.0	Richard Bull
Others		1,935	4.9	

An Essex marginal captured by Jerry Hayes at the height of the 1983 Tory landslide and lost to Labour in 1997, the Conservatives failed to win the seat by 97 votes at the last election. A New Town with high-speed rail links to London which grew rapidly in the post-war years, Harlow would not win any prices for its aesthetic beauty. Despite a third of local residents living in local authority housing, Conservative support in the town and its surrounding villages is strong with the party dominating the borough council and holding all of the constituency's county council seats. Conservative candidate Robert Halfon will hope to make it third time lucky by capturing the seat from Armed Forces Minister Bill Rammell.

Harwich & North Essex

Conservative notional majority of 5,583; notional turnout: 66.9%

PARTY	2005 CANDIDATE	NOTIONAL 2005 VOTES	NOTIONAL 2005 % VOTE	PPC FOR NEXT GE
Conservative	Bernard Jenkin MP	20,285	42.6	Bernard Jenkin MP
Labour	Elizabeth Hughes	14,702	30.9	Darren Barrenger
Lib Dem	James Raven	9,162	19.2	n/a
Others		3,453	7.3	

Huntingdon

Conservative notional majority of 11,652; notional turnout: 62.6%

PARTY	2005 CANDIDATE	NOTIONAL 2005 VOTES	NOTIONAL 2005 % VOTE	PPC FOR NEXT GE
Conservative	Jonathan Djanogly MP	24,541	50.8	Jonathan Djanogly MP
Lib Dem	Julian Huppert	12,889	26.7	n/a
Labour	Stephen Sartain	8,898	18.4	Anthea Cox
Others		2,021	4.2	

Ipswich

PARTY	2005 CANDIDATE	NOTIONAL 2005 VOTES	NOTIONAL 2005 % VOTE	PPC FOR NEXT GE
Labour notional majority of 5,235; notional turnout: 60.0%				
Labour	Chris Mole MP	19,020	42.9	Chris Mole MP
Conservative	Paul West	13,785	31.1	Ben Gummer
Lib Dem	Richard Atkins	9,368	21.1	n/a
Others		2,147	4.8	

With more than 120,000 residents, Ipswich is easily the largest town in Suffolk. Traditionally a Labour seat but for a short spells in 1970–74 and 1987–92, Ipswich is home to a working port and has a strong industrial sector. Labour's support is concentrated on around the tough Gainsborough and Priory Heath areas in the south of the city, both of which contain the bulk of the constituency's substantial social housing stock. While the majority of the town's upscale residential areas are found in the neighbouring Central Suffolk & North Ipswich constituency, the Bixley ward provides the Conservatives with near-slavish loyalty. Despite Labour's widespread decimation in the 2009 Suffolk County Council elections, the party clung on to two urban seats in the centre of this seat while the Conservatives swept the board elsewhere. Incumbent Labour MP and government whip Chris Mole will face opposition from Conservative Ben Gummer, son of former Tory Cabinet minister John Gummer.

Maldon

PARTY	2005 CANDIDATE	NOTIONAL 2005 VOTES	NOTIONAL 2005 % VOTE	PPC FOR NEXT GE
Conservative notional majority of 13,631; notional turnout: 62.8%				
Conservative	John Whittingdale MP	23,889	56.3	John Whittingdale MP
Labour	Sue Tibballs	10,258	24.2	Swatantra Nandanwar
Lib Dem	Matthew Lambert	6,360	15.0	n/a
Others		1,917	4.5	

Mid Norfolk

PARTY	2005 CANDIDATE	NOTIONAL 2005 VOTES	NOTIONAL 2005 % VOTE	PPC FOR NEXT GE
Conservative notional majority of 7,793; notional turnout: 65.5%				
Conservative	n/a	22,265	46.5	George Freeman
Labour	n/a	14,472	30.3	Elizabeth Hughes
Lib Dem	n/a	9,186	19.2	n/a
Others		1,914	4.0	

North Norfolk

PARTY	2005 CANDIDATE	NOTIONAL 2005 VOTES	NOTIONAL 2005 % VOTE	PPC FOR NEXT GE
Lib Dem notional majority of 8,575; notional turnout: 72.7%				
Lib Dem	Norman Lamb MP	26,410	53.2	Norman Lamb MP
Conservative	Iain Dale	17,835	35.9	Trevor Ivory
Labour	Phil Harris	4,439	8.9	Phil Harris
Others		933	1.9	

Third-time Liberal Democrat candidate Norman Lamb proved in 2001 that persistence works, seizing North Norfolk from the Conservative by 483 votes before increasing his majority to 10,606 in 2005. An incredibly remote constituency by English standards, North Norfolk stretches more than 50 miles along the coast, extending only narrowly inland to include much of the Broads National Park. There are no large towns in this constituency, the most populous being sleepy Cromer with fewer than 8,000 residents. With ornithology and fishing popular local pursuits, the tourist sector is an important employer. A Liberal Democrat stronghold on a local government level, North Norfolk has one of the highest concentrations of second homes in the country and a remarkably high proportion of elderly residents.

North West Norfolk

Conservative notional majority of 8,417; notional turnout: 61.6%

PARTY	2005 CANDIDATE	NOTIONAL 2005 VOTES	NOTIONAL 2005 % VOTE	PPC FOR NEXT GE
Conservative	Henry Bellingham MP	22,920	49.9	Henry Bellingham MP
Labour	Damien Welfare	14,503	31.6	Manish Sood
Lib Dem	Simon Higginson	6,780	14.8	n/a
Others		1,694	3.7	

South Norfolk

Conservative notional majority of 6,719; notional turnout: 69.0%

PARTY	2005 CANDIDATE	NOTIONAL 2005 VOTES	NOTIONAL 2005 % VOTE	PPC FOR NEXT GE
Conservative	Richard Bacon MP	22,172	44.2	Richard Bacon MP
Lib Dem	Ian Mack	15,453	30.8	n/a
Labour	John Morgan	11,153	22.2	Michael Castle
Others		1,407	2.8	

South West Norfolk

Conservative notional majority of 6,817; notional turnout: 62.0%

PARTY	2005 CANDIDATE	NOTIONAL 2005 VOTES	NOTIONAL 2005 % VOTE	PPC FOR NEXT GE
Conservative	Christopher Fraser MP	20,435	45.0	n/a
Labour	Charmaine Morgan	13,618	30.0	Peter Smith
Lib Dem	April Pond	8,719	19.2	n/a
Others		2,672	5.9	

Norwich North

Labour notional majority of 6,769; notional turnout: 61.8%

PARTY	2005 CANDIDATE	NOTIONAL 2005 VOTES	NOTIONAL 2005 % VOTE	PPC FOR NEXT GE
Labour	Ian Gibson MP	19,212	47.1	n/a
Conservative	James Tumbridge	12,443	30.5	Chloe Smith MP
Lib Dem	Robin Whitmore	6,551	16.1	n/a
Others		2,578	6.3	

Despite sharing the same name as the constituency seized by Conservative Chloe Smith in a July 2009 by-election following the resignation of Labour's Dr Ian Gibson, the newly drawn Norwich North constituency is rather a different beast than its existing namesake. Frustratingly for Smith, boundary changes transfer the safely Conservative wards of Drayton and Taversham to the newly drawn Broadland constituency yet retain the urban Norwich Crome, Mile Cross and Sewell wards, in which her party battles with the Liberal Democrats for second place behind Labour. Conservative support is strongest in the pleasant suburbs of Hellesdon and Sprowston, both located in the Broadland District Council area. Unlike neighbouring Norwich South, where almost a quarter of residents are full-time students, the student community here is tiny. An interesting mix of wealthy suburbs, council estates and Norfolk farmland, no party is safe here.

Norwich South

PARTY	2005 CANDIDATE	NOTIONAL 2005 VOTES	NOTIONAL 2005 % VOTE	PPC FOR NEXT GE
Labour notional majority of 3,023; notional turnout: 58.9%				
Labour	Charles Clarke MP	15,275	37.4	Charles Clarke MP
Lib Dem	Andrew Aalders-Dunthorne	12,252	30.0	Simon Wright
Conservative	Antony Little	8,917	21.8	Antony Little
Others		4,398	10.8	

Held since 1997 by tough-talking Home Secretary Charles Clarke, Norwich South is traditionally the more Labour-inclined of the town's two constituencies, having been in Labour hands for all but one term since 1974. This seat is predominantly urban, taking in the majority of the city of Norwich and the suburb of New Costessey. At 50.6%, levels of owner occupation are extremely low for an East of England constituency. Fuelled by anger at the introduction of student tuition fees and the war in Iraq, the Liberal Democrats have made considerable advances in this university-dominated constituency in recent years. The seat is now a three-way marginal with 6,000 votes separating Clarke from the third-placed Conservatives. Clarke will be opposed by Liberal Democrat Simon Wright and Antony Little, the Conservative group leader on Norwich City Council. The Green Party, who have gained several council seats in the constituency in recent years, are likely to save their deposit.

Peterborough

PARTY	2005 CANDIDATE	NOTIONAL 2005 VOTES	NOTIONAL 2005 % VOTE	PPC FOR NEXT GE
Conservative notional majority of 4,005; notional turnout: 59.0%				
Conservative	Stewart Jackson	19,414	43.3	Stewart Jackson MP
Labour	Helen Clark MP	15,409	34.4	Ed Murphy
Lib Dem	Nick Sandford	7,487	16.7	Nick Sandford
Others		2,534	5.7	

Rayleigh & Wickford

PARTY	2005 CANDIDATE	NOTIONAL 2005 VOTES	NOTIONAL 2005 % VOTE	PPC FOR NEXT GE
Conservative notional majority of 12,983; notional turnout: 63.9%				
Conservative	Mark Francois MP	25,556	53.9	Mark Francois MP
Labour	Julian Ware-Lane	12,573	26.5	Mike Le-Surf
Lib Dem	Sid Cumberland	7,336	15.5	n/a
Others		1,972	4.2	

Rochford & Southend East

PARTY	2005 CANDIDATE	NOTIONAL 2005 VOTES	NOTIONAL 2005 % VOTE	PPC FOR NEXT GE
Conservative notional majority of 5,307; notional turnout: 55.4%				
Conservative	James Duddidge	17,449	45.4	James Duddidge MP
Labour	Fred Grindrod	12,142	31.6	Kevin Bonavia
Lib Dem	Graham Longley	5,668	14.7	n/a
Others		3,191	8.3	

Saffron Walden

PARTY	2005 CANDIDATE	NOTIONAL 2005 VOTES	NOTIONAL 2005 % VOTE	PPC FOR NEXT GE
Conservative notional majority of 10,483; notional turnout: 68.8%				
Conservative	Alan Haselhurst MP	25,086	50.8	Alan Haselhurst MP
Lib Dem	Elfreda Tealby-Watson	14,603	29.6	Peter Wilcock
Labour	Swatantra Nandanwar	6,995	14.2	n/a
Others		2,655	5.4	

Southend West

Conservative notional majority of 9,008; notional turnout: 61.1%

PARTY	2005 CANDIDATE	NOTIONAL 2005 VOTES	NOTIONAL 2005 % VOTE	PPC FOR NEXT GE
Conservative	David Amess MP	18,726	46.2	David Amess MP
Lib Dem	Peter Wexham	9,718	24.0	Peter Welch
Labour	Jan Etienne	9,190	22.7	Thomas Flynn
Others		2,935	7.2	

Central Suffolk & North Ipswich

Conservative notional majority of 7,786; notional turnout: 67.0%

PARTY	2005 CANDIDATE	NOTIONAL 2005 VOTES	NOTIONAL 2005 % VOTE	PPC FOR NEXT GE
Conservative	Michael Lord MP	21,570	44.5	Michael Lord MP
Labour	Neil MacDonald	13,784	28.5	Bhavna Joshi
Lib Dem	Andrew Houseley	9,808	20.2	Andrew Aalders-Dunthorne
Others		3,274	6.8	

Suffolk Coastal

Conservative notional majority of 9,674; notional turnout: 67.2%

PARTY	2005 CANDIDATE	NOTIONAL 2005 VOTES	NOTIONAL 2005 % VOTE	PPC FOR NEXT GE
Conservative	John Gummer MP	23,391	44.6	John Gummer MP
Labour	David Rowe	13,717	26.1	David Rowe
Lib Dem	David Young	11,610	22.1	n/a
Others		3,767	7.2	

South Suffolk

Conservative notional majority of 6,664; notional turnout: 68.8%

PARTY	2005 CANDIDATE	NOTIONAL 2005 VOTES	NOTIONAL 2005 % VOTE	PPC FOR NEXT GE
Conservative	Tim Yeo MP	20,551	42.1	Tim Yeo MP
Lib Dem	Kathy Pollard	13,887	28.4	Nigel Bennett
Labour	Kevin Craig	11,954	24.5	Kevin Craig
Others		2,461	5.0	

West Suffolk

Conservative notional majority of 8,735; notional turnout: 60.7%

PARTY	2005 CANDIDATE	NOTIONAL 2005 VOTES	NOTIONAL 2005 % VOTE	PPC FOR NEXT GE
Conservative	Richard Spring MP	21,439	48.9	Richard Spring MP
Labour	Michael Jeffreys	12,704	29.0	Abul Monsur Ohid Ahmed
Lib Dem	Adrian Graves	7,539	17.2	n/a
Others		2,161	4.9	

Thurrock

PARTY	2005 CANDIDATE	NOTIONAL 2005 VOTES	NOTIONAL 2005 % VOTE	PPC FOR NEXT GE
Labour notional majority of 5,358; notional turnout: 54.4%				
Labour	Andrew MacKinlay MP	19,017	46.2	n/a
Conservative	Garry Hague	13,659	33.2	Jackie Doyle-Price
Lib Dem	Earnshaw Palmer	4,555	11.1	n/a
Others		3,935	9.6	

A bastion of the white working class, the Thames Gateway town of Thurrock has abandoned its Labour roots only once in the past 40 years, electing hard-line Conservative Tim Janman for a single term in 1987. The majority of the pebbledashed towns of Thurrock and nearby Grays are loyal to Labour with the Conservatives strongest in Ockendon, Aveley and Uplands. At the 2009 European elections, the Conservatives, UKIP, Labour and the BNP were within six points of one another. Hoping to capitalise upon his party's strong local support, BNP chairman Nick Griffin MEP has declared he will contest this seat. Jackie Doyle-Price will fight the seat for the Conservatives while sitting Labour MP Andrew MacKinlay has announced his retirement.

Waveney

PARTY	2005 CANDIDATE	NOTIONAL 2005 VOTES	NOTIONAL 2005 % VOTE	PPC FOR NEXT GE
Labour notional majority of 5,950; notional turnout: 63.6%				
Labour	Bob Blizzard MP	22,492	45.4	Bob Blizzard MP
Conservative	Peter Aldous	16,542	33.4	Peter Aldous
Lib Dem	Nick Bromley	7,495	15.1	n/a
Others		3,060	6.2	

Best known as home to the seaside town of Lowestoft, the Waveney constituency has been held by Labour's Bob Blizzard since the 1997 general election. Located in north Suffolk on the edge of the Broads National Park, Lowestoft has seen better days. Its once-bustling tourist trade has all but disappeared and the area has been plagued by job losses since Shell's decision to cease its local oil and gas operations in 2003. Predictably, Lowestoft provides the base of Labour support locally, delivering the party landslide margins in the town's Harbour and Normanston wards while the Conservatives are strongest in the villages of Carlton and Worlingham. In his bid for a fourth term Blizzard will face former Waverley councillor Peter Aldous, who is contesting the seat for the Conservatives.

Witham

PARTY	2005 CANDIDATE	NOTIONAL 2005 VOTES	NOTIONAL 2005 % VOTE	PPC FOR NEXT GE
Conservative notional majority of 7,241; notional turnout: 63.5%				
Conservative	n/a	20,822	49.7	Priti Patel
Labour	n/a	13,581	32.4	n/a
Lib Dem	n/a	6,345	15.2	n/a
Others		1,131	2.7	

East Midlands

Here we define the East Midlands as the three counties of Northamptonshire, Leicestershire and Lincolnshire (except for the northernmost part, analysed under Yorkshire and Humberside) – or four, if one counts Rutland, which forms part of Alan Duncan's very safe seat, together with Melton. For many purposes, the region is extended to include Derbyshire and Nottinghamshire as well, but we treat these, together with Cheshire, under 'North Midlands'. One reason for this split is that there will be so much of electoral interest in the next general election in this highly marginal part of the country. Each county does in fact deserve detailed consideration.

There is always added need for coverage when new seats are created by the Boundary Commission. This is the case in Northamptonshire, which in any case has a remarkably high number of marginal seats – in fact the highest proportion of any county. In 2005, six out of its seven constituencies could fairly be placed in the category of those critical to the choice of government. It is true that the eighth and additional seat to be fought for the first time in 2010 will itself be safe for the Conservatives. It is to be called South Northamptonshire (rather confusingly, as there is already a Northampton South borough division). As 61 per cent of the newcomer is carved out of the one safe Tory seat in the county (Daventry), and the other 39 per cent is derived from the burgeoning private estates, such as East and West Hunsbury, currently in Northampton South, it will provide a secure berth for Andrea Leadsom, a member of the Conservative candidates 'A-list'.

However, as is often the case with the creation of brand new constituencies, the main interest lies in the knock-on effects elsewhere in the county. In this case, the transfer of over 32 per cent of its electorate (27,000 voters) has a profound effect on the urban seat of Northampton South. Notional calculations of a hypothetical result here for 2005 suggest that Labour would actually have won, by nearly 1,500 votes. Rather bravely, the man who actually took the former South seat then, Brian Binley (at sixty-three the oldest entrant to the Commons that year) decided to seek this nomination rather than that for the much safer South Northamptonshire. The only parallel of this opposite phenomenon to the 'chicken run' would appear to be the Sarah Teather's choice to fight Brent Central for the Liberal Democrats. It has to be said, though, that it looks as if things will turn out well for Binley, as all recent national polls suggest the Conservatives will gain Northampton South for the second consecutive election.

Nor is this likely to be their only success in the county. In 2005, although they did not make much headway nationally, the Tories did take two of Northamptonshire's many marginals: Kettering and Wellingborough. Their position in both has been made weaker by the boundary review. In the case of Kettering, the first-term MP Philip Hollobone's majority has been reduced from 3,301 to a notional 176, as 14,000 voters in seven rural wards are transferred to Daventry, which reduces it to half its previous acreage as a much more compact urban seat. In Wellingborough, Peter Bone won by scarcely more than the notional 600 anyway. However with the national Tory strength and the first-term incumbency effect of two active MPs, neither implicated in the expenses scandal, both should win easily next time. For example, we can tell that the new Kettering seat, which is coterminous with the local council, gave 35 per cent of its votes to the Conservatives in the Euro elections in June 2009, while Labour were only in third place (behind UKIP) with 15 per cent. In the council elections in 2007 the Tories were also nearly 20 per cent ahead of Labour, and returned twenty-eight councillors to Labour's six; all this in a seat that the notionals suggest was super-marginal in 2005.

All this suggests that Labour are likely to lose all their seats in Northamptonshire at the next general election. The Conservative candidate Louise Bagshawe, the 'chick-lit' novelist, only needs a 2 per cent swing to take Corby, based on the troubled town whose council was ruled in July 2009 to be culpable with regard to child deformity in its handling of demolition and disposal of the former steelworks, in a case redolent of Thalidomide. In the same year, the MP Phil Hope returned £41,709 to the taxpayer, although he said he had not broken the rules laid down by Parliament. Northampton North is still the safer of the two Labour seats in the county town, but Sally Keeble will still lose it to Michael Ellis on a swing of less than 5 per cent.

No excuses need to be made for extensive coverage of Northamptonshire, the most marginal county in Britain. However, there is also much of interest in the rest of the East Midlands, although there have been no extensive boundary changes in the other two counties discussed here. The Conservatives must take two seats in Leicestershire if they are to form a government, whether with an overall majority or as clearly the largest party. A swing of just 2 per cent will see Labour's Andy Reed dislodged in Loughborough, once known best for its engineering industry (including bell-founding) but where the largest employer is now the increasingly respected high-tech university. A more challenging swing of 5 per cent is needed by Andrew Bridgen in North West Leicestershire (centred on the former mining communities around the aptly named Coalville), but here the popular MP David Taylor has announced his retirement after three terms.

The Liberal Democrats have two targets in Leicestershire, one from each of the major parties. The East Midlands is not one of their stronger regions in municipal or parliamentary terms. However they did make a concerted effort to target Edward Garnier's Harborough (south-east Leicestershire, and the largely affluent Oadby-Wigston southern suburbs of Leicester) in 2005, with activists being drawn from as far afield as Nottingham. They were disappointed to achieve a swing of less than 2 per cent and although it remains one of their top twenty Tory-held targets in Britain, their opponents are now nearly 10 per cent stronger in the national polls than they were at the time of the last election. The Lib Dems did strengthen their control of Oadby & Wigston borough in the most recent elections there in 2007, but at the same time the Tories seized an overall majority of the more rural Harborough District Council. The Liberal Democrats are also unlikely to retake Leicester South, where their task is harder than the 4.4 per cent target swing implies, as the 2005 result itself represented a gain for Labour's former city council leader Sir Peter Soulsby from Parmjit Singh Gill, who had gained South in a July 2004 by-election. It should also be noted that Labour's vote appears to be holding up better in Leicester than anywhere else in Britain. In the June 2009 European elections, when they reached an unprecedented low of less than 16 per cent nationally, Labour still polled 37 per cent in the city s a whole, a figure exceeded only in Newham and Knowsley. It is probably no coincidence that around 40 per cent of Leicester's population is currently made up of ethnic minority groups, and Leicester is expected to become 'majority-minority' within a couple of decades. The seats held by Keith Vaz (East) and to be vacated by Patricia Hewitt (West) are also likely to remain safe.

Turning finally to Lincolnshire, the Conservatives won six of the seven seats easily in 2005 – though UKIP achieved their best result anywhere, and pushed the Lib Dems into fourth place, in Boston & Skegness. This is largely due to the influx of eastern European migrant workers in agriculture and packing businesses; the polyglot nature of Boston reflects a curious kind of reversal considering the town's history as the origin of some of the founders of the American colonies. One other oddity is that technically the rural, affluent Grantham & Stamford has been represented by a Labour MP since 26 June 2007, when Quentin Davies defected. However, there seems to be no suggestion that he will contest the seat again, and it appears very safe for the new Conservative candidate Nick Boles. The other seat in Lincolnshire which might change hands is the nationally archetypal cathedral city and county town (see *One to Watch* below).

There seems a good chance that these three East Midland counties will return a full slate of Conservative MPs at the next election, with the exception of the three Labour seats in Leicester. This is very bad news indeed for the government, which has relied for its victories since 1997 on extending its appeal throughout Britain, beyond its heartlands, to include classic marginals in the 'shires', of which those discussed here are exceptionally relevant.

Target seats

SEAT	SWING REQUIRED %	MP	CHALLENGER
Conservative from Labour			
Corby	1.6	Phil Hope	Louise Bagshawe
Northampton South	1.9	(Clyde Loakes)	Brian Binley MP
Loughborough	2.0	Andy Reed	Nicky Morgan
Northampton North	4.6	Sally Keeble	Michael Ellis
Lincoln	4.8	Gillian Merron	Karl McCartney
North West Leicestershire	4.8	David Taylor*	Andrew Bridgen
Lib Dem from Labour			
Leicester South	4.4	Sir Peter Soulsby	Jeremy Evans
Labour from Conservatives			
Kettering	0.2	Philip Hollobone	Phil Sawford
Wellingborough	0.7	Peter Bone	Jayne Buckland
Lib Dems from Conservatives			
Harborough	4.1	Edward Garnier	

One to watch: Lincoln

Actual majority 2005: Labour 4,614 (12.5%)
Notional majority 2005: Labour 3,806 (9.5%)
Labour candidate: Gillian Merron MP
Conservative candidate: Karl McCartney

A short story. During the 1983 general election campaign, just after the publication of the first edition of the *Almanac of British Politics*, I was asked by the *Times* newspaper to pick a constituency they could follow as the most politically typical in Britain, the most likely to replicate the national trends and outcome. I had little doubt which one to recommend: Lincoln. In addition to casting votes in shares close to the national average for all three main parties, its social, economic and demographic percentages were (and still are) very representative of the country as a whole. As Lincoln is also photogenic, and the seat closely follows the easily recognisable and defined boundaries of the famous cathedral city, the mighty 'Thunderer' seemed happy. Then a few days later they asked me if I could pick a typical seat within closer range of London, for greater convenience of reporting. I did as asked (choosing Medway); but when the results came in three weeks later, it was indeed Lincoln which was the closest to the national result. This was not quite the case in 2005, but a Conservative capture of Lincoln would still be the best augury in the East Midlands of a change of government. Labour controlled the council from 1982 to 2007, and Gillian Merron has been the MP since the Blairite revolution of 1997. Karl McCartney needs a swing of 5 per cent; his task has been made a little easier by boundary changes which bring in 4,800 voters from villages and suburbs outside the city's historic boundaries. The age, housing tenure, and patterns of ethnicity and class are still very typical of the nation as a whole; and I shall again venture to say that whoever wins the seat next time will form the national government.

Boston & Skegness

Conservative notional majority of 6,391; notional turnout: 58.9%

PARTY	2005 CANDIDATE	NOTIONAL 2005 VOTES	NOTIONAL 2005 % VOTE	PPC FOR NEXT GE
Conservative	Mark Simmonds MP	19,991	46.3	Mark Simmonds MP
Labour	Paul Kenny	13,600	31.5	Paul Kenny
UKIP	Richard Horsnell	4,081	9.5	Christopher Pain
Others		5,479	12.7	

Bosworth

Conservative notional majority of 5,335; notional turnout: 65.6%

PARTY	2005 CANDIDATE	NOTIONAL 2005 VOTES	NOTIONAL 2005 % VOTE	PPC FOR NEXT GE
Conservative	David Tredinnick MP	21,210	42.6	David Tredinnick MP
Labour	Rupert Herd	15,875	31.9	Rory Palmer
Lib Dem	James Moore	10,750	21.6	Michael Mullaney
Others		1,933	3.9	

Charnwood

Conservative notional majority of 8,613; notional turnout: 63.9%

PARTY	2005 CANDIDATE	NOTIONAL 2005 VOTES	NOTIONAL 2005 % VOTE	PPC FOR NEXT GE
Conservative	Stephen Dorrell MP	22,230	48.3	Stephen Dorrell MP
Labour	Richard Robinson	13,617	29.6	Eric Neal Goodyer
Lib Dem	Sue King	8,739	19.0	n/a
Others		1,404	3.1	

Corby

Labour notional majority of 1,517; notional turnout: 65.5%

PARTY	2005 CANDIDATE	NOTIONAL 2005 VOTES	NOTIONAL 2005 % VOTE	PPC FOR NEXT GE
Labour	Phil Hope MP	20,913	43.1	Phil Hope MP
Conservative	Andrew Griffith	19,396	40.0	Louise Bagshawe
Lib Dem	David Radcliffe	6,184	12.7	n/a
Others		2,034	4.2	

One of the most politically polarised seats in the United Kingdom, the Corby constituency is split down the middle between working-class Corby town and rural east Northamptonshire. Corby, a heavily industrial town whose economy was decimated by the closure of its steelworks in the 1980s, is tribally loyal to the Labour Party. Labour has controlled Corby Borough Council outright since 1979 and convincingly triumphed in the town's county council wards in 2009. It is on Corby's rural fringes that the Conservatives are all-conquering, running up huge margins of victory in the east Northamptonshire market towns of Oundle, Raunds and Irthlingborough. Sitting Labour MP Phil Hope will aim to retain his seat against an aggressive challenge from glamorous chick-lit author Louise Bagshawe.

Daventry

Conservative notional majority of 11,776; notional turnout: 67.8%

PARTY	2005 CANDIDATE	NOTIONAL 2005 VOTES	NOTIONAL 2005 % VOTE	PPC FOR NEXT GE
Conservative	n/a	24,809	53.0	Chris Heaton-Harris
Labour	n/a	13,033	27.8	Paul Corazzo
Lib Dem	n/a	6,797	14.5	n/a
Others		2,179	4.7	

Gainsborough

Conservative notional majority of 7,895; notional turnout: 64.6%

PARTY	2005 CANDIDATE	NOTIONAL 2005 VOTES	NOTIONAL 2005 % VOTE	PPC FOR NEXT GE
Conservative	Edward Leigh MP	19,524	43.8	Edward Leigh MP
Labour	John Knight	11,629	26.1	Jamie McMahon
Lib Dem	Adrian Heath	11,578	26.0	Pat O'Connor
Others		1,803	4.0	

Grantham & Stamford

Conservative notional majority of 7,308; notional turnout: 62.9%

PARTY	2005 CANDIDATE	NOTIONAL 2005 VOTES	NOTIONAL 2005 % VOTE	PPC FOR NEXT GE
Conservative	Quentin Davies MP	21,746	46.9	Nick Boles
Labour	Ian Selby	14,438	31.2	n/a
Lib Dem	Patrick O'Connor	7,640	16.5	Harrish Bisnauthsing
Others		2,520	5.4	

Harborough

Conservative notional majority of 4,047; notional turnout: 66.3%

PARTY	2005 CANDIDATE	NOTIONAL 2005 VOTES	NOTIONAL 2005 % VOTE	PPC FOR NEXT GE
Conservative	Edward Garnier MP	20,749	41.5	Edward Garnier MP
Lib Dem	Jill Hope	16,702	33.4	n/a
Labour	Peter Evans	9,334	18.7	Kevin McKeever
Others		3,262	6.5	

Kettering

Conservative notional majority of 176; notional turnout: 69.1%

PARTY	2005 CANDIDATE	NOTIONAL 2005 VOTES	NOTIONAL 2005 % VOTE	PPC FOR NEXT GE
Conservative	Philip Hollobone	19,274	43.0	Philip Hollobone MP
Labour	Phil Sawford MP	19,098	42.6	Phil Sawford
Lib Dem	Roger Aron	5,488	12.2	n/a
Others		1,015	2.3	

Leicester East

Labour notional majority of 16,400; notional turnout: 61.9%

PARTY	2005 CANDIDATE	NOTIONAL 2005 VOTES	NOTIONAL 2005 % VOTE	PPC FOR NEXT GE
Labour	Keith Vaz MP	24,765	58.7	Keith Vaz MP
Conservative	Suella Fernandes	8,365	19.8	n/a
Lib Dem	Susan Cooper	6,945	16.5	n/a
Others		2,100	5.0	

Leicester South

Labour notional majority of 3,727; notional turnout: 57.7%

PARTY	2005 CANDIDATE	NOTIONAL 2005 VOTES	NOTIONAL 2005 % VOTE	PPC FOR NEXT GE
Labour	Peter Soulsby	16,702	39.3	Peter Soulsby MP
Lib Dem	Parmjit Singh Gill MP	12,975	30.6	Parmjit Singh Gill
Conservative	Martin McElwee	7,556	17.8	n/a
Others		5,213	12.3	

Leicester West

Labour notional majority of 8,539; notional turnout: 52.5%

PARTY	2005 CANDIDATE	NOTIONAL 2005 VOTES	NOTIONAL 2005 % VOTE	PPC FOR NEXT GE
Labour	Patrcia Hewiitt MP	16,420	50.8	n/a
Conservative	Sarah Richardson	7,881	24.4	n/a
Lib Dem	Zuffar Haq	5,906	18.3	Peter Coley
Others		2,113	6.5	

North West Leicestershire

Labour notional majority of 4,477; notional turnout: 66.8%

PARTY	2005 CANDIDATE	NOTIONAL 2005 VOTES	NOTIONAL 2005 % VOTE	PPC FOR NEXT GE
Labour	David Taylor MP	21,449	45.5	Ross Wilmott
Conservative	Nicola Le Page	16,972	36.0	Andrew Bridgen
Lib Dem	Rod Keys	5,682	12.1	Paul Reynolds
Others		3,037	6.4	

Seized by Labour's David Taylor at the 1997 general election, the North West Leicestershire constituency is largely formed out of the small towns Coalville and Ashby-de-la-Zouch and the surrounding rural areas. The constituency has a rich industrial heritage, having at one time been home to an active coal-mining industry as well as substantial amounts of gravel and brick clay extraction. While many of the seat's traditional industries have long vanished, the manufacturing sector remains vibrant and provides a considerable amount of employment. The fast-growing East Midlands airport is located inside the constituency. Labour failed to win a single seat here in the 2009 local elections, even losing their former Coalville bastion to the BNP. Conservative Andrew Brigden will face Labour's Ross Wilmott, the leader of Leicester City Council.

South Leicestershire

Conservative notional majority of 7,704; notional turnout: 65.2%

PARTY	2005 CANDIDATE	NOTIONAL 2005 VOTES	NOTIONAL 2005 % VOTE	PPC FOR NEXT GE
Conservative	Andrew Robathan MP	22,183	45.4	Andrew Robathan MP
Labour	J David Morgan	14,479	29.6	Sally Gimson
Lib Dem	Jeff Stephenson	9,294	19.0	n/a
Others		2,892	5.9	

Lincoln

Labour notional majority of 3,806; notional turnout: 57.2%

PARTY	2005 CANDIDATE	NOTIONAL 2005 VOTES	NOTIONAL 2005 % VOTE	PPC FOR NEXT GE
Labour	Gillian Merron MP	17,563	43.7	Gillian Merron MP
Conservative	Karl McCartney	13,757	34.2	Karl McCartney
Lib Dem	Lisa Gabriel	7,387	18.4	Reginald Shore
Others		1,475	3.7	

Situated in the centre of Lincolnshire and with a population of approaching 100,000, Lincoln was lost by the Conservatives to Labour at the 1997 general election. Dominated by its enormous cathedral, the historic city is home to a mix of light industries, professional services and a growing university. Around two thirds of the homes here are owner occupied with around a fifth of residents living in social housing. Despite the town's pleasant architecture, one should not assume this is a wealthy area: many jobs pay low wages and unemployment is above the national average. Locally, Labour's support is strongest in the Park and Boultham areas in the centre of the city while the Conservatives dominate the areas to the north, east and south of the constituency. The Conservatives won seven seats to Labour's three at the 2009 Lincolnshire County Council elections. Labour minister Gillian Merron will face a challenge from Conservative Karl McCartney.

Loughborough

Labour notional majority of 1,816; notional turnout: 63.0%

PARTY	2005 CANDIDATE	NOTIONAL 2005 VOTES	NOTIONAL 2005 % VOTE	PPC FOR NEXT GE
Labour	Andy Reed MP	19,261	41.2	Andy Reed MP
Conservative	Nicky Morgan	17,445	37.3	Nicky Morgan
Lib Dem	Graeme Smith	8,354	17.9	n/a
Others		1,700	3.6	

Located midway between Leicester and Nottingham in the heart of the East Midlands, Loughborough is a vibrant engineering town with significant pharmaceutical and scientific research facilities. With a university located here and 15.6% of residents engaged in full-time studies, education is also a significant local employer. Loughborough town is generally loyal to the Labour Party, with the Garendon, Hastings and Lemyington wards providing the party with the basis of its support ,while the Conservatives dominate in town's suburbs and rural Sileby, Quorn and Mountsorrel Castle wards. The next election will be a rerun of the 2005 contest with sitting MP Labour's Andy Reed again facing Conservative Nicky Morgan.

Louth & Horncastle

Conservative notional majority of 9,813; notional turnout: 62.2%

PARTY	2005 CANDIDATE	NOTIONAL 2005 VOTES	NOTIONAL 2005 % VOTE	PPC FOR NEXT GE
Conservative	Peter Tapsell MP	21,598	46.4	Peter Tapsell MP
Labour	Frank Hodgkiss	11,785	25.3	Patrick Mountain
Lib Dem	Fiona Martin	9,554	20.5	Fiona Martin
Others		3,611	7.8	

Northampton North

Labour notional majority of 3,340; notional turnout: 57.1%

PARTY	2005 CANDIDATE	NOTIONAL 2005 VOTES	NOTIONAL 2005 % VOTE	PPC FOR NEXT GE
Labour	Sally Keeble MP	14,352	38.7	Sally Keeble MP
Conservative	Damien Collins	11,012	29.7	Michael Ellis
Lib Dem	Andrew Simpson	10,000	26.9	Andrew Simpson
Others		1,752	4.7	

Won by Labour in 1997 with a majority of exactly 10,000 votes, Northampton North has alternated between the two major parties for nearly half a century. Both of the main parties find pockets of considerable support here, Labour in the Dallington and Links areas and the Conservatives in the suburban districts to the north of the seat. While this is a Conservative–Labour marginal, the Liberal Democrats, who sit in third place, less than 5,000 votes off victory and hold the majority of council seats locally, cannot be completely counted out. Sitting Labour MP and former Transport Minister Sally Keeble will hope to retain her seat in the face of a challenge from Conservative Michael Ellis and Liberal Democrat Andrew Simpson.

Northampton South

Labour notional majority of 1,445; notional turnout: 58.8%

PARTY	2005 CANDIDATE	NOTIONAL 2005 VOTES	NOTIONAL 2005 % VOTE	PPC FOR NEXT GE
Labour	Tony Clarke MP	15,906	41.6	Clyde Loakes
Conservative	Brian Binley	14,461	37.8	Brian Binley MP
Lib Dem	Kevin Barron	5,199	13.6	Paul Varnsverry
Others		2,696	7.0	

A socially mixed seat, the Northampton South constituency stretches from socially depressed wards such as Castle and St Crispin in the centre of the former manufacturing town to Conservative bastions such as Weston. Owner occupation levels in the constituency are below the regional average and a fifth of residents live in social housing. The next general election will see a rematch between Conservative incumbent Brian Binley and Tony Clarke, the man he defeated five years ago. It is, however, not exactly the rematch either man would have wanted. Binley has watched the Boundary Commission transfer the most strongly Tory third of his constituency to the new South Northamptonshire seat while Clarke now sits as an Independent councillor following his expulsion from the Labour Party. Clyde Loakes, the leader of Waltham Forest Borough Council, will stand for Labour.

South Northamptonshire

Conservative notional majority of 11,356; notional turnout: 67.5%

PARTY	2005 CANDIDATE	NOTIONAL 2005 VOTES	NOTIONAL 2005 % VOTE	PPC FOR NEXT GE
Conservative	n/a	25,628	51.6	Andrea Leadsom
Labour	n/a	14,272	28.7	Matthew May
Lib Dem	n/a	8,516	17.1	Scott Collins
Others		1,277	2.6	

Rutland & Melton

Conservative notional majority of 12,998; notional turnout: 65.3%

PARTY	2005 CANDIDATE	NOTIONAL 2005 VOTES	NOTIONAL 2005 % VOTE	PPC FOR NEXT GE
Conservative	Alan Duncan MP	25,328	51.2	Alan Duncan MP
Labour	Linda Arnold	12,330	24.9	Tom Sleigh
Lib Dem	Grahame Hudson	9,183	18.6	Grahame Hudson
Others		2,595	5.2	

Sleaford & North Hykeham

Conservative notional majority of 12,687; notional turnout: 66.7%

PARTY	2005 CANDIDATE	NOTIONAL 2005 VOTES	NOTIONAL 2005 % VOTE	PPC FOR NEXT GE
Conservative	Douglas Hogg MP	26,566	50.6	Douglas Hogg MP
Labour	Katrina Bull	13,879	26.4	James Normington
Lib Dem	David Harding-Price	9,485	18.1	David Harding-Price
Others		2,614	5.0	

South Holland & the Deepings

Conservative notional majority of 15,127; notional turnout: 61.4%

PARTY	2005 CANDIDATE	NOTIONAL 2005 VOTES	NOTIONAL 2005 % VOTE	PPC FOR NEXT GE
Conservative	John Hayes MP	26,549	57.0	John Hayes MP
Labour	Linda Woodings	11,422	24.5	n/a
Lib Dem	Steve Jarvis	5,995	12.9	n/a
Others		2,614	5.6	

Wellingborough

Conservative notional majority of 610; notional turnout: 65.8%

PARTY	2005 CANDIDATE	NOTIONAL 2005 VOTES	NOTIONAL 2005 % VOTE	PPC FOR NEXT GE
Conservative	Peter Bone MP	20,860	42.7	Peter Bone MP
Labour	Paul Stinchcombe	20,250	41.4	Jayne Buckland
Lib Dem	Richard Church	5,637	11.5	n/a
Others		2,108	4.3	

West Midlands

Every opinion poll published over the past year indicates that it is probable that for the first time in over a decade there will be a change of a government in Britain at the forthcoming general election. However questions remain: what do the Conservatives need to do to achieve an overall majority, or as a lesser ambition to become the largest party in a hung parliament? What might count as a meltdown for the Labour Party? How are the Liberal Democrats likely to do, having changed their leader twice since the 2005 general election?

An important way of assessing these questions is to go beyond national polls to consider individual constituency outcomes, as this is how the formation of a new government will actually be decided. This exercise is made even more interesting by the fact that the 2009 or 2010 election will be the first to be fought on new boundaries since 1997, with all but a hundred or so seats having been redrawn. What is more, results may vary from region to region, where the key issues and also the patterns of contest will be different: for example in Scotland the performance of the SNP will be one of the most vital factors, while in the West of England the main battle will be between the Conservatives and the Liberal Democrats.

The West Midlands (here defined as covering Herefordshire, Shropshire, Staffordshire, Warwickshire and Worcestershire as well as the Birmingham metropolitan area) is often regarded as the vital swing region in English politics. For example, its preferences moved more strikingly and effectively than any other in both 1970 and February 1974, paving the way for the national changes of government in favour of the Tories and Labour respectively, with the influence of that saturnine son of Birmingham, Enoch Powell, a far from negligible factor on both occasions, due to the impact first of his anti-immigration campaign from 1968 then of his defection from the Conservatives over Edward Heath's entry into Europe. In the 2005 election, despite the well-publicised collapse of Rover cars, both a symbolic and an actual indicator of the economic health of this historically manufacturing region, there was relatively little in the way of punishment for the Labour government, as only four of their forty-three seats in the region were lost. Perhaps Labour had not been blamed for Rover's plight, and the more general prosperity of the economy saved them – on that occasion. This is not likely to be the case in the depths of a full-blown recession next time.

After taking into account the boundary changes, over the whole of Britain the Conservatives will need to gain seventy seats to become the largest party, requiring a swing from Labour of 5 per cent, and a further forty-six for a bare overall majority, which would need 8 per cent – huge, but not unprecedented in the era of volatile electoral choice. Assuming for the moment that these are all to be at Labour's expense, no fewer than 17 of these 116 key constituencies are located in the West Midlands; so it remains a true cockpit of the struggle to win the next general election, for this is the largest number in any region in Britain except the North West of England.

These crucial seventeen are divided between the metropolitan boroughs of the West Midlands conurbation (seven) and the shire counties which make up the rest of the region (ten). Of the former, by far the most important is the borough of Dudley, in the south-western quadrant of the metropolitan core of the region, which the Tories have already taken at local government level. None of Labour's MPs here is safe. The most likely to fall to the Tories is Stourbridge, where first-term member Lynda Waltho would lose on a swing of only 1.5 per cent. Arguably, however, constituencies like this should not be regarded as the true key marginals, as Labour could lose them and still retain an overall majority. More vital are places like Dudley South, which is right on the cusp of the percentage majority needed for the Conservatives to become the largest party, should they be able to defeat a Dudley native, Ian Pearson, who is currently a parliamentary under-secretary shared between the key departments of Business and the Exchequer. To become the largest party the Tories will also need to take Halesowen & Rowley Regis, divided between Dudley and Sandwell boroughs, and to gain an overall majority they have to add Dudley North.

No other metropolitan borough has more than one marginal. In Birmingham itself, the key Conservative target is Edgbaston, site of famous institutions like the university and the Test cricket ground, and also of the classic west end of the city, with mansions once built for captains of industry such as the Chamberlain family. In 1997 this was a notable gain for the German-born (but now relatively EU-sceptic) Gisela Stuart, but her majority was exactly halved in 2005 and with minor but adverse boundary adjustment it would now fall on a swing of just two per cent to the new Tory candidate Deirdre Alden. Another famous name to watch out for is Wolverhampton South West. The Tories can regain Enoch Powell's old seat from Rob Marris with a swing of 3 per cent, which would deny Labour an overall majority. However, given what was said above about the true key marginals required for a change of government, we need to long at the other end of their spectrum of difficulty. Should they re-establish a presence in Coventry by taking the South division, the 8 per cent swing required would be of the order for David Cameron to enter 10 Downing Street with an overall majority.

Out in the shire counties (though most of the seats here are also still urban in nature), there are even more Tory targets from Labour. The heart of England in many ways is Warwickshire. Not only does it harbour a claim to be the geographical centre of the country, and of course holding a special role as the birthplace of the national Bard, it also is the most likely to be the basis for the symbolic and indeed mythical location of Tolkien's embodiment of peaceful harmony, the 'Shire'. It also has more vulnerable Labour seats than any other of the counties outside the conurbation, four in all.

This is partly because in the boundary changes, which see Birmingham lose one currently Labour seat, Warwickshire restores the region's representation by being awarded an extra one. These are the only major changes the Boundary Commission has made in the region. They have mixed political effects. Although a new, very safe Conservative seat has been created, Kenilworth & Southam, mainly from parts of the oversized Stratford-on-Avon and Rugby & Kenilworth, these voters have to come from somewhere, and one consequence has been to move the later back to being a Labour win on the 'notional' figures calculated by Professors Rallings and Thrasher, which will be used by the media. The Rugby & Kenilworth MP, Jeremy Wright, has secured his own safety with the nomination for the safe extra seat, but the redrawn core of Rugby will need to be won all over again by Mark Pawsey, requiring a swing of about 3 per cent.

In addition, the same changes mean that Warwick & Leamington will be rather harder to gain, now being in the range enabling the Conservatives to be the largest party (see *One to Watch* below). The same applies to Nuneaton, where Labour's Bill Olner is retiring. If the Tories can take North Warwickshire on an 8 per cent movement, they should have an overall majority.

Elsewhere in the region, the Boundary Commission has already effectively given the Tories one gain in Staffordshire Moorlands, where Karen Bradley will start with a notional lead of 1,618 against the sitting Labour MP Charlotte Atkins. There are in addition three key targets in Staffordshire, two in Worcestershire, and one in Shropshire. The easiest in the first named is Stafford, where David Cameron first tried to enter Parliament in 1997, only to fail like so many others in his party in the Labour landslide of that year. Burton and Tamworth would also involve the reversal of the results then. All three in Staffordshire are relatively easy prospects, falling on a swing of between 2 and 3 per cent. The same, perhaps surprisingly, applies to Redditch in north Worcestershire, which would involve perhaps the most senior Labour figure in danger of ejection from Parliament itself, former Home Secretary Jacqui Smith. A swing of 4 per cent would also lead to the gain of Worcester, one of those constituencies subject to the targeting beloved of marketing experts as the home of a type of voter identified as crucial, 'Worcester woman'. For an overall majority, one needs to look to see if Labour loses their only remaining seat in Shropshire, the New Town of Telford set beneath the glowering mound of the Wrekin, an extinct volcano visible for many miles around. That would truly signify a political eruption, with new Labour buried under the detritus like the destroyed civilisation of Pompeii.

Although the West Midlands is chiefly a Labour–Conservative battleground, other parties' hopes and fears should never be forgotten. The Tories' aims would be made easier if they can also make gains from the Liberal Democrats. Technically, though, these would not include their surprise loss of Solihull, as the notional figures suggest that they may just have held it, by 124 votes, on the slightly redrawn lines; with the Lib Dem MP Lorely Burt having built up a personal vote, though, it would feel like a regain if she could be beaten. The one seat which is clearly on the Tory 'gain' target list is the renamed Hereford & South Herefordshire, where Paul Keetch held off the spirited challenge of Virginia Taylor by just a thousand votes in the last two contests. This is wide open, with two new candidates, but Mr Keetch's retirement may be a fatal blow for the LDs, a party which more than the others benefits from personal votes.

Meanwhile, the Liberal Democrats themselves would like to regain Ludlow from the

Conservatives, and maybe to take the very redrawn Birmingham, Hall Green, which now includes much of the heavily Asian east inner city, from Labour; this seat bears little resemblance to the former seat of the same name, which was much more outer leafy suburban and held by the Conservatives until 1997. Much will now depend on the political negotiations with and within the Muslim community, including the strength of Respect, which polled strongly in 2005. Finally, one more possible Conservative gain may come in Wyre Forest: the Independent health service campaigner Dr Richard Taylor, now seventy-four years old, has it held since 2001, but he may not stand again.

If the Conservatives can become the largest party in the West Midlands, they will also be in a position to form the next government of the UK. The above survey demonstrates that the Tories emphatically do not need to take inner city seats to win the election. If Labour, under whoever is leader, is driven back into its strongholds here, it will have lost power for the first time in twelve or thirteen years, and this critical region will undoubtedly have again played a leading part in another electoral transformation.

Target seats

SEAT	SWING REQUIRED %	MP	CHALLENGER
Conservative from Labour			
Stourbridge	1.5	Lynda Waltho	Margot James
Birmingham, Edgbaston	2.1	Gisela Stuart	Deirdre Alden
Stafford	2.1	David Kidney	Jeremy Lefroy
Burton	2.5	Janet Dean*	Andrew Griffiths
Redditch	2.7	Jacqui Smith	Karen Lumley
Rugby	2.7	(Andy King)	Mark Pawsey
Wolverhampton South West	2.7	Rob Marris	Paul Uppal
Tamworth	3.0	Brian Jenkins	Christopher Pincher
Worcester	3.4	Michael Foster	Robin Walker
Dudley South	4.6	Ian Pearson	Chris Kelly
Halesowen & Rowley Regis	4.9	Sylvia Heal	James Morris
Nuneaton	4.9	Bill Olner*	Marcus Jones
Warwick & Leamington	5.2	James Plaskitt	Chris White
Dudley North	5.6	Ian Austin	John Perry
Telford	7.6	Dave Wright	Tom Biggins
Coventry South	7.6	Jim Cunningham	Kevin Foster
North Warwickshire	7.7	Mike O'Brien	Daniel Byles
Conservative from Lib Dem			
Hereford & South Herefordshire	1.2	Paul Keetch*	Jesse Norman
Conservative from Independent			
Wyre Forest	4.8	Richard Taylor	Mark Garnier
Lib Dem from Labour			
Birmingham, Hall Green	8.0	Roger Godsiff	Jeremy Evans
Lib Dem from Conservatives			
Solihull	0.2	(Maggie Throup)	Lorely Burt MP
Ludlow	2.2	Philip Dunne	Heather Kidd
West Worcestershire	3.1	Sir Michael Spicer* (Harriet Baldwin)	Richard Burt

One to watch: Warwick & Leamington

Actual majority 2005: Labour 266 (0.5%) – James Plaskitt MP
Notional majority 2005: Labour 4,393 (10.3%)
Conservative candidate: Mark Pawsey

Warwick & Leamington is typical of the seats Labour gained in 1997: it had never been won by that party before, among the distinguished former MPs being Sir Anthony Eden, member here for thirty-four years, and Sir Dudley Smith. It had always had areas where Labour were competitive, though, such as the southern section of Leamington itself, with its Asian community and working-class estate of Sydenham, and its industrial employers such as AP (Automotive Products), linking with the region's manufacturing tradition. With its share of students from the University of Warwick, although that is actually nearer Coventry, this seat proved clearly winnable at the high water mark of Labour success in 1997 and 2001. Although James Plaskitt's majority was reduced to 266 in 2005, the loss of over 16,000 rural voters in the boundary changes which have given Warwickshire an extra seat increases Labour's notional lead from 2005 to a level which means that if the Tories can win it, they will be at least the largest party nationally. We therefore have an absolutely key marginal at the very heart of England, where the major parties will battle for a crucial outcome around the setting of one of our most famous, and most visited, castles.

Aldridge-Brownhills

Conservative notional majority of 5,732; notional turnout: 63.5%

PARTY	2005 CANDIDATE	NOTIONAL 2005 VOTES	NOTIONAL 2005 % VOTE	PPC FOR NEXT GE
Conservative	Richard Shepherd MP	17,845	48.2	Richard Shepherd MP
Labour	John Phillips	12,113	32.7	Ashiq Hussain
Lib Dem	Roy Sheward	4,406	11.9	n/a
Others		2,652	7.2	

Birmingham, Edgbaston

Labour notional majority of 1,555; notional turnout: 57.3%

PARTY	2005 CANDIDATE	NOTIONAL 2005 VOTES	NOTIONAL 2005 % VOTE	PPC FOR NEXT GE
Labour	Gisela Stuart MP	16,732	43.1	Gisela Stuart MP
Conservative	Deirdre Alden	15,177	39.1	Deirdre Alden
Lib Dem	Mike Dixon	4,972	12.8	n/a
Others		1,944	5.0	

Located in Birmingham's south-western suburbs, German-born and -accented Gisela Stuart succeeded Tory grandee Dame Jill Knight at the 1997 general election. Home to the University of Birmingham, the area is largely middle class in nature. With her party holding all the constituency's 12 council seats, Conservative candidate Deirdre Alden is well placed to capture the seat and maintain Edgbaston's 57-year record of electing a female member of Parliament. The Tories cannot, however, afford to relax. With almost a third of the constituency's residents living in social housing and many of area's elegant town houses being converted into flats, it is likely that the area will continue to be a closely fought marginal for many election cycles to come.

Birmingham, Erdington

Labour notional majority of 9,677; notional turnout: 48.4%

PARTY	2005 CANDIDATE	NOTIONAL 2005 VOTES	NOTIONAL 2005 % VOTE	PPC FOR NEXT GE
Labour	Sion Simon MP	17,037	52.9	Sion Simon MP
Conservative	Victoria Elvidge	7,360	22.9	Robert Alden
Lib Dem	Jerry Evans	5,089	15.8	n/a
Others		2,964	8.4	

Birmingham, Hall Green

Labour notional majority of 6,649; notional turnout: 55.9%

PARTY	2005 CANDIDATE	NOTIONAL 2005 VOTES	NOTIONAL 2005 % VOTE	PPC FOR NEXT GE
Labour	n/a	17,708	42.4	Roger Godsiff MP
Lib Dem	n/a	11,059	26.5	Jerry Evans
Conservative	n/a	6,226	14.9	Jo Barker
Others		6,816	16.3	

Despite baring the name of an existing constituency, the Birmingham, Hall Green seat which will be fought in 2010 bares little similarity to that contested five years ago. Significant boundary changes mean that this seat is composed of around half of the current Sparkbrook & Small Heath constituency (whose sitting Labour MP, Roger Godsiff, will contest this seat), two fifths of Hall Green and a quarter of Selly Oak. Under the redrawn boundaries, more than a third of local residents are Muslims – one of the highest proportions of any British seat. This constituency is not a serious prospect for the Tories, the notional Labour majority having been suppressed by the 27.5% vote for George Galloway's Respect coalition in Sparkbrook & Small Heath in 2005. Jo Barker will fight this seat for the Conservatives.

Birmingham, Hodge Hill

Labour notional majority of 7,063; notional turnout: 55.7%

PARTY	2005 CANDIDATE	NOTIONAL 2005 VOTES	NOTIONAL 2005 % VOTE	PPC FOR NEXT GE
Labour	Liam Byrne MP	19,437	46.9	Liam Byrne MP
Lib Dem	Nicola Davies	12,374	29.9	Tariq Khan
Conservative	Deborah Thomas	4,394	10.6	Shailesh Parekh
Others		5,230	12.7	

Birmingham, Ladywood

Labour notional majority of 6,804; notional turnout: 45.1%

PARTY	2005 CANDIDATE	NOTIONAL 2005 VOTES	NOTIONAL 2005 % VOTE	PPC FOR NEXT GE
Labour	Clare Short MP	15,422	52.6	Shabana Mahmood
Lib Dem	Ayoub Khan	8,618	29.4	Ayoub Khan
Conservative	Phillipa Stroud	2,470	8.4	Colin Hughes
Others		2,786	9.5	

Birmingham, Northfield

Labour notional majority of 7,879; notional turnout: 55.2%

PARTY	2005 CANDIDATE	NOTIONAL 2005 VOTES	NOTIONAL 2005 % VOTE	PPC FOR NEXT GE
Labour	Richard Burden MP	19,900	50.3	Richard Burden MP
Conservative	Vicky Ford	12,021	30.4	Keely Huxtable
Lib Dem	Trevor Sword	4,875	12.3	n/a
Others		2,738	6.9	

Located in south-west Birmingham, and taking in the suburbs of Weoley and King's Norton as well as the former Rover plant at Longbridge, sitting Labour MP Richard Burden gained the Northfield constituency from Conservative Roger King in 1992 – a election in which the Tory party suffered heavy losses in the city. At only 7.2%, the constituency has one of the lowest ethnic minority populations of any Birmingham constituency and recorded the lowest anti-Labour swing of any of the city's seats at the 2005 general election. Despite Richard Burden's healthy grip on the parliamentary seat, the Conservatives enjoy absolute hegemony on a local government level, providing all 12 councillors in the constituency. Conservative candidate and life-long Northfield resident Keely Huxtable needs a swing of 10.35% to take the seat from Labour.

Birmingham, Perry Barr

Labour notional majority of 7,825; notional turnout: 53.8%

PARTY	2005 CANDIDATE	NOTIONAL 2005 VOTES	NOTIONAL 2005 % VOTE	PPC FOR NEXT GE
Labour	Khalid Mahmood MP	17,919	46.3	Khalid Mahmood MP
Lib Dem	Jon Hunt	10,094	26.1	Karen Hamilton
Conservative	Naweed Khan	6,702	17.3	William Norton
Others		3,983	10.3	

Birmingham, Selly Oak

Labour notional majority of 7,564; notional turnout: 60.3%

PARTY	2005 CANDIDATE	NOTIONAL 2005 VOTES	NOTIONAL 2005 % VOTE	PPC FOR NEXT GE
Labour	n/a	20,672	46.8	Steve McCabe MP
Conservative	n/a	13,108	29.7	Nigel Dawkins
Lib Dem	n/a	7,651	17.3	David Radcliffe
Others		2,700	6.1	

Selly Oak, like many other constituencies in the south of Birmingham, has been subject to considerable boundary changes which make the seat almost unrecognisable from that fought at the last election. This reconfigured seat includes two thirds of the present Hall Green constituency, half of the current territory of Selly Oak and negligibly small parts of Edgbaston and Northfield. The new constituency comprises the Billesley, Bournville, Brandwood and Selly Oak districts, resulting in a diverse mix of affluent detached and poor social housing. At 6.1%, the ethnic minority population of this seat is relatively low in comparison to the remainder of the city. On Birmingham City Council, the Conservatives hold eight council seats locally to the Liberal Democrat's three and Labour's one. Government whip and sitting Hall Green MP Steve McCabe will be challenged by Conservative Nigel Dawkins.

Birmingham, Yardley

Lib Dem notional majority of 2,864; notional turnout: 54.5%

PARTY	2005 CANDIDATE	NOTIONAL 2005 VOTES	NOTIONAL 2005 % VOTE	PPC FOR NEXT GE
Lib Dem	John Hemming	16,485	42.0	John Hemming MP
Labour	Jayne Innes	13,621	34.7	Jean Helme
Conservative	Paul Uppal	4,142	10.6	Meirion Jenkins
Other		4,975	12.7	

Bromsgrove

Conservative notional majority of 10,080; notional turnout: 67.5%

PARTY	2005 CANDIDATE	NOTIONAL 2005 VOTES	NOTIONAL 2005 % VOTE	PPC FOR NEXT GE
Conservative	Julie Kirkbride MP	24,387	51.0	n/a
Labour	David Jones	14,307	29.9	n/a
Lib Dem	Sue Haswell	7,197	15.1	Ray Geoffrey
Others		1,919	4.0	

Burton

Labour notional majority of 2,132; notional turnout: 60.4%

PARTY	2005 CANDIDATE	NOTIONAL 2005 VOTES	NOTIONAL 2005 % VOTE	PPC FOR NEXT GE
Labour	Janet Dean MP	18,677	42.1	Ruth Smeeth
Conservative	Adrian Pepper	16,545	37.3	Andrew Griffiths
Lib Dem	Sandra Johnson	5,538	12.5	Gavin Webb
Others		3,608	8.1	

Formerly represented by Tory grandee Sir Ivan Lawrence, the Burton constituency has been held by Labour's Janet Dean since the 1997 general election. The seat is largely centred on Burton upon Trent, the centre of the country's beer-brewing industry, and the market town of Uttoxeter. A politically divided seat, Labour's support is greatest in the Horninglow and Stapenhill areas of Burton, which are dominated by social housing, while the strength of the Conservative vote in rural east Staffordshire ensures that this will always be a closely fought marginal. The 2009 Staffordshire County Council election results were encouraging for the Conservatives, who won six of the eight seats contested. Ruth Smeeth will attempt to hold this seat for Labour while Andrew Griffiths, a former chief of staff to Theresa May, will fight this seat for the Tories.

Cannock Chase

Labour notional majority of 8,726; notional turnout: 57.4%

PARTY	2005 CANDIDATE	NOTIONAL 2005 VOTES	NOTIONAL 2005 % VOTE	PPC FOR NEXT GE
Labour	Tony Wright MP	21,187	51.0	Sue Woodward
Conservative	Ian Collard	12,461	30.0	Aidan Burley
Lib Dem	Jenny Pinkett	5,820	14.0	n/a
Others		2,088	5.0	

Traditionally Labour territory, this constituency was last held by the Conservatives between 1983 and 1992 in the form of right-winger Gerald Howarth. Located in the south of Staffordshire, the Labour-dominated town of Cannock grew rapidly in the post-war years on the back of rapid industrial expansion. North of the town is the rugged Cannock Chase heathland, which mixes upmarket Tory-inclined villages with Labour-dominated former coal-mining areas, and has been designated an area of outstanding natural beauty. Labour were roundly defeated here in the 2009 county council elections, winning only one of the constituency's six seats. Sue Woodward, who narrowly failed to be elected by a handful votes in nearby Lichfield in 1997, will hope to defeat Conservative Hammersmith & Fulham councillor Aidan Burley to keep this seat in the Labour column. Sitting MP Tony Wright is retiring.

Coventry North East

Labour notional majority of 14,621; notional turnout: 53.3%

PARTY	2005 CANDIDATE	NOTIONAL 2005 VOTES	NOTIONAL 2005 % VOTE	PPC FOR NEXT GE
Labour	Bob Ainsworth MP	21,859	56.9	Bob Ainsworth MP
Conservative	Jaswant Singh Birdi	7,238	18.8	Hazel Noonan
Lib Dem	Russell Field	6,352	16.5	n/a
Others		2,950	7.7	

Coventry North West

Labour notional majority of 8,934; notional turnout: 60.0%

PARTY	2005 CANDIDATE	NOTIONAL 2005 VOTES	NOTIONAL 2005 % VOTE	PPC FOR NEXT GE
Labour	Geoffrey Robinson MP	20,084	48.0	Geoffrey Robinson MP
Conservative	Brian Connell	11,150	26.6	Gary Ridley
Lib Dem	Iona Anderson	7,702	18.4	n/a
Others		2,908	6.9	

Coventry South

Labour notional majority of 6,237; notional turnout: 59.3%

PARTY	2005 CANDIDATE	NOTIONAL 2005 VOTES	NOTIONAL 2005 % VOTE	PPC FOR NEXT GE
Labour	Jim Cunningham MP	18,826	45.8	Jim Cunningham MP
Conservative	Heather Wheeler	12,589	30.6	Kevin Foster
Lib Dem	Vincent McKee	7,229	17.6	n/a
Others		2,431	6.0	

The Coventry South constituency is one of the country's most varied seats, including wealthy commuter suburbs, inner-city council estates, heavy manufacturing and a sizeable student population. The birthplace of the British motor industry, the city saw its last car manufacturing plant at Ryton close its doors in April 2006, leading to an increase in unemployment locally. Coventry South is an ethnically diverse constituency with an Asian population of 9.3%. Around one in ten homes in the constituency is privately rented, largely as a result of the substantial number of University of Warwick students opting to live off campus. Conservative support here is strongest in the suburban Wainbody and Earlsdon areas while Labour dominates the wards in the city centre. Former Coventry council leader and MP since 1992 Jim Cunningham will be opposed by Conservative councillor Kevin Foster.

Dudley North

Labour notional majority of 4,106; notional turnout: 61.2%

PARTY	2005 CANDIDATE	NOTIONAL 2005 VOTES	NOTIONAL 2005 % VOTE	PPC FOR NEXT GE
Labour	Ian Austin	15,682	42.6	Ian Austin MP
Conservative	Ian Hillas	11,576	31.4	n/a
Lib Dem	Gerry Lewis	3,868	10.5	n/a
Others		5,719	15.5	

The safer for Labour of the town's two constituencies, the party gained Dudley North from the Conservatives at the 1997 general election. Both the Conservatives and Labour have significant support here, Labour leading in the urban Gornal, Castle and Priory areas while the Tories are ahead by strong margins in the commuter suburb of Sedgley. At 64.1%, levels of home ownership are considerably lower here than in the south of the town. Conservative chances here are slightly improved by the transfer of the safe Labour ward of Coseley East to the neighbouring Wolverhampton South East constituency. Ian Austin, a former parliamentary private secretary to the Prime Minister, will defend his seat for Labour. The British National Party are active locally and may save their deposit.

Dudley South

Labour notional majority of 3,222; notional turnout: 60.2%

PARTY	2005 CANDIDATE	NOTIONAL 2005 VOTES	NOTIONAL 2005 % VOTE	PPC FOR NEXT GE
Labour	Ian Pearson MP	15,896	44.0	Ian Pearson MP
Conservative	Marco Longhi	12,674	35.0	Chris D. Kelly
Lib Dem	Jonathan Bramall	4,587	12.7	n/a
Others		3,006	8.3	

Situated just west of Birmingham and on the edge of the Black Country, the Dudley South constituency is formed of the bulk of the former Dudley West seat, which the Conservatives lost to Labour in a 1994 by-election on a 30% swing. Labour is strongest here in the Brierley Hill area, a former steel and glass manufacturing town which is plagued by high unemployment. Even in a bad year, the Conservatives are strongly competitive in the Birmingham commuter town of Kingswinford – an area which is expected to expand rapidly in the coming decades. Conservative chances here are boosted slightly by the transfer of the safe Labour ward of Coseley East to Wolverhampton North East. Government minister Ian Pearson will be challenged by avowed Thatcherite right-winger Chris D. Kelly for the Conservatives.

Halesowen & Rowley Regis

Labour notional majority of 4,010; notional turnout: 63.1%

PARTY	2005 CANDIDATE	NOTIONAL 2005 VOTES	NOTIONAL 2005 % VOTE	PPC FOR NEXT GE
Labour	Sylvia Heal MP	19,199	46.2	Sylvia Heal MP
Conservative	Leslie Jones	15,189	36.6	James Morris
Lib Dem	Martin Turner	5,187	12.5	n/a
Others		1,940	4.7	

Located in the heart of the Black Country and gained by Labour at the 1997 general election, this constituency is comprised of the parts of Sandwell and Dudley boroughs. This is a socially divided constituency, the middle-class town of Halesowen largely comprising detached homes for Birmingham commuters while Rowley Regis and Cradley Heath are dominated by council housing. A political divide is apparent here too, Halesowen supporting the Tories and Rowley Regis backing Labour. At 70.8%, levels of owner occupation are high in the constituency yet almost a quarter of residents live in social housing. Sylvia Heal, the deputy Speaker of the House of Commons and incumbent Labour MP here, will be challenged by Conservative James Morris.

Hereford & South Herefordshire

Lib Dem notional majority of 1,089; notional turnout: 66.0%

PARTY	2005 CANDIDATE	NOTIONAL 2005 VOTES	NOTIONAL 2005 % VOTE	PPC FOR NEXT GE
Lib Dem	Paul Keetch MP	19,793	43.4	Sarah Carr
Conservative	Virginia Taylor	18,704	41.0	Jesse Norman
Labour	Tom Calver	4,678	10.3	n/a
Others		2,445	5.4	

On paper, this wealthy, predominantly rural constituency looks like a classic Conservative stronghold. In reality, it is has been a closely fought marginal for the past three decades with the winning majority exceeding 3,000 votes in only one of the last seven general elections. The constituency's two largest towns of Hereford and Ross-on-Wye are both pleasant historic places which, due to a mix of the party's decades-long dominance on a local government level and a sizeable left-leaning literary community, favour the Liberal Democrats. The Conservatives record their strongest performance in rural areas, scoring large majorities in the Wye and Golden Valley areas. Paul Keetch, the MP here since 1997, is retiring and is replaced as Liberal Democrat candidate by Sarah Carr. The Conservatives are fielding author Jesse Norman.

North Herefordshire

Conservative notional majority of 12,688; notional turnout: 69.2%

PARTY	2005 CANDIDATE	NOTIONAL 2005 VOTES	NOTIONAL 2005 % VOTE	PPC FOR NEXT GE
Conservative	Bill Wiggin MP	23,422	52.5	Bill Wiggin MP
Lib Dem	Caroline Williams	10,734	24.1	Lucy Hurds
Labour	Paul Bell	6,926	15.5	Sam Greenwood
Others		3,541	7.9	

Kenilworth & Southam

Conservative notional majority of 10,956; notional turnout: 70.2%

PARTY	2005 CANDIDATE	NOTIONAL 2005 VOTES	NOTIONAL 2005 % VOTE	PPC FOR NEXT GE
Conservative	n/a	22,245	50.4	Jeremy Wright MP
Labour	n/a	11,289	25.6	Nicholas Milton
Lib Dem	n/a	9,736	22.0	Nigel Rock
Others		910	2.1	

Lichfield

Conservative notional majority of 7,791; notional turnout: 66.7%

PARTY	2005 CANDIDATE	NOTIONAL 2005 VOTES	NOTIONAL 2005 % VOTE	PPC FOR NEXT GE
Conservative	Michael Fabricant MP	23,009	48.7	Michael Fabricant MP
Labour	Nigel Gardner	15,218	32.2	Steve Hyden
Lib Dem	Ian Jackson	7,502	15.9	n/a
Others		1,529	3.2	

Ludlow

Conservative notional majority of 2,027; notional turnout: 71.9%

PARTY	2005 CANDIDATE	NOTIONAL 2005 VOTES	NOTIONAL 2005 % VOTE	PPC FOR NEXT GE
Conservative	Philip Dunne	20,979	45.1	Philip Dunne MP
Lib Dem	Matthew Green MP	18,952	40.7	Heather Kidd
Labour	Nigel Knowles	4,974	10.7	n/a
Others		1,635	3.5	

Meriden

Conservative notional majority of 7,412; notional turnout: 60.1%

PARTY	2005 CANDIDATE	NOTIONAL 2005 VOTES	NOTIONAL 2005 % VOTE	PPC FOR NEXT GE
Conservative	Caroline Spelman MP	22,975	47.6	Caroline Spelman MP
Labour	Jim Brown	15,563	32.3	Ed Williams
Lib Dem	William Laitinen	8,075	16.7	n/a
Others		1,620	3.4	

Newcastle-under-Lyme

Labour notional majority of 8,108; notional turnout: 58.2%

PARTY	2005 CANDIDATE	NOTIONAL 2005 VOTES	NOTIONAL 2005 % VOTE	PPC FOR NEXT GE
Labour	Paul Farrelly MP	18,053	45.4	Paul Farrelly MP
Conservative	Jeremy Lefroy	9,945	25.0	Robert Jenrick
Lib Dem	Trevor Johnson	7,528	18.9	Elizabeth Shenton
Others		4,262	10.7	

Located in Staffordshire's north-eastern corner, Newcastle-under-Lyme is a socially mixed constituency which has, throughout its electoral history, been steadfastly loyal to the Labour Party. Parts of this constituency fall within the former Staffordshire coalfield, notably Silverdale, whose colliery closed for the last time in 1998. This is not a wealthy area, less than half of all homes being owner occupied and unemployment being some way above the national average. Despite the area's natural inclination towards Labour, the seat is not entirely hostile to the Conservatives, with the rural western portion heavily favouring the party. The Conservatives are the largest party on Newcastle-under-Lyme council, holding 25 seats to the Liberal Democrats' 19 and Labour's 12. Labour MP Paul Farrelly will be challenged by Conservative Robert Jenrick, one of his party's youngest candidates.

Nuneaton

Labour notional majority of 3,894; notional turnout: 58.9%

PARTY	2005 CANDIDATE	NOTIONAL 2005 VOTES	NOTIONAL 2005 % VOTE	PPC FOR NEXT GE
Labour	Bill Olner MP	18,652	46.6	Jayne Innes
Conservative	Mark Pawsey	14,758	36.9	Marcus Jones
Lib Dem	Ali Asghar	5,008	12.5	n/a
Others		1,574	3.9	

The largest town in Warwickshire, Nuneaton was gained by Labour from the Conservatives at the 1992 general election. Once an important manufacturing and textiles town, these industries have now largely disappeared and the constituency is now largely home to commuters to nearby Birmingham and Coventry. Labour have traditionally performed best in the Nuneaton town wards, especially around the former National Coal Board housing estate of Camp Hill, while the Conservatives are convincingly ahead in the affluent suburb of Whitestone. The Conservatives gained control of Nuneaton & Bedworth Council from Labour in 2008, the same elections in which the British National Party secured its first two councillors locally. Incumbent MP Bill Olner is retiring and is replaced as Labour candidate by Jayne Innes. The Conservative candidate will be Marcus Jones.

Redditch

Labour notional majority of 2,163; notional turnout: 63.5%

PARTY	2005 CANDIDATE	NOTIONAL 2005 VOTES	NOTIONAL 2005 % VOTE	PPC FOR NEXT GE
Labour	Jacqui Smith MP	18,166	43.7	Jacqui Smith MP
Conservative	Karen Lumly	16,003	38.5	Karen Lumley
Lib Dem	Nigel Hicks	5,975	14.4	Malcolm Hal
Others		1,432	3.4	

The constituency of former Home Secretary Jacqui Smith, this seat is high on the Conservative Party's wish list. Located 15 miles south of Birmingham, the Redditch constituency is neither particularly wealthy nor poor in terms of its composition. A classic New Town, Redditch's population grew substantially during the 1960s as demand for housing close to Birmingham accelerated, while more upscale housing developments on the town's fringes have sprung up in recent years. A fifth of residents live in social housing, yet owner occupation levels remain above average for a Midlands constituency. Neither party can claim domination on a local level, the Conservatives holding a majority of one on Redditch Borough Council. Karen Lumley, who fought the seat for the Conservatives at the past two general elections, will hope to make it third time lucky.

Rugby

Labour notional majority of 2,397; notional turnout: 67.3%

PARTY	2005 CANDIDATE	NOTIONAL 2005 VOTES	NOTIONAL 2005 % VOTE	PPC FOR NEXT GE
Labour	Andy King MP	20,047	43.5	Andy King
Conservative	Jeremy Wright	17,650	38.3	Mark Pawsey
Lib Dem	Richard Allanach	6,896	15.0	Jerry Roodhouse
Others		1,462	3.2	

Shrewsbury & Atcham

Conservative notional majority of 1,808; notional turnout: 69.3%

PARTY	2005 CANDIDATE	NOTIONAL 2005 VOTES	NOTIONAL 2005 % VOTE	PPC FOR NEXT GE
Conservative	Daniel Kawczynski	18,960	37.7	Daniel Kawczynski MP
Labour	Michael Ion	17,152	34.1	Jon Tandy
Lib Dem	Richard Burt	11,487	22.8	Charles West
Others		2,697	5.4	

North Shropshire

Conservative notional majority of 11,020; notional turnout: 63.2%

PARTY	2005 CANDIDATE	NOTIONAL 2005 VOTES	NOTIONAL 2005 % VOTE	PPC FOR NEXT GE
Conservative	Owen Paterson MP	23,061	49.6	Owen Paterson MP
Labour	Sandra Samuels	12,041	25.9	Ian McLaughlan
Lib Dem	Steve Bourne	9,175	19.7	n/a
Others		2,233	4.8	

Solihull

Conservative notional majority of 124; notional turnout: 67.4%

PARTY	2005 CANDIDATE	NOTIONAL 2005 VOTES	NOTIONAL 2005 % VOTE	PPC FOR NEXT GE
Conservative	John Taylor MP	20,058	39.7	Maggie Throup
Lib Dem	Lorely Burt	19,934	39.4	Lorely Burt MP
Labour	Rory Vaughan	7,902	15.6	Sarah Merrill
Others		2,689	5.3	

Stafford

Labour notional majority of 1,852; notional turnout: 66.9%

PARTY	2005 CANDIDATE	NOTIONAL 2005 VOTES	NOTIONAL 2005 % VOTE	PPC FOR NEXT GE
Labour	David Kidney MP	19,970	43.2	David Kidney MP
Conservative	David Chambers	18,118	39.2	Jeremy Lefroy
Lib Dem	Barry Stamp	6,613	14.3	n/a
Others		1,525	3.3	

The county town of Staffordshire, here sitting MP David Kidney defeated a young Conservative Central Office staffer named David Cameron in order to win the seat for Labour at the 1997 general election. A largely middle-class town, many local people find employment in the electrical engineering and light industrial sector. Labour has traditionally dominated in Stafford town, holding wide leads over the Conservatives in the Highfields, Western Downs and Manor districts, while the Conservatives are strongest in the town's suburbs and outlying villages. Conservative chances in Stafford are improved slightly by the Boundary Commission's decision to transfer the heavily Tory Seighford and Haywood & Hixon wards into the constituency from neighbouring Stone. The Conservatives swept the boards in the 2009 county council elections, winning every seat in the constituency. Chartered accountant Jeremy Lefroy will fight this seat for the Conservatives.

Staffordshire Moorlands

Conservative notional majority of 1,618; notional turnout: 67.7%

PARTY	2005 CANDIDATE	NOTIONAL 2005 VOTES	NOTIONAL 2005 % VOTE	PPC FOR NEXT GE
Conservative	Marcus Hayes	16,671	39.7	Karen Bradley
Labour	Charlotte Atkins MP	15,053	35.9	Charlotte Atkins MP
Lib Dem	John Fisher	7,377	17.6	Steve Povey
Others		2,862	6.8	

South Staffordshire

Conservative notional majority of 8,346; notional turnout: 37.6%

PARTY	2005 CANDIDATE	NOTIONAL 2005 VOTES	NOTIONAL 2005 % VOTE	PPC FOR NEXT GE
Conservative	Patrick Cormack MP	13,794	50.6	Patrick Cormack MP
Labour	Paul Kalinauckas	5,448	20.0	Kevin McElduff
Lib Dem	Jo Crotty	3,654	13.4	n/a
Others		4,338	15.9	

Stoke-on-Trent Central

Labour notional majority of 9,717; notional turnout: 48.6%

PARTY	2005 CANDIDATE	NOTIONAL 2005 VOTES	NOTIONAL 2005 % VOTE	PPC FOR NEXT GE
Labour	Mark Fisher MP	15,068	52.4	Mark Fisher MP
Lib Dem	John Redfern	5,351	18.6	John Redfern
Conservative	Esther Baroudy	4,977	17.3	n/a
Others		3,354	11.7	

Stoke-on-Trent North

Labour notional majority of 13,666; notional turnout: 50.8%

PARTY	2005 CANDIDATE	NOTIONAL 2005 VOTES	NOTIONAL 2005 % VOTE	PPC FOR NEXT GE
Labour	Joan Walley MP	20,064	55.8	Joan Walley MP
Conservative	Benjamin Browning	6,398	17.8	n/a
Lib Dem	Henry Jebb	4,845	13.5	David Jack
Others		4,626	12.9	

Stoke-on-Trent South

Labour notional majority of 8,324; notional turnout: 54.2%

PARTY	2005 CANDIDATE	NOTIONAL 2005 VOTES	NOTIONAL 2005 % VOTE	PPC FOR NEXT GE
Labour	Robert Flello	17,195	46.8	Robert Flello MP
Conservative	Mark Deaville	8,871	24.2	n/a
Lib Dem	Andrew Martin	5,529	15.1	n/a
Others		5,119	13.9	

Stone

Conservative notional majority of 8,191; notional turnout: 66.9%

PARTY	2005 CANDIDATE	NOTIONAL 2005 VOTES	NOTIONAL 2005 % VOTE	PPC FOR NEXT GE
Conservative	Bill Cash MP	21,178	48.4	Bill Cash MP
Labour	Mark Davis	12,987	29.7	n/a
Lib Dem	Richard Stevens	8,154	18.6	Christine Tinker
Others		1,425	3.3	

Stourbridge

Labour notional majority of 1,280; notional turnout: 63.8%

PARTY	2005 CANDIDATE	NOTIONAL 2005 VOTES	NOTIONAL 2005 % VOTE	PPC FOR NEXT GE
Labour	Lynda Waltho	18,469	42.2	Lynda Waltho MP
Conservative	Diana Coad	17,189	39.2	Margot James
Lib Dem	Chris Bramall	6,982	15.9	n/a
Others		1,163	2.7	

An increasingly aspirational seat, the Stourbridge constituency typifies the mix of wealthy commuter suburbs, social housing and light industry increasingly common to many seats on the fringes of the West Midlands conurbation. Lost to Labour in 1997 on an average swing, Labour's long-term prospects here are not helped by the near-frenetic construction of private housing estates, which have tended to favour the Conservatives. Surrounded by pleasant countryside, three quarters of homes in this middle-class constituency are owner occupied. Conservative support is strongest in Amblecote, Pedmore and Kingswinford while Labour dominates in Stourbridge town and Dudley Wood. Sitting MP Lynda Waltho, selected to fight the seat for Labour only days before the 2005 general election, will be challenged by Conservative Party vice-chairman Margot James.

Stratford-on-Avon

Conservative notional majority of 10,928; notional turnout: 69.1%

PARTY	2005 CANDIDATE	NOTIONAL 2005 VOTES	NOTIONAL 2005 % VOTE	PPC FOR NEXT GE
Conservative	John Maples MP	23,452	51.3	John Maples MP
Lib Dem	Susan Juned	12,524	27.4	Martin Turner
Labour	Rachel Blackmore	7,077	15.5	n/a
Others		2,675	5.8	

Sutton Coldfield

Conservative notional majority of 12,318; notional turnout: 62.7%

PARTY	2005 CANDIDATE	NOTIONAL 2005 VOTES	NOTIONAL 2005 % VOTE	PPC FOR NEXT GE
Conservative	Andrew Mitchell MP	24,235	52.6	Andrew Mitchell MP
Labour	Robert Pocock	11,917	25.9	n/a
Lib Dem	Craig Drury	7,679	16.7	n/a
Others		2,262	4.9	

Tamworth

Labour notional majority of 2,569; notional turnout: 61.0%

PARTY	2005 CANDIDATE	NOTIONAL 2005 VOTES	NOTIONAL 2005 % VOTE	PPC FOR NEXT GE
Labour	Brian Jenkins MP	18,801	43.0	n/a
Conservative	Christopher Pincher	16,232	37.1	Christopher Pincher
Lib Dem	Phillip Bennion	6,175	14.1	n/a
Others		2,532	5.8	

Lost by the Conservatives to local council leader Brian Jenkins on a 22% swing at a 1996 by-election, Tamworth is a perfect example of the type of West Midlands marginal the Conservatives will need in order to form a majority in the House of Commons. The constituency is a mix of an elegant town centre, wealthy Birmingham commuter villages and pockets of real deprivation in Tamworth's Bolehill, Castle and Glascote areas. The Conservatives dominate at the local government level, holding 24 seats to Labour's five on Tamworth Borough Council. Not unusually for a Midlands seat, the Liberal Democrat presence is almost non-existent. Dapper IT consultant Christopher Pincher, whose party scored a clean sweep of Tamworth's six Staffordshire County Council wards at the 2009 elections, will fight the seat for the Conservatives.

Telford

Labour notional majority of 5,651; notional turnout: 58.6%

PARTY	2005 CANDIDATE	NOTIONAL 2005 VOTES	NOTIONAL 2005 % VOTE	PPC FOR NEXT GE
Labour	David Wright MP	18,119	48.1	David Wright MP
Conservative	Stella Kyriazis	12,468	33.1	Tom Biggins
Lib Dem	Ian Jenkins	5,301	14.1	n/a
Others		1,748	4.6	

A relatively safe Labour seat for most of its existence, Telford supported the Conservatives for Margaret Thatcher's first two terms before being recaptured by future Lords Chief Whip Bruce Grocott in 1987. Located around 30 miles east of Birmingham, Telford has carved itself a niche as a centre for the high-tech and IT sector. The town's population is projected to grow from 104,000 in 1980 to 200,000 within the next 20 years. Despite recent investment, high unemployment has been a long-term problem for Telford with only one in ten residents holding university degrees (12.1%) and more than a third (34.1%) having no qualifications. Ultra-local MP David Wright will stand again for Labour while former Shropshire county councillor Tom Biggins will challenge for the Conservatives.

Walsall North

Labour notional majority of 6,901; notional turnout: 52.1%

PARTY	2005 CANDIDATE	NOTIONAL 2005 VOTES	NOTIONAL 2005 % VOTE	PPC FOR NEXT GE
Labour	David Winnick MP	16,008	48.2	David Winnick MP
Conservative	Ian Lucas	9,107	27.4	Helen Clack
Lib Dem	Douglas Taylor	4,102	12.4	n/a
Others		3,977	12.0	

Held for the past 30 years by David Winnick, a mild-mannered Labour rebel with an independent mind, only a Cameron landslide would deliver this seat to the Conservatives. Despite a having a Conservative-controlled council, it's easy to see why Labour do well here. More than a third of residents live in social housing and a fifth of homes have no central heating or private bathrooms. One of the few West Midlands towns still dominated by manufacturing, Willenhall has been the centre of the UK lock-making industry for more than 200 years. Labour dominates in the Walsall town wards while the Conservatives perform well in Bloxwich, home to large-scale new housing developments. Surrey county councillor Helen Clack will challenge for the Conservatives.

Walsall South

Labour notional majority of 7,910; notional turnout: 59.9%

PARTY	2005 CANDIDATE	NOTIONAL 2005 VOTES	NOTIONAL 2005 % VOTE	PPC FOR NEXT GE
Labour	Bruce George MP	18,739	49.2	Bruce George MP
Conservative	Kabir Sabar	10,829	28.4	Thelma Matuk
Lib Dem	Mohamed Hanif Asmal	3,738	9.8	n/a
Others		4,783	12.6	

Comprising the southern wards of the industrial town of Walsall, this is a constituency the Conservatives could only hope to win in a landslide election year. The reason for Labour's traditional strength here is clear: more than a quarter of local residents occupy social housing and manufacturing dominates the local employment market. There is a diverse ethnic mix in this constituency with substantial amounts of Muslims (12.6%), Sikhs (5.1%) and Hindus (3.6%) making their homes here. While traditionally a solid Labour seat, Walsall North is ordinarily less susceptible to large swings than other seats and rarely returns its MPs with overwhelming majorities. One of the longest-serving members of Parliament, Labour incumbent Bruce George will hope to defeat Conservative Richard Hunt to secure a tenth term in the House of Commons.

Warley

Labour notional majority of 11,206; notional turnout: 57.2%

PARTY	2005 CANDIDATE	NOTIONAL 2005 VOTES	NOTIONAL 2005 % VOTE	PPC FOR NEXT GE
Labour	John Spellar MP	19,232	54.9	John Spellar MP
Conservative	Karen Bissell	8,026	22.9	Jas Parmer
Lib Dem	Tony Ferguson	4,635	13.2	n/a
Others		3,133	8.9	

Warwick & Leamington

Labour notional majority of 4,393; notional turnout: 65.7%

PARTY	2005 CANDIDATE	NOTIONAL 2005 VOTES	NOTIONAL 2005 % VOTE	PPC FOR NEXT GE
Labour	James Plaskitt MP	18,980	44.7	James Plaskitt MP
Conservative	Chris White	14,587	34.4	Chris White
Lib Dem	Linda Forbes	6,739	15.9	Alan Beddow
Others		2,156	5.1	

One of the Conservative Party's narrowest misses at the 2005 general election, major boundary changes which transfer the safe Tory wards of Lapworth, Leek Wootton and Radford Semele to the new Kenilworth & Southam seat have boosted the notional Labour majority here from 266 to more than 5,000. Despite their outward attractiveness – and a considerable amount of residual Conservative support – both the towns of Warwick and Leamington include pockets of pockets of real poverty in the Clarendon and Willes areas, which boosts Labour. This seat will see a rematch of the 2005 contest with sitting Labour MP James Plaskitt again battling Conservative Chris White to retain his seat.

North Warwickshire

Labour notional majority of 6,684; notional turnout: 62.8%

PARTY	2005 CANDIDATE	NOTIONAL 2005 VOTES	NOTIONAL 2005 % VOTE	PPC FOR NEXT GE
Labour	Mike O'Brien MP	20,735	47.4	Mike O'Brien MP
Conservative	Ian Gibb	14,051	32.1	Dan Byles
Lib Dem	Jerry Roodhouse	5,923	13.5	n/a
Others		3,065	7.0	

Gained by shadow Cabinet Office Secretary Francis Maude at the height of the 1983 Conservative landslide, North Warwickshire returned to its Labour roots in 1992. The constituency is set in the heart of the former Warwickshire coalfield, taking in the towns of Bedworth, Atherstone and Coleshill. While coal-mining has long since vanished, the area retains a strong link with light manufacturing and industry. The Conservatives have made strong advances in the past years, taking control of both Nuneaton & Bedworth and North Warwickshire councils from Labour. As a rule, urban areas in this constituency tend to favour Labour while the many rural areas which house commuters to Birmingham and Coventry are more inclined towards the Tories. Dan Byles, who will contest the seat for the Conservatives, earned a place in *Guinness World Records* by trekking to the North Pole and rowing across the Atlantic Ocean.

West Bromwich East

Labour notional majority of 11,947; notional turnout: 58.2%

PARTY	2005 CANDIDATE	NOTIONAL 2005 VOTES	NOTIONAL 2005 % VOTE	PPC FOR NEXT GE
Labour	Tom Watson MP	20,183	55.8	Tom Watson MP
Conservative	Rosemary Bromwich	8,236	22.8	n/a
Lib Dem	Ian Garrett	4,464	12.3	n/a
Others		3,317	9.2	

West Bromwich West

Labour notional majority of 9,821; notional turnout: 51.6%

PARTY	2005 CANDIDATE	NOTIONAL 2005 VOTES	NOTIONAL 2005 % VOTE	PPC FOR NEXT GE
Labour	Adrian Bailey MP	17,058	53.7	Adrian Bailey MP
Conservative	Mimi Harker	7,237	22.8	n/a
Lib Dem	Martyn Smith	3,229	10.2	n/a
Others		4,258	13.4	

Wolverhampton North East

Labour notional majority of 8,628; notional turnout: 55.0%

PARTY	2005 CANDIDATE	NOTIONAL 2005 VOTES	NOTIONAL 2005 % VOTE	PPC FOR NEXT GE
Labour	Ken Purchase MP	18,787	54.7	Emma Reynolds
Conservative	Alexander Robson	10,159	29.6	Julie Rook
Lib Dem	David Jack	3,996	11.6	n/a
Others		1,402	4.1	

Wolverhampton South East

Labour notional majority of 12,309; notional turnout: 52.2%

PARTY	2005 CANDIDATE	NOTIONAL 2005 VOTES	NOTIONAL 2005 % VOTE	PPC FOR NEXT GE
Labour	Pat McFadden MP	20,025	59.5	Pat McFadden MP
Conservative	James Fairbairn	7,716	22.9	Ken Wood
Lib Dem	David Murray	4,148	12.3	n/a
Others		1,761	5.2	

Wolverhampton South West

Labour notional majority of 2,114; notional turnout: 63.0%

PARTY	2005 CANDIDATE	NOTIONAL 2005 VOTES	NOTIONAL 2005 % VOTE	PPC FOR NEXT GE
Labour	Rob Marris MP	17,288	43.4	Rob Marris MP
Conservative	Sandip Verma	15,174	38.1	Paul Uppal
Lib Dem	Colin Ross	5,364	13.5	n/a
Others		1,967	4.9	

A socially polarised West Midlands marginal, Wolverhampton South West will be forever known as Enoch Powell's former constituency. Labour support here is strongest in the densely populated St Peter's ward, a city centre area with an unemployment rate of nearly four times the national average. The Conservatives could not possibly be more dominant in Tettenhall, a pleasant suburb whose detached houses, tree-lined avenues and ornate village green are faintly reminiscent of the Surrey commuter belt. Wolverhampton South West is an ethnically diverse constituency with one of the highest Sikh populations in the country (8.2%) as well as a substantial number of Hindu (4.4%), black (4.4%) and Muslim (3.6%) residents. It is a mark of how far things have come since Mr Powell's time as MP here that the Conservatives' candidate will be Sikh businessman Paul Uppal. He will face Labour incumbent and 2008 Backbencher of the Year Rob Marris MP.

Worcester

Labour notional majority of 3,144; notional turnout: 64.4%

PARTY	2005 CANDIDATE	NOTIONAL 2005 VOTES	NOTIONAL 2005 % VOTE	PPC FOR NEXT GE
Labour	Michael Foster MP	19,421	41.9	Michael Foster MP
Conservative	Margaret Harper	16,277	35.1	Robin Walker
Lib Dem	Mary Dhonau	7,557	16.3	n/a
Others		3,133	6.8	

From 'pebbledash man' to 'Holby City woman', every election has a stereotypical voter political parties declare key to their election-winning efforts. In 1997 it was the turn of 'Worcester woman' – a middle income West Midlands woman. The Worcester constituency, which broke decisively for Labour in 1997, is a diverse mix of manufacturing and professional industries, inner-city terraces and pleasant commuter suburbia. Labour are strongest in the urban Worcester wards, scoring big leads in the Gorse Hill and Nunnery areas, while the Conservatives perform best in Warndon Parish and Bedwardine just outside the city. While the 2009 Worcestershire County Council elections were deeply disappointing for Labour, the party retained the social housing-dominated St John and Gorse Hill & Warndon wards. Incumbent Labour MP and international Development Minister Michael Foster will face a challenge from Conservative Robin Walker.

Mid Worcestershire

Conservative notional majority of 12,906; notional turnout: 66.5%

PARTY	2005 CANDIDATE	NOTIONAL 2005 VOTES	NOTIONAL 2005 % VOTE	PPC FOR NEXT GE
Conservative	Peter Luff MP	24,246	51.3	Peter Luff MP
Labour	Matthew Gregson	11,340	24.0	Karl Turner
Lib Dem	Margaret Rowley	9,575	20.3	Margaret Rowley
Others		2,060	4.4	

West Worcestershire

Conservative notional majority of 3,053; notional turnout: 70.0%

PARTY	2005 CANDIDATE	NOTIONAL 2005 VOTES	NOTIONAL 2005 % VOTE	PPC FOR NEXT GE
Conservative	Michael Spicer MP	22,756	45.0	Harriet Baldwin
Lib Dem	Tom Wells	19,703	38.9	Richard Burt
Labour	Qamar Bhatti	5,299	10.5	n/a
Others		2,865	5.7	

The Wrekin

Conservative notional majority of 1,187; notional turnout: 65.8%

PARTY	2005 CANDIDATE	NOTIONAL 2005 VOTES	NOTIONAL 2005 % VOTE	PPC FOR NEXT GE
Conservative	Mark Pritchard MP	17,531	42.1	Mark Pritchard MP
Labour	Peter Bradley	16,344	39.3	Paul Kalinauckas
Lib Dem	Bill Tomlinson	6,248	15.0	n/a
Others		1,501	3.6	

Wyre Forest

Independent notional majority of 4,613; notional turnout: 63.9%

PARTY	2005 CANDIDATE	NOTIONAL 2005 VOTES	NOTIONAL 2005 % VOTE	PPC FOR NEXT GE
Independent	Richard Taylor MP	18,739	38.6	Richard Taylor MP
Conservative	Mark Garnier	14,126	29.1	Mark Garnier
Labour	Marc Bayliss	10,944	22.6	Nigel Knowles
Others		4,697	9.7	

In 2001, retired consultant physician Dr Richard Taylor shocked the political establishment by seizing the Wyre Forest constituency from Labour on an Independent ticket, protesting at the closure of the local hospital's A&E department. Re-elected in 2005, he is the first Independent MP to secure a second term since the 1945 general election. The constituency is centred on the light-industrial town of Kidderminster, large parts of rural Worcestershire and the attractive town of Stourport. Until recently the largest party on Wyre Forest District Council, Dr Taylor's Independent Kidderminster Hospital and Health Concern are now placed second behind the Conservatives, who took outright control in 2008. This is one of the few strongholds of the old Liberal Party, who hold six council seats here to Labour's and the Liberal Democrats' two apiece. The incumbent will be challenged by Conservative Mark Garnier and Labour county councillor Nigel Knowles.

North Midlands

Three critically important counties form our North Midlands region: Cheshire, Derbyshire and Nottinghamshire (although in the Registrar General's standard regions of England, the first named is included in the North West and the latter two in the East Midlands). In 2005, Labour won twenty-four of the thirty-two constituencies, and the Tories just seven – the Liberal Democrats' sole victory was at Chesterfield. This shows that Labour's national success in forming a government has been based on extending their achievement beyond the big cities and metropolitan areas. However, no fewer than eleven of their seats are vulnerable to a Conservative breakthrough at the next general election – and if the majority tenure does indeed shift between the major parties in the North Midlands, it will both symbolise and play a significant part in the first shift in power for thirteen years.

Two developments since 2005 need to be addressed. The first is that at Crewe & Nantwich on 22 May 2008 the Conservatives achieved their first by-election gain from Labour for no less than thirty years (Ilford North, 1978), and their first of any kind since beating Bruce Douglas-Mann, who had offered himself for re-election during the Falklands War in 1982 following his defection to the SDP. Edward Timpson achieved a swing of nearly 18 per cent, defeating the daughter of the formidable late MP Gwyneth Dunwoody. This was widely seen as proof of the establishment of David Cameron's remodelled Conservative party as the likely next government, but much more significant would be the retention of Crewe & Nantwich at the general election itself.

Secondly, boundary changes mean that there will now be one more seat in the region, making thirty-three in all. The extra constituency is Mid Derbyshire. Although this seems certain to provide a safe seat for the Tory candidate Pauline Latham, in fact paradoxically it is the result of something of a Labour coup in the review process. Mid Derbyshire includes largely Conservative parts of four current seats including three Labour marginals: Derby North, Erewash and Amber Valley. Labour's idea was to make each of these safer, and they managed to persuade the neutral Boundary Commission to accept their plan, even though there is little other rhyme or reason to the new seat. In a final twist, though, the plot may backfire, as even on new boundaries Labour could still lose Erewash and Amber Valley now the required 8 per cent swing to the Tories seems plausible; while Derby North has been converted into a three-way marginal, with the Liberal Democrats notionally just in second place (see *One to Watch* below).

There are two other Labour seats in Derbyshire that will fall on much lesser swings. Despite its name, the High Peak constituency is more dominated by the five towns of Buxton, Glossop, New Mills, Chapel-en-le-Frith and Whaley Bridge than by the National Park – most of the best known parts of which are either in safely Conservative West Derbyshire (which is indeed to be renamed Derbyshire Dales, like its council) or beyond the county boundaries. High Peak is only won by Labour when they form a comfortable overall majority government, as in 1966 and since 1997. With the largest employer – Turner & Newall brake linings – having suffered from serious problems with its pension plan, there is little doubt that Andrew Bingham will regain it for the Tories. At the other end of the county, South Derbyshire, which was Edwina Currie's seat, is also likely to fall; her conqueror (in a political sense) Mark Todd has already announced his retirement. It could well be that Labour only hold Margaret Beckett's Derby South, made much safer by the boundary changes, and their seats on the former coalfield in the east of the county, including, of course, the Beast's lair in Bolsover.

The Nottingham conurbation is so drawn in parliamentary terms that there are three fairly safe Labour seats in the city itself, and two suburban marginals which swing with the tide. If they do so again, this will be bad news for Vernon Coaker in Gedling (the eastern suburbs) and Broxtowe to the west – despite the activity of Nick Palmer, the resident MP, on Politicalbetting.com, a fashionable website for political habitués. In order for David Cameron to win a substantial overall majority, two other Nottinghamshire divisions may fall. An 8 per cent swing is required in Sherwood, known in recent decades less for Robin Hood than for the coalfield which defied Arthur Scargill in the 1980s. Sherwood has been won by the Tories before, on both sides of that strike, in 1983 and 1987. However Bassetlaw in the far north of the county (named after a medieval hundred, or group of parishes) has been held by Labour since 1935, and its capture on a swing of over 9 per cent would be a sure indicator of a Conservative landslide, although they have been helped by the boundary changes which bring in the market town of Retford and lose ex-mining Warsop. Patrick Mercer's Newark becomes even safer, taking 11,000 largely Conservative voters that Kenneth Clarke can easily afford to lose in Rushcliffe.

There are three Tory targets in Cheshire, as at present constituted – leaving aside those parts of the historic county in Merseyside and Greater Manchester, but including Halton and Warrington boroughs which straddle the old border with Lancashire on the river Mersey. One of these only requires a 1 per cent swing, one will be won by whoever becomes the largest party, and one will only be won if the Conservatives are strong enough to gain an overall majority; this means that Cheshire will offer series of benchmarks by which to judge the next election result. Labour will win again unless the Tories take City of Chester, which they last held when Gyles Brandreth was MP up to 1997. Minor boundary changes reduce the constituency to be identical with the old city council area (since April 2009 Cheshire has been reorganised solely in unitary authorities), which at least pushes

Labour's overall majority into four figures, but they were fully 30 per cent behind the Conservatives in the final council elections in May 2007 – in fact they were in third place. A swing of just over 4 per cent would lead to a change of hands in Warrington South, which mainly consists of middle-class suburbs such as Stockton Heath and Grappenhall south of the Mersey and the Manchester Ship Canal. Helen Southworth is one of a surprisingly large number of the 1997 intake retiring from the Commons, which may make David Mowat's chances of a gain easier. A much harder task, but one which will need to be achieved if the Conservatives are to win an overall majority, is to be found in Ellesmere Port & Neston at the southern end of the Wirral peninsula. This challenge has been entrusted to a young Bury councillor and ex-naval officer, Stuart Penketh.

Overall, the North Midlands is one of the regions most typified by two-party contests. Apart from Derby North, the Liberal Democrats' main interest lies in holding Chesterfield for a third term, Paul Holmes having originally gained the seat when Tony Benn finally retired from Parliament after over fifty years' (interrupted) service in 2001. 'Minor' parties are likely to make relatively little impact, although there is a pocket of BNP support around Heanor in Derbyshire's Amber Valley. More than a third of the seats in this region are marginal, and if the opinion poll ratings through most of 2009 prove a lasting indicator, the Conservatives may win nearly all of them – and this will put David Cameron into 10 Downing Street.

Target seats

SEAT	SWING REQUIRED %	MP	CHALLENGER
Conservative from Labour			
City of Chester	1.2	Christine Russell	Stephen Mosley
High Peak	2.0	Tom Levitt	Andrew Bingham
Broxtowe	2.3	Nick Palmer	Anna Soubry
South Derbyshire	2.8	Mark Todd*	Heather Wheeler
Warrington South	4.1	Helen Southworth*	David Mowat
Gedling	4.9	Vernon Coaker	Bruce Laughton
Amber Valley	6.3	Judy Mallaber	Nigel Mills
Erewash	7.9	Liz Blackman	Jessica Lee
Sherwood	8.0	Paddy Tipping	Mark Spencer
Ellesmere Port & Neston	8.0	Andrew Miller	Stuart Penketh
Derby North	8.1	Bob Laxton	Stephen Mold
Bassetlaw	9.0	John Mann	Keith Girling
Lib Dem from Labour			
Derby North	7.3	Bob Laxton	Lucy Care
Labour from Conservatives			
Crewe & Nantwich	9.5**	Edward Timpson	
Labour from Lib Dems			
Chesterfield	3.2	Paul Holmes	Toby Perkins

**since 2008 by-election*

Derby North

Labour notional majority of 5,691; notional turnout: 62.4%

PARTY	2005 CANDIDATE	NOTIONAL 2005 VOTES	NOTIONAL 2005 % VOTE	PPC FOR NEXT GE
Labour	Robert Laxton MP	16,420	42.1	Robert Laxton MP
Lib Dem	Jeremy Beckett	10,729	27.5	Lucy Care
Conservative	Richard Aitken-Davies	10,120	25.9	Stephen Mold
Others		1,763	4.5	

Traditionally a Labour–Conservative marginal, this constituency is considerably more middle class and residential than Margaret Beckett's Derby South berth. Labour chances of retaining the seat are helped considerably by boundary changes which transfer many of the constituency's safest Tory wards – namely Allestree, Oakwood and Spondon – to the newly formed Mid Derbyshire constituency. Following boundary changes, this is now a three-way marginal with little more than 5,000 votes separating Labour from the third-placed Conservatives. Support for Labour and the Liberal Democrats is strongest in the Abbey and Darley areas in the city centre, while the Conservatives perform strongest in the village of Mickleover to the west of the city. The Conservatives and Liberal Democrats were essentially tied at the 2008 city council elections with Labour trailing far behind. Incumbent Labour MP Bob Laxton will face a challenge from Conservative Stephen Mold and Liberal Democrat Lucy Care.

Derby South

Labour notional majority of 11,655; notional turnout: 64.6%

PARTY	2005 CANDIDATE	NOTIONAL 2005 VOTES	NOTIONAL 2005 % VOTE	PPC FOR NEXT GE
Labour	Margaret Beckett MP	21,370	53.2	Margaret Beckett MP
Lib Dem	Lucy Care	9,715	24.2	n/a
Conservative	David Brackenbury	7,946	19.8	Jack Perschke
Others		1,170	2.9	

Derbyshire Dales

Conservative notional majority of 8,810; notional turnout: 67.5%

PARTY	2005 CANDIDATE	NOTIONAL 2005 VOTES	NOTIONAL 2005 % VOTE	PPC FOR NEXT GE
Conservative	Patrick McLoughlin MP	19,684	46.5	Patrick McLoughlin MP
Labour	David Menon	10,874	25.7	Colin Swindell
Lib Dem	Ray Dring	10,308	24.4	n/a
Others		1,459	3.4	

Derbyshire

Conservative notional majority of 5,329; notional turnout: 66.5%

	2005 CANDIDATE	NOTIONAL 2005 VOTES	NOTIONAL 2005 % VOTE	PPC FOR NEXT GE
Conservative	n/a	20,050	47.2	Pauline Latham
	n/a	14,721	34.6	Hardyal Dhindsa
	n/a	6,809	16.0	Sally McIntosh
		923	2.2	

Derbyshire

notional majority of 9,564; notional turnout: 61.1%

	2005 CANDIDATE	NOTIONAL 2005 VOTES	NOTIONAL 2005 % VOTE	PPC FOR NEXT GE
	Natascha Engel	20,675	48.2	Natascha Engel MP
	Dominic Johnson	11,111	25.9	Huw Merriman
	Tom Snowdon	9,206	21.5	Richard Bull
		1,871	4.4	

One to watch: Derby North

Actual majority 2005: Labour 3,757 (8.6%) over Con
Notional majority 2005: Labour 5,691 (14.6%) over LD
Labour candidate: Bob Laxton MP
Lib Dem candidate: Lucy Care
Conservative candidate: Stephen Mold

Beware; this is not the Labour–Conservative marginal Derby North that existed up to and including the 2005 election. As a political contest it has been transformed by the major boundary changes in the county which involve the creation of a new Mid Derbyshire constituency, the largest single element (47 per cent) of which come from the old North. Knock-on effects mean that over a third of the new North (that is, 30,500 voters) is taken from the former Derby South. The wards which are removed from this constituency are Allestree, the most middle class and affluent residential neighbourhood in the whole city, Spondon (generally Conservative despite the impression given by the dominance of the British Celanese (now Acordis) factory and the sewage works responsible for the infamous 'Spondon pong') and Oakwood, the huge modern estate carved out of the old Breadsall ward. In exchange Derby North gains 26,000 voters (over a third of its total electorate) from South, including the Liberal Democrats' two strongest areas – Littleover, a south-western suburb, and the inner heart of the city. These wards helped make the Lib Dems strong challengers to Margaret Beckett in Derby South in 2005, and propel that party into a narrow second place in the notional figures for Derby North. However the Conservatives are not far behind in third place – they need an 8 per cent wing from Labour, the Lib Dems 7 per cent. If the Labour vote collapses in 2010, as seems entirely possible, either rival could take advantage. In the May 2008 council elections, the Liberal Democrats were first in the wards which make up the new Derby North with 9,805 votes, the Tories second with 7.026, and Labour slumped to third with 5,656. However, the Lib Dems are known to do disproportionately well in local elections, and in fact they then became the largest party on Derby council. The Conservatives can advance from third to first in Derby North – and if they do, they will be on course for an overall majority in the Commons.

Amber Valley

Labour notional majority of 5,512; notional turnout: 64.0%

PARTY	2005 CANDIDATE	NOTIONAL 2005 VOTES	NOTIONAL 2005 % VOTE	PPC FOR NEXT GE
Labour	Judy Mallaber MP	20,427	46.5	Judy Mallaber MP
Conservative	Gillian Shaw	14,915	33.9	Nigel Mills
Lib Dem	Kate Smith	5,446	12.4	Tom Snowdon
Others		3,185	7.2	

Ashfield

Labour notional majority of 10,370; notional turnout: 57.1%

PARTY	2005 CANDIDATE	NOTIONAL 2005 VOTES	NOTIONAL 2005 % VOTE	PPC FOR NEXT GE
Labour	Geoff Hoon MP	20,801	48.7	Geoff Hoon MP
Conservative	Giles Inglis-Jones	10,431	24.4	n/a
Lib Dem	Wendy Johnson	5,910	13.8	Jason Zadrozny
Others		5,569	13.0	

Bassetlaw

Labour notional majority of 8,256; notional turnout: 60.8%

PARTY	2005 CANDIDATE	NOTIONAL 2005 VOTES	NOTIONAL 2005 % VOTE	PPC FOR NEXT GE
Labour	John Mann MP	24,413	53.0	John Mann MP
Conservative	Jonathan Sheppard	16,157	35.1	Keith Girling
Lib Dem	David Dobbie	5,507	12.0	n/a
Others				

The name of a council area rather than a town, the Bassetlaw constituency is largely centred on the town of Worksop and the surrounding rural area. Located around 20 miles south-east of Sheffield, Bassetlaw is a former coal-mining area whose economy has adjusted radically in the past two decades to focus on light industry. Labour's support is strongest in Worksop, although recent Conservative advances in the town have helped the party gain overall control of Bassetlaw District Council. Boundary changes which shift the safe Labour Meden ward to neighbouring Mansfield slightly improve Conservative chances here. John Mann, the Labour MP here since 2001, will be challenged by Conservative Keith Girling.

Bolsover

Labour notional majority of 19,260; notional turnout: 56.1%

PARTY	2005 CANDIDATE	NOTIONAL 2005 VOTES	NOTIONAL 2005 % VOTE	PPC FOR NEXT GE
Labour	Dennis Skinner MP	26,331	65.2	Dennis Skinner MP
Lib Dem	Denise Hawksworth	7,071	17.5	Denise Hawksworth
Conservative	Hasan Imam	6,993	17.3	n/a
Others		0	0.0	

Broxtowe

Labour notional majority of 2,139; notional turnout: 68.9%

PARTY	2005 CANDIDATE	NOTIONAL 2005 VOTES	NOTIONAL 2005 % VOTE	PPC FOR NEXT GE
Labour	Nick Palmer MP	20,089	41.7	Nick Palmer MP
Conservative	Bob Seely	17,950	37.3	Anna Soubry
Lib Dem	David Watts	7,756	16.1	David Watts
Others		2,351	4.9	

Located in Nottingham's eastern suburbs close to the border with Derbyshire, the Broxtowe constituency has been represented by Labour's Dr Nick Palmer since the 1997 general election. With around 20,000 residents apiece, the two largest towns here are Beeston and Stapleford – both of which are largely populated by professional and managerial workers. The constituency is generally suburban in nature, although patches of Conservative-inclined rural territory are found towards the north. Aside from commuters to nearby Nottingham, a large number of local jobs are provided by the software industry. More than three quarters of homes in the constituency are owner occupied, with only one in ten residents living in social housing stock. Dr Palmer, a sexilingual former world-champion of the boardgame Diplomacy and regular commentator on PoliticalBetting.com, will be challenged by Conservative barrister Anna Soubry, a former regional television presenter.

City of Chester

Labour notional majority of 973; notional turnout: 64.3%

PARTY	2005 CANDIDATE	NOTIONAL 2005 VOTES	NOTIONAL 2005 % VOTE	PPC FOR NEXT GE
Labour	Christine Russell MP	17,263	39.0	Christine Russell MP
Conservative	Paul Offer	16,290	36.8	Stephen Mosley
Lib Dem	Mia Jones	9,657	21.8	Lizzie Jewkes
Others		1,074	2.4	

Formerly held by television presenter and well-known raconteur Gyles Brandreth, this constituency takes in the historic city of Chester and a slew of attractive villages just outside the city's walls. While Chester is considerably more middle-class than the majority of nearby Merseyside, the constituency is not without pockets of deprivation, particularly in the social housing-dominated wards of Lache Park, Blacon Lodge and Blacon Hall, which heavily favour the Labour Party. The Conservatives, who won a decisive victory in the inaugural 2009 Cheshire West & Chester unitary authority elections, are strongest in the city's suburbs, amassing large leads in the Curzon, Westminster and Saughall areas. While sitting Labour MP Christine Russell has opted for retirement, former Chester City Council deputy leader Stephen Mosley will fight the seat for the Conservatives.

Chesterfield

Lib Dem notional majority of 2,733; notional turnout: 59.9%

PARTY	2005 CANDIDATE	NOTIONAL 2005 VOTES	NOTIONAL 2005 % VOTE	PPC FOR NEXT GE
Lib Dem	Paul Holmes MP	20,190	47.0	Paul Holmes MP
Labour	Simon Rich	17,457	40.6	Toby Perkins
Conservative	Mark Kreling	3,554	8.3	n/a
Others		1,791	4.2	

Congleton

Conservative notional majority of 8,246; notional turnout: 64.1%

PARTY	2005 CANDIDATE	NOTIONAL 2005 VOTES	NOTIONAL 2005 % VOTE	PPC F
Conservative	Ann Winterton MP	21,189	45.4	n/a
Labour	Nicholas Milton	12,943	27.7	Da
Lib Dem	Eleanor Key	12,550	26.9	P
Others		0	0.0	

Crewe & Nantwich

Labour notional majority of 6,999; notional turnout: 59.9%

PARTY	2005 CANDIDATE	NOTIONAL 2005 VOTES	NOTIONAL 2005 % V
Labour	Gwyneth Dunwoody MP	21,860	48.4
Conservative	Eveleigh Moore-Dutton	14,861	32.9
Lib Dem	Paul Roberts	8,421	18
Others		0	

Nominally a Labour-held seat, Crewe & Nantwich has been represented by majority of 7,860 since his by-election in May 2008. Prior to Mr Timpson been represented for 34 years by the formidable Gwyneth Dunwoody, who throughout the 1980s. Located on the direct train line from London, Cr mix of traditionally Labour-supporting terraces and immaculate new h market town of Nantwich, strongly favour the Conservatives. While t' elections for the new Cheshire East unitary authority in May 2008, the party will always be strong here.

South Derbyshire

Labour notional majority of 2,436; notional turnout: 66.9%

PARTY	2005 CANDIDATE	NOTIONAL 2005 VOTES	NOTIONAL 2005 % VOTE	PPC FOR NEXT GE
Labour	Mark Todd MP	19,146	42.9	Michael Edwards
Conservative	Simon Spencer	16,710	37.4	Heather Wheeler
Lib Dem	Deborah Newton-Cook	5,738	12.8	Alexis Diouf
Others		3,069	6.9	

Held for 13 years by controversial former minister Edwina Currie, South Derbyshire delivered Labour a 14,000 majority at the 1997 general election. While a large portion of the constituency is rural and Conservative inclined, the once-thriving industrial town of Swadlincote and former coal-mining area of Woodville lean strongly towards the Labour Party. The 2009 Derbyshire County Council results were a disaster for Labour with the Conservatives gaining seats they had not held since the late 1970s. Conservative Heather Wheeler, the leader of South Derbyshire District Council, will hope to defeat Labour's Michael Edwards to take the seat. The sitting MP, Mark Todd, is retiring.

Eddisbury

Conservative notional majority of 6,408; notional turnout: 65.1%

PARTY	2005 CANDIDATE	NOTIONAL 2005 VOTES	NOTIONAL 2005 % VOTE	PPC FOR NEXT GE
Conservative	Stephen O'Brien MP	20,272	46.9	Stephen O'Brien MP
Labour	Mark Green	13,864	32.1	Pat Merrick
Lib Dem	Joanne Crotty	7,775	18.0	
Others		1,292	3.0	

Ellesmere Port & Neston

Labour notional majority of 6,713; notional turnout: 61.3%

PARTY	2005 CANDIDATE	NOTIONAL 2005 VOTES	NOTIONAL 2005 % VOTE	PPC FOR NEXT GE
Labour	Andrew Miller MP	20,449	48.7	Andrew Miller MP
Conservative	Myles Hogg	13,736	32.7	Stuart Penketh
Lib Dem	Steve Cooke	6,600	15.7	n/a
Others		1,201	2.9	

Andrew Miller captured Ellesmere Port & Neston, a Conservative seat throughout the Thatcher years, for Labour at the 1992 general election and expanded his winning margin to 16,000 votes in 1997. The industry town of Ellesmere Port is home to the country's largest oil and petrol refinery at Stanlow and several chemical production facilities, all major sources of employment locally, although with the decline of British manufacturing, unemployment has become an endemic problem in this constituency. The west of the constituency fits much more easily with Cheshire's 'gin and Jags' image, wards like Parkgate, Willaston and Thornton on the border with the Wirral breaking overwhelmingly for the Conservatives. Bury councillor Stuart Penketh will contest the seat for the Conservatives.

Erewash

Labour notional majority of 6,782; notional turnout: 62.6%

PARTY	2005 CANDIDATE	NOTIONAL 2005 VOTES	NOTIONAL 2005 % VOTE	PPC FOR NEXT GE
Labour	Liz Blackman MP	19,369	44.7	Liz Blackman MP
Conservative	David Simmonds	12,587	29.1	Jessica Lee
Lib Dem	Martin Garnett	5,850	13.5	Martin Garnett
Others		5,503	12.7	

Nestled between Derby and Nottingham, Erewash is a strange name for a constituency that would be better referred to as South East Derbyshire. The seat is largely based around the towns of Ilkeston and Long Eaton, which share dramatically different party political loyalties. Ilkeston, formerly the home to the Stanton ironworks, which closed for the last time in May 2007, is a Labour bastion while Long Eaton and the rural areas surrounding the two towns are considerably more Tory friendly. TV personality and MEP Robert Kilroy-Silk stood for the seat at the last election, achieving a humiliating 5.8% of the vote. Former government whip Liz Blackman will hope to defeat barrister Jessica Lee in her quest to secure a fourth term.

Gedling

Labour notional majority of 4,335; notional turnout: 63.8%

PARTY	2005 CANDIDATE	NOTIONAL 2005 VOTES	NOTIONAL 2005 % VOTE	PPC FOR NEXT GE
Labour	Vernon Coaker MP	20,982	46.6	Vernon Coaker MP
Conservative	Anna Soubry	16,647	37.0	Bruce Laughton
Lib Dem	Raymond Poynter	6,169	13.7	n/a
Others		1,196	2.7	

Located just to the west of Nottingham, the previously safe Conservative seat of Gedling was gained from Andrew Mitchell by Labour at the 1997 general election. The constituency is generally middle class and suburban in nature, taking in the towns of Gedling, Arnold and Carlton and substantial rural areas. The Conservatives are strongest in the semi-rural Woodthorpe and Ravenshead wards while Labour's strength is built around the industrial Netherfield & Colwick. Labour's chances of holding this seat are slightly improved by the loss of the Conservative ward of Lambley to neighbouring Sherwood. Locally, Gedling Borough Council has been narrowly controlled by the Conservatives since May 2007. Sitting MP and Home Office minister Vernon Coaker will face a challenge from Conservative Bruce Laughton.

Halton

Labour notional majority of 16,060; notional turnout: 53.6%

PARTY	2005 CANDIDATE	NOTIONAL 2005 VOTES	NOTIONAL 2005 % VOTE	PPC FOR NEXT GE
Labour	Derek Twigg MP	23,436	63.1	Derek Twigg MP
Conservative	Colin Bloom	7,376	19.9	Ben Jones
Lib Dem	Roger Barlow	6,317	17.0	n/a
Others		0	0.0	

High Peak

Labour notional majority of 1,750; notional turnout: 66.1%

PARTY	2005 CANDIDATE	NOTIONAL 2005 VOTES	NOTIONAL 2005 % VOTE	PPC FOR NEXT GE
Labour	Tom Levitt MP	18,950	41.1	Tom Levitt MP
Conservative	Andrew Bingham	17,200	37.3	Andrew Bingham
Lib Dem	Marc Godwin	8,946	19.4	Steve Sharp
Others		989	2.1	

A curiously named constituency, High Peak is formed of the bulk of the Peak District National Park. As one might expect, the seat is predominantly rural and characterised by dramatic open landscapes yet several small towns are also found within its boundaries. Labour support is generally drawn from the small towns of Buxton, New Mills, Hadfield and Glossop while the Conservatives are strongest in the Manchester commuter villages on the seat's north-west edge. In the 2009 county council elections, the Conservatives outpolled Labour by more than 5,000 votes. While many seats close to large cities have witnessed rapid housing growth in recent years, High Peak's status as a National Park will likely preserve its rural feel for decades to come. Local councillor Andrew Bingham will contest the seat for the Conservatives against sitting Labour MP Tom Levitt.

Macclesfield

Conservative notional majority of 9,464; notional turnout: 62.4%

PARTY	2005 CANDIDATE	NOTIONAL 2005 VOTES	NOTIONAL 2005 % VOTE	PPC FOR NEXT GE
Conservative	Nicholas Winterton MP	22,735	49.6	n/a
Labour	Stephen Carter	13,271	29.0	Alex Bryce
Lib Dem	Catherine O'Brien	8,945	19.5	n/a
Others		848	1.9	

Mansfield

Labour notional majority of 13,776; notional turnout: 56.9%

PARTY	2005 CANDIDATE	NOTIONAL 2005 VOTES	NOTIONAL 2005 % VOTE	PPC FOR NEXT GE
Labour	Alan Meale MP	21,988	50.1	Alan Meale MP
Conservative	Anne Wright	8,212	18.7	n/a
Independent	Stewart Rickersey	7,525	17.1	n/a
Others		6,157	14.0	

Newark

Conservative notional majority of 10,077; notional turnout: 63.3%

PARTY	2005 CANDIDATE	NOTIONAL 2005 VOTES	NOTIONAL 2005 % VOTE	PPC FOR NEXT GE
Conservative	Patrick Mercer MP	22,950	50.5	Patrick Mercer MP
Labour	Jason Reece	12,873	28.3	Ian Campbell
Lib Dem	Stuart Thompstone	8,354	18.4	n/a
Others		1,267	2.8	

Nottingham East

Labour notional majority of 7,083; notional turnout: 48.9%

PARTY	2005 CANDIDATE	NOTIONAL 2005 VOTES	NOTIONAL 2005 % VOTE	PPC FOR NEXT GE
Labour	John Heppell MP	13,651	46.7	John Heppell MP
Conservative	Jim Thornton	6,568	22.5	n/a
Lib Dem	Issan Ghazni	6,389	21.9	n/a
Others		2,632	9.0	

Nottingham North

Labour notional majority of 12,870; notional turnout: 48.4%

PARTY	2005 CANDIDATE	NOTIONAL 2005 VOTES	NOTIONAL 2005 % VOTE	PPC FOR NEXT GE
Labour	Graham Allen MP	18,545	59.1	Graham Allen MP
Conservative	Priti Patel	5,675	18.1	Martin Curtis
Lib Dem	Tim Ball	5,452	17.4	Tim Ball
Others		1,684	5.4	

Nottingham South

Labour notional majority of 6,665; notional turnout: 51.4%

PARTY	2005 CANDIDATE	NOTIONAL 2005 VOTES	NOTIONAL 2005 % VOTE	PPC FOR NEXT GE
Labour	Alan Simpson MP	15,939	45.9	Lilian Greenwood
Conservative	Sudesh Mattu	9,274	26.7	Rowena Holland
Lib Dem	Tony Sutton	8,158	23.5	Tony Sutton
Others		1,347	3.9	

Last held by the Conservatives by the magnificently named Martin Brandon-Bravo, Nottingham South has been represented by Labour's Alan Simpson since the 1992 general election. The constituency takes in the Nottingham's vibrant town centre and the city's growing university in Lenton. Labour support is particularly strong in the Clifton, Radford and Park areas, where a large amount of student and social housing can be found. Conservative support is far more robust in Wollaton, a leafy suburb on the city's western edge. Just over half of the housing in the constituency is owner occupied while almost a fifth is privately rented – unsurprising given that a quarter of local residents are full-time students. With Simpson retiring, Lillian Greenwood will be the Labour candidate while the Conservatives are fielding Rowena Holland.

Rushcliffe

Conservative notional majority of 9,932; notional turnout: 69.9%

PARTY	2005 CANDIDATE	NOTIONAL 2005 VOTES	NOTIONAL 2005 % VOTE	PPC FOR NEXT GE
Conservative	Kenneth Clarke MP	23,156	48.0	Kenneth Clarke MP
Labour	Edward Gamble	13,224	27.4	Andrew Clayworth
Lib Dem	Karrar Khan	8,351	17.3	n/a
Others		3,491	7.2	

Sherwood

Labour notional majority of 6,869; notional turnout: 61.8%

PARTY	2005 CANDIDATE	NOTIONAL 2005 VOTES	NOTIONAL 2005 % VOTE	PPC FOR NEXT GE
Labour	Paddy Tipping MP	21,327	49.4	Paddy Tipping MP
Conservative	Bruce Laughton	14,458	33.5	Mark Spencer
Lib Dem	Peter Harris	5,806	13.4	n/a
Others		1,601	3.7	

Located at the heart of the Nottinghamshire coalfield and taking in parts of the Newark & Sherwood, Ashfield and Gedling council areas, the Sherwood constituency has been held by Labour's Paddy Tipping since the 1992 general election. With almost 30,000 residents, the town of Hucknall is the largest population centre in the constituency. Located seven miles north-west of Nottingham on the city's tramline, the town has moved away from its coal-mining past and is now regarded as a relatively quiet slice of suburbia. At the 2009 Nottinghamshire County Council elections Labour managed to win only one seat in the constituency, in the rural former mining village of Ollerton. The Conservative candidate will be local councillor Mark Spencer.

Tatton

Conservative notional majority of 1,1537; notional turnout: 63.9%

PARTY	2005 CANDIDATE	NOTIONAL 2005 VOTES	NOTIONAL 2005 % VOTE	PPC FOR NEXT GE
Conservative	George Osborne MP	21,415	51.5	George Osborne MP
Labour	Justin Madders	9,878	23.7	Richard Jackson
Lib Dem	Ainsley Arnold	9,066	21.8	Craig Browne
Others		1,245	3.0	

Warrington North

Labour notional majority of 11,382; notional turnout: 55.3%

PARTY	2005 CANDIDATE	NOTIONAL 2005 VOTES	NOTIONAL 2005 % VOTE	PPC FOR NEXT GE
Labour	Helen Jones MP	21,101	52.9	Helen Jones MP
Conservative	Andrew Ferryman	9,719	24.4	Paul Campbell
Lib Dem	Peter Walker	7,449	18.7	Dave Eccles
Others		1,630	4.1	

Warrington South

Labour notional majority of 4,337; notional turnout: 61.5%

PARTY	2005 CANDIDATE	NOTIONAL 2005 VOTES	NOTIONAL 2005 % VOTE	PPC FOR NEXT GE
Labour	Helen Southworth MP	19,503	41.2	n/a
Conservative	Fiona Bruce	15,166	32.1	David Mowat
Lib Dem	Ian Marks	11,361	24.0	Jo Crotty
Others		1,286	2.7	

Last won by the Conservatives at the 1987 general election, the Warrington South constituency is largely middle class, populated by commuters to nearby Manchester and Liverpool. While lacking in local amenities, this is a broadly pleasant residential seat in which more than four in five homes are owner occupied. Conservative support is at its strongest in the semi-rural areas abutting the neighbouring Tatton constituency, while the Warrington town wards are safe for Labour. Boundary changes which transfer the Bewsey & Whitecross ward into this seat from Warrington South mean that this constituency is now slightly more favourable towards Labour. While on a parliamentary level this seat is a battle between Labour and the Tories, the Liberal Democrats are fast gathering pace in local government. With the sitting Labour MP, Helen Southworth, opting for retirement, Conservative businessman David Mowat will hope to take the seat.

Weaver Vale

Labour notional majority of 5,277; notional turnout: 55.6%

PARTY	2005 CANDIDATE	NOTIONAL 2005 VOTES	NOTIONAL 2005 % VOTE	PPC FOR NEXT GE
Labour	Mike Hall MP	17,196	45.7	Mike Hall MP
Conservative	Jonathan Mackie	11,919	31.7	Graham Evans
Lib Dem	Trevor Griffiths	7,435	19.8	n/a
Others		1,072	2.8	

The name of a council area rather than a town, the Weaver Vale constituency is largely composed of the western Cheshire towns of Northwich and Frodsham. Held by Labour since its creation in 1997, this constituency is an uneasy mix of wealthy Cheshire villages and heavy industry. Northwich, the largest town in the seat, is home to a thriving industrial sector with chemical processing providing a major source of jobs in the area. Located between Chester and Warrington, the attractive town of Frodsham is considerably more middle class, ordinarily offering the Conservatives its steadfast support. The area is nearly exclusively white with owner occupation levels standing at close to three quarters. The Conservatives control the Cheshire West & Chester unitary authority with a commanding majority. Sitting Labour MP Mike Hall will be challenged by Conservative Graham Evans.

North West England

The North West of England – here defined as the metropolitan boroughs within Greater Manchester and Merseyside, and the administratively separate county of Lancashire (a geographical entity which historically included the first two areas, of course) – has always been a key region in deciding the democratic choice of government of the people of Britain. The next general election will prove no exception. David Cameron's Conservatives will have to demonstrate an ability to make a very large number of gains in the north of England as well as the Midlands and south; and there are indeed a plethora of opportunities in the tight marginals of the North West.

Two features of the pattern of contest here may be picked out immediately. One is that there are actually fewer super-close seats based on 2005 notional results than might be expected. For example, the 'easiest' Tory gain, Bury North, ranks only at number 33 on the national Conservative target list of currently Labour seats. However this fact does not in any way suggest the marginals in this region are any the less important; quite the reverse, in fact. Most of those seats throughout Britain requiring a very small swing will not decide who forms the new government, as the Tories could take the twenty or so with the smallest majorities and still leave Labour with an overall majority. The most important constituencies are those which need to fall in order to make the Conservatives the largest party, or give them an overall majority. There are many in these key categories in the North West – in fact nearly twenty, if potential gains from the Liberal Democrats are also counted. This number is not exceeded in any other region.

Secondly, there is a myth that the Tories will need to make substantial advances in the big northern cities and metropolitan boroughs if they are to win the general election. This is not true. The majority of their vital targets even within this predominantly urban region are not in Merseyside or Greater Manchester, but in the shire county of Lancashire. This applies both to seats needed to become the largest party, and in those needed to go on and secure an overall majority. Indeed well over half of the sixteen seats now to be allocated to Lancashire are critical marginals – the highest proportion of any county.

The Conservatives could be said to have already benefited in Lancashire from the gain of an extra constituency awarded by the boundary commission. This is Wyre & Preston North, just over half of which is drawn from the marginal Lancaster &

Wyre, gained from Labour at the 2005 election, and the rest from a reduction in the electorate of true-blue Ribble Valley. This converts Ben Wallace's tenure here to utter safety. On the other hand, the Tories will have to take the city of Lancaster all over again, now that it is paired with Fleetwood, with a swing of over 4 per cent. The knock-on effects of a major boundary change such as this addition of a seat are further shown by the effect as one moves down the coast further into the Fylde peninsula. Fleetwood is a Labour-inclined and somewhat depressed port, previously paired with Blackpool North. Its loss makes Joan Humble's seat more vulnerable, as indicated by it being renamed Blackpool North & Cleveleys. It is all a matter of swings and roundabouts in this part of Lancashire.

Elsewhere, all other parts of the county are full of marginals. In the east, in the tight-knit communities of owner-occupied terraced houses in valleys carved by the rivers flowing down from the Pennines, Labour are striving with some desperation to hold on to Pendle, Rossendale & Darwen and Hyndburn. Pendle is named after the great and mysterious hill of that name, historically known for its witches, that looms above the communities which include Nelson and Colne; Gordon Prentice may have to resort to sorcery to ward off the challenge of the Tory candidate, Andrew Stephenson, who needs a swing of less than 3 per cent since 2005. In Rossendale and Darwen, almost all the wards which make up the seat are marginal, and the Conservatives won almost all of them in 2008. Hyndburn, based on Accrington and containing the very heart of the famous Lancashire cricket league, needs a larger swing of 7 per cent, but the Tories will need to take seats like this for the overall majority that many opinion polls suggest is within their grasp; and Greg Pope is one of four Labour MPs in key seats who have already announced their intention to stand down at the next election. Chorley presents an even harder task, but it was held by for the Conservatives until 1997 on only slightly more favourable boundaries by Den Dover (who has recently been expelled from the party after a fraud charge incurred during his time as Chief Whip of the Tories in the European Parliament).

In the north of Lancashire, a classic swing marginal, likely to be won by whichever party comes out of the election as the largest, is South Ribble, centred on Leyland (as in commercial road vehicles), where David Borrow defends a majority of just over 2,000. Harder for the Tories will be Morecambe & Lunesdale, which despite the image of the seaside and its attractive rural hinterland remains almost drawn to give Labour a good chance. Not only is Morecambe itself battling to reverse a long period of depression, but the seat includes the most deprived suburb of the city of Lancaster, Skerton, as it is located on the west bank of the Lune.

The location of the West Lancashire division speaks for itself, but it is made up of two very disparate parts, whose relative balance influences the outcome: the very Conservative communities around Ormskirk on the flat rich dark soil of the 'moss' or plain, versus the massively Labour (but low-turnout) wards of the new town of Skelmersdale in a more windy, hilly, bleak setting. Overall Adrian Owens will need a swing of just over 7 per cent to displace Rosie Cooper, but much depends on which half of the seat is keener to vote. Finally, before moving to the metropolitan areas, it is worth mentioning that at the very outer edge of marginality are two larger towns with significant Asian populations. In Blackburn, Jack Straw's position is not quite completely safe, with the Tories in second place, while in Burnley the Liberal Democrats are best placed to advance if the traditional Labour vote should threaten to defect to Independents or to the BNP, as it notably has in local elections in the borough. The announced retirement of Labour MP Kitty Ussher (at the age of thirty-eight) in the wake of the expenses issue has further muddied the waters here.

All this interest in Lancashire is not to say that there is none in Merseyside and Greater Manchester. It is true that most seats in the two conurbations will remain safe for Labour, but both Conservatives and Liberal Democrats do have irons in the fire. In addition (or perhaps subtraction), in both metropolitan areas a Labour seat has been removed in the boundary changes – the awkwardly named Knowsley North & Sefton East in Merseyside, and Eccles in Greater Manchester. What is more, minor changes have notionally moved Wirral West (the affluent commuting belt around Hoylake) into the Tory column for 2005, so the TV presenter Esther McVey technically had to defend rather than gain the seat from Stephen Hesford MP. The Conservatives will also have to gain the South division of the Wirral in order to become the largest party in the Commons, and another vital marginal target in Merseyside is Sefton Central (see *One to Watch* below). They will also hope to make a gain from the Liberal Democrats in the upmarket seaside resort of Southport, but the former philosophy teacher John Pugh now looks well established there in the northernmost – and most reluctant – part of the borough of Sefton. If the Tories do win, the new MP will probably be the oldest member of the new intake – the active and well-regarded Ainsdale ward councillor Brenda Porter will be seventy-one at the likely time of the next election.

We should not leave Merseyside without considering the Lib Dems' own chances of advance. Since the first successes of Cyril Carr in establishing a presence for the Liberals on the city council back in the 1960s, followed by the rise of the Alliance, SLD and now the Liberal Democrats in municipal politics, they have always threatened a breakthrough in parliamentary terms in Liverpool. The Lib Dems have now been in control of the council (once known for the antics of Derek Hatton and the Militant Far Left) since 1998. Yet with the single exception of David Alton, an MP from 1979 to 1997, they have flattered to deceive in general elections. Now, boundary changes have concentrated their strongest support in the Liverpool, Wavertree seat (where their local success started four decades ago), and Colin Eldridge needs a swing of just 4.5 per cent to oust Jane Kennedy; but for all the fact that they polled twice as many votes as Labour in the wards making up Wavertree in 2008, one has the suspicion that they will be disappointed once again.

The Liberal Democrats may have more success in Greater Manchester, where they currently hold four seats, though on narrow notional figures Paul Rowen will have to 'regain' Rochdale. The advantages of first-term incumbency may also help them to hold Cheadle against the Conservatives (Mark Hunter having retained it in the first by-election of the 2005 parliament) and the university-influenced Manchester, Withington from Labour. The Lib Dems also have a chance of taking Oldham East & Saddleworth from Labour's Phil Woolas, having selected a new candidate for the challenge in this seat which climbs into the desirable villages on the very edge of the Pennine hills and moors.

The Conservatives are well known to have no councillors at all in the city of Manchester, and they have no chance of a gain there either. However, they do have winnable targets within the other boroughs in Greater Manchester. A swing of only 2.6 per cent would be enough to take Bury North, which consists of the home of black puddings itself together with the small town of Ramsbottom, which is more upmarket a residential area than the name might imply. However, the key to whether the Tories can take power at Westminster probably lies most of all in Bolton, a town known for producing the comedian Peter Kay of *Phoenix Nights*, as well as a ringful of professional wrestlers. It also harbours two key marginal seats, North East and West (where Ruth Kelly is retiring despite favourable boundary changes), each requiring a swing of exactly 6 per cent. If the Conservatives can win both of these, it will be no laughing matter for Labour, who will be in a hammer-lock or 'full nelson' which will probably force them to submit – not just in Bolton, but in the grapple for government itself.

Target seats

SEAT	SWING REQUIRED %	MP	CHALLENGER
Conservative from Labour			
Bury North	2.6	David Chaytor*	David Nuttall
Pendle	2.8	Gordon Prentice	Andrew Stephenson
South Ribble	3.8	David Borrow	Lorraine Fullbrook
Rossendale & Darwen	4.2	Janet Anderson	Jake Berry
Blackpool North & Cleveleys	4.3	Joan Humble	Paul Maynard
Lancaster & Fleetwood	4.5	(Clive Grunshaw)	Eric Ollerenshaw
Wirral South	4.7	Ben Chapman*	Jeff Clarke
Morecambe & Lunesdale	5.8	Geraldine Smith	David Morris
Bolton West	6.0	Ruth Kelly*	Susan Williams
Bolton North East	6.0	David Crausby	Deborah Dunleavy
Sefton Central	6.1	Claire Curtis-Thomas	Debi Jones
Hyndburn	7.0	Greg Pope*	
West Lancashire	7.2	Rosie Cooper	Adrian Owens
Chorley	8.3	Lindsay Hoyle	Alan Cullens
Blackpool South	8.9	Gordon Marsden	Ron Bell
Blackburn	9.8	Jack Straw	
Labour from Conservatives			
Wirral West	0.8	(Esther McVey)	Stephen Hesford MP
Conservative from Lib Dems			
Cheadle	3.8	Mark Hunter	Ben Jeffreys
Southport	4.7	John Pugh	Brenda Porter
Lib Dem from Labour			
Rochdale	0.2	(Simon Danczuk)	Paul Rowen MP
Liverpool, Wavertree	4.5	Jane Kennedy	Colin Eldridge
Oldham East & Saddleworth	5.2	Phil Woolas	Elwyn Watkins
Burnley	7.5	Kitty Ussher*	Gordon Birtwhistle
Labour from Lib Dems			
Manchester, Withington	0.7	John Leech	Lucy Powell

One to watch: Sefton Central
Actual majority 2005 (Crosby): Labour 5,840 (16.1%) – Claire Curtis-Thomas MP
Notional majority 2005: Labour 4,950 (12.0%)
Conservative candidate: Debi Jones

Although Sefton Central is a new (and rather anonymous) name, this seat contains over two thirds of the electorate of the former Crosby, and is in political makeup not too different from that famous constituency name. In 1981 one of the SDP's founding Gang of Four, Shirley Williams, triumphantly returned to Parliament with a swing of over 25 per cent from the Conservatives in a national blaze of publicity. However, the Tories regained the Crosby seat less than two years later, and in 1997 it was Labour who benefited from a stunning swing, increasing their share by 22 per cent to seize what had been thought of as a solidly middle-class swathe of suburbia north of Liverpool, the childhood home of such contrasting celebrities as Kenny Everett and Anne Robinson. Claire Curtis-Thomas has held on with surprising comfort since, but next time it may be a different story. In the boundary changes which have occasioned the seat's name change, the southern and less fashionable half of the eponymous town of Crosby has been transferred to Bootle (Labour's safest seat anywhere in the UK), and replaced by the more middle-class dormitory town of Maghull, which had previously sat uneasily with the larger, solidly working-class, Kirkby in the awkwardly named Knowsley North & Sefton East. Although this has only reduced the notional swing needed to 6 per cent, this figure may be inflated, as there was little incentive for Conservatives to turn out to vote in Maghull when it was so overwhelmed – whereas now local councillor Debi Jones has a real chance of turning the political wheel full circle, and laying to rest the historic disasters here in 1981 and 1997.

Altrincham & Sale West

Conservative notional majority of 7,618; notional turnout: 67.8%

PARTY	2005 CANDIDATE	NOTIONAL 2005 VOTES	NOTIONAL 2005 % VOTE	PPC FOR NEXT GE
Conservative	Graham Brady MP	20,384	47.0	Graham Brady MP
Labour	John Stockton	12,766	29.4	n/a
Lib Dem	Ian Chappell	9,489	21.9	n/a
Others		718	1.7	

Ashton-under-Lyne

Labour notional majority of 13,199; notional turnout: 51.5%

PARTY	2005 CANDIDATE	NOTIONAL 2005 VOTES	NOTIONAL 2005 % VOTE	PPC FOR NEXT GE
Labour	David Heyes MP	20,136	58.5	David Heyes MP
Conservative	Graeme Brown	6,937	20.1	n/a
Lib Dem	Les Jones	4,017	11.7	n/a
Others		3,342	9.7	

Birkenhead

Labour notional majority of 14,638; notional turnout: 49.9%

PARTY	2005 CANDIDATE	NOTIONAL 2005 VOTES	NOTIONAL 2005 % VOTE	PPC FOR NEXT GE
Labour	Frank Field MP	20,534	64.8	Frank Field MP
Lib Dem	Stuart Kelly	5,896	18.6	Stuart Kelly
Conservative	Howard Morton	5,246	16.6	Andrew Gilbert
Others		0	0.0	

Blackburn

Labour notional majority of 8,048; notional turnout: 57.6%

PARTY	2005 CANDIDATE	NOTIONAL 2005 VOTES	NOTIONAL 2005 % VOTE	PPC FOR NEXT GE
Labour	Jack Straw MP	17,439	42.1	Jack Straw MP
Conservative	Imtiaz Ameen	9,391	22.7	Michael Law-Riding
Lib Dem	Tony Melia	8,518	20.6	Paul English
Others		6,040	14.6	

Held by Justice Secretary Jack Straw for the past 30 years, Blackburn is an economically depressed former textile town in central Lancashire. The housing stock, generally comprised of poorly maintained terraces, is of exceptionally low quality with 15.5% of homes having no central heating or private bathroom. Two in five Blackburn residents have no qualifications and a quarter of the town's population are Muslims, the majority of them British born. The BNP have so far failed to establish a strong local government base here, yet have seen their support in the town rise in recent years. Despite their weakness in Blackburn town, the Conservatives are not entirely irrelevant here, holding several wards in the town's rural suburbs. Jack Straw, despite being returned to Parliament with a low 42% vote share in 2005 against a backdrop of anger over the Iraq war, should benefit from the town's fractured political allegiances to win an eighth term.

Blackley & Broughton

Labour notional majority of 13,060; notional turnout: 45.8%

PARTY	2005 CANDIDATE	NOTIONAL 2005 VOTES	NOTIONAL 2005 % VOTE	PPC FOR NEXT GE
Labour	Graham Stringer MP	18,825	62.5	Graham Stringer MP
Lib Dem	Iain Donaldson	5,765	19.1	n/a
Conservative	Amar Ahmed	3,927	13.0	n/a
Others		1,607	5.3	

Blackpool North & Cleveleys

Labour notional majority of 3,241; notional turnout: 57.6%

PARTY	2005 CANDIDATE	NOTIONAL 2005 VOTES	NOTIONAL 2005 % VOTE	PPC FOR NEXT GE
Labour	n/a	17,470	45.7	Joan Humble MP
Conservative	n/a	14,229	37.2	Paul Maynard
Lib Dem	n/a	5,222	13.7	n/a
Others		1,278	3.3	

A newly created constituency, the loss of Labour-inclined areas in the north of the constituency to the new Lancaster & Fleetwood seat makes this easily the more marginal of the two Blackpool constituencies. On a local government level, the Conservatives easily lead Labour; holding 14 out of 18 of the constituency's seats on Blackpool Borough Council and all 11 of the seats which fall inside the boundaries of Wyre borough. Conservative strength grows precipitously the further north one travels in the constituency with the densely populated Blackpool town centre wards providing the base of Labour's support. As with neighbouring Blackpool South, the tourist trade is important here, which can lead to significant seasonal unemployment. Despite being a low-wage constituency, less than one in ten residents live in social housing, although private housing is often in a poor state of repair. Sitting Blackpool North & Fleetwood MP Joan Humble (Labour) will face Conservative Paul Maynard.

Blackpool South

Labour notional majority of 5,911; notional turnout: 52.3%

PARTY	2005 CANDIDATE	NOTIONAL 2005 VOTES	NOTIONAL 2005 % VOTE	PPC FOR NEXT GE
Labour	Gordon Marsden MP	16,232	48.5	Gordon Marsden MP
Conservative	Michael Winstanley	10,321	30.9	Ron Bell
Lib Dem	Doreen Holt	5,054	15.1	n/a
Others		1,844	5.5	

In winning the constituency by almost 12,000 votes at the 1997 general election, Labour's Gordon Marsden brought to an end more than 50 years of Conservative dominance in Blackpool South. Taking in the Tower and Pleasure Beach amusement park, the constituency is home to the majority of the town's tourist attractions. Decades have passed since Blackpool's heyday as the destination of choice for British holidaymakers yet tourism still provides a large number of jobs locally. Wages, as one may expect from a declining seaside area where two fifths of local residents have no qualifications, are low yet owner occupation is higher than average at almost 70%. The Conservatives have made solid advances here in recent years, outpacing Labour by 10% at the 2007 council elections. Blackpool councillor Ron Bell will fight the seat for the Conservatives.

Bolton North East

Labour notional majority of 4,527; notional turnout: 54.4%

PARTY	2005 CANDIDATE	NOTIONAL 2005 VOTES	NOTIONAL 2005 % VOTE	PPC FOR NEXT GE
Labour	David Crausby MP	17,486	46.3	David Crausby MP
Conservative	Paul Brierley	12,959	34.3	Deborah Dunleavy
Lib Dem	Adam Killeya	6,083	16.1	n/a
Others		1,244	3.3	

Bolton North East has been a key marginal for almost 30 years, electing the Conservatives by small majorities between 1979 and 1992 and Labour ever since. Considerably more urban than the neighbouring marginal of Bolton West, the stretches from the city's Labour-friendly urban centre out to Astley Bridge and Bradshaw on the edge of the Pennine Hills, where tree-lined avenues and 4x4 vehicles are the order of the day. There is a large and relatively affluent ethnic minority population in the constituency, one in ten residents being Asian. Two thirds of homes are owner occupied, although much of the terraced housing in the central Bolton wards is of a poor quality. Conservative candidate Deborah Dunleavy will hope to unseat incumbent Labour MP David Crausby.

Bolton South East

Labour notional majority of 11,483; notional turnout: 51.3%

PARTY	2005 CANDIDATE	NOTIONAL 2005 VOTES	NOTIONAL 2005 % VOTE	PPC FOR NEXT GE
Labour	Brian Iddon MP	19,366	55.7	Yasmin Qureshi
Conservative	Deborah Dunleavy	7,883	22.7	Andy Morgan
Lib Dem	Frank Harasiwka	6,298	18.1	Donal O'Hanlon
Others		1,218	3.5	

Bolton West

Labour notional majority of 5,041; notional turnout: 61.2%

PARTY	2005 CANDIDATE	NOTIONAL 2005 VOTES	NOTIONAL 2005 % VOTE	PPC FOR NEXT GE
Labour	Ruth Kelly MP	19,137	45.4	Julie Hilling
Conservative	Philip Allott	14,096	33.4	Susan Williams
Lib Dem	Tim Perkins	7,990	18.9	Jackie Pearcy
Others		961	2.3	

The constituency of former Communities Secretary Ruth Kelly, this Greater Manchester seat is a mix of wealthy commuter belt villages such as Heaton and working-class enclaves of the city of Bolton. Boundary changes have seen Labour's notional majority rise from 2,000 to 4,000 following the addition of Atherton ward from Leigh and loss of parts of the Tory-inclined Hulton to Bolton South East. Unlike other parts of the city, Bolton West is almost entirely white (97%) and more than three quarters of homes (76.6%) are owner occupied. With Ruth Kelly opting to retire from the Commons, this seat will be a battle between trade unionist Julie Hilling for Labour and Trafford Borough Council leader Susan Williams for the Tories. The Conservatives dominate here on a local government level.

Bootle

Labour notional majority of 20,125; notional turnout: 50.8%

PARTY	2005 CANDIDATE	NOTIONAL 2005 VOTES	NOTIONAL 2005 % VOTE	PPC FOR NEXT GE
Labour	Joe Benton MP	26,243	71.0	Joe Benton MP
Lib Dem	Chris Newby	6,118	16.6	James Murray
Conservative	Wafik Moustafa	2,719	7.4	n/a
Others		1,857	5.0	

Burnley

Labour notional majority of 4,818; notional turnout: 59.5%

PARTY	2005 CANDIDATE	NOTIONAL 2005 VOTES	NOTIONAL 2005 % VOTE	PPC FOR NEXT GE
Labour	Kitty Ussher	14,999	38.5	n/a
Lib Dem	Gordon Birtwistle	9,221	23.7	Gordon Birtwistle
Independent	Harry Brooks	5,786	14.8	n/a
Others		4,582	11.8	

Bury North

Labour notional majority of 2,059; notional turnout: 61.6%

PARTY	2005 CANDIDATE	NOTIONAL 2005 VOTES	NOTIONAL 2005 % VOTE	PPC FOR NEXT GE
Labour	David Chaytor MP	17,064	41.8	n/a
Conservative	David Nuttall	15,005	36.8	David Nuttall
Lib Dem	Wilf Davison	6,156	15.1	Richard Baum
Others		2,553	6.3	

Located at the northern edge of the Greater Manchester conurbation, Bury North was gained by Labour at the 1997 general election. As a whole, the constituency is broadly middle-class in nature, taking in Bury town centre in the south before gradually moving northwards to the villages of Tottington and Ramsbottom in the shadow of the Rossendale valley and west Pennine moors. Labour is strongest in the east of Bury town while the Conservatives run up huge leads in the constituency's commuter-populated rural areas. More than three quarters of homes here are owner occupied. A high profile casualty of the *Telegraph*'s investigation into alleged expenses abuses, sitting MP David Chaytor has opted to retire. Solicitor David Nuttall will hope to take the seat for the Conservatives.

Bury South

Labour notional majority of 9,779; notional turnout: 58.4%

PARTY	2005 CANDIDATE	NOTIONAL 2005 VOTES	NOTIONAL 2005 % VOTE	PPC FOR NEXT GE
Labour	Ivan Lewis MP	21,807	50.9	Ivan Lewis MP
Conservative	Alex Williams	12,028	28.1	Michelle Wiseman
Lib Dem	Victor D'Albert	7,326	17.1	Victor D'Albert
Others		1,654	3.9	

Cheadle

Lib Dem notional majority of 3,672; notional turnout: 68.7%

PARTY	2005 CANDIDATE	NOTIONAL 2005 VOTES	NOTIONAL 2005 % VOTE	PPC FOR NEXT GE
Lib Dem	Patsy Calton MP	23,671	47.8	Mark Hunter MP
Conservative	Stephen Day	19,999	40.3	Ben Jeffreys
Labour	Martin Miller	4,889	9.9	Hark Singh-Raud
Others		1,005	2.0	

This is a pleasant seat in the south of Greater Manchester, although many of the residents of the constituency's detached, owner-occupied properties on tree-lined avenues would much rather claim association with Cheshire than nearby Stockport. After decades of domination at a local government level, local councillor Patsy Calton finally seized the seat from Conservative Stephen Day by 33 votes at the 2001 election. Despite gains elsewhere in suburban Manchester, Conservative progress on a local government level has been largely limited to Bramall with the Liberal Democrats dominating Cheadle town and Hulme. Former Stockport Council leader Mark Hunter, who retained the seat for the Liberal Democrats in a July 2005 by-election following Calton's death, will hope to hold off a challenge from Conservative candidate teacher Ben Jeffreys.

Chorley

Labour notional majority of 7,285; notional turnout: 62.1%

PARTY	2005 CANDIDATE	NOTIONAL 2005 VOTES	NOTIONAL 2005 % VOTE	PPC FOR NEXT GE
Labour	Lindsay Hoyle MP	22,568	50.8	Lindsay Hoyle MP
Conservative	Simon Mallett	15,283	34.4	Alan Cullens
Lib Dem	Alexander Wilson-Fletcher	6,537	14.7	Stephen Fenn
Others		0	0.0	

Situated in south Lancashire, the Chorley constituency is one of the longest-standing candidates for bellwether seat in the country, having followed the winner of each general election since 1964. Chorley is a former mining and industrial town which is now a key logistical hub for the north-west of England. The constituency also includes a number of villages such as Whittle-le-Woods and Euxton which are home to large numbers of commuters to Manchester, Preston and Bolton. Owner occupation levels are, at 78.2%, extremely high and unemployment is slightly below the national average. Locally, the Conservatives control Chorley Borough Council outright and swept the boards at the 2009 Lancashire County Council elections, winning all but one of the constituency's seats. Incumbent Labour MP Lindsay Hoyle will be challenged by Conservative local councillor Alan Cullens.

Denton & Reddish

Labour notional majority of 13,128; notional turnout: 52.5%

PARTY	2005 CANDIDATE	NOTIONAL 2005 VOTES	NOTIONAL 2005 % VOTE	PPC FOR NEXT GE
Labour	Andrew Gwynne	19,595	57.6	Andrew Gwynne MP
Conservative	Alex Story	6,467	19.0	n/a
Lib Dem	Allison Seabourne	5,541	16.3	n/a
Others		2,391	7.0	

Fylde

Conservative notional majority of 11,117; notional turnout: 59.3%

PARTY	2005 CANDIDATE	NOTIONAL 2005 VOTES	NOTIONAL 2005 % VOTE	PPC FOR NEXT GE
Conservative	Michael Jack MP	21,053	54.3	Mark Menzies
Labour	William Parbury	9,936	25.6	Liam Robinson
Lib Dem	Bill Winlow	6,137	15.8	Bill Winlow
Others		1,647	4.2	

Garston & Halewood

Labour notional majority of 10,814; notional turnout: 53.2%

PARTY	2005 CANDIDATE	NOTIONAL 2005 VOTES	NOTIONAL 2005 % VOTE	PPC FOR NEXT GE
Labour	Maria Eagle MP	22,433	57.9	Maria Eagle MP
Lib Dem	Paul Keaveney	11,619	30.0	n/a
Conservative	Amber Rudd	3,818	9.9	n/a
Others		860	2.2	

Hazel Grove

Lib Dem notional majority of 7,694; notional turnout: 61.3%

PARTY	2005 CANDIDATE	NOTIONAL 2005 VOTES	NOTIONAL 2005 % VOTE	PPC FOR NEXT GE
Lib Dem	Andrew Stunell MP	19,423	50.3	Andrew Stunell MP
Conservative	Alan White	11,729	30.4	Annesley Abercorn
Labour	Andrew Graystone	6,219	16.1	Richard Scorer
Others		1,258	3.3	

Located on the south-east fringes of Greater Manchester, the Hazel Grove constituency enjoys relative independence from the city's urban sprawl while still providing a home to thousands of middle-class professionals who commute to work in the city each day. Composed of pleasant suburbs and several semi-rural wards, the constituency has been held by bookish Liberal Democrat MP Andrew Stunell since 1997. A close marginal for more than 20 years, Hazel Grove is now the safest Liberal Democrat seat in the North West with the party holding all but one of the constituency's 18 council seats. Annesley Abercorn, a feisty campaigner whose local profile has been boosted by his double-decker campaign bus, will contest the seat for the Conservatives.

Heywood & Middleton

Labour notional majority of 11,034; notional turnout: 53.8%

PARTY	2005 CANDIDATE	NOTIONAL 2005 VOTES	NOTIONAL 2005 % VOTE	PPC FOR NEXT GE
Labour	Jim Dobbin MP	20,059	48.3	Jim Dobbin MP
Conservative	Stephen Pathmarajah	9,025	21.7	n/a
Lib Dem	Crea Lavin	8,403	20.2	Wera Hobhouse
Others		4,032	9.7	

Hyndburn

Labour notional majority of 5,528; notional turnout: 58.7%

PARTY	2005 CANDIDATE	NOTIONAL 2005 VOTES	NOTIONAL 2005 % VOTE	PPC FOR NEXT GE
Labour	Greg Pope MP	18,308	45.7	n/a
Conservative	James Mawdsley	12,780	31.9	n/a
Lib Dem	Bill Greene	5,750	14.4	n/a
Others		3,221	8.0	

Named after its local government area, the Hyndburn constituency is largely composed of the towns of Accrington, Oswaldtwistle and Great Harwood. The constituency has traditionally been loyal to Labour, falling to Conservative Ken Hargreaves by the narrowest of margins in 1983. The largest town in the constituency is Accrington, a manufacturing town located some 20 miles north of Manchester. The Tories, who have controlled Hyndburn Borough Council outright since 2003, are strongest in the rural portions of the seat. Labour will have been sorely disappointed by their performance here at the 2009 Lancashire County Council elections, in which the party captured only two seats locally, in their strongholds of Rishton & Clayton-le-Moors and Great Harwood, both typified by the traditional terraced housing so commonly associated with Lancashire. Labour incumbent Greg Pope will retire at the general election.

Knowsley

Labour notional majority of 24,333; notional turnout: 53.7%

Party	2005 Candidate	Notional 2005 Votes	Notional 2005 % Vote	PPC for next GE
Labour	n/a	30,112	71.8	George Howarth MP
Lib Dem	n/a	5,779	13.8	n/a
Conservative	n/a	4,709	11.2	n/a
Others		1,336	3.2	

West Lancashire

Labour notional majority of 6,084; notional turnout: 58.0%

Party	2005 Candidate	Notional 2005 Votes	Notional 2005 % Vote	PPC for next GE
Labour	Rosie Cooper	20,746	48.1	Rosie Cooper MP
Conservative	Alf Doran	14,662	34.0	Adrian Owens
Lib Dem	Richard Kemp	6,059	14.0	n/a
Others		1,688	3.9	

Formed around the towns of Ormskirk and Skelmersdale, West Lancashire has been held by Labour since the 1992 general election. With a history of coal-mining and a sizeable amount of social housing, Skelmersdale is a Labour stronghold while Ormskirk, which has evolved into a commuter town for those working in nearby Liverpool and Manchester, is far more favourable towards the Conservatives. In delivering Labour a 17,000 majority at the 1997 election, it appeared that this seat would be safe for Labour for many years to come, yet Conservative advances on a local government level (they hold a 16-seat majority on West Lancashire Borough Council) put this seat very much in contention. First elected for Labour in 2005, former Liverpool mayor Rosie Cooper will be challenged by local Conservative councillor Adrian Owens.

Lancaster & Fleetwood

Labour notional majority of 3,428; notional turnout: 59.5%

Party	2005 Candidate	Notional 2005 Votes	Notional 2005 % Vote	PPC for next GE
Labour	Anne Sacks	16,496	42.4	Clive Grunshaw
Conservative	Ben Wallace	13,068	33.6	Eric Ollerenshaw
Lib Dem	Stuart Langhorn	6,081	15.6	Stuart Langhorn
Others		3,231	8.3	

A newly created constituency, Lancaster & Fleetwood is comprised of arguably the most Labour-leaning portions of the current Blackpool North & Fleetwood and Lancaster & Wyre seats. This one of the strangest-shaped constituencies, with the two towns physically divided from one other by the Wyre estuary. Fleetwood, at the end of the Blackpool tramline, has suffered considerably from the near-collapse of its traditional fishing industry, three of its five wards being ranked in the top 5% most deprived areas in the UK. Lancaster, a pleasant, stone-clad Lancashire city, is home to a large university whose student and academic population have not traditionally favoured the Tories. The Green Party are particularly strong in the Lancaster portion of the seat and may save their deposit. Labour has selected local councillor Clive Grunshaw while the Conservatives are fielding Lancashire-born Eric Ollerenshaw, his party's former leader on the London Assembly.

Leigh

Labour notional majority of 15,098; notional turnout: 51.3%

PARTY	2005 CANDIDATE	NOTIONAL 2005 VOTES	NOTIONAL 2005 % VOTE	PPC FOR NEXT GE
Labour	Andy Burnham MP	22,544	57.8	Andy Burnham MP
Lib Dem	Dave Crowther	7,446	19.1	n/a
Conservative	Laurance Wedderburn	6,393	16.4	n/a
Others		2,604	6.7	

Liverpool, Riverside

Labour notional majority of 11,731; notional turnout: 42.6%

PARTY	2005 CANDIDATE	NOTIONAL 2005 VOTES	NOTIONAL 2005 % VOTE	PPC FOR NEXT GE
Labour	Louise Ellman MP	19,342	59.2	Louise Ellman MP
Lib Dem	Richard Marbrow	7,611	23.3	Richard Marbrow
Conservative	Gabrielle Howatson	2,963	9.1	n/a
Others		2,733	8.4	

Liverpool, Walton

Labour notional majority of 17,611; notional turnout: 46.7%

PARTY	2005 CANDIDATE	NOTIONAL 2005 VOTES	NOTIONAL 2005 % VOTE	PPC FOR NEXT GE
Labour	Peter Kilfoyle MP	23,070	71.8	Peter Kilfoyle MP
Lib Dem	Kiron Reid	5,459	17.0	n/a
Conservative	Sharon Buckle	2,069	6.4	n/a
Others		1,555	4.8	

Liverpool, Wavertree

Labour notional majority of 2,911; notional turnout: 47.8%

PARTY	2005 CANDIDATE	NOTIONAL 2005 VOTES	NOTIONAL 2005 % VOTE	PPC FOR NEXT GE
Labour	Jane Kennedy MP	16,181	49.5	Jane Kennedy MP
Lib Dem	Colin Eldridge	13,270	40.6	Colin Eldridge
Conservative	Jason Steen	2,107	6.4	n/a
Others		1,123	3.4	

Liverpool, West Derby

Labour notional majority of 13,874; notional turnout: 45.6%

PARTY	2005 CANDIDATE	NOTIONAL 2005 VOTES	NOTIONAL 2005 % VOTE	PPC FOR NEXT GE
Labour	Robert Wareing MP	18,547	60.5	Stephen Twigg
Independent				Robert Wareing MP
Lib Dem	Patrick Moloney	4,673	15.3	n/a
Liberal	Steve Radford	4,304	14.1	n/a
Others		3,108	10.1	

Makerfield

Labour notional majority of 17,903; notional turnout: 49.6%

PARTY	2005 CANDIDATE	NOTIONAL 2005 VOTES	NOTIONAL 2005 % VOTE	PPC FOR NEXT GE
Labour	Ian McCartney MP	22,913	62.1	n/a
Conservative	Kulveer Ranger	5,010	13.6	n/a
Lib Dem	Trevor Beswick	4,215	11.4	n/a
Others		4,780	12.9	

Manchester Central

Labour notional majority of 11,636; notional turnout: 41.7%

PARTY	2005 CANDIDATE	NOTIONAL 2005 VOTES	NOTIONAL 2005 % VOTE	PPC FOR NEXT GE
Labour	Tony Lloyd MP	18,004	59.3	Tony Lloyd MP
Lib Dem	Mark Ramsbottom	6,368	21.0	Mark Ramsbottom
Conservative	Tom Jackson	3,168	10.4	n/a
Others		2,797	9.2	

Manchester, Gorton

Labour notional majority of 6,355; notional turnout: 45.7%

PARTY	2005 CANDIDATE	NOTIONAL 2005 VOTES	NOTIONAL 2005 % VOTE	PPC FOR NEXT GE
Labour	Gerald Kaufman MP	17,224	53.1	Gerald Kaufman MP
Lib Dem	Qassim Afzal	10,869	33.5	Qassim Afzal
Conservative	Amanda Byrne	3,194	9.9	n/a
Others		1,125	3.5	

Manchester, Withington

Lib Dem notional majority of 531; notional turnout: 55.3%

PARTY	2005 CANDIDATE	NOTIONAL 2005 VOTES	NOTIONAL 2005 % VOTE	PPC FOR NEXT GE
Lib Dem	John Leech	16,195	42.3	John Leech MP
Labour	Keith Bradley MP	15,664	40.9	Lucy Powell
Conservative	Karen Bradley	3,972	10.4	n/a
Others		2,495	6.5	

Morecambe & Lunesdale

Labour notional majority of 4,849; notional turnout: 61.5%

PARTY	2005 CANDIDATE	NOTIONAL 2005 VOTES	NOTIONAL 2005 % VOTE	PPC FOR NEXT GE
Labour	Geraldine Smith MP	20,266	49.1	Geraldine Smith MP
Conservative	James Airey	15,417	37.3	David Morris
Lib Dem	Alex Stone	5,627	13.6	n/a
Others		0	0.0	

Located in a remote part of north-west Lancashire, Morecambe & Lunesdale has been held by independent-minded Labour MP Geraldine Smith since her ousting of veteran Tory Mark Lennox-Boyd in 1997. While almost three quarters of homes are owner occupied and fewer than one in ten residents lives in social housing, this is a low-wage area where many residents struggle to make a living from the area's declining levels of tourism. Industry remains comparatively healthy here, with a functioning port and nuclear power station operating in Heysham. The Conservatives are strong in the town of Carnforth and the many inland villages scattered to the east of Morecambe Bay. David Morris, a businessman and former Stock, Aitken and Waterman songwriter, will contest the seat for the Conservatives.

Oldham East & Saddleworth

Labour notional majority of 4,245; notional turnout: 56.7%

PARTY	2005 CANDIDATE	NOTIONAL 2005 VOTES	NOTIONAL 2005 % VOTE	PPC FOR NEXT GE
Labour	Phil Woolas MP	17,381	42.5	Phil Woolas MP
Lib Dem	Tony Dawson	13,136	32.1	Elwyn Watkins
Conservative	Keith Chapman	7,256	17.8	n/a
Others		3,090	7.6	

Oldham West & Royton

Labour notional majority of 10,454; notional turnout: 54.0%

PARTY	2005 CANDIDATE	NOTIONAL 2005 VOTES	NOTIONAL 2005 % VOTE	PPC FOR NEXT GE
Labour	Michael Meacher MP	18,637	48.4	Michael Meacher MP
Lib Dem	Stuart Bodsworth	8,183	21.2	Mark Alcock
Conservative	Sean Moore	8,127	21.1	n/a
Others		3,587	9.3	

Pendle

Labour notional majority of 2,180; notional turnout: 63.6%

PARTY	2005 CANDIDATE	NOTIONAL 2005 VOTES	NOTIONAL 2005 % VOTE	PPC FOR NEXT GE
Labour	Gordon Prentice MP	15,250	37.1	Gordon Prentice MP
Conservative	Jane Ellison	13,070	31.8	Andrew Stephenson
Lib Dem	Shazad Anwar	9,528	23.2	Afzal Anwar
Others		3,284	8.0	

The Pendle constituency, which was gained by Scots-born Labour MP Gordon Prentice in 1992, is far better described by its former name of Nelson & Colne. Archetypal Lancashire towns set against the background of the picturesque hills, Nelson and Colne are both traditional mill towns whose fortunes have risen and fallen with the decline of the British textile industry. The seat's sizeable Muslim community (13.4%) and industrial past makes it favourable to Labour yet the Conservatives are strongly dominant in rural areas. Whilst this is a poor area, where more than a third of local residents have no qualifications, three quarters of homes are owner occupied – well above average for a North West constituency. Andy Stephenson, a former Macclesfield councillor and chairman of the Tatton Conservative Association, will fight the seat for the Conservatives.

Preston

Labour notional majority of 8,338; notional turnout: 54.1%

PARTY	2005 CANDIDATE	NOTIONAL 2005 VOTES	NOTIONAL 2005 % VOTE	PPC FOR NEXT GE
Labour	Mark Henrick MP	14,663	48.7	Mark Henrick MP
Conservative	Fiona Bryce	6,325	21.0	Nerissa Warner-O'Neill
Lib Dem	William Parkinson	5,986	19.9	Mark Jewell
Others		3,163	10.5	

South Ribble

Labour notional majority of 2,528; notional turnout: 63.4%

PARTY	2005 CANDIDATE	NOTIONAL 2005 VOTES	NOTIONAL 2005 % VOTE	PPC FOR NEXT GE
Labour	David Borrow MP	20,642	44.3	David Borrow MP
Conservative	Lorraine Fullbrook	18,114	38.8	Lorraine Fullbrook
Lib Dem	Mark Alcock	6,854	14.7	n/a
Others		1,029	2.2	

Formed around the town of Leyland and wealthy suburbs north of Preston, Labour gained South Ribble from Conservative minister Sir Robert Atkins at the 1997 general election. Leyland itself is a medium-sized industrial town which has suffered over the past years from substantial job losses in the manufacturing sector. As one moves south of Leyland and into the Lancashire countryside surrounding Preston, Conservative prospects improve dramatically with the party receiving overwhelming support in the towns of Longton and Hutton. Owner occupation rates, at 83.4%, are exceptionally high with only one in ten people living in social housing. Sitting Labour MP David Borrow will face his second challenge from former Hart Council leader Lorraine Fullbrook.

Ribble Valley

Conservative notional majority of 6,953; notional turnout: 61.5%

PARTY	2005 CANDIDATE	NOTIONAL 2005 VOTES	NOTIONAL 2005 % VOTE	PPC FOR NEXT GE
Conservative	Nigel Evans MP	20,693	44.9	Nigel Evans MP
Labour	Jack Davenport	13,740	29.8	Paul Foster
Lib Dem	Julie Young	10,404	22.6	Allan Knox
Others		1,229	2.7	

Rochdale

Labour notional majority of 149; notional turnout: 57.2%

PARTY	2005 CANDIDATE	NOTIONAL 2005 VOTES	NOTIONAL 2005 % VOTE	PPC FOR NEXT GE
Labour	Lorna Fitzsimons MP	17,547	40.9	Simon Danczuk
Lib Dem	Paul Rowen	17,398	40.5	Paul Rowen MP
Conservative	Khalid Hussain	4,493	10.5	n/a
Others		3,503	8.2	

Rossendale & Darwen

Labour notional majority of 3,696; notional turnout: 61.6%

PARTY	2005 CANDIDATE	NOTIONAL 2005 VOTES	NOTIONAL 2005 % VOTE	PPC FOR NEXT GE
Labour	Janet Anderson MP	19,024	43.0	Janet Anderson MP
Conservative	Nigel Adams	15,328	34.6	Jake Berry
Lib Dem	Mike Carr	6,587	14.9	Dale Mulgrew
Others		3,305	7.5	

Gained from Conservative minister Sir David Trippier by 120 votes at the 1992 general election, Rossendale & Darwen is a striking rural constituency located in the north of Greater Manchester. Darwen, Rawtenstall and Bacup are the largest towns here, all of them former textile towns which have gradually diversified into light manufacturing industries over the past two decades. Whilst three quarters of homes are owner occupied, around a third of residents have no qualifications and youth unemployment is a problem locally. In contrast with other Lancashire mill towns, the Asian population here is extremely low, only 2% at the time of the 2001 census. The Conservatives performed extremely well here at the 2009 Lancashire County Council elections, winning every seat in the constituency. Labour's Janet Anderson will face a challenge from Conservative Jake Berry.

St Helens North

Labour notional majority of 15,265; notional turnout: 55.6%

PARTY	2005 CANDIDATE	NOTIONAL 2005 VOTES	NOTIONAL 2005 % VOTE	PPC FOR NEXT GE
Labour	David Watts MP	23,993	57.4	David Watts MP
Lib Dem	John Beirne	8,728	20.9	John Beirne
Conservative	Paul Oakley	7,884	18.8	n/a
Others		1,231	2.9	

St Helens South & Whiston

Labour notional majority of 10,987; notional turnout: 53.2%

PARTY	2005 CANDIDATE	NOTIONAL 2005 VOTES	NOTIONAL 2005 % VOTE	PPC FOR NEXT GE
Labour	Shaun Woodward MP	22,820	55.6	Shaun Woodward MP
Lib Dem	Brian Spencer	11,833	28.8	Brian Spencer
Conservative	Una Riley	4,977	12.1	n/a
Others		1,424	3.5	

Salford & Eccles

Labour notional majority of 10,707; notional turnout: 45.5%

PARTY	2005 CANDIDATE	NOTIONAL 2005 VOTES	NOTIONAL 2005 % VOTE	PPC FOR NEXT GE
Labour	n/a	18,183	55.4	Hazel Blears MP
Lib Dem	n/a	7,476	22.8	n/a
Conservative	n/a	5,528	16.9	n/a
Others		1,618	4.9	

Sefton Central

Labour notional majority of 4,950; notional turnout: 60.7%

PARTY	2005 CANDIDATE	NOTIONAL 2005 VOTES	NOTIONAL 2005 % VOTE	PPC FOR NEXT GE
Labour	Claire Curtis-Thomas MP	18,776	45.6	Claire Curtis-Thomas MP
Conservative	Debi Jones	13,826	33.6	Debi Jones
Lib Dem	Richard Clein	7,915	19.2	Richard Clein
Others		662	1.6	

A rather anonymously named seat, the newly formed Sefton Central constituency is comprised of roughly two thirds of the current Crosby and two fifths of the Knowsley North and Sefton East seats – both of which are currently held by Labour. In reality, this Merseyside constituency can be best described as the middle-class Liverpool suburbs with affluent areas like Ruvonmeols and Blundellsands housing many professional commuters to the city. Geographical proximity is all this seat has in common with Liverpool, for an astonishing 87.2% of homes in this constituency are owner occupied and the majority of residents work in comfortable professional occupations. On a local government level, the Conservatives are the largest party here by quite some distance. Local councillor and TV presenter Debi Jones, one of her party's most glamorous candidates, will fight the seat for the Conservatives. Incumbent Crosby MP Claire Curtis-Thomas will seek to hold it for Labour.

Southport

Lib Dem notional majority of 3,838; notional turnout: 61.0%

PARTY	2005 CANDIDATE	NOTIONAL 2005 VOTES	NOTIONAL 2005 % VOTE	PPC FOR NEXT GE
Lib Dem	John Pugh MP	19,093	46.3	John Pugh MP
Conservative	Mark Bigley	15,255	37.0	Brenda Porter
Labour	Paul Brant	5,277	12.8	Jim Conalty
Others		1,576	3.8	

Located on the Lancashire coast some 14 miles north of Liverpool, Southport's tree-lined avenues have played host to a closely fought battle between the Liberal Democrats and Conservatives for the past three decades. Local residents angrily reject any association with Merseyside and vocally oppose their inclusion within the boundaries of Sefton Borough Council, which may explain the Labour Party's traditionally poor performance here. At 7.6% the level of social housing is extremely low, while a third of the population are of pensionable age. Mirroring the closeness of the parliamentary race, Conservative and Liberal Democrat support is fairly even on a local government level. Tory councillor Brenda Porter, who would be among the oldest members of the 2010 intake, will oppose socially conservative Lib Dem MP John Pugh.

Stalybridge & Hyde

Labour notional majority of 8,455; notional turnout: 53.8%

PARTY	2005 CANDIDATE	NOTIONAL 2005 VOTES	NOTIONAL 2005 % VOTE	PPC FOR NEXT GE
Labour	James Purnell MP	17,779	49.7	James Purnell MP
Conservative	Lisa Boardman	9,324	26.1	n/a
Lib Dem	Viv Binghan	5,584	15.6	n/a
Others		3,073	8.6	

Stockport

Labour notional majority of 9,982; notional turnout: 53.9%

PARTY	2005 CANDIDATE	NOTIONAL 2005 VOTES	NOTIONAL 2005 % VOTE	PPC FOR NEXT GE
Labour	Ann Coffey MP	18,119	52.3	n/a
Conservative	Elizabeth Berridge	8,137	23.5	Stephen Holland
Lib Dem	Lyn-Su Floodgate	7,419	21.4	Stuart Bodsworth
Others		955	2.8	

Stretford & Urmston

Labour notional majority of 8,310; notional turnout: 63.8%

PARTY	2005 CANDIDATE	NOTIONAL 2005 VOTES	NOTIONAL 2005 % VOTE	PPC FOR NEXT GE
Labour	Beverley Hughes MP	20,061	51.4	n/a
Conservative	Damien Hinds	11,751	30.1	Mark Versallion
Lib Dem	Faraz Bhatti	5,429	13.9	Steven Cooke
Others		1,813	4.6	

Home to Manchester United's Old Trafford football ground, this is a largely residential constituency located in the southern part of the city. Created at the 1997 general election, the bulk of this constituency is formed out of the old Manchester, Davyhulme constituency, which was held by the Conservatives until its demise. Politically speaking, both main parties have pockets of firm support here, the Tories dominating in suburban Davyhulme and Labour strongly ahead in Clifford and Bucklow St Martins. An economically vibrant area, the seat is home to a large number of light industrial and high-tech industries, particularly around the sprawling Trafford Park business park. The Tories, who have controlled Trafford Borough Council since 2004, have selected local councillor Mark Versallion to contest the seat. Incumbent MP Beverley Hughes is retiring.

Wallasey

Labour notional majority of 91,30; notional turnout: 57.7%

PARTY	2005 CANDIDATE	NOTIONAL 2005 VOTES	NOTIONAL 2005 % VOTE	PPC FOR NEXT GE
Labour	Angela Eagle MP	20,752	54.5	Angela Eagle MP
Conservative	Leah Fraser	11,622	30.5	Leah Fraser
Lib Dem	Joanna Pemberton	4,843	12.7	n/a
Others		855	2.2	

Wigan

Labour notional majority of 15,501; notional turnout: 52.0%

PARTY	2005 CANDIDATE	NOTIONAL 2005 VOTES	NOTIONAL 2005 % VOTE	PPC FOR NEXT GE
Labour	Neil Turner MP	23,017	58.1	Neil Turner MP
Conservative	John Coombes	7,516	19.0	n/a
Lib Dem	Denise Capstick	6,699	16.9	n/a
Others		2,364	6.0	

Wirral South

Labour notional majority of 3,538; notional turnout: 67.7%

PARTY	2005 CANDIDATE	NOTIONAL 2005 VOTES	NOTIONAL 2005 % VOTE	PPC FOR NEXT GE
Labour	Ben Chapman MP	16,157	42.5	n/a
Conservative	Carl Cross	12,619	33.2	Jeff Clarke
Lib Dem	Simon Holbrook	8,218	21.6	Paula Southwood
Others		1,053	2.8	

If the political establishment needed any evidence of the coming landslide, the 17.24% swing Labour's Ben Chapman achieved at the February 1997 Wirral South by-election was the perfect tell-tale sign. Historically a solidly Conservative seat, the constituency is made up of a number of middle-class towns set against the backdrop of some stunning scenery. The Conservatives are all-conquering in Heswall, in the southern part of the Wirral peninsula, while Labour is strongest in the former dock town of Bromborough. The constituency is within easy reach of both Manchester and Liverpool and is home to many commuters. The Conservatives are fielding Jeff Clarke, who was the Liberal Democrat candidate in Wirral West at the last election.

Wirral West

Conservative notional majority of 569; notional turnout: 68.1%

PARTY	2005 CANDIDATE	NOTIONAL 2005 VOTES	NOTIONAL 2005 % VOTE	PPC FOR NEXT GE
Conservative	Esther McVey	15,705	41.8	Esther McVey
Labour	Stephen Hesford MP	15,136	40.3	Stephen Hesford MP
Lib Dem	Jeff Clarke	6,158	16.4	Peter Reisdorf
Others		600	1.6	

Worsley & Eccles South

Labour notional majority of 10,001; notional turnout: 54.2%

PARTY	2005 CANDIDATE	NOTIONAL 2005 VOTES	NOTIONAL 2005 % VOTE	PPC FOR NEXT GE
Labour	n/a	20,804	53.3	Barbara Keeley MP
Conservative	n/a	10,803	27.7	Iain Lindley
Lib Dem	n/a	5,044	12.9	n/a
Others		2,386	6.1	

Wyre & Preston North

Conservative notional majority of 12,082; notional turnout: 63.2%

PARTY	2005 CANDIDATE	NOTIONAL 2005 VOTES	NOTIONAL 2005 % VOTE	PPC FOR NEXT GE
Conservative	n/a	24,011	54.7	Ben Wallace MP
Labour	n/a	11,929	27.2	Jack Davenport
Lib Dem	n/a	7,055	16.1	n/a
Others		931	2.1	

Wythenshawe & Sale East

Labour notional majority of 10,827; notional turnout: 51.1%

PARTY	2005 CANDIDATE	NOTIONAL 2005 VOTES	NOTIONAL 2005 % VOTE	PPC FOR NEXT GE
Labour	Paul Goggins MP	18,878	52.2	Paul Goggins MP
Conservative	Jane Meehan	8,051	22.3	n/a
Lib Dem	Alison Firth	7,766	21.5	Martin Eakins
Others		1,489	4.1	

Yorkshire and Humberside

The denizens of the 'broad acres' of Yorkshire have never been accused of underestimating the importance of their county, the largest by far in England geographically though traditionally divided into its three ridings (a term also used for constituencies in the Canadian parliament, though rather oddly, as strictly speaking it originally meant a tripartite division). Their pride and self-confidence is not misplaced in terms of the significance of Yorkshire for the forthcoming general election, as it has many key marginals for all the main English parties. Also included in this region is 'Humberside'; we do know that this artificial and far from popular entity has not existed, even for administrative purposes, since 1996, but the fact is that the Boundary Commission did still use it as a unit for their latest review.

It looks as if the first sea-change in British politics since 1997 is in the air, and the Conservatives' chief aim is to reverse the landslide, and erase the memory, of that dramatic general election. The Labour MPs elected then, and not seriously challenged since, are now in the spotlight in more ways than one. One striking feature, seen more in Yorkshire than elsewhere, is the number who are not even going to try to continue their career in Parliament, and have for a variety of reasons already announced their retirement. These already include five of the nine most vulnerable seats in Yorkshire, and in another, Dewsbury, the Communities and Local Government Minister Shahid Malik came under severe pressure in the expenses scandal of early summer 2009. All in all, Labour's belief that they can hold their key seats must be in doubt.

The first two seats on the Tory shopping list are both currently held by members of that class of '97 that some placed in the sub-category of 'Blair babes' – but both Kali Mountford and Christine McCafferty are retiring. Both seats too, are West Yorkshire 'valley' constituencies, hugging the rivers Colne and Calder respectively, and linking small towns that had grown up around the mills of the textile industry of the industrial revolution, using the fast-flowing streams pouring down the eastern slopes of the Pennines. Colne Valley, in the borough of Kirklees, also extends into the western suburbs of Huddersfield, where it was once rumoured, unlikely though it may seem, that more millionaires lived than in any other British neighbourhood. Meanwhile Calder Valley (in the similarly named Calderdale borough) almost reaches Halifax, at Sowerby Bridge. Both seats seem almost certain to fall to the Tory candidates Jason

McCartney and Craig Whittaker. However, to become the largest party and even win an overall majority the challengers need to reverse far more 1997 losses.

Slightly harder nuts to crack will be the larger ex-mill towns of West Yorkshire: Halifax, Dewsbury, Denis Healey and Alastair Campbell's home town of Keighley, and Batley & Spen. One reason for their larger majorities is that unlike in the valley seats, all now have significant minorities of Asian residents (ranging from 9 to 14 per cent), which has itself given rise to a substantial BNP presence. In fact in 2005 party leader Nick Griffin chose to stand in Keighley, though his 6.8 per cent of the vote was scarcely half that polled in Dewsbury (13.1 per cent). Dewsbury is a troubled town, sharply divided between a Muslim minority and a deprived white working class, the home both of one of the July 2005 bombers and of the kidnapped nine-year-old Shannon Matthews. All four seats would fall to the Tories on swings of between 4 and 7 per cent, although the picture may here as elsewhere be made more complex by minor parties.

A West Riding seat with a much larger Asian presence is Bradford West, and technically it requires a smaller swing, though its politics have been rendered unpredictable by an element of the clan or 'birideri' system. In contrast to Labour's Sikh MP, Marsha Singh, the Conservatives have selected a Muslim candidate, Zahid Iqbal, though it would be simplistic to assume that he can automatically gain all or even most of the 38 per cent of the population who follow his religion (only 1 per cent is Sikh, though).

The next two Yorkshire Tory targets, both needing swings of just under 6 per cent, will also both be vacated by their sitting MPs: Elmet & Rothwell, to the east of Leeds, and the cricketing constituency of Pudsey (Sir Len Hutton, Brian Close, Raymond Illingworth and Matthew Hoggard were all born in the seat). If these can be gained, the Conservatives will become the largest party nationally. To secure an overall majority, they need to go on to regain the two north Leeds seats lost in 1997, North East and North West (where they are now third), and even perhaps Wakefield, where they have not come closer since 1935 than 360 votes, in 1983. Finally, two Labour seats in the 'Humberside' section should fall, Cleethorpes in north-east Lincolnshire, and the truly cross-county (and cross-class) dichotomy that is Brigg & Goole.

The main reason the Boundary Commission retained the anachronistic Humberside was, one suspects, to preclude the need for major boundary changes, but they could not avoid these in various parts of Yorkshire. For a start, West Yorkshire, like all the 'metropolitan' areas, needed to lose a seat. This turned out to be that of Gordon Brown's right-hand man and would-be heir apparent, Ed Balls – Normanton. Nearly a quarter of the abolished division, including the eponymous town, went into Pontefract & Castleford, which happens to be held by Mr Balls's wife, Yvette Cooper. However instead of becoming involved in an odd kind of marital dispute, he found a different berth in the new seat of Morley & Outwood. The 'owner' of the largest portion here (two thirds), 56-year-old Colin Challen, did not contest the nomination and will retire; but net Labour has lost a seat.

They have also effectively lost Selby, which gains 9,000 voters from Conservative seats and is obscurely renamed Selby & Ainsty (a historic wapentake or Anglo-Saxon administrative unit containing thirty-five villages west of York). John Grogan, MP since 1997, is also standing down, though still in his forties. Meanwhile, a much stranger creation is that of the doughnut-shaped York Outer seat (see *One to Watch* below). The multiple knock-on effects in North Yorkshire involve the selection for the Conservatives of Anne McIntosh of the abolished and six-way split Vale of York seat in the re-created Thirsk & Malton, ahead of John Greenway of Ryedale, even though his seat had contained much more of its electorate.

It seems unlikely at present that Labour can hope to gain any of its own target seats in 2010, even Leeds North West, including the very heavily student ward of Headingley, which was lost to the Liberal Democrat Greg Mulholland in 2005. However the Liberal Democrats do have both hopes and fears. Their main fear is probably that they could lose Harrogate & Knaresborough to the Tory Andrew Jones. Though there was a healthy majority in 2005, one of only six over 10,000 in fact, they have suffered from two blows: the addition of over 8,000 voters from Tory seats, and far worse, the retirement of their popular MP, Phil Willis, who originally denied a displaced Norman Lamont in 1997. On the positive side, the Lib Dems entertain hopes in two thoroughly urban constituencies, Bradford East (effectively the old North) and Sheffield Central, where they control the city council and where the former Sports Minister Richard Caborn is not standing again.

Standing down . . . retiring . . . giving way. There seems to have been a theme running through this regional survey, and though it is not atypical of the rest of the country, one wonders just how many members will be new to the House of Commons in the next Parliament. Incumbents who do place themselves before their electorate may well find that this is no longer an advantage due to the discredit of the Commons in 2009. While the impact of minor parties may have subsided by the general election campaign, and indeed none is likely to win a seat, the outcome in Yorkshire and Humberside will still be more unpredictable, and hence exciting, than in any election since at least 1945.

Target seats

SEAT	SWING REQUIRED %	MP	CHALLENGER
Conservative from Labour			
Colne Valley	1.3	Kali Mountford*	Jason McCartney
Calder Valley	1.4	Chris McCafferty*	Craig Whittaker
Cleethorpes	3.1	Shona McIsaac	Martin Vickers
Brigg & Goole	4.0	Ian Cawsey	Andrew Percy
Bradford West	4.2	Marsha Singh	Zahid Iqbal
Halifax	4.4	Linda Riordan	Philip Allott
Dewsbury	4.5	Shahid Malik	Simon Reevell
Keighley	5.3	Ann Cryer*	Kris Hopkins
Elmet & Rothwell	5.8	Colin Burgon*	Alec Shelbrooke
Pudsey	5.9	Paul Truswell*	Stuart Andrew
Batley & Spen	6.8	Mike Wood	Janice Small
Leeds North East	7.8	Fabian Hamilton	Matthew Lobley
Wakefield	8.8	Mary Creagh	Alex Story
Labour from Conservatives			
Shipley	0.5	Philip Davies	Susan Hinchcliffe
Scarborough & Whitby	1.4	Robert Goodwill	AnnaJoy David
Selby & Ainsty	2.2	(Nigel Adams)	Wendy Nichols
Conservative from Lib Dems			
York Outer	0.3	(Madeleine Kirk)	Julian Sturdy
Leeds North West	5.1	Greg Mulholland	Julia Mulligan
Sheffield, Hallam	8.2	Nick Clegg	
Harrogate & Knaresborough	8.2	Phil Willis*	Andrew Jones
Lib Dem from Labour			
Bradford East	7.2	Terry Rooney	David Ward
Sheffield Central	7.6	Richard Caborn*	Paul Scriven
Lab target from Lib Dem			
Leeds North West	2.5	Greg Mulholland	Judith Blake

One to watch: York Outer

Notional majority 2005: Lib Dem 203 (0.4%) over C
Liberal Democrat candidate: Madeleine Kirk
Conservative candidate: Julian Sturdy
Labour candidate: James Alexander

The phrase 'gerrymandering' is well known in the USA, where it combines the idea of the creation of electoral districts with very strange (even animal) shapes with party political bias. No-one would accuse our Boundary Commission of the latter, but the enlargement of the City of York council area so that it deserved two seats has led them to an unprecedented solution. For the first time we have a 'doughnut': a constituency entirely surrounding the urban core of York, which now looks like the bullseye in the centre of a dartboard. However the target for at least two parties is the new York Outer seat (the nomenclature is another first, more reminiscent of an Australian sports ground). The renamed York Central should remain safely Labour, needing a pro-Tory swing of 13 per cent, though with some of the wilder predictions and possible outcomes of the next election one can never tell. York Outer, however, is such a strange creature that it deserves the closest of watches. Its electorate is taken from no fewer than four old seats, none providing more than 35 per cent. It contains no towns, but a series of villages and suburbs radiating from the cathedral city. Notional results here are exceptionally hard to calculate, but the Liberal Democrats have done well enough in the local elections on which these are partially based that the 'official' figures calculate at Plymouth University place them 203 votes ahead of the Conservatives, had the seat existed in 2005. But the truth is that no-one really knows what the baseline is. The Tory candidate, Julian Sturdy, does realise, though, that if he should take York Outer, it will count as a vital gain in his party's quest for government after thirteen years in the outer darkness of opposition.

Barnsley Central

Labour notional majority of 11,839; notional turnout: 47.7%

PARTY	2005 CANDIDATE	NOTIONAL 2005 VOTES	NOTIONAL 2005 % VOTE	PPC FOR NEXT GE
Labour	Eric Illsley MP	17,805	57.6	Eric Illsley MP
Lib Dem	Miles Crompton	5,966	19.3	n/a
Conservative	Peter Morel	4,548	14.7	n/a
Others		2,578	8.3	

Barnsley East

Labour notional majority of 18,298; notional turnout: 48.8%

PARTY	2005 CANDIDATE	NOTIONAL 2005 VOTES	NOTIONAL 2005 % VOTE	PPC FOR NEXT GE
Labour	n/a	22,808	71.0	Jeff Ennis MP
Lib Dem	n/a	4,510	14.0	n/a
Conservative	n/a	4,078	12.7	n/a
Others		740	2.3	

Batley & Spen

Labour notional majority of 6,060; notional turnout: 60.8%

PARTY	2005 CANDIDATE	NOTIONAL 2005 VOTES	NOTIONAL 2005 % VOTE	PPC FOR NEXT GE
Labour	Mike Wood MP	20,249	45.3	Mike Wood MP
Conservative	Robert Light	14,189	31.7	Janice Small
Lib Dem	Neil Bentley	6,888	15.4	n/a
Others		3,418	7.7	

Located in the Leeds, Bradford and Huddersfield triangle, Batley & Spen is typical of the working-class northern constituencies which fell to the Conservatives in the 1983 Thatcher landslide. Characterised by pebbledashed terraces, working men's clubs and light industry, the constituency has proved itself curiously resistant to producing large swings. Conservative firebrand Elizabeth Peacock held the seat with majorities of under 1,500 for three elections until her defeat in 1997 on a below-average 7.4% swing. Fomenting hostility towards the sizeable Muslim community (14.7%), the BNP has made advances at a local government level in recent years, securing a councillor in Heckmondwike in 2007. Public relations consultant and Conservative candidate Janice Small will challenge the incumbent MP, Labour's Mike Wood.

Beverley & Holderness

Conservative notional majority of 3,097; notional turnout: 64.2%

PARTY	2005 CANDIDATE	NOTIONAL 2005 VOTES	NOTIONAL 2005 % VOTE	PPC FOR NEXT GE
Conservative	Graham Stuart	20,345	40.9	Graham Stuart MP
Labour	George McManus	17,248	34.7	Ian Saunders
Lib Dem	Stewart Willie	9,784	19.7	John Beacroft-Mitchell
Others		2,312	4.7	

Bradford East

Labour notional majority of 5,227; notional turnout: 54.1%

PARTY	2005 CANDIDATE	NOTIONAL 2005 VOTES	NOTIONAL 2005 % VOTE	PPC FOR NEXT GE
Labour	Terry Rooney MP	16,172	44.1	Terry Rooney MP
Lib Dem	David Ward	10,945	29.8	David Ward
Conservative	Teck Khong	6,392	17.4	n/a
Others		3,196	8.7	

Bradford South

Labour notional majority of 8,444; notional turnout: 53.4%

PARTY	2005 CANDIDATE	NOTIONAL 2005 VOTES	NOTIONAL 2005 % VOTE	PPC FOR NEXT GE
Labour	Gerry Sutcliffe MP	17,009	48.3	Gerry Sutcliffe MP
Conservative	Geraldine Carter	8,565	24.3	n/a
Lib Dem	Mike Doyle	5,112	14.5	Mike Doyle
Others		4,512	12.8	

Bradford West

Labour notional majority of 3,050; notional turnout: 56.0%

PARTY	2005 CANDIDATE	NOTIONAL 2005 VOTES	NOTIONAL 2005 % VOTE	PPC FOR NEXT GE
Labour	Marsha Singh MP	14,524	39.7	Marsha Singh MP
Conservative	Haroon Rashid	11,474	31.4	Zahid Iqbal
Lib Dem	Mukhtar Ali	6,967	19.0	Mukhtar Ali
Others		3,618	9.9	

Demographically speaking, Bradford West is a textbook Labour constituency. Unemployment is high, a fifth of homes are council owned and almost a quarter of dwellings have no central heating. Outside Northern Ireland, however, Bradford West is one of the few constituencies where religious affiliations have played a significant role in recent elections. At 38%, the constituency is home to one of the highest proportion of Muslims in the country, many of whom have opted in recent years to support Islamic Conservative candidates over the sitting Sikh Labour MP Marsha Singh. Some observers have suggested that Mr Singh owes his past margins of victory to support from white, working-class voters. The Conservatives have again opted for a Muslim candidate in local property developer Zahid Iqbal.

Brigg & Goole

Labour notional majority of 3,217; notional turnout: 62.7%

PARTY	2005 CANDIDATE	NOTIONAL 2005 VOTES	NOTIONAL 2005 % VOTE	PPC FOR NEXT GE
Labour	Ian Cawsey MP	18,795	45.8	Ian Cawsey MP
Conservative	Matthew Bean	15,578	38.0	Andrew Percy
Lib Dem	Gary Johnson	5,411	13.2	n/a
Others		1,226	3.0	

Taking in Lincolnshire's bleak north-eastern corner and the southern portion of the East Riding of Yorkshire, this seat has been held by Labour since the 1997 general election. The incumbent party's support is unassailable in Goole, a town whose skyline is dominated by the cranes which service its active container port, while the Conservatives are strongest in Axholme and the market town of Brigg. There is a diverse range of employment here, including light manufacturing, chemical production and farming. Eurosceptic sentiment is strong here, UKIP having come close to topping the poll at the 2009 European elections. Labour's notional majority here is slightly boosted by the transfer of the solidly Conservative Ridge ward to neighbouring Scunthorpe. Teacher Andrew Percy is the Conservative Party's choice to take on sitting Labour MP Ian Cawsey.

Calder Valley

Labour notional majority of 1,303; notional turnout: 66.0%

PARTY	2005 CANDIDATE	NOTIONAL 2005 VOTES	NOTIONAL 2005 % VOTE	PPC FOR NEXT GE
Labour	Christine McCafferty MP	18,347	38.5	Stephanie Booth
Conservative	Liz Truss	17,044	35.8	Craig Whittaker
Lib Dem	Liz Ingleton	9,007	18.9	Hilary Myers
Others		3,258	6.8	

An attractive West Yorkshire constituency located on the border with Lancashire, Calder Valley has been represented by a Labour MP since the 1997 general election. The constituency is largely rural in nature, taking in the small Pennine towns of Brighouse and Todmorden. Once sustained by thriving textiles industries, the area is now popular with commuters to Manchester, Bradford and Leeds. Both major parties are fairly evenly divided in both the rural and urban portions of this seat, although both have pockets of firm support. Unlike the majority of West Yorkshire constituencies, there is an almost total absence of ethnic minority residents here. Incumbent MP Christine McCafferty is retiring and will be replaced as Labour candidate by Cherie Blair's stepmother, Stephanie Booth. Craig Whittaker will hope to take the seat for the Conservatives.

Cleethorpes

Labour notional majority of 2,640; notional turnout: 61.6%

PARTY	2005 CANDIDATE	NOTIONAL 2005 VOTES	NOTIONAL 2005 % VOTE	PPC FOR NEXT GE
Labour	Shona McIsaac MP	18,887	43.3	Shona McIsaac MP
Conservative	Martin Vickers	16,247	37.3	Martin Vickers
Lib Dem	Geoff Lowis	6,437	14.8	Doug Pickett
Others		2,016	4.6	

Located just south of Grimsby, the Cleethorpes constituency was wrestled by Labour from Conservative MP-turned-journalist Michael Brown at the 1997 general election. Cleethorpes itself is a small, middle-class town located alongside the Humber estuary which is virtually contiguous with neighbouring Grimsby. The constituency also includes the country's largest deep-water port in the country at Immingham and the Lindsey oil refinery, site of 2009's 'wildcat' strikes in protest at the decision of the facility to hire largely non-British workers. Support for the two main parties is fairly evenly divided locally with Labour strongest in the Crosby and Park areas of Cleethorpes and the Conservatives dominating in the constituency's rather humdrum rural areas. At the 2009 European elections, the Conservatives outpolled Labour here by a two-to-one margin. Labour MP Shona McIssac will be challenged by North Lincolnshire Conservative councillor Martin Vickers.

Colne Valley

Labour notional majority of 1,267; notional turnout: 65.2%

PARTY	2005 CANDIDATE	NOTIONAL 2005 VOTES	NOTIONAL 2005 % VOTE	PPC FOR NEXT GE
Labour	Kali Mountford MP	17,862	35.4	Debbie Abrahams
Conservative	Maggie Throup	16,595	32.9	Jason McCartney
Lib Dem	Elisabeth Wilson	12,370	24.5	Nicola Turner
Others		3,603	7.1	

Politically speaking, this picturesque rural constituency is something of a political oddity, having been represented by each of the three major parties in the last 25 years. With no particularly large towns here, the seat comprises scores of villages along the Colne and Holme valleys. With the area's industrial sector long since having disappeared, many local residents commute to work in nearby Huddersfield. Levels of owner occupation are extremely high at 77.5% yet much of the stone-clad housing here is of poor quality, a fifth of homes having no central heating. The Liberal Democrats, whose predecessor party held this seat until 1987, remain strong here on a local government level. Debbie Abrahams has been selected as the Labour candidate, replacing retiring MP Kali Mountford. The Conservatives are fielding Jason McCartney.

Dewsbury

Labour notional majority of 3,999; notional turnout: 59.2%

PARTY	2005 CANDIDATE	NOTIONAL 2005 VOTES	NOTIONAL 2005 % VOTE	PPC FOR NEXT GE
Labour	Shahid Malik	18,278	40.6	Shahid Malik MP
Conservative	Sayeeda Warsi	14,279	31.7	n/a
Lib Dem	Kingsley Hill	6,187	13.7	n/a
Others		6,292	14.0	

Situated in the heart of West Yorkshire, Dewsbury is a former textile town in easy reach of both Leeds and Bradford. At 12.1%, the constituency has one of the largest Muslim populations in the country, which has led to significant local tensions with the predominantly white population in the town's eastern suburbs. Having received 13.1% of the vote here in 2005, the BNP has Dewsbury as one of its top target seats. Labour and the BNP are strong in Dewsbury town while the Conservatives dominate in the outlying villages. The proportion of residents living in social housing, 18.5%, is around average for a Yorkshire constituency. Much of the privately owned terraced housing in Dewsbury town is of poor quality with almost of a quarter of residents having no central heating systems. Labour minister Shahid Malik will seek re-election.

Don Valley

Labour notional majority of 11,333; notional turnout: 53.3%

PARTY	2005 CANDIDATE	NOTIONAL 2005 VOTES	NOTIONAL 2005 % VOTE	PPC FOR NEXT GE
Labour	Caroline Flint MP	21,674	56.5	Caroline Flint MP
Conservative	Adam Duguid	10,341	27.0	n/a
Lib Dem	Stewart Arnold	6,330	16.5	n/a
Others		0	0.0	

Doncaster Central

Labour notional majority of 10,325; notional turnout: 52.0%

PARTY	2005 CANDIDATE	NOTIONAL 2005 VOTES	NOTIONAL 2005 % VOTE	PPC FOR NEXT GE
Labour	Rosie Winterton MP	19,265	51.0	Rosie Winterton MP
Lib Dem	Patrick Wilson	8,940	23.7	n/a
Conservative	Stefan Kerner	7,040	18.6	n/a
Others		2,529	6.7	

Doncaster North

Labour notional majority of 12,027; notional turnout: 52.6%

PARTY	2005 CANDIDATE	NOTIONAL 2005 VOTES	NOTIONAL 2005 % VOTE	PPC FOR NEXT GE
Labour	Ed Miliband	19,300	51.1	Ed Miliband MP
Conservative	Martin Drake	7,273	19.3	n/a
Lib Dem	Doug Pickett	5,919	15.7	n/a
Others		5,273	14.0	

Elmet & Rothwell

Labour notional majority of 6,078; notional turnout: 69.7%

PARTY	2005 CANDIDATE	NOTIONAL 2005 VOTES	NOTIONAL 2005 % VOTE	PPC FOR NEXT GE
Labour	Colin Burgon MP	24,416	45.9	n/a
Conservative	Andrew Millard	18,338	34.5	Alec Shelbrooke
Lib Dem	Madeleine Kirk	9,202	17.3	Stewart Golton
Others		1,231	2.3	

Formed out of the Labour-held seats of Elmet and Morley & Rothwell, the new Elmet & Rothwell constituency will be contested for the first time at the forthcoming general election. This is a politically mixed constituency with the Conservatives dominating in the market town of Wetherby while Labour lead in Rothwell, only a short distance from Leeds's deprived city centre. Located in the north-eastern corner of West Yorkshire, the constituency lies on the outermost boundaries of the city of Leeds. As one might expect in a relatively affluent commuter constituency, almost four out of five homes are owner occupied and unemployment is below the national average. Incumbent Labour MP Colin Burgon has opted for retirement. Alec Shelbrooke will contest the seat for the Conservatives.

Great Grimsby

Labour notional majority of 7,654; notional turnout: 51.7%

PARTY	2005 CANDIDATE	NOTIONAL 2005 VOTES	NOTIONAL 2005 % VOTE	PPC FOR NEXT GE
Labour	Austin Mitchell MP	15,512	47.1	Austin Mitchell MP
Conservative	Giles Taylor	7,858	23.8	Victoria Ayling
Lib Dem	Andrew de Freitas	6,356	19.3	Andrew de Freitas
Others		3,238	9.8	

Halifax

Labour notional majority of 3,481; notional turnout: 61.0%

PARTY	2005 CANDIDATE	NOTIONAL 2005 VOTES	NOTIONAL 2005 % VOTE	PPC FOR NEXT GE
Labour	Linda Riordan MP	16,658	41.9	Linda Riordan MP
Conservative	Kris Hopkins	13,177	33.1	Philip Allott
Lib Dem	Michael Taylor	7,120	17.9	Diane Park
Others		2,818	7.1	

Situated in West Yorkshire and once the centre of the UK's wool-manufacturing sector, Halifax has been loyal to the Labour Party in all but one election since 1964. Labour are strongest in the urban Halifax town portion of the seat while the Conservatives lead in rural Northowram and Shelf and the town of Sowerby Bridge. As with many other former textile towns in West Yorkshire, the constituency has a substantial ethnic minority population with almost one in ten residents being Muslims. The BNP has secured a foothold here, gaining a councillor in the Illingworth & Mixenden ward. While all constituencies have been hit by the economic slump, residents here are braced for significant job losses at the headquarters of the Halifax, the HBOS-owned former building society. Sitting MP Linda Riordan will defend her seat for Labour against Conservative businessman Philip Allot.

Haltemprice & Howden

Conservative notional majority of 5,080; notional turnout: 70.4%

PARTY	2005 CANDIDATE	NOTIONAL 2005 VOTES	NOTIONAL 2005 % VOTE	PPC FOR NEXT GE
Conservative	David Davis MP	22,687	47.0	David Davis MP
Lib Dem	Jon Neal	17,607	36.5	n/a
Labour	Edward Hart	6,514	13.5	Daniel Marten
Others		1,463	3.0	

Harrogate & Knaresborough

Lib Dem notional majority of 7,980; notional turnout: 66.6%

PARTY	2005 CANDIDATE	NOTIONAL 2005 VOTES	NOTIONAL 2005 % VOTE	PPC FOR NEXT GE
Lib Dem	Phil Willis MP	25,639	52.1	Claire Kelley
Conservative	Maggie Punyer	17,659	35.9	Andrew Jones
Labour	Lorraine Ferris	4,480	9.1	Kevin McNerney
Others		1,434	2.9	

Once safe for the Conservatives, this sumptuously wealthy constituency spectacularly deserted the party in 1997, electing Liberal Democrat headteacher Phil Willis on a 15.7% swing. The home of the famous Betty's Tearoom, elegant stone-clad terraces and beautifully manicured gardens, the spa town of Harrogate is a major tourist and conference destination. The nearby town of Knaresborough is similarly ornate with stunning views of the Yorkshire Dales. On a local government level, the Conservatives have rebuilt substantially in recent years, wresting outright control of Harrogate Borough Council from the Liberal Democrats and winning convincingly at the 2009 county council elections. With owner occupation rates of almost 80%, Labour support is virtually non-existent. The Liberal Democrats have selected Claire Kelley while the Conservative candidate will be marketing professional Andrew Jones.

Hemsworth

Labour notional majority of 14,026; notional turnout: 54.3%

PARTY	2005 CANDIDATE	NOTIONAL 2005 VOTES	NOTIONAL 2005 % VOTE	PPC FOR NEXT GE
Labour	Jon Trickett MP	22,542	58.7	Jon Trickett MP
Conservative	Jonathan Mortimer	8,516	22.2	n/a
Lib Dem	David Hall-Matthews	6,034	15.7	n/a
Others		1,329	3.5	

Huddersfield

Labour notional majority of 7,883; notional turnout: 56.6%

PARTY	2005 CANDIDATE	NOTIONAL 2005 VOTES	NOTIONAL 2005 % VOTE	PPC FOR NEXT GE
Labour	Barry Sheerman MP	16,402	46.4	Barry Sheerman MP
Lib Dem	Emma Bone	8,519	24.1	James Blanchard
Conservative	David Meacock	7,447	21.1	Karen Tweed
Others		2,994	8.5	

Kingston upon Hull East

Labour notional majority of 11,740; notional turnout: 47.6%

PARTY	2005 CANDIDATE	NOTIONAL 2005 VOTES	NOTIONAL 2005 % VOTE	PPC FOR NEXT GE
Labour	John Prescott MP	18,361	56.1	Karl Turner
Lib Dem	Andy Sloan	6,621	20.2	n/a
Conservative	Katy Lindsay	4,258	13.0	n/a
Others		3,513	10.7	

Kingston upon Hull North

Labour notional majority of 7,384; notional turnout: 46.1%

PARTY	2005 CANDIDATE	NOTIONAL 2005 VOTES	NOTIONAL 2005 % VOTE	PPC FOR NEXT GE
Labour	Diana Johnson	14,679	52.3	Diana Johnson MP
Lib Dem	Denis Healy	7,295	26.0	Denis Healy
Conservative	Lydia Rivlin	3,730	13.3	n/a
Others		2,385	8.5	

Kingston upon Hull West & Hessle

Labour notional majority of 9,430; notional turnout: 44.7%

PARTY	2005 CANDIDATE	NOTIONAL 2005 VOTES	NOTIONAL 2005 % VOTE	PPC FOR NEXT GE
Labour	Alan Johnson MP	15,244	55.1	Alan Johnson MP
Lib Dem	David Nolan	5,814	21.0	Mike Ross
Conservative	Karen Woods	5,741	20.7	n/a
Others		889	3.2	

Keighley

Labour notional majority of 4,852; notional turnout: 69.1%

PARTY	2005 CANDIDATE	NOTIONAL 2005 VOTES	NOTIONAL 2005 % VOTE	PPC FOR NEXT GE
Labour	Ann Cryer MP	20,720	44.7	Jane Thomas
Conservative	Karl Poulsen	15,868	34.3	Kris Hopkins
Lib Dem	Nader Fekri	5,484	11.8	Nader Fekri
Others		4,240	9.2	

Previously held by Conservative Gary Waller, Keighley was gained by Labour's Ann Cryer at the 1997 general election. Located around 10 miles north of the city of Bradford, the Keighley constituency is a mix of former textile towns and pleasant countryside set against the backdrop of the southern Pennines. On a political level, Keighley town is a relatively safe bet for Labour while the Conservatives dominate in the tourist town of Ilkley and in the rural Worth valley. As with many West Yorkshire constituencies, the area has sadly suffered for significant racial tensions between the majority white and 9.4% Asian community. BNP leader Nick Griffin contested this seat at the last election, securing 9.2% of the vote. With Mrs Cryer opting for retirement, Labour has selected Jane Thomas. Bradford City Council leader Kris Hopkins is standing for the Conservatives.

Leeds Central

Labour notional majority of 12,916; notional turnout: 44.3%

PARTY	2005 CANDIDATE	NOTIONAL 2005 VOTES	NOTIONAL 2005 % VOTE	PPC FOR NEXT GE
Labour	Hilary Benn MP	20,236	59.5	Hilary Benn MP
Lib Dem	Ruth Coleman	7,320	21.5	Ryk Downes
Conservative	Brian Cattell	4,320	12.7	n/a
Others		2,132	6.3	

Leeds East

Labour notional majority of 13,689; notional turnout: 56.1%

PARTY	2005 CANDIDATE	NOTIONAL 2005 VOTES	NOTIONAL 2005 % VOTE	PPC FOR NEXT GE
Labour	George Mudie MP	21,423	59.8	George Mudie MP
Conservative	Dominic Ponniah	7,734	21.6	n/a
Lib Dem	Andrew Tear	6,172	17.2	n/a
Others		500	1.4	

Leeds North East

Labour notional majority of 6,762; notional turnout: 64.5%

PARTY	2005 CANDIDATE	NOTIONAL 2005 VOTES	NOTIONAL 2005 % VOTE	PPC FOR NEXT GE
Labour	Fabian Hamilton MP	19,937	45.7	Fabian Hamilton MP
Conservative	Matthew Lobley	13,175	30.2	Matthew Lobley
Lib Dem	Jonathan Brown	9,454	21.7	Aqila Choudhry
Others		1,038	2.4	

Fabian Hamilton gained Leeds North East, historically a Conservative constituency, from Tory Home Office minister Timothy Kirkhope at the 1997 general election. Despite its name, the constituency encompasses far more than urban Leeds, taking in the semi-rural Alwoodley, which has the highest house prices in the Yorkshire and Humber region. Labour support is strongest in the Moortown ward, which includes substantial amounts of low-rise council housing, while Roundhay is more evenly divided between the parties. Leeds North East is home to sizeable Jewish (7%), Muslim (5.5%), black (4.6%) and Sikh (3.7%) populations and enjoys an above-average owner occupation rate (70%). Local councillor Matthew Lobley, whose party's chances are not helped by the changing demographics locally, will fight the seat for the Conservatives.

Leeds North West

Lib Dem notional majority of 2,064; notional turnout: 62.7%

PARTY	2005 CANDIDATE	NOTIONAL 2005 VOTES	NOTIONAL 2005 % VOTE	PPC FOR NEXT GE
Lib Dem	Greg Mulholland	15,328	36.9	Greg Mulholland MP
Labour	Judith Blake	13,204	31.9	Judith Blake
Conservative	George Lee	11,151	26.8	Julia Mulligan
Others		1,829	4.4	

Held for almost three decades by leading Tory 'wet' Dr Keith Hampson, the voters of Leeds North West followed the rest of the city in electing a Labour MP in 1997. Conservative fortunes have not improved since. Capitalising upon widespread anger at student top-up fees (a quarter of residents are full-time students) and the Iraq War, the Liberal Democrats rose from third place to take the seat in 2005. Now a three-way marginal, as little more than 4,000 votes separate the three main parties, all of whom have robust pockets of support locally. The constituency stretches from the poor and densely populated inner-city areas out to the rural wilds of Adel & Wharfedale ward, one of Yorkshire's most prosperous residential areas. The sitting Liberal Democrat MP, Greg Mulholland, will fight local Labour councillor Judith Blake and Conservative Julia Mulligan.

Leeds West

Labour notional majority of 13,699; notional turnout: 52.7%

PARTY	2005 CANDIDATE	NOTIONAL 2005 VOTES	NOTIONAL 2005 % VOTE	PPC FOR NEXT GE
Labour	John Battle MP	19,831	56.2	Rachel Reeves
Lib Dem	Darren Finlay	6,132	17.4	Ruth Coleman
Conservative	Tim Metcalfe	4,967	14.1	n/a
Others		4,353	12.3	

Morley & Outwood

Labour notional majority of 8,669; notional turnout: 58.4%

PARTY	2005 CANDIDATE	NOTIONAL 2005 VOTES	NOTIONAL 2005 % VOTE	PPC FOR NEXT GE
Labour	Colin Challen MP	19,024	46.0	Ed Balls MP
Conservative	Nick Vineall	10,355	25.0	Antony Calvert
Lib Dem	Stewart Golton	4,159	10.0	James Monaghan
Others		7,851	19.0	

Normanton, Pontefract & Castleford

Labour notional majority of 20,608; notional turnout: 53.3%

PARTY	2005 CANDIDATE	NOTIONAL 2005 VOTES	NOTIONAL 2005 % VOTE	PPC FOR NEXT GE
Labour	Yvette Cooper MP	27,630	65.3	Yvette Cooper MP
Conservative	Simon Jones	7,022	16.6	n/a
Lib Dem	Wesley Paxton	4,704	11.1	n/a
Others		2,931	6.9	

Penistone & Stocksbridge

Labour notional majority of 8,617; notional turnout: 62.0%

PARTY	2005 CANDIDATE	NOTIONAL 2005 VOTES	NOTIONAL 2005 % VOTE	PPC FOR NEXT GE
Labour	n/a	19,047	45.2	Angela C. Smith MP
Lib Dem	n/a	10,430	24.7	Ian Cuthbertson
Conservative	n/a	9,996	23.7	Spencer Pitifield
Others		2,706	6.4	

Pudsey

Labour notional majority of 5,204; notional turnout: 65.9%

PARTY	2005 CANDIDATE	NOTIONAL 2005 VOTES	NOTIONAL 2005 % VOTE	PPC FOR NEXT GE
Labour	Paul Truswell MP	20,120	45.4	n/a
Conservative	Pamela Singleton	14,916	33.7	Stuart Andrew
Lib Dem	James Keeley	8,044	18.2	David Morton
Others		1,229	2.8	

Located mid-way between Leeds and Bradford, Pudsey was gained from the Conservatives by Labour's Paul Truswell at the 1997 general election. Pudsey itself is a small working-class town which is ordinarily loyal to the Labour Party, whereas the commuter suburbs of Guiseley and Horsforth generally favour the Conservatives. Levels of owner occupation here are high, yet a high proportion of the constituency's stone-clad homes are in a poor condition, with one in five having no central heating or private bathroom. Despite almost no swing-back to the Conservatives having been recorded at the 2001 or 2005 elections, the Tories outpolled Labour two-to-one at the 2008 council elections and will be hopeful of reclaiming this seat. The Conservative candidate will be Stuart Andrew, a member of Leeds City Council.

Richmond (Yorks)

Conservative notional majority of 19,450; notional turnout: 64.5%

PARTY	2005 CANDIDATE	NOTIONAL 2005 VOTES	NOTIONAL 2005 % VOTE	PPC FOR NEXT GE
Conservative	William Hague MP	29,793	59.3	William Hague MP
Labour	Neil Foster	10,343	20.6	Eileen Driver
Lib Dem	Jacquie Bell	8,500	16.9	Linda Curran
Others		1,581	3.1	

Rother Valley

Labour notional majority of 11,558; notional turnout: 57.6%

PARTY	2005 CANDIDATE	NOTIONAL 2005 VOTES	NOTIONAL 2005 % VOTE	PPC FOR NEXT GE
Labour	Kevin Barron MP	20,929	51.6	Kevin Barron MP
Conservative	Colin Phillips	9,371	23.1	Lynda Donaldson
Lib Dem	Phil Bristow	6,549	16.1	Phil Bristow
Others		3,748	9.2	

Rotherham

Labour notional majority of 13,865; notional turnout: 54.1%

PARTY	2005 CANDIDATE	NOTIONAL 2005 VOTES	NOTIONAL 2005 % VOTE	PPC FOR NEXT GE
Labour	Denis MacShane MP	19,371	57.7	Denis MacShane MP
Lib Dem	Tim Gordon	5,506	16.4	Tim Gordon
Conservative	Lee Rotheram	4,464	13.3	Lee Rotheram
Others		4,209	12.5	

Scarborough & Whitby

Conservative notional majority of 1,245; notional turnout: 63.5%

PARTY	2005 CANDIDATE	NOTIONAL 2005 VOTES	NOTIONAL 2005 % VOTE	PPC FOR NEXT GE
Conservative	Robert Goodwill	19,248	41.0	Robert Goodwill MP
Labour	Lawrence Quinn	18,003	38.4	Annajoy David
Lib Dem	Tani Exley-Moore	7,495	16.0	Tani Exley-Moore
Others		2,166	4.6	

Scunthorpe

Labour notional majority of 8,638; notional turnout: 54.4%

PARTY	2005 CANDIDATE	NOTIONAL 2005 VOTES	NOTIONAL 2005 % VOTE	PPC FOR NEXT GE
Labour	Elliot Morley MP	17,815	52.0	n/a
Conservative	Julian Sturdy	9,177	26.8	Caroline Johnson
Lib Dem	Neil Poole	5,835	17.0	Neil Poole
Others		1,403	4.1	

Selby & Ainsty

Conservative notional majority of 2,060; notional turnout: 68.9%

PARTY	2005 CANDIDATE	NOTIONAL 2005 VOTES	NOTIONAL 2005 % VOTE	PPC FOR NEXT GE
Conservative	John Grogan MP	22,554	47.2	Nigel Adams
Labour	Mark Menzies	20,494	42.8	Wendy Nichols
Lib Dem	Ian Cuthbertson	4,785	10.0	Nicholas Emmerson
Others		0	0.0	

Sheffield, Brightside & Hillsborough

Labour notional majority of 18,801; notional turnout: 49.9%

PARTY	2005 CANDIDATE	NOTIONAL 2005 VOTES	NOTIONAL 2005 % VOTE	PPC FOR NEXT GE
Labour	David Blunkett MP	23,126	69.6	David Blunkett MP
Lib Dem	Jonathan Harston	4,325	13.0	Jonathon Harston
Conservative	Tim Clark	3,250	9.8	n/a
Others		2,529	7.6	

Sheffield Central

Labour notional majority of 5,025; notional turnout: 55.0%

PARTY	2005 CANDIDATE	NOTIONAL 2005 VOTES	NOTIONAL 2005 % VOTE	PPC FOR NEXT GE
Labour	Richard Carborn MP	15,463	46.5	Paul Blomfield
Lib Dem	Ali Qadar	10,438	31.4	Paul Scriven
Conservative	Samantha George	3,046	9.2	n/a
Others		4,278	12.9	

Sheffield, Hallam

Lib Dem notional majority of 7,416; notional turnout: 67.9%

PARTY	2005 CANDIDATE	NOTIONAL 2005 VOTES	NOTIONAL 2005 % VOTE	PPC FOR NEXT GE
Lib Dem	Nick Clegg	21,253	46.4	Nick Clegg MP
Conservative	Spencer Pitifield	13,837	30.2	n/a
Labour	Mahroof Hussain	8,160	17.8	Jack Scott
Others		2,602	5.7	

The constituency of Liberal Democrat leader Nick Clegg, Sheffield, Hallam is one of the wealthiest seats in the United Kingdom. Home to many of the city's professional classes, owner occupation levels hover around 80% and a third of residents are university educated. The seat stretches from the city's south-eastern suburbs of Dore, Ecclesall and Totley to take in part of the Peak District National Park to the west. The seat also has a large student population (11.9%) with the University of Sheffield and Sheffield Hallam University being located nearby. For decades a Conservative seat, the Liberal Democrats finally capitalised upon years of local government domination by ousting sitting MP Sir Irvine Patnick in 1997. With the Liberal Democrats continuing to hold every council seat in the constituency it is almost inconceivable to see Nick Clegg losing.

Sheffield, Heeley

Labour notional majority of 12,340; notional turnout: 57.7%

PARTY	2005 CANDIDATE	NOTIONAL 2005 VOTES	NOTIONAL 2005 % VOTE	PPC FOR NEXT GE
Labour	Meg Munn MP	20,418	54.1	Meg Munn MP
Lib Dem	Colin Ross	8,078	21.4	n/a
Conservative	Aster Crawshaw	5,428	14.4	n/a
Others		3,849	10.2	

Sheffield South East

Labour notional majority of 15,843; notional turnout: 54.6%

PARTY	2005 CANDIDATE	NOTIONAL 2005 VOTES	NOTIONAL 2005 % VOTE	PPC FOR NEXT GE
Labour	Clive Betts MP	22,023	60.3	Clive Betts MP
Lib Dem	Kevin Moore	6,180	16.9	n/a
Conservative	Tracy Critchlow	5,250	14.4	n/a
Others		3,083	8.4	

Shipley

Conservative notional majority of 450; notional turnout: 68.0%

PARTY	2005 CANDIDATE	NOTIONAL 2005 VOTES	NOTIONAL 2005 % VOTE	PPC FOR NEXT GE
Conservative	Phillip Davis	18,077	38.8	Philip Davies MP
Labour	Christopher Leslie	17,627	37.9	Susan Hinchcliffe
Lib Dem	John Briggs	7,059	15.2	John Harris
Others		3,788	8.1	

Skipton & Ripon

Conservative notional majority of 11,596; notional turnout: 66.1%

PARTY	2005 CANDIDATE	NOTIONAL 2005 VOTES	NOTIONAL 2005 % VOTE	PPC FOR NEXT GE
Conservative	David Curry MP	24,747	50.0	n/a
Lib Dem	Paul English	13,151	26.6	James Keeley
Labour	Paul Baptie	9,038	18.3	Claire Hazlegrove
Others		2,548	5.1	

Thirsk & Malton

Conservative notional majority of 14,117; notional turnout: 65.8%

PARTY	2005 CANDIDATE	NOTIONAL 2005 VOTES	NOTIONAL 2005 % VOTE	PPC FOR NEXT GE
Conservative	John Greenway MP	25,702	51.9	Anne McIntosh MP
Labour	Paul Blanchard	11,585	23.4	Jonathon Roberts
Lib Dem	Gordon Beever	9,314	18.8	Howard Keal
Others		2,939	5.9	

Wakefield

Labour notional majority of 7,349; notional turnout: 61.4%

PARTY	2005 CANDIDATE	NOTIONAL 2005 VOTES	NOTIONAL 2005 % VOTE	PPC FOR NEXT GE
Labour	Mary Creagh	18,497	44.1	Mary Creagh MP
Conservative	Alec Shelbrooke	11,148	26.5	Alex Story
Lib Dem	David Ridgway	7,889	18.8	n/a
Others		4,456	10.6	

Situated in the south-western portion of West Yorkshire, Wakefield is a once-thriving industrial town which has successfully capitalised upon its excellent transport links to reinvent itself in recent years as an important retail and commuter centre. The town's 75,000 residents are predominantly employed in the service sector although wages are below the national average, and the city centre juxtaposes an ornate and imposing cathedral with a plethora of rather more low-rent bars and clubs. Politically speaking, Wakefield city is a Labour bastion, delivering the party overwhelming support, while the surrounding rural areas of Horbury and Ossett are considerably more inclined towards the Tories. Three fifths of homes in the constituency are owner occupied, while council properties house a third of residents. Currently held by Labour's Mary Creigh, she will face a challenge from former Olympic rower Alex Story for the Conservatives.

Wentworth & Dearne

Labour notional majority of 17,551; notional turnout: 54.3%

PARTY	2005 CANDIDATE	NOTIONAL 2005 VOTES	NOTIONAL 2005 % VOTE	PPC FOR NEXT GE
Labour	John Healey MP	23,810	61.8	John Healey MP
Lib Dem	Keith Orrell	6,259	16.2	n/a
Conservative	Mark Hughes	5,301	13.8	n/a
Others		3,163	8.2	

York Central

Labour notional majority of 10,344; notional turnout: 60.6%

PARTY	2005 CANDIDATE	NOTIONAL 2005 VOTES	NOTIONAL 2005 % VOTE	PPC FOR NEXT GE
Labour	Hugh Bayley MP	19,490	48.8	Hugh Bayley MP
Conservative	Clive Booth	9,146	22.9	Susan Wade-Weeks
Lib Dem	Andrew Waller	8,040	20.1	Christian Vassie
Others		3,231	8.1	

York Outer

Lib Dem notional majority of 203; notional turnout: 64.4%

PARTY	2005 CANDIDATE	NOTIONAL 2005 VOTES	NOTIONAL 2005 % VOTE	PPC FOR NEXT GE
Lib Dem	n/a	16,904	36.7	Madeleine Kirk
Conservative	n/a	16,701	36.3	Julian Sturdy
Labour	n/a	12,425	27.0	James Alexander
Others		0	0.0	

One of the strangest creations the Boundary Commission has dreamed up for many years, York Outer encircles the urban City of York seat in a doughnut-like fashion, taking in many attractive villages from the Vale of York and Ryedale as well as the University of York campus in Heslington from Selby. At 83%, the level of home ownership is extremely high while the local population is 98% white. In theory a three-way marginal, the Liberal Democrats the dominant force at a local government level with the Conservatives far behind. Long-serving Liberal Democrat councillor Madeleine Kirk will fight Conservative farmer Julian Sturdy for the right to become this new constituency's first MP. Former York University Students' Union president James Alexander contests for Labour.

East Yorkshire

Conservative notional majority of 6,284; notional turnout: 61.1%

PARTY	2005 CANDIDATE	NOTIONAL 2005 VOTES	NOTIONAL 2005 % VOTE	PPC FOR NEXT GE
Conservative	Gregory Knight MP	21,410	45.4	Gregory Knight MP
Labour	Emma Hoddinott	15,126	32.1	Paul Rounding
Lib Dem	Jim Wastling	8,938	18.9	Robert Adamson
Others		1,721	3.6	

North of England

The far north of England is one of the smaller regions in terms of numbers of parliamentary constituencies, and is remote from media centres of 'opinion-formers' such as London, but it will be as important as any other in deciding the outcome of the next election; and although historically and presently one of their weakest areas, the Conservatives realise they must pick up a substantial proportion of seats here if they are to form a government, especially if their ambitions extend to an overall majority.

Currently they can boast only two MPs (for Hexham and Penrith & the Border) in Cumbria, Northumberland, Tyne and Wear, Durham, and Teesside and the former county of Cleveland. This is the same number as the Liberal Democrats, who added Westmorland & Lonsdale in 2005 to the veteran Alan Beith's Berwick upon Tweed. Labour won all the other thirty-one seats in that year. In 2010, however, this dominance could be sapped, as between them their rivals have at least ten plausible targets. What is more, whatever happens in the polling booths, Labour will lose one constituency in the extensive boundary changes in this region: the allocation for Tyne and Wear is reduced due to population shifts, although it is not quite clear which seat should be defined as having been abolished.

There will no longer be a parliamentary division called Tyne Bridge, spanning the river, which sounds like bad news for its MP since a 1985 by-election, Dave Clelland. However, most of Tyne Bridge forms the largest part of the new Gateshead, and Mr Clelland has duly been selected there. Meanwhile, the current Gateshead East & Washington West MP, Sharon Hodgson, has moved a little eastwards to be the candidate for the new Washington & Sunderland West, which consists of fairly equal portions drawn from four seats. If this sounds complicated – it is. Nor is that the end of it. As the last name mentioned may imply, the community to be most affected by the boundary changes in the north-east of England is the city of Sunderland. At present there are simply two clearly drawn North and South constituencies, which are better known than their safe Labour status might indicate because in recent general elections they have usually been the first to declare. Neither continues in anything like its present form, though. The novelist and diarist Chris Mullin retires from North, which is partly incorporated in Washington & Sunderland West but mainly in a new

Sunderland Central. Bill Etherington's South may in fact be the best nominee as the seat to disappear entirely, as it forms the major part of no new successor seat, its largest portion becoming a minority in Houghton & Sunderland South.

That is surely enough in the way of compass points for a while (though boundary changes will also play a part in the discussion of Cumbrian seats below). All the changes above, though resulting in a net loss of one for Labour in the game of musical chairs, do not really produce opportunities for other parties – though some optimistic Tories entertain hopes for the new Sunderland Central, remembering that the Conservatives could win seats in the town (as it was then) in the 1950s. However, the Rallings & Thrasher notional figures for 2005 suggest that a mighty swing of 13 per cent would be required.

The main Conservative targets in the North East are Tynemouth (swing needed: 6 per cent), Stockton South (7 per cent) and Middlesbrough South & East Cleveland (9.3 per cent). None of these will be easy to gain. The main reason for hope in Tynemouth lies in the Tories' good performances in elections for North Tyneside Borough Council, and in its direct mayoral elections: in June 2009 Linda Arkley regained this post with a majority of nearly 5,000 over her Labour predecessor (and successor) John Harrison, and this in an area covering Stephen Byers's safe North Tyneside parliamentary seat as well as Tynemouth. Stockton South was one of only half a dozen SDP constituencies in 1983, but Tim Devlin won it for the Conservatives in 1987 and 1992. Middlesbrough South & East Cleveland – an unwieldy name to replace an unpronounceable one, for it was called Langbaurgh before 1997 – has bounced back and forth between Labour's Dr Ashok Kumar and his Tory opponents since he first won it in a 1991 by-election. While the 9-plus per cent swing needed looks steep, it would be foolish to write off Paul Bristow's chances given recent mid-term election results and opinion polls.

Over in Cumbria in the far north-west of England, the chief focus of attention is probably Carlisle (see *One to Watch* below). However, there are two other Conservative targets from Labour there that require almost identical swings to Carlisle after the boundary changes, one outside possibility of a change of hands, and one Liberal Democrat versus Tory contest which may well buck the national tide.

The former Cabinet minister John Hutton has decided to end his parliamentary career voluntarily at the age of fifty-four; but he may have lost his seat in any case. The addition of 3,000 staunchly non-Labour voters around the old-fashioned town of Broughton-in-Furness, with its leafy sloping central square, reduces the swing needed for a Tory gain from 9 to 7 per cent. Although most of the town of Barrow, founded on iron and shipbuilding, looks resolutely working class, it does in fact have strong Conservative wards such as Hawcoat – and another clue to its marginality is to be found in the full name of the constituency, as most of the Furness peninsula is now included as well. This seat has historically been subject to large swings, usually connected with the health of its main employing industry and the fortunes of Vickers, all much influenced by government policy. Barrow was held by Cecil Franks for the Tories between 1983 and 1992.

Another possible change may occur in Copeland, though it has less of such a tradition, having been won by Labour ever since 1935, previously under the name of its largest town, Whitehaven. Again, though, the task facing the Conservative candidate Chris Whiteside has been made easier by the Boundary Commission, which has increased the amount of the Lake District included in Copeland. It will now include Keswick and Derwent Water as well as England's highest point at Scafell Pike. Mountains and lakes do not of course have votes, and the rural inland dependent on farming and tourism has previously been outvoted by the economically depressed communities on the west Cumbrian coast. This may not happen next time. Copeland was the first area in the country to be switched over to digital television, and a historic political switch in 2010 should not be ruled out either.

Workington is Labour's safest seat in Cumbria, made even more so by the same boundary changes, although unlike Copeland it has briefly been held by the Tories within living memory, following a by-election in 1976. It will be an uphill task for Judith Pattinson to repeat this in a general election, and the evidence suggests that the much easier task on paper of regaining Westmorland & Lonsdale from the Liberal Democrats may be as well. First-term Lib Dem MPs like Tim Farron have a reputation for strengthening their position dramatically (see, for example, Norman Lamb in North Norfolk in 2005). In Westmorland, the incumbent party has also done extremely well in recent local council elections as well. The Liberal Democrats took control of South Lakeland district for the first time in May 2006, and by 2008 had thirty-six councillors to the Tories' fourteen. The also achieved their highest percentage anywhere in Britain here in the June 2009 Euro elections: 36.8 per cent, higher even than Orkney and Shetland.

Another of the few council areas where the Liberal Democrats finished first then in term of votes (in elections where they are always disadvantaged by the electorate's undoubted Eurosceptic hue) was Newcastle upon Tyne, where they have also been in control of the city authority since 2004. This gives them hopes of gaining parliamentary seats from Labour too, although municipal success can have a counter-effect if the council is unpopular, and the swings needed to beat any of the Newcastle MPs, including Chief Whip Nick Brown, are all in double figures. Perhaps a more likely gain is City of Durham, with its increasing middle class and university presence as the memory of the north eastern coalfield as epitomised in the Durham Gala gradually fades. In 2005 Roberta Blackman-Woods had a distinctly vulnerable majority of 3,000 here.

Despite the fading of the economic dominance of heavy industry in the north of England, Labour will still return most of the MPs in the region; but that is not the point. In order to win a fourth term they will need to win almost 90 per cent of the seats, as they have since 1997. There are no easy gains here, but the key seats are all the more vital for lying in that crucial range which determines whether the Conservatives can become comfortably the largest party, or leap to an overall majority for the first time since the 1992 election – which seems, and is, a very long time ago.

Target seats

SEAT	SWING REQUIRED %	MP	CHALLENGER
Conservative from Labour			
Tynemouth	5.9	Alan Campbell	Wendy Morton
Barrow & Furness	6.3	John Hutton*	John Gough
Copeland	6.7	Jamie Reed	Chris Whiteside
Stockton South	6.8	Dari Taylor	James Wharton
Carlisle	6.8	Eric Martlew*	John Stephenson
Middlesbrough South & East Cleveland	9.3	Ashok Kumar	Paul Bristow
Workington	11.5	Tony Cunningham	Judith Pattinson
Sunderland Central	12.8	(Julie Elliott)	Lee Martin
Lib Dem from Labour			
City of Durham	3.7	Roberta Blackman-Woods	Carol Woods
Blaydon	6.9	David Anderson	Neil Bradbury
Newcastle upon Tyne East	10.5	Nick Brown	Greg Stone
Conservative from Lib Dems			
Westmorland & Lonsdale	0.9	Tim Farron	Gareth McKeever

One to watch: Carlisle

Actual majority 2005: Labour 5,695 (16.1%) – Eric Martlew MP (retiring)
Notional majority 2005: Labour 5,085 (13.5%)
Conservative candidate: John Stephenson

Carlisle is a rather unusual place. The city strategically placed near the Anglo-Scottish border has also been a key fortress in electoral terms. The Conservative Party has found it a hard nut to crack. It remained in Labour hands in 1970 and through Mrs Thatcher's three victories, although by only 71 votes in 1983 and 916 in 1987. Now, however, there is a belief that the redoubt may finally fall. One reason is that Carlisle has long been rather small in electorate, only 59,500 in 2005, for example, some 10,000 below the average quota. Although the county of Cumbria has been ruled by the Boundary Commission to be worthy of over-representation due to its difficult mountainous terrain, this rather oddly benefited Carlisle, maintained as a compact urban seat. In the boundary changes brought in for 2010, though, this anomaly was at least partially rectified as 3,650 voters were added from rural and suburban wards, enough to reduce the swing needed from over 8 to under 7 per cent. With the MP of twenty-two years' standing, Eric Martlew, announcing his retirement in 2009, it seems that Labour's sequence of twelve election victories may come to an end. Carlisle's pubs were uniquely state run from the First World War till 1971 – but its long connection with the once-socialist party is now in jeopardy.

Barrow & Furness

Labour notional majority of 4,843; notional turnout: 58.9%

PARTY	2005 CANDIDATE	NOTIONAL 2005 VOTES	NOTIONAL 2005 % VOTE	PPC FOR NEXT GE
Labour	John Hutton MP	17,445	45.2	n/a
Conservative	William Dorman	12,602	32.6	John Gough
Lib Dem	Barry Rabone	6,870	17.8	Barry Rabone
Others		1,708	4.4	

Located at the end of an eerie peninsula, Cumbria's largest town has been described as the most working-class town in Britain. Formerly reliant upon the iron and steel industries, manufacturing in Barrow has been in steady decline for decades, although significant employment can still be found in specialist ship- and nuclear submarine-building. The constituency has traditionally remained loyal to Labour yet backed the Tories in 1983 and 1987 in protest at the party's commitment to unilateral nuclear disarmament. Conservatives John Gough, whose party won five seats to Labour's three in the 2009 Cumbria County Council elections, will hope to succeed former Defence Secretary John Hutton, who has announced his intention to retire next year.

Berwick-upon-Tweed

Lib Dem notional majority of 8,585; notional turnout: 63.3%

PARTY	2005 CANDIDATE	NOTIONAL 2005 VOTES	NOTIONAL 2005 % VOTE	PPC FOR NEXT GE
Lib Dem	Alan Beith MP	19,147	52.6	Alan Beith MP
Conservative	Mike Elliott	10,562	29.0	Anne-Marie Trevelyan
Labour	Glen Reynolds	6,697	18.4	Alan Strickland
Other		0	0.0	

Bishop Auckland

Labour notional majority of 10,047; notional turnout: 56.1%

PARTY	2005 CANDIDATE	NOTIONAL 2005 VOTES	NOTIONAL 2005 % VOTE	PPC FOR NEXT GE
Labour	Helen Goodman	19,065	50.0	Helen Goodman MP
Lib Dem	Chris Foote Wood	9,018	23.7	n/a
Conservative	Richard Bell	8,736	22.9	Barbara Harrison
Others		1,309	3.4	

Blaydon

Labour notional majority of 5,748; notional turnout: 62.2%

PARTY	2005 CANDIDATE	NOTIONAL 2005 VOTES	NOTIONAL 2005 % VOTE	PPC FOR NEXT GE
Labour	David Anderson	21,591	51.6	David Anderson MP
Lib Dem	Peter Maughan	15,843	37.9	Neil Bradbury
Conservative	Dorothy Luckhurst	3,356	8.0	n/a
Others		1,028	2.5	

Blyth Valley

Labour notional majority of 8,527; notional turnout: 56.2%

PARTY	2005 CANDIDATE	NOTIONAL 2005 VOTES	NOTIONAL 2005 % VOTE	PPC FOR NEXT GE
Labour	Ronnie Campbell MP	19,659	55.0	Ronnie Campbell MP
Lib Dem	Jeffrey Reid	11,132	31.1	Jeffrey Reid
Conservative	Michael Windridge	4,982	13.9	Barry Flux
Others		0	0.0	

Carlisle

PARTY	2005 CANDIDATE	NOTIONAL 2005 VOTES	NOTIONAL 2005 % VOTE	PPC FOR NEXT GE
Labour notional majority of 5,085; notional turnout: 58.5%				
Labour	Eric Martlew MP	17,701	46.8	n/a
Conservative	Mike Mitchelson	12,616	33.4	John Stevenson
Lib Dem	Steven Tweedie	6,257	16.6	Stephen Tweedie
Others		1,217	3.2	

The most northerly Labour constituency in England, Carlisle is an isolated town located in the rural wilderness just south of the Scottish border. It is a working-class town with a 99% white population in which the manufacturing sector still provides much employment, yet Labour repelled Tory challenges by less than 1,000 votes at the 1983 and 1987 elections. While Labour are likely to continue their dominance in urban Carlisle, beneficial boundary changes which add several rural wards to the seat give the Conservatives their first chance to take the seat for almost 50 years. The town's MP since 1987, Eric Martlew, is retiring and Conservative solicitor John Stevenson is aiming to take his place.

Copeland

PARTY	2005 CANDIDATE	NOTIONAL 2005 VOTES	NOTIONAL 2005 % VOTE	PPC FOR NEXT GE
Labour notional majority of 5,157; notional turnout: 62.1%				
Labour	Jamie Reed	18,198	46.7	Jamie Reed MP
Conservative	Chris Whiteside	13,041	33.5	Chris Whiteside
Lib Dem	Frank Hollowell	5,432	13.9	Frank Hollowell
Others		2,287	5.9	

The Copeland constituency is formed around the town of Whitehaven, an economically depressed fishing port whose economy has struggled in recent years following job losses in the coal-mining and chemical sectors. Despite being formally decommissioned in 2003, the Sellafield nuclear facility remains the largest employer in the constituency and the construction of a new power station is at the top of the local wish-list. Unlike nearby Barrow & Furness, which was sufficiently put off by Labour's anti-nuclear stance to elect a Conservative MP, the constituency remained loyal to pro-nuclear former MP Jack Cunningham throughout the 1980s. Conservative economist Chris Whiteside will challenge sitting MP Jamie Reed, a former press officer for British Nuclear Fuels.

Darlington

PARTY	2005 CANDIDATE	NOTIONAL 2005 VOTES	NOTIONAL 2005 % VOTE	PPC FOR NEXT GE
Labour notional majority of 10,417; notional turnout: 59.4%				
Labour	Alan Milburn MP	20,811	52.3	n/a
Conservative	Anthony Frieze	10,394	26.1	Edward Legard
Lib Dem	Robert Adamson	7,346	18.5	Mike Barker
Others		1,246	3.1	

North Durham

PARTY	2005 CANDIDATE	NOTIONAL 2005 VOTES	NOTIONAL 2005 % VOTE	PPC FOR NEXT GE
Labour notional majority of 16,781; notional turnout: 55.3%				
Labour	Kevan Jones MP	23,932	64.1	Kevan Jones MP
Lib Dem	Philip Latham	7,151	19.2	n/a
Conservative	Mark Watson	6,258	16.8	David Skelton
Others		0	0.0	

North West Durham

Labour notional majority of 13,443; notional turnout: 57.8%

PARTY	2005 CANDIDATE	NOTIONAL 2005 VOTES	NOTIONAL 2005 % VOTE	PPC FOR NEXT GE
Labour	Hilary Armstrong MP	21,312	53.9	n/a
Lib Dem	Alan Ord	7,869	19.9	Owen Temple
Conservative	Jamie Devlin	6,463	16.4	Michelle Tempest
Others		3,865	9.8	

City of Durham

Labour notional majority of 3,274; notional turnout: 63.4%

PARTY	2005 CANDIDATE	NOTIONAL 2005 VOTES	NOTIONAL 2005 % VOTE	PPC FOR NEXT GE
Labour	Roberta Blackman-Woods	20,928	47.2	Roberta Blackman-Woods MP
Lib Dem	Carol Woods	17,654	39.8	Carol Woods
Conservative	Ben Rogers	4,179	9.4	Nick Varley
Others		1,603	3.6	

Easington

Labour notional majority of 18,874; notional turnout: 51.8%

PARTY	2005 CANDIDATE	NOTIONAL 2005 VOTES	NOTIONAL 2005 % VOTE	PPC FOR NEXT GE
Labour	John Cummings MP	23,043	71.3	Grahame Morris
Lib Dem	Christopher Ord	4,169	12.9	n/a
Conservative	Lucille Nicholson	3,472	10.7	n/a
Others		1,638	5.1	

Gateshead

Labour notional majority of 14,245; notional turnout: 53.6%

PARTY	2005 CANDIDATE	NOTIONAL 2005 VOTES	NOTIONAL 2005 % VOTE	PPC FOR NEXT GE
Labour	n/a	21,510	61.4	Sharon Hodgson MP
Lib Dem	n/a	7,265	20.7	n/a
Conservative	n/a	3,564	10.2	n/a
Others		2,682	7.7	

Hartlepool

Labour notional majority of 7,478; notional turnout: 51.3%

PARTY	2005 CANDIDATE	NOTIONAL 2005 VOTES	NOTIONAL 2005 % VOTE	PPC FOR NEXT GE
Labour	Iain Wright MP	18,251	51.5	Iain Wright MP
Lib Dem	Jody Dunn	10,773	30.4	Reg Clark
Conservative	Amanda Vigar	4,058	11.5	n/a
Others		2,354	6.6	

Hexham

Conservative notional majority of 4,957; notional turnout: 68.6%

PARTY	2005 CANDIDATE	NOTIONAL 2005 VOTES	NOTIONAL 2005 % VOTE	PPC FOR NEXT GE
Conservative	Peter Atkinson MP	17,463	42.4	Guy Opperman
Labour	Kevin Graham	12,506	30.4	Antoine Tinnion
Lib Dem	Andrew Duffield	10,578	25.7	Andrew Duffield
Others		650	1.6	

Houghton & Sunderland South

Labour notional majority of 16,986; notional turnout: 53.2%

Party	2005 Candidate	Notional 2005 Votes	Notional 2005 % Vote	PPC for next GE
Labour	n/a	23,007	62.0	Bridget Phillipson
Conservative	n/a	6,021	16.2	Robert Oliver
Lib Dem	n/a	5,395	14.5	n/a
Others		2,682	7.2	

Jarrow

Labour notional majority of 12,749; notional turnout: 54.7%

PARTY	2005 CANDIDATE	NOTIONAL 2005 VOTES	NOTIONAL 2005 % VOTE	PPC FOR NEXT GE
Labour	Stephen Hepburn MP	20,637	58.8	Stephen Hepburn MP
Lib Dem	Bill Schardt	7,888	22.5	n/a
Conservative	Linkson Jack	4,485	12.8	n/a
Others		2,064	5.9	

Middlesbrough

Labour notional majority of 12,476; notional turnout: 48.6%

PARTY	2005 CANDIDATE	NOTIONAL 2005 VOTES	NOTIONAL 2005 % VOTE	PPC FOR NEXT GE
Labour	Stuart Bell MP	18,486	57.6	Stuart Bell MP
Lib Dem	Joe Michna	6,010	18.7	n/a
Conservative	Caroline Flynn-Macleod	5,283	16.5	n/a
Others		2,320	7.2	

Middlesbrough South & East Cleveland

Labour notional majority of 8,096; notional turnout: 60.8%

PARTY	2005 CANDIDATE	NOTIONAL 2005 VOTES	NOTIONAL 2005 % VOTE	PPC FOR NEXT GE
Labour	Ashok Kumar MP	22,021	50.3	Ashok Kumar MP
Conservative	Mark Brooks	13,925	31.8	Paul Bristow
Lib Dem	Carl Minns	6,034	13.8	n/a
Others		1,757	4.0	

Held by the Conservative Michael Bates until 1997, the cumbersomely named Middlesbrough South & East Cleveland seat is a constituency of contrasts. Both Labour and the Conservatives have a solid core vote here, the poverty of southern Middlesbrough's council estates lying in stark contrast to the opulence of the towns and villages dotted along the North Yorkshire Moors and the Cleveland coast. More than a third of local residents have no qualifications, a quarter live in council housing and unemployment is higher than the national average. Hammersmith and Fulham councillor Paul Bristow has been selected to fight Labour's Dr Ashok Kumar in this 98.6% white constituency.

Newcastle upon Tyne Central

Labour notional majority of 7,509; notional turnout: 56.5%

PARTY	2005 CANDIDATE	NOTIONAL 2005 VOTES	NOTIONAL 2005 % VOTE	PPC FOR NEXT GE
Labour	Jim Cousins MP	16,466	50.6	n/a
Lib Dem	Greg Stone	8,957	27.5	Gareth Kane
Conservative	Wendy Morton	5,400	16.6	n/a
Others		1,731	5.3	

Newcastle upon Tyne East

Labour notional majority of 6,987; notional turnout: 55.2%

PARTY	2005 CANDIDATE	NOTIONAL 2005 VOTES	NOTIONAL 2005 % VOTE	PPC FOR NEXT GE
Labour	Nick Brown MP	17,588	52.8	Nick Brown MP
Lib Dem	David Ord	10,601	31.8	Greg Stone
Conservative	Norma Dias	4,344	13.0	n/a
Others		787	2.4	

Newcastle upon Tyne North

Labour notional majority of 6,878; notional turnout: 61.6%

PARTY	2005 CANDIDATE	NOTIONAL 2005 VOTES	NOTIONAL 2005 % VOTE	PPC FOR NEXT GE
Labour	Doug Henderson MP	20,361	49.8	n/a
Lib Dem	Ron Beadle	13,483	33.0	Ron Beadle
Conservative	Neil Hudson	6,004	14.7	n/a
Others		997	2.4	

Penrith & the Border

Conservative notional majority of 10,795; notional turnout: 66.7%

PARTY	2005 CANDIDATE	NOTIONAL 2005 VOTES	NOTIONAL 2005 % VOTE	PPC FOR NEXT GE
Conservative	David Maclean MP	21,689	51.4	David Maclean MP
Lib Dem	Geyve Walker	10,894	25.8	Kate Clarkson
Labour	Michael Boaden	8,042	19.1	Barbara Cannon
Others		1,581	3.7	

Redcar

Labour notional majority of 12,116; notional turnout: 57.9%

PARTY	2005 CANDIDATE	NOTIONAL 2005 VOTES	NOTIONAL 2005 % VOTE	PPC FOR NEXT GE
Labour	Vera Baird MP	19,968	51.4	Vera Baird MP
Lib Dem	Ian Swales	7,852	20.2	Ian Swales
Conservative	Jonathan Lehrle	6,954	17.9	n/a
Others		4,087	10.5	

Sedgefield

Labour notional majority of 18,198; notional turnout: 62.3%

PARTY	2005 CANDIDATE	NOTIONAL 2005 VOTES	NOTIONAL 2005 % VOTE	PPC FOR NEXT GE
Labour	Tony Blair MP	23,943	59.0	Phil Wilson MP
Conservative	Gp CAPT Al Lockwood	5,745	14.2	Neil Mahapatra
Independent	Reg Keys	5,486	13.5	n/a
Others		5,425	13.4	

South Shields

Labour notional majority of 13,368; notional turnout: 50.7%

PARTY	2005 CANDIDATE	NOTIONAL 2005 VOTES	NOTIONAL 2005 % VOTE	PPC FOR NEXT GE
Labour	David Miliband MP	19,529	60.8	David Miliband MP
Lib Dem	Stephen Psallidas	6,161	19.2	n/a
Conservative	Richard Lewis	5,667	17.6	Karen Allen
Others		773	2.4	

Stockton North

Labour notional majority of 12,742; notional turnout: 58.1%

PARTY	2005 CANDIDATE	NOTIONAL 2005 VOTES	NOTIONAL 2005 % VOTE	PPC FOR NEXT GE
Labour	Frank Cook MP	20,800	54.8	Alex Cunningham
Conservative	Harriet Baldwin	8,058	21.2	Ian Galletley
Lib Dem	Neil Hughes	7,061	18.6	Gordon Parkin
Others		2,009	5.3	

Stockton South

Labour notional majority of 5,834; notional turnout: 62.4%

PARTY	2005 CANDIDATE	NOTIONAL 2005 VOTES	NOTIONAL 2005 % VOTE	PPC FOR NEXT GE
Labour	Dari Taylor MP	20,692	47.7	Dari Taylor MP
Conservative	James Gaddas	14,858	34.2	James Wharton
Lib Dem	Mike Barker	6,979	16.1	Jacquie Bell
Others		894	2.1	

Held by Labour since the 1997 general election, Stockton South is the one of the most affluent and middle-class constituencies in the north-east of England. Despite its rather urban name, the constituency includes only a small portion of the industrial Stockton, taking in the pleasant villages of Eaglescliffe, Hartburn and Yarm, which house many commuters to nearby Middlesbrough and Newcastle-upon-Tyne. Perhaps unsurprisingly, it is in these rural areas that the Conservatives find the bulk of their support. Levels of owner occupation are high in this constituency (78.1%) and the proportion of university graduates (18.5%) is well above average for a North East seat. Conservative chances here are boosted slightly by the boundary changes, which transfer portions of the Labour-inclined Town Centre and Newtown wards to the already impregnable Labour seat of Stockton North. Sitting MP Dari Taylor will face Conservative James Wharton, one of his party's youngest candidates.

Sunderland Central

Labour notional majority of 9,464; notional turnout: 50.6%

PARTY	2005 CANDIDATE	NOTIONAL 2005 VOTES	NOTIONAL 2005 % VOTE	PPC FOR NEXT GE
Labour	n/a	18,543	50.0	Julie Elliot
Conservative	n/a	9,079	24.5	Lee Martin
Lib Dem	n/a	6,249	16.9	n/a
Others		3,193	8.6	

Tynemouth

Labour notional majority of 5,490; notional turnout: 66.0%

PARTY	2005 CANDIDATE	NOTIONAL 2005 VOTES	NOTIONAL 2005 % VOTE	PPC FOR NEXT GE
Labour	Alan Campbell MP	22,752	48.3	Alan Campbell MP
Conservative	Michael McIntyre	17,262	36.6	Wendy Morton
Lib Dem	Colin Finlay	7,109	15.1	John Appleby
Others		0	0.0	

Historically one of the Conservative Party's strongest seats in the North East, Tynemouth delivered Labour an 11,000 majority at the 1997 general election. This is a socially polarised constituency, mixing the middle-class Newcastle commuter suburbs of Whitley Bay and Cullercoats with impoverished council estates in the south of the seat. While the decline of the Newcastle shipbuilding industry hit Tynemouth hard, it remains a relatively prosperous seat with high levels of owner occupation, a well-educated population and unemployment rates considerably lower than the regional average. Following the Conservatives' decisive win at the 2009 North Tyneside mayoral election, the party will be upbeat about their chances of reclaiming this seat. Home Office Minister and sitting MP Alan Campbell will face a challenge from former Conservative North Yorkshire councillor Wendy Morton.

North Tyneside

Labour notional majority of 14,929; notional turnout: 55.3%

PARTY	2005 CANDIDATE	NOTIONAL 2005 VOTES	NOTIONAL 2005 % VOTE	PPC FOR NEXT GE
Labour	Stephen Byers MP	23,713	59.4	Stephen Byers MP
Lib Dem	Gillian Ferguson	8,784	22.0	David Ord
Conservative	Duncan McLellan	7,438	18.6	n/a
Others		0	0.0	

Wansbeck

Labour notional majority of 10,581; notional turnout: 58.4%

PARTY	2005 CANDIDATE	NOTIONAL 2005 VOTES	NOTIONAL 2005 % VOTE	PPC FOR NEXT GE
Labour	Denis Murphy MP	20,315	55.2	Denis Murphy MP
Lib Dem	Simon Reed	9,734	26.4	Simon Reed
Conservative	Ginny Scrope	5,515	15.0	Campbell Storey
Others		1,245	3.4	

Washington & Sunderland West

Labour notional majority of 17,060; notional turnout: 47.4%

PARTY	2005 CANDIDATE	NOTIONAL 2005 VOTES	NOTIONAL 2005 % VOTE	PPC FOR NEXT GE
Labour	n/a	22,327	68.8	Sharon Hodgson
Lib Dem	n/a	5,267	16.2	n/a
Conservative	n/a	4,864	15.0	Ian Cuthbert
Others		0	0.0	

Westmorland & Lonsdale

Lib Dem notional majority of 806; notional turnout: 70.7%

PARTY	2005 CANDIDATE	NOTIONAL 2005 VOTES	NOTIONAL 2005 % VOTE	PPC FOR NEXT GE
Lib Dem	Tim Farron	21,829	46.0	Tim Farron MP
Conservative	Tim Collins MP	21,023	44.3	Gareth McKeever
Labour	John Reardon	3,712	7.8	John Wiseman
Others		941	2.0	

The only high-profile casualty of the Liberal Democrats' 'decapitation strategy', Conservative shadow Education Secretary Tim Collins will have been devastated to lose the sprawling Westmorland & Lonsdale constituency to Tim Farron at the last general election by only 267 votes. One of the most aesthetically stunning seats in the country, it is home to part of the Yorkshire Dales National Park, Windermere and the picturesque towns of Kendal and Kirkby Lonsdale. With agriculture and tourism the largest local employers, the Liberal Democrats have continued to consolidate their position on a local level, steadily increasing their lead over the Tories on South Lakeland District Council since 2006. Gareth McKeever, an executive director at Morgan Stanley, will fight the seat for the Conservatives.

Workington

PARTY	2005 CANDIDATE	NOTIONAL 2005 VOTES	NOTIONAL 2005 % VOTE	PPC FOR NEXT GE
Labour notional majority of 8,226; notional turnout: 62.4%				
Labour	Tony Cunningham MP	18,622	52.0	Tony Cunningham MP
Conservative	Judith Pattinson	10,396	29.0	Judith Pattinson
Lib Dem	Kate Clakson	5,170	14.4	Mark Richardson
Others		1,626	4.5	

Situated on the isolated west Cumbria coast, the Workington constituency was last won by the Conservatives at a 1976 by-election, only to quickly revert back to its Labour roots at the following general election. Workington has a rich industrial past, having once been home to thriving coal-mining, steel and iron-casting industries. Having been in decline for many years, Workington town has recently undergone significant regeneration work which has bolstered the town's service sector, yet with almost two in five residents having no qualifications this remains a relatively poor area. Allerdale Borough Council is jointly controlled by a coalition of Conservatives, Liberal Democrats and Independent councillors. Elected as the town's MP at the 2001 election after serving one term in the European Parliament, Tony Cunningham will defend his seat for Labour. The Conservative PPC will be former Carlisle mayor Judith Pattinson.

Wales

The Conservatives – until relatively recently proudly the Conservative and Unionist Party, defenders of the territorial integrity of the UK – currently have only three MPs in Wales, this having increased in 2005 from precisely zero. At the last general election, Labour won twenty-nine of the forty seats in the principality, dwarfing the Tories' total, and those of the Liberal Democrats (four), the Welsh Nationalists (three) and the solitary Independent in Blaenau Gwent. If there is to be a change of government at the next election in 2009 or, more likely, 2010, this hegemony will have to be weakened substantially.

If the Conservatives are to become the largest party across the UK, which would in all probability be enough to put David Cameron into 10 Downing Street, there are four target constituencies that they must gain; and for a bare overall majority, at least two more, with four outside possibilities should they be the beneficiaries of a national landslide.

Three of the four 'must-wins' for the Tories are in seats which are effectively unaltered in the boundary changes which come into force next time. Cardiff North would appear to be the easiest. Labour's Julie Morgan (wife of First Secretary Rhodri) only held on by 1,146 votes in 2005, and the seat is completely unchanged. North includes most of the more affluent residential areas of the Welsh capital, and indeed with a third of its workers in professional and managerial occupations and fully three quarters classed as non-manual, it is one of the most middle-class constituencies currently held by Labour, and one suspects that if it were in England it would already have been regained by the Tories, who lost it in the 1997 cataclysm. In the 2007 National Assembly for Wales elections, they won the parallel seat with a majority of nearly 5,000.

At first sight, it should be as easy to recapture Vale of Glamorgan too, which also requires a general election swing since 2005 of less than 2 per cent, and also includes the gentle farming land and rather twee small towns (by Welsh standards) of the vale as well as the more gritty port of Barry. However in 2007, the Labour AM Jane Hutt held on, albeit by just eighty-three votes, which means that the Tories have not won a constituency-wide contest here for over eleven years. Nevertheless, if Labour held on to Vale of Glamorgan it would be a major surprise, as it would suggest they have a decent chance of winning an unprecedented, and highly unexpected, fourth consecutive term in UK government.

The third of the established Tory targets is the rather mixed Carmarthen West & South Pembrokeshire, which as the name implies combines the substantially Welsh-speaking former section, which harbours a substantial Plaid Cymru vote, and the latter part of 'Little England beyond Wales'. In the 2007 assembly elections, the Conservatives did achieve a gain, but by only a wafer-thin 98 margin, polling 8,590 to Labour's 8,492, with the Nationalists completing a three-way near dead heat with 8,340.

The fourth seat on the Tory 'top-hit' list raises the question of boundary changes. Wales retains forty seats at the next election, which means that it is still heavily over-represented compared with the rest of the UK. The quota set by the Boundary Commission in the latest review as the average target electorate for each constituency was only 55,640, compared with nearly 70,000 for England. On strict parity this means that Wales would have only thirty-one or thirty-two MPs. The Commission's rules allow it to reduce the number of Welsh seats to thirty-five, but it decided largely to avoid disturbing existing arrangements in most areas – with the single exception of the north-west of the country, where there are major changes. One of these is to create a new seat of Aberconwy, drawn almost entirely from the existing marginal of Conwy; but a third of Conwy is now to be in Arfon, and this is the section around Bangor, which was much better ground for Labour. Notionally it has been calculated (by Professors Colin Rallings and Michael Thrasher of Plymouth University) that Labour would have beaten the Conservatives by just 1,070 votes if Aberconwy had existed in 2005, but in the 2007 Assembly elections Plaid Cymru actually won, with the Tories second and Labour in a poor third. Given that the nationalists tend to do better in Assembly elections, where they have a chance of at least a share in power (as eventually was the case) this still suggests that the Conservatives could well be favourites in a UK general election in Aberconwy – which has, incidentally, one of the smallest electorates even in Wales at just 44,000.

If the Tories are to become the largest party across the UK, and assuming a uniform swing applied to Wales as well, they need to gain more than these four seats. The next on their list, requiring a much larger swing from Labour of 8 per cent, are Vale of Clwyd and Newport West. That such targets are not impossible is suggested by yet another photo-finish in 2007, in Vale of Clwyd, where they failed to oust Labour by only 92 votes; in Newport West they were 1,400 behind, but Labour have suffered yet more traumas and slumped further in the national polls in the last eighteen months. In order to win a working overall majority, the Tories would also be looking to add at least some of Delyn, Bridgend, Gower and Clwyd South, which need swings of between 8 and 10 per cent. Only the first two were won by the Conservative candidates even in the heyday of the Thatcher landslides, so these must represent the outer edge of the party's ambitions against the current government.

There is an alternative source of possible Conservative gains in the shape of Liberal Democrat seats. Back in the 1980s they did achieve victories in Brecon & Radnorshire and Montgomeryshire, though in these rural inland constituencies they must overcome the substantial personal votes of sitting MPs Roger Williams and Lembit

Opik, whose two-edged celebrity is also underpinned by a long and deep tradition of Liberalism in a seat only once lost to the Tories in well over a century.

The other main area of interest in Wales will be the performance of Plaid Cymru, particularly against their somewhat reluctant executive partners since 2007, Labour. In the 2007 Assembly (fought on the new boundaries for the first time) the nationalists won seven constituency seats and finished almost level with the Tories in second place in the share of the vote, with between 21 and 22 per cent compared with 12.6 per cent in 2005. As well as taking all four in the majority Welsh-speaking north-west (which used to be called Gwynedd), they also won Ceredigion (held in parliament by the Liberal Democrats since 2005), Carmarthen East & Dinefwr (Adam Price's seat at Westminster) – and moved into the valleys to take Llanelli, in the shape of the charismatic Helen Mary Jones. At the next general election they are unlikely to repeat the latter success, but given Labour's weakness throughout Britain, Plaid must have a good chance of unseating Albert Owen in Ynys Môn (Anglesey) and taking the new Arfon in its first contest, and as we have seen they will have a major role to play in Aberconwy and Carmarthen West & South Pembrokeshire.

As well as their concerns about possible losses to the Conservatives and Plaid Cymru, Labour will need to guard a couple of other flanks too. The Liberal Democrats' best hope of a gain in Wales is Swansea West, where they need a swing of over 6 per cent even after their advance in 2005 (typical of seats with a university presence, following the Iraq War), but they did cut Labour's lead to 1,500 in 2007, and may be assisted by the retirement of the Father of the House of Commons, Alan Williams, who has represented the division since 1964.

Finally, Labour have now lost four elections in a row in Blaenau Gwent, following their original decree that there should be an all-woman short list, which led to the Independent candidacy of the AM Peter Law in 2005, and further defeats in both by-elections on his death in April 2006 and in the Assembly seat in 2007, when his widow Trish held on by over 5,000. Blaenau Gwent is a classic valley seat of multiple deprivation, having suffered from the loss of both its coal and then its steel industry. The seat was formerly called Ebbw Vale, and held from 1929 to 1992 by just two famous MPs, Aneurin Bevan and Michael Foot. In 1983 and 1992 it was Labour's safest constituency of all. That the party has managed to lose it recently suggests that in some circumstances nothing is safe, even in one of Labour's most ancestral of heartlands, and they will indeed be belaboured on all sides in their attempt to hang on to power at Westminster in well under a year's time.

Target seats

SEAT	SWING REQUIRED %	MP	CHALLENGER
Conservative from Labour			
Cardiff North	1.3	Julie Morgan	Jonathan Evans
Vale of Glamorgan	1.7	John Smith*	Alun Cairns
Aberconwy	2.0	Betty Williams*	Guto Bebb
Carmarthen West & South Pembrokeshire	2.7	Nick Ainger	Simon Hart
Vale of Clwyd	7.1	Chris Ruane	Matt Wright
Newport West	7.7	Paul Flynn	Matthew Williams
Gower	8.5	Martin Caton	Byron Davies
Bridgend	9.0	Madeleine Moon	Helen Baker
Delyn	9.8	David Hanson	Antoinette Sandbach
Clwyd South	10.0	Martyn Jones*	John Bell
Conservative from Lib Dems			
Brecon & Radnorshire	5.1	Roger Williams	Suzy Davies
Montgomeryshire	11.4	Lembit Opik	Glyn Davies
Lib Dem from Labour			
Swansea West	6.5	Alan Williams*	Peter May
PC from Labour			
Arfon	1.0	Hywel Williams MP	
Ynys Mon	1.8	Albert Owen	Dylan Rees
Llanelli	10.3	Nia Griffith	Myfanwy Davies
Aberconwy	15.1	Betty Williams*	Phil Edwards
Carmarthen West & South Pembrokeshire	15.9	Nick Ainger	John Dixon
PC from Lib Dems			
Ceredigion	0.4	Mark Williams	Penri James
Labour from Independent			
Blaenau Gwent	4.7**	Dai Davies	Nick Smith

** from 2006 by-election

One to watch: Carmarthen West & Pembrokeshire South

Actual majority 2005: Labour 1,910 (5.0%) – Nick Ainger MP
Notional majority 2005: Labour 2,063 (5.4%)
Conservative candidate: Simon Hart
Plaid Cymru candidate: John Dixon

Fourth on the Conservative target list of Labour seats, requiring a swing from 2005 of 2 per cent, this south-west Wales seat would seem to be an easy gain. However, there are complicating factors. In the 2007 National Assembly for Wales elections, the Tory Angela Burns did win – but only by 98 votes from Labour, with the Welsh Nationalists just another 152 behind, which gives the constituency the status of a three-way marginal. The reason for this lies in the divided nature of the seat. Pembrokeshire, especially its southern section below the Preseli hills, is a predominantly English-speaking county, and the Conservatives can expect to benefit from the kind of swing indicated by national polls across England and Wales. However, west Carmarthenshire, including the county town of Carmarthen, has far more Welsh speakers, more similar to the neighbouring Carmarthen East & Dinefwr seat, which is now a Plaid Cymru stronghold. The nationalists are unlikely actually to win our 'one to watch' in the next Westminster election, but their strength could bear on the chances of the other two parties. This is a seat of castles, at Saundersfoot and Tenby and Pembroke itself, but no party can regard it as a stronghold. The Conservative candidate Simon Hart must win it from sitting Labour MP Nick Ainger, and by a majority well into four figures, if his party are to form the next government of the UK.

Aberavon

Labour notional majority of 13,937; notional turnout: 59.4%

PARTY	2005 CANDIDATE	NOTIONAL 2005 VOTES	NOTIONAL 2005 % VOTE	PPC FOR NEXT GE
Labour	Hywel Francis MP	18,077	60.0	Hywel Francis MP
Lib Dem	Claire Waller	4,140	13.8	n/a
Plaid Cymru	Philip Evans	3,545	11.8	n/a
Others		4,823	14.5	

Aberconwy

Labour notional majority of 1,070; notional turnout: 62.0%

PARTY	2005 CANDIDATE	NOTIONAL 2005 VOTES	NOTIONAL 2005 % VOTE	PPC FOR NEXT GE
Labour	Betty Williams MP	8,994	33.0	Ronnie Hughes
Conservative	Guto Bebb	7,924	29.1	Guto Bebb
Lib Dem	n/a	5,197	19.1	Mike Priestley
Others		5,143	18.9	

Located on Wales's north coast, the newly created Aberconwy constituency is a curious one. Formed around the current Conwy constituency, a Labour–Conservative marginal on a Westminster level which is held by Plaid Cymru in the Welsh Assembly, much of its territory has traditionally been a closely fought battle between Conservatives and Liberal Democrats. Conservative prospects in this Welsh-speaking and 99% white seat are strengthened by the loss of Labour-inclined Bangor to the new Arfon seat. Retiring MP Betty Williams, who came from third place in 1997 to capture the Conwy seat from the Tories, is replaced as Labour candidate by former council leader Ronnie Hughes. Plaid Cymru defector Guto Bebb will contest the constituency for the Conservatives.

Alyn & Deeside

Labour notional majority of 8,378; notional turnout: 59.7%

PARTY	2005 CANDIDATE	NOTIONAL 2005 VOTES	NOTIONAL 2005 % VOTE	PPC FOR NEXT GE
Labour	Mark Tami MP	17,331	48.8	Mark Tami MP
Conservative	Lynne Hale	8,953	25.2	n/a
Lib Dem	Paul Brighton	6,174	17.4	n/a
Others		3,038	8.6	

Arfon

Labour notional majority of 456; notional turnout: 58.2%

PARTY	2005 CANDIDATE	NOTIONAL 2005 VOTES	NOTIONAL 2005 % VOTE	PPC FOR NEXT GE
Labour	n/a	8,484	33.9	n/a
Plaid Cymru	n/a	8,028	32.1	Hywel Williams MP
Conservative	n/a	4,106	16.4	Sarah Green
Others	n/a	4,424	17.6	

Largely based upon the current Caernarfon constituency, this newly formed constituency will be a closely fought Plaid Cymru—Conservative marginal. Previously safe for Plaid Cymru, the party's position has been weakened by the transfer of the Labour-inclined town of Bangor from neighbouring Conwy to this seat. The largest employer in the constituency is the agricultural sector but tourism also plays a key role here with many visitors drawn to the area for hill-walking and seaside holidays. This constituency is one of the closest things Britain has to an American-style 'minority district', the below-average size of seats in north-west Wales seats being tolerated by the Boundary Commission after widespread local demands for a majority Welsh-speaking representation. Incumbent MP Hywel Williams will attempt to 'retake' this seat for Plaid Cymru against what has become a Labour notional hold because of boundary changes.

Blaenau Gwent

Independent notional majority of 9,121; notional turnout: 66.1%

PARTY	2005 CANDIDATE	NOTIONAL 2005 VOTES	NOTIONAL 2005 % VOTE	PPC FOR NEXT GE
Independent	Peter Law	20,505	58.2	Dai Davies MP
Labour	Maggie Jones	11,384	32.3	Nick Smith
Lib Dem	Brian Thomas	1,511	4.3	n/a
Others		1,851	2.8	

Brecon & Radnorshire

Lib Dem notional majority of 3,905; notional turnout: 69.4%

PARTY	2005 CANDIDATE	NOTIONAL 2005 VOTES	NOTIONAL 2005 % VOTE	PPC FOR NEXT GE
Lib Dem	Roger Williams MP	17,182	44.8	Roger Williams MP
Conservative	Andrew Davies	13,277	34.6	Suzy Davies
Labour	Leighton Veale	5,755	15.0	Chris Lloyd
Others		2,127	5.5	

One of the largest, most rural and most picturesque constituencies in the United Kingdom, the sprawling Brecon & Radnorshire constituency has been a closely fought marginal for decades. Based around the Brecon Beacons National Park, the seat was gained from Labour by the Conservatives in 1979, flipped to the Liberal Democrats in a 1985 by-election, returned to the Tories in 1992 and has backed the Liberal Democrats since 1997. Unsurprisingly, the largest source of local employment is agriculture and tourism although there is a sizeable manufacturing base in the Labour-supporting town of Ystradgynlais. As with many remote rural constituencies, personal votes matter a great deal here. Conservative Suzy Davies will battle it out against sitting MP and NFU Cymru chairman Roger Williams.

Bridgend

Labour notional majority of 6,089; notional turnout: 59.7%

PARTY	2005 CANDIDATE	NOTIONAL 2005 VOTES	NOTIONAL 2005 % VOTE	PPC FOR NEXT GE
Labour	Madeleine Moon	14,621	42.9	Madeleine Moon MP
Conservative	Helen Baker	8,532	25.0	Helen Baker
Lib Dem	Paul Warren	7,512	22.0	n/a
Others		3,414	10.0	

Located mid-way between Cardiff and Swansea, Labour gained the Bridgend seat from one-term Conservative MP Peter Hubbard-Miles at the 1987 general election. Once an intersection railway town for the coal mining and quarrying industries, Bridgend has been more successful than many other south Wales towns in recent years, reinventing itself as base for the electronics and light manufacturing sector. Despite many local people working in low-wage jobs, almost four in five homes here are owner occupied with only 13.9% of residents living in social housing. As memories of Bridgend's industrial past fade, and new estates housing middle-class commuters continue to grow, one might expect to see a steady improvement in Conservative fortunes locally. Unlike the majority of south Wales constituencies, Labour has rarely recorded large majorities here. Sitting Labour MP Madeleine Moon will face a challenge from Conservative Helen Baker.

Caerphilly

Labour notional majority of 13,517; notional turnout: 56.4%

PARTY	2005 CANDIDATE	NOTIONAL 2005 VOTES	NOTIONAL 2005 % VOTE	PPC FOR NEXT GE
Labour	Wayne David MP	20,082	55.4	Wayne David MP
Plaid Cymru	Lindsay Whittle	6,565	18.1	Lindsay Whittle
Conservative	Stephen Watson	5,334	14.7	Craig Piper
Others		4,242	11.8	

Cardiff Central

Lib Dem notional majority of 5,593; notional turnout: 59.1%

PARTY	2005 CANDIDATE	NOTIONAL 2005 VOTES	NOTIONAL 2005 % VOTE	PPC FOR NEXT GE
Lib Dem	Jenny Willott	17,991	49.8	Jenny Willott MP
Labour	Jon Owen Jones MP	12,398	34.3	Jenny Rathbone
Conservative	Gotz Mohindra	3,339	9.2	n/a
Others		2,404	6.7	

Cardiff North

Labour notional majority of 1,146; notional turnout: 70.4%

PARTY	2005 CANDIDATE	NOTIONAL 2005 VOTES	NOTIONAL 2005 % VOTE	PPC FOR NEXT GE
Labour	Julie Morgan MP	17,707	39.0	Julie Morgan MP
Conservative	Jonathan Morgan	16,561	36.5	Jonathan Evans
Lib Dem	John Dixon	8,483	18.7	n/a
Others		2,609	5.8	

Captured by Julie Morgan in Labour's 1997 election, Cardiff North is to the Welsh capital what Bromley is to London. Easily the most middle-class seat in the principality, 83% of homes are owner occupied and unemployment is low. The constituency stretches from Labour-inclined urban areas out to the Rhiwbina, Tongwynlais and Whitchurch wards, which have long since been part of Cardiff's urban sprawl but still retain a pleasant village feel. Conservative Jonathan Morgan romped home at the 2007 Welsh Assembly elections, outpacing Labour by almost 5,000 votes and won the 2008 city council elections by an 18% margin. Former Welsh Office Minister Jonathan Evans, who held nearby Brecon & Randorshire for a term and led his party in the European Parliament until 2004, will challenge for the Conservatives.

Cardiff South & Penarth

Labour notional majority of 8,955; notional turnout: 58.1%

PARTY	2005 CANDIDATE	NOTIONAL 2005 VOTES	NOTIONAL 2005 % VOTE	PPC FOR NEXT GE
Labour	Alun Michael MP	18,402	46.6	Alun Michael MP
Conservative	Victoria Green	9,447	23.9	Simon Hoare
Lib Dem	Gavin Cox	7,824	19.8	Dominic Hannigan
Others		3,814	9.7	

Cardiff West

Labour notional majority of 8,361; notional turnout: 58.1%

PARTY	2005 CANDIDATE	NOTIONAL 2005 VOTES	NOTIONAL 2005 % VOTE	PPC FOR NEXT GE
Labour	Kevin Brennan MP	16,859	44.9	Kevin Brennan MP
Conservative	Simon Baker	8,498	22.6	Angela Jones-Evans
Lib Dem	Alison Goldsworthy	6,392	17.0	Alison Goldsworthy
Others		5,829	15.5	

The former constituency of Welsh First Minister Rhodri Morgan, Cardiff West has been held by his protégé Business, Innovation and Skills Minister Kevin Brennan since 2001. Mirroring the political landscape of each of the Cardiff's seats, the seat is home to dramatic extremes of poverty and affluence. Labour is all-conquering in Caerau and Ely, the site of early 1990s race rioting, while the Conservatives find rich pickings in Llandaff and Radyr. The constituency also includes Canton, one of the most ethnically diverse wards in Wales. Despite Labour's recent dominance, Ukrainian Soviet defector Stefan Terlezki held the seat for the Conservatives from the 1983 Thatcher landslide until his defeat by Morgan in 1987.

Carmarthen East & Dinefwr

Plaid Cymru notional majority of 6,551; notional turnout: 70.8%

PARTY	2005 CANDIDATE	NOTIONAL 2005 VOTES	NOTIONAL 2005 % VOTE	PPC FOR NEXT GE
Plaid Cymru	Adam Price MP	17,124	45.9	Adam Price MP
Labour	Ross Hendry	10,573	28.3	Rhys Williams
Conservative	Suzy Davies	5,105	13.7	n/a
Others		4,542	12.1	

Carmarthen West & South Pembrokeshire

Labour notional majority of 2,043; notional turnout: 67.2%

PARTY	2005 CANDIDATE	NOTIONAL 2005 VOTES	NOTIONAL 2005 % VOTE	PPC FOR NEXT GE
Labour	Nicholas Ainger MP	14,090	36.7	Nicholas Ainger MP
Conservative	David Morris	12,047	31.3	Simon Hart
Plaid Cymru	John Dixon	5,960	15.5	John Dixon
Others		6,332	16.4	

A wonderfully varied constituency, Carmarthen West & South Pembrokeshire stretches from West Wales's stunning coast, and the port of Pembroke Dock, inland to the Welsh-speaking town of Carmarthen. More than a quarter of local residents are of pensionable age with many retirees choosing to make their homes on the Pembrokeshire coast. The Tories and Plaid Cymru are fairly evenly divided in rural areas while Labour's support is chiefly drawn from Pembroke Dock, a working-class town scarred by the decline of the British maritime industry. The 2007 Welsh Assembly elections produced a nail-biting result with 250 votes separating the successful Conservative candidate from third-placed Plaid Cymru. Countryside Alliance chief executive and Conservative candidate Simon Hart will hope to seize this constituency from sitting Labour MP Nick Ainger.

Ceredigion

Lib Dem notional majority of 218; notional turnout: 68%

PARTY	2005 CANDIDATE	NOTIONAL 2005 VOTES	NOTIONAL 2005 % VOTE	PPC FOR NEXT GE
Lib Dem	Mark Williams	13,045	36.5	Mark Williams MP
Plaid Cymru	Simon Thomas MP	12,827	35.9	Penri James
Conservative	John Harrison	4,426	12.4	n/a
Others		5,418	15.3	

Clwyd South

Labour notional majority of 6,220; notional turnout: 61.2%

PARTY	2005 CANDIDATE	NOTIONAL 2005 VOTES	NOTIONAL 2005 % VOTE	PPC FOR NEXT GE
Labour	Martyn Jones MP	14,172	45.2	n/a
Conservative	Tom Biggins	7,952	25.4	John Bell
Lib Dem	Deric Burnham	4,853	15.5	n/a
Others		4,373	13.9	

Traditionally a coal mining and industrial constituency, the Clwyd South constituency has been held by Labour since its creation at the 1997 general election. This is a diverse constituency, stretching from the Denbighshire town of Llangollen on the edge of the Berwyn mountain range to the outskirts of the city of Wrexham, close to the border with England. Fought and lost by Boris Johnson at the 1997 election, this has never been traditional Conservative territory: more than a quarter of homes are council owned and unemployment has long been above the national average. Sitting Labour MP Martyn Jones will stand down at the next election and his successor will be selected from an all-women shortlist. Conservative candidate John Bell will hope to replace him.

Clwyd West

Conservative notional majority of 51; notional turnout: 65.0%

PARTY	2005 CANDIDATE	NOTIONAL 2005 VOTES	NOTIONAL 2005 % VOTE	PPC FOR NEXT GE
Conservative	David Jones	13,021	36.1	David Jones MP
Labour	Gareth Thomas MP	12,970	36.0	Donna Hutton
Lib Dem	Frank Taylor	4,801	13.3	n/a
Others		5,255	14.6	

Cynon Valley

Labour notional majority of 14,390; notional turnout: 60.2%

PARTY	2005 CANDIDATE	NOTIONAL 2005 VOTES	NOTIONAL 2005 % VOTE	PPC FOR NEXT GE
Labour	Ann Clwyd MP	18,329	63.0	Ann Clwyd MP
Plaid Cymru	Geraint Benney	3,939	13.5	Dafydd Trystan Davies
Lib Dem	Margaret Phelps	3,547	12.2	n/a
Others		3,265	11.2	

Delyn

Labour notional majority of 6,644; notional turnout: 63.6%

PARTY	2005 CANDIDATE	NOTIONAL 2005 VOTES	NOTIONAL 2005 % VOTE	PPC FOR NEXT GE
Labour	David Hanson MP	15,540	45.7	David Hanson MP
Conservative	John Bell	8,896	26.2	Antoinette Sandbach
Lib Dem	Tudor Jones	6,089	17.9	n/a
Others		3,479	10.2	

Previously held by the Conservative Keith Raffan, this north Wales constituency fell to Labour at the 1992 general election. This is a fairly bleak and industrial area separated from neighbouring England by the river Dee. The largest towns in the constituency are Flint, Holywell and Mold, each of which suffers from higher than average unemployment following the decline of traditional manufacturing industries. Labour enjoy robust support in the constituency's coastal and urban areas while the Conservatives tend to lead in the rural areas found inland and closest to the English border. Incumbent Labour MP David Hanson, a former parliamentary private secretary to Tony Blair, will be opposed by Conservative Antoinette Sandbach, who very narrowly failed to win the constituency's Welsh Assembly seat in 2007.

Dwyfor Meirionnydd

Plaid Cymru notional majority of 8,706; notional turnout: 61.4%

PARTY	2005 CANDIDATE	NOTIONAL 2005 VOTES	NOTIONAL 2005 % VOTE	PPC FOR NEXT GE
Plaid Cymru	Elfyn Llwyd MP	15,228	50.8	Steve Churchman
Labour	Rhodri Jones	6,522	21.7	n/a
Conservative	Dan Munford	4,253	14.2	Lisa Francis
Others		3,993	13.3	

Gower

Labour notional majority of 6,703; notional turnout: 65.4%

PARTY	2005 CANDIDATE	NOTIONAL 2005 VOTES	NOTIONAL 2005 % VOTE	PPC FOR NEXT GE
Labour	Martin Caton MP	16,786	42.5	Martin Caton MP
Conservative	Mike Murray	10,083	25.5	Byron Davies
Lib Dem	Nick Tregoning	7,291	18.4	n/a
Others		5,382	13.6	

Located in south-west Wales, Gower is one of the principality's most breathtaking constituencies. Spanning more than 70 square miles, the constituency is largely composed of scores of small and often sparsely populated villages although some more urban areas exist in the Swansea suburbs in the east of the seat. The tourist industry here is growing rapidly, as is the proportion of elderly residents, who now number almost a quarter of the population. This is a constituency steeped in trade unionist history, having once been home to large coal and steel industries. Curiously, this is one of Labour's three longest-standing seats, having been held by the party since the 1906 general election. Buoyed by a near-10% swing to the party at the 2007 Welsh Assembly elections, the Conservatives will be hopeful of making inroads here. Martin Caton will defend his seat for Labour against opposition from Conservative Byron Davies.

Islwyn

Labour notional majority of 17,582; notional turnout: 60.2%

PARTY	2005 CANDIDATE	NOTIONAL 2005 VOTES	NOTIONAL 2005 % VOTE	PPC FOR NEXT GE
Labour	Don Touhig MP	21,795	64.3	Don Touhig MP
Plaid Cymru	Jim Criddle	4,213	12.4	Steffan Lewis
Lib Dem	Lee Dillon	4,128	12.2	n/a
Others		3,735	11.0	

Llanelli

Labour notional majority of 7,234; notional turnout: 63.9%

PARTY	2005 CANDIDATE	NOTIONAL 2005 VOTES	NOTIONAL 2005 % VOTE	PPC FOR NEXT GE
Labour	Nia Griffth	16,592	46.9	Nia Griffth MP
Plaid Cymru	Neil Baker	9,358	26.5	Myfanwy Davies
Conservative	Adrian Phillips	4,844	13.7	
Others		4,550	12.9	

Merthyr Tydfil & Rhymney

Labour notional majority of 13,934; notional turnout: 55.4%

PARTY	2005 CANDIDATE	NOTIONAL 2005 VOTES	NOTIONAL 2005 % VOTE	PPC FOR NEXT GE
Labour	Dai Harvard MP	18,129	60.5	Dai Harvard MP
Lib Dem	Ceirion Rees	4,195	14.0	Amy Kitcher
Plaid Cymru	Noel Turner	2,972	9.9	n/a
Others		4,680	15.5	

Monmouth

Conservative notional majority of 4,527; notional turnout: 73.3%

PARTY	2005 CANDIDATE	NOTIONAL 2005 VOTES	NOTIONAL 2005 % VOTE	PPC FOR NEXT GE
Conservative	David Davies	21,396	46.9	David Davies MP
Labour	Huw Edwards MP	16,869	37.0	Hamish Sandison
Lib Dem	Phylip A.D.Hobson	5,852	12.8	Phylip Hobson
Others		1,536	3.4	

Montgomeryshire

Lib Dem notional majority of 7,048; notional turnout: 66.2%

PARTY	2005 CANDIDATE	NOTIONAL 2005 VOTES	NOTIONAL 2005 % VOTE	PPC FOR NEXT GE
Lib Dem	Lembit Opik MP	15,548	50.3	Lembit Opik MP
Conservative	Simon Baynes	8,500	27.5	Glyn Davies
Labour	David Tinline	3,794	12.3	Nick Colbourne
Others		3,072	9.9	

Neath

Labour notional majority of 12,710; notional turnout: 62.5%

PARTY	2005 CANDIDATE	NOTIONAL 2005 VOTES	NOTIONAL 2005 % VOTE	PPC FOR NEXT GE
Labour	Peter Hain MP	18,835	52.6	Peter Hain MP
Plaid Cymru	Geraint Owen	6,125	17.1	Alun Llwelyn
Lib Dem	Sheila Wayne	5,112	14.3	Frank Little
Others		5,745	16.0	

Newport East

Labour notional majority of 6,838; notional turnout: 57.9%

PARTY	2005 CANDIDATE	NOTIONAL 2005 VOTES	NOTIONAL 2005 % VOTE	PPC FOR NEXT GE
Labour	Jessica Morden	14,389	45.2	Jessica Morden MP
Lib Dem	Ed Townsend	7,551	23.7	Ed Townsend
Conservative	Matthew Collings	7,459	23.4	n/a
Others		2,426	7.6	

Newport West

Labour notional majority of 5,458; notional turnout: 59.2%

PARTY	2005 CANDIDATE	NOTIONAL 2005 VOTES	NOTIONAL 2005 % VOTE	PPC FOR NEXT GE
Labour	Paul Flynn MP	16,021	44.8	Paul Flynn MP
Conservative	William Morgan	10,563	29.6	Matthew Williams
Lib Dem	Nigel Flanagan	6,398	17.9	Veronica Watkins
Others		2,750	7.7	

Situated in south-east Wales, the Newport West constituency was last won by the Conservatives at the height of Margaret Thatcher's 1983 landslide. Regaining it for Labour at the following election, Paul Flynn expanded his majority to almost 15,000 votes in 1997. The constituency is considerably more middle class than neighbouring Newport East, taking in the town's attractive centre and the Tory-inclined areas of Langstone and Llanwern along the border with Monmouthshire. Newport is, however, a traditionally Labour-supporting town whose residents have long been employed in the docking and industrial sectors, which continue to dominate the town today. The Conservatives failed to gain the Welsh Assembly constituency by 1,401 votes in 2007, yet are the largest party in the constituency at a local government level. Matthew Williams will stand for the Conservatives.

Ogmore

Labour notional majority of 14,839; notional turnout: 59.5%

PARTY	2005 CANDIDATE	NOTIONAL 2005 VOTES	NOTIONAL 2005 % VOTE	PPC FOR NEXT GE
Labour	Huw Irranca-Davies MP	19,542	61.0	Huw Irranca-Davies MP
Lib Dem	Jackie Radford	4,703	14.7	n/a
Conservative	Norma Lloyd-Nesling	4,540	14.2	n/a
Others		3,274	10.2	

Pontypridd

Labour notional majority of 11,694; notional turnout: 63.1%

PARTY	2005 CANDIDATE	NOTIONAL 2005 VOTES	NOTIONAL 2005 % VOTE	PPC FOR NEXT GE
Labour	Kim Howells MP	18,534	54.2	Kim Howells MP
Lib Dem	Mike Powell	6,840	20.0	Mike Powell
Conservative	Quentin Edwards	3,949	11.6	n/a
Others		4,861	14.2	

Preseli Pembrokeshire

Conservative notional majority of 601; notional turnout: 69.9%

PARTY	2005 CANDIDATE	NOTIONAL 2005 VOTES	NOTIONAL 2005 % VOTE	PPC FOR NEXT GE
Conservative	Stephen Crabb	14,261	36.4	Stephen Crabb MP
Labour	Sue Hayman	13,660	34.8	Mari Rees
Lib Dem	Dewi Smith	5,105	13.0	n/a
Others		6,173	15.7	

Rhondda

Labour notional majority of 16,242; notional turnout: 61.7%

PARTY	2005 CANDIDATE	NOTIONAL 2005 VOTES	NOTIONAL 2005 % VOTE	PPC FOR NEXT GE
Labour	Chris Bryant MP	21,198	68.1	Chris Bryant MP
Plaid Cymru	Percy Jones	4,956	15.9	n/a
Lib Dem	Karen Roberts	3,264	10.5	n/a
Others		1,730	5.6	

Swansea East

Labour notional majority of 11,249; notional turnout: 53.6%

PARTY	2005 CANDIDATE	NOTIONAL 2005 VOTES	NOTIONAL 2005 % VOTE	PPC FOR NEXT GE
Labour	Siân James	17,457	56.6	Siân James MP
Lib Dem	Robert Speht	6,208	20.1	Rob Speht
Conservative	Ellenor Bland	3,103	10.1	Christian Holliday
Others		4,066	13.2	

Swansea West

Labour notional majority of 4,269; notional turnout: 56.6%

PARTY	2005 CANDIDATE	NOTIONAL 2005 VOTES	NOTIONAL 2005 % VOTE	PPC FOR NEXT GE
Labour	Alan Williams MP	13,833	41.8	Geraint Davies
Lib Dem	Rene Kinzett	9,564	28.9	Peter May
Conservative	Mohammed Abdel-Haq	5,285	16.0	Rene Kinzett
Others		4,404	13.3	

Torfaen

Labour notional majority of 14,791; notional turnout: 59.3%

PARTY	2005 CANDIDATE	NOTIONAL 2005 VOTES	NOTIONAL 2005 % VOTE	PPC FOR NEXT GE
Labour	Paul Murphy MP	20,472	56.9	Paul Murphy MP
Conservative	Nick Ramsay	5,681	15.8	n/a
Lib Dem	Veronica Watkins	5,678	15.8	n/a
Others		4,148	11.5	

Vale of Clwyd

Labour notional majority of 4,629; notional turnout: 65.7%

PARTY	2005 CANDIDATE	NOTIONAL 2005 VOTES	NOTIONAL 2005 % VOTE	PPC FOR NEXT GE
Labour	Chris Ruane MP	14,977	45.9	Chris Ruane MP
Conservative	Felicity Elphick	10,348	31.7	Matt Wright
Lib Dem	Elizabeth Jewkes	3,865	11.8	Mark Young
Others		3,454	10.6	

One of Labour's first gains from the Conservatives on election night 1997, this constituency is one of the three marginal seats in the ancient county of Clwyd. Rhyl, a depressed seaside town which suffers from a high level of unemployment and drug dependency, is the largest town in the constituency. The other significant settlement, Prestatyn, is a considerably more upmarket resort than nearby Rhyl and still attracts a large number of tourists each year. The Conservatives have made considerable advances here in recent years, topping the poll at the 2009 European elections and forming the largest party on Denbighshire County Council. Incumbent Labour MP Chris Ruane will hope to defend his seat against a challenge from Conservative Matt Wright, who missed out on gaining the area's Welsh Assembly seat by 92 votes in 2007.

Vale of Glamorgan

Labour notional majority of 1,574; notional turnout: 68.5%

PARTY	2005 CANDIDATE	NOTIONAL 2005 VOTES	NOTIONAL 2005 % VOTE	PPC FOR NEXT GE
Labour	John Smith MP	19,068	40.8	n/a
Conservative	Alan Cairns	17,494	37.4	Alun Cairns
Lib Dem	Mark Hooper	6,171	13.2	n/a
Others		4,015	8.6	

Located at Wales's most southerly point, the Vale of Glamorgan constituency is a mixture of pleasant Cardiff commuter villages and the gritty dock town of Barry. Barry, with its cargo-handling docks and manufacturing industries, provides the basis of Labour's support while the Tories are stronger in rural areas. Barry's once-thriving tourist industry is now in terminal decline. Cardiff International airport, whose growth is expected to provide a considerable number more local jobs in the coming years, is also located here. This is a constituency used to close races, the Conservatives having won by 19 votes in 1992 and Labour holding the Welsh Assembly seat by 83 votes in 2007. John Smith, the Labour MP here since 1997, has announced his retirement. Welsh Assembly member Alun Cairns will contest this seat for the Conservatives.

Wrexham

Labour notional majority of 6,819; notional turnout: 63.2%

PARTY	2005 CANDIDATE	NOTIONAL 2005 VOTES	NOTIONAL 2005 % VOTE	PPC FOR NEXT GE
Labour	Ian Lucas MP	13,993	46.1	Ian Lucas MP
Lib Dem	Tom Rippeth	7,174	23.6	Tom Rippeth
Conservative	Therese Coffey	6,079	20.0	Gareth Hughes
Others		3,139	10.3	

Ynys Môn

Labour notional majority of 1,242; notional turnout: 67.5%

PARTY	2005 CANDIDATE	NOTIONAL 2005 VOTES	NOTIONAL 2005 % VOTE	PPC FOR NEXT GE
Labour	Albert Owen MP	12,278	34.6	Albert Owen MP
Plaid Cymru	Eurig Wyn	11,036	31.1	Dylan Rees
Independent	Peter Rogers	5,448	15.4	n/a
Others		6,700	18.8	

Scotland

There may well be those, especially north of the border, who balk at the idea of covering the whole of Scotland in a single regional survey. They do of course have a point. However, apart from the constraints of the sands of time running out as the next general election inevitably approaches, there are a couple of justifications for the coverage which can be advanced. One that is undeniably true is that in Scotland alone there are no boundary changes at all to analyse, as the review there was completed before the 2005 general election, which saw the number of seats reduced from seventy-two to fifty-nine, to compensate for the previous over-representation and to acknowledge the increasing powers of the now established Scottish Parliament.

The other excuse is that if looked at in terms of conventional uniform swing since 2005, there are no more marginal seats in Scotland than in the other regions we have defined. However, this is more dubious, as the 2007 Scottish Parliament elections showed that abnormally large swings are very much possible, in this case largely from Labour to the SNP. Also with no fewer than four major competing parties, the permutations of the challenges are complex and fascinating, with a number of seats featuring on target lists of more than one challenger.

Without further ado, then, we should perhaps start with the battle between undoubtedly the two leading competitors in this nation – Labour and the SNP, who pipped them by one seat in 2007 to form a minority government at Holyrood (and yes, it is now called a government, not merely an executive). If we start from the 2005 Westminster contest, it looks as if the SNP would need very large swings to take any significant number of Labour seats, and thus make Gordon Brown's task of retaining power even harder. The Nationalists were in a close second place only in one seat, Ochil & South Perthshire, in that general election. However in 2007 they made no fewer than nine gains from Labour, in similar constituencies (in fact the Scottish Parliament was still elected on the basis of the seats which existed before the boundary changes). Such seats as North Ayrshire & Arran, Dundee West, Edinburgh East, Glasgow Govan, Kilmarnock & Loudoun (where former Defence Secretary Des Browne is MP), Livingston (whose Labour MP, Jim Devine, has been deselected following the expenses revelations) and Stirling should therefore be regarded as Westminster targets too, despite the huge swings since 2005 needed in most.

In July 2008, the SNP gained Glasgow East, the forty-fourth seat of their target list, in a traditional heartland of Labour support. With Labour's percentage in the polls even lower in 2009, and with the impact of the expenses scandal, there remains the possibility of a raft of SNP gains in the next general election. No wonder the enforced resignation in May 2009 of Speaker Michael Martin, the MP for the even more multiply deprived Glasgow North East, caused tremors throughout the Scottish Labour party. In more than one sense, they wondered if anyone was safe.

However, it should also be observed that for understandable reasons the SNP tend to do better in Holyrood contests. They do not have a chance of gaining power in the Commons, a body they do not believe should rule over Scotland in any case. Nor did they win the second Scottish by-election in 2008 in Glenrothes in November, where they made little impact at the height of the brief 'Brown bounce' after the G20 summit. Therefore, although the SNP are clearly Labour's main rivals for votes north of the border, we can move on to consider the Conservatives' chances, as the party chiefly competing to change the ownership of the government of the whole United Kingdom.

If Scotland is to provide its fair share of Tory gains in order for them to form a government with an overall majority, several Labour seats would have to fall. However there are two major problems which may well prevent this from happening. The first is that, given the multi-party competition in Scotland, the Conservatives were actually in third place in some of the seats highest on their target list, including some which they held before the 1997 election, like Edinburgh South and South West (the former Pentlands seat of Sir Malcolm Rifkind). The second difficulty is that there has been a long-term and powerful trend against them in Scotland. It is hard to believe now that in 1955 they actually held more than half of all Scottish constituencies. In 1979, the year of the historic Thatcher triumph, her designated Secretary of State for Scotland, Teddy Taylor of Glasgow Cathcart, was the single Tory casualty throughout Britain. Under Mrs Thatcher, the Conservatives seemed more than ever an English party, for example with the early imposition of the poll tax by a government holding hardly any north of the border. It now seems clear that if David Cameron does become Prime Minister, it will also be with very few MPs from Scotland in his ranks. This can do nothing but strengthen doubts regarding the legitimacy of Westminster power there – and develop the 'West Lothian question' with the influence of opposition Scottish MPs on matters elsewhere.

It is hard to see the Conservatives winning more than half a dozen seats at the very most. To add to their single existing MP, David Mundell of Dumfriesshire, Clydesdale & Tweeddale, they have a good chance in Dumfries (the town) & Galloway in the form of Peter Duncan, who was himself a lone Tory Scottish MP there from 2001 to 2005. However any more gains from Labour would be both against the odds and against the tide of history, including the most recent Scottish Parliament results in 2007 – this applies to East Renfrewshire (the former Eastwood, in Glasgow's most upmarket southern suburbs) and Stirling (see *One to Watch* below). However, the Tories did take a Borders seat from the Liberal Democrats that year, so Michael Moore will have to treat Berwickshire, Roxburgh & Selkirk as a tight marginal. Finally, the Tories could hope their national surge reaches far enough northwards to take two seats in the Tayside area from the SNP: Perth & North Perthshire, which needs a swing of just less than 2 per cent since 2005, and the historic county of Angus, a little over 2 per cent.

The Liberal Democrats do themselves have a number of targets, in attempts to add to the eleven they already hold (which makes them currently second in terms of seats, though not of votes, in Scotland). Fred Mackintosh has a much better chance of taking Edinburgh South (a mixture of the elite Morningside of Muriel Spark's 'Miss Jean Brodie' and peripheral council estates) from Labour than the Tories do; and they are not much further behind on the other side of the city at Edinburgh North & Leith, whose contrasting literary and social ambience from the south side is encapsulated by the reference to Leith station in the title of Irvine Welsh's *Trainspotting*. Last time the Lib Dems also finished just over 1,000 votes behind Anne Begg in Aberdeen South.

In Scotland, the landscape of politics is unique, with different issues and patterns of contest to the fore, and a contrasting take from England on the whole question of 'who is to govern'. It is quite likely, indeed probable, that in a year's time there will be a Conservative government of the United Kingdom, resting in Scotland on a most slender basis of being the fourth best represented party, with only a handful of seats. The problems of legitimacy and practicality this would cause will unfold over the years to come.

Target seats

SEAT	SWING REQUIRED %	MP	CHALLENGER
Conservative from Labour			
Dumfries & Galloway	2.9	Russell Brown	Peter Duncan
Stirling	5.5	Anne McGuire	Bob Dalrymple
East Renfrewshire	7.1	Jim Murphy	Richard Cook
Edinburgh South	8.2	Nigel Griffiths	Neil Hudson
Edinburgh South West	8.3	Alistair Darling	Jason Rust
Conservative from SNP			
Perth & North Perthshire	1.7	Pete Wishart	Peter Lyburn
Angus	2.1	Mike Weir	Alberto Costa
Conservative from Liberal Democrats			
Berwickshire, Roxburgh & Selkirk	6.5	Michael Moore	
SNP from Labour			
Ochil & South Perthshire	0.8	Gordon Banks	Annabelle Ewing
Dundee West	7.3	Jim McGovern	Jim Barrie
Kilmarnock & Loudoun	9.8	Des Browne	George Leslie
Aberdeen North	10.1	Frank Doran	Kevin Stewart
Lib Dem from Labour			
Edinburgh South	0.5	Nigel Griffiths	Fred Mackintosh
Aberdeen South	1.7	Anne Begg	John Sleigh
Edinburgh North & Leith	2.6	Mark Lazarowicz	Kevin Lang
Glasgow North	6.0	Ann McKechin	Katy Gordon
Labour from SNP			
Dundee East	0.5	Stewart Hosie	Katrina Murray
SNP from Lib Dem			
Argyll & Bute	10.5	Alan Reid	Mike Mackenzie

One to watch: Stirling

Actual majority 2005: Labour 4,767 (10.9%) – Anne McGuire MP
No boundary changes
Conservative candidate: Bob Dalrymple

Anywhere but Scotland, Stirling would be seen as a classic Labour–Conservative marginal, which the Tories held till the Blair landslide of 1997, when Michael Forsyth, as Scottish Secretary in the Cabinet, was one of the highest profile of the many casualties. With a technical swing of under 6 per cent, it would return to the Tories on almost any of the figures recorded in national (British) opinion polls. This impression would also be reinforced by a tour of the constituency. As well as Stirling itself, with its commanding castle on a dominant crag, the seat includes some very affluent communities, such as Bridge of Allan near the university, and Dunblane, whose fame through the massacre at the school of the young Andy Murray is entirely belied by its comfortable and solid middle-class ambience. The seat even ascends into the Highlands to include the magnificent scenery of the Trossachs beyond Callander, the fictional Tannochbrae of *Dr Finlay's Casebook*, to reach Killin at the west end of Loch Tay. Yet these impressions should not trap the unwary. Not only does Stirling have its working-class suburbs, but there is also a strong Nationalist tradition, as befits the home of the monument to William Wallace – indeed it was the SNP who took the seat in the 2007 elections, with the Conservatives third. Another feature of the seat is Bannockburn – and we should not write off the possibility that the SNP may deal another violent blow to one or both 'English' parties within this crucial battleground.

Aberdeen North

Labour notional majority of 6,795; notional turnout: 55.7%

PARTY	2005 CANDIDATE	NOTIONAL 2005 VOTES	NOTIONAL 2005 % VOTE	PPC FOR NEXT GE
Labour	Frank Doran	15,557	42.5	Frank Doran MP
Lib Dem	Steve Delaney	8,762	23.9	n/a
SNP	Kevin Stewart	8,168	22.3	n/a
Others		4,147	11.3	

Aberdeen South

Labour notional majority of 1,348; notional turnout: 62.1%

PARTY	2005 CANDIDATE	NOTIONAL 2005 VOTES	NOTIONAL 2005 % VOTE	PPC FOR NEXT GE
Labour	Anne Begg MP	15,272	36.7	Anne Begg MP
Lib Dem	Vicki Harris	13,924	33.5	John Sleigh
Conservative	Stewart Whyte	7,134	17.1	Mark Jones
Others		5,291	12.7	

Located on Scotland's north-eastern coastline, Aberdeen South has one of the most exciting electoral histories of any seat in recent times. While boundaries have shifted over time, Conservative, Liberal Democrat and Labour MPs have all represented large parts of this seat during the past two decades. Stretching southwards and westwards from the city of Aberdeen, this seat takes in Labour-friendly inner city areas, Liberal Democrat-inclined suburbs and Conservative-dominated farmland. Despite its appearance on the Conservative target list, this well-educated constituency would now be better described as a Labour–Liberal Democrat marginal. Former Scottish Liberal Democrat leader Nicol Stephen has held the broadly coplanar Aberdeen South constituency in the Scottish Parliament since 1999. Current MP Anne Begg will contest the seat again for Labour, John Sleigh will carry the Liberal Democrat standard, and farmer Mark Jones will fight for the Conservatives.

West Aberdeenshire & Kincardine

Lib Dem notional majority of 7,471; notional turnout: 63.5%

PARTY	2005 CANDIDATE	NOTIONAL 2005 VOTES	NOTIONAL 2005 % VOTE	PPC FOR NEXT GE
Lib Dem	Robert Smith MP	19,285	46.3	Robert Smith MP
Conservative	Alan Johnstone	11,814	28.4	Alan Johnstone
Labour	James Barrowman	5,470	13.1	n/a
Others		5,079	12.2	

A large rural constituency comprising small towns and villages on the edge of the Grampian mountain range and along the Dee valley, the Liberal Democrats took this seat at the 1997 general election. West Aberdeenshire & Kincardine is a largely prosperous constituency, taking in the Queen's estate at Balmoral and the attractive towns of Banchor, Stonehaven and Braemar – none of which have populations above 10,000. The majority of the constituency's residents are employed in the agricultural sector, although tourism is also important here with the Cairngorms National Park located inside the seat's boundaries. With the city of Aberdeen located just north of this seat, many commuters have chosen to make their homes here. Incumbent Liberal Democrat MP Sir Robert Smith will face Conservative MSP and local farmer Alex Johnstone.

Airdrie & Shotts

Labour notional majority of 14,084; notional turnout: 54.7%

PARTY	2005 CANDIDATE	NOTIONAL 2005 VOTES	NOTIONAL 2005 % VOTE	PPC FOR NEXT GE
Labour	John Reid MP	19,568	59.0	n/a
SNP	Malcolm Balfour	5,404	16.5	n/a
Lib Dem	Helen Watt	3,792	11.4	n/a
Others		4,314	13.0	

Angus

SNP notional majority of 1,601; notional turnout: 60.5%

PARTY	2005 CANDIDATE	NOTIONAL 2005 VOTES	NOTIONAL 2005 % VOTE	PPC FOR NEXT GE
SNP	Michael Weir MP	12,840	33.7	Michael Weir MP
Conservative	Sandy Bushby	11,239	29.5	Alberto Costa
Labour	Douglas Bradley	6,850	18.0	n/a
Others		7,216	19.0	

Nestled on Scotland's remote eastern coast, Angus is one of the Scottish National Party's longest-standing constituencies, having first been won by the party in 1974. A largely rural constituency, the Dundee commuter town of Arbroath is the largest settlement here with a little over 20,000 residents. The port of Montrose and ornate market town of Forfar are also found within the seat's boundaries. Unsurprisingly, agriculture is the largest local employer here yet tourism is likely to grow in importance in the coming years. The SNP are the largest party on Angus Council, holding 13 seats to the Conservatives' five. Sitting MP Mike Weir will be challenged by Conservative Alberto Costa.

Argyll & Bute

Lib Dem notional majority of 5,636; notional turnout: 64.3%

PARTY	2005 CANDIDATE	NOTIONAL 2005 VOTES	NOTIONAL 2005 % VOTE	PPC FOR NEXT GE
Lib Dem	Alan Reid MP	15,786	36.5	Alan Reid MP
Conservative	Jamie McGrigor	10,150	23.5	Gary Mulvaney
Labour	Carolyn Manson	9,696	22.4	n/a
Others		7,597	17.5	

One of the largest and most remote constituencies in the United Kingdom, Argyll & Bute takes in almost a third of western Scotland's coastline and scores of sparsely populated islands. There are no particularly large settlements in this constituency, with even the Glasgow commuter towns of Oban and Helensburgh being home to less than 15,000 residents. Around one in ten residents of this constituency is fluent in Gaelic. On a Westminster level, this seat was gained from the Conservatives by the Liberal Democrats in 1987 yet elected the SNP's Jim Mather at the 2007 Scottish Parliament elections. With all the main parties – Labour, Conservative, Liberal Democrat and SNP – having solid support bases here this is a rare four-way marginal. Sitting Liberal Democrat MP Alan Reid will defend his seat against Conservative Gary Mulvaney and the SNP's Michael MacKenzie.

Ayr, Carrick & Cumnock

Labour notional majority of 9,997; notional turnout: 61.9%

PARTY	2005 CANDIDATE	NOTIONAL 2005 VOTES	NOTIONAL 2005 % VOTE	PPC FOR NEXT GE
Labour	Sandra Osborne MP	20,433	45.4	Sandra Osborne MP
Conservative	Mark Jones	10,436	23.2	William Grant
Lib Dem	Colin Waugh	6,341	14.1	n/a
Others		7,838	17.4	

Central Ayrshire

Labour notional majority of 10,423; notional turnout: 63.2%

PARTY	2005 CANDIDATE	NOTIONAL 2005 VOTES	NOTIONAL 2005 % VOTE	PPC FOR NEXT GE
Labour	Brian Donohoe MP	19,905	46.4	Brian Donohoe MP
Conservative	Garry Clark	9,482	22.1	Maurice Golden
Lib Dem	Iain Kennedy	6,881	16.1	n/a
Others		6,603	15.4	

North Ayrshire & Arran

Labour notional majority of 11,296; notional turnout: 60.6%

PARTY	2005 CANDIDATE	NOTIONAL 2005 VOTES	NOTIONAL 2005 % VOTE	PPC FOR NEXT GE
Labour	Katy Clark	19,417	43.9	Katy Clark MP
Conservative	Stewart Connell	8,121	18.4	Philip Lardner
SNP	Tony Gurney	7,938	18.0	n/a
Others		8,729	19.8	

Banff & Buchan

SNP notional majority of 11,837; notional turnout: 56.6%

PARTY	2005 CANDIDATE	NOTIONAL 2005 VOTES	NOTIONAL 2005 % VOTE	PPC FOR NEXT GE
SNP	Alex Salmond MP	19,044	51.2	Dr Eilidh Whiteford
Conservative	Sandy Wallace	7,207	19.4	Jimmy Buchan
Lib Dem	Eleanor Anderson	4,952	13.3	Galen Milne
Others		6,013	16.1	

Berwickshire, Roxburgh & Selkirk

Lib Dem notional majority of 5,901; notional turnout: 64.1%

PARTY	2005 CANDIDATE	NOTIONAL 2005 VOTES	NOTIONAL 2005 % VOTE	PPC FOR NEXT GE
Lib Dem	Michael Moore MP	18,993	41.8	Michael Moore MP
Conservative	John Lamont	13,092	28.8	n/a
Labour	Sam Held	7,206	15.9	n/a
Other		6,097	13.4	

A rare Conservative target seat in Scotland, the scale of the party's recovery in Berwickshire, Roxburgh & Selkirk has far outpaced that in any other constituency north of the border. Held by the Liberal Democrats in its various incarnations since 1983, Conservative John Lamont surprised many by seizing the broadly coplanar Scottish Parliament constituency of Roxburgh & Berwickshire in 2007 on a 9.4% swing. Unsurprisingly, the sprawling seat is largely rural in nature although it does contain the attractive towns of Jedburgh, Kelso and Hawick, each of which still plays host to the traditional Scottish knitwear industry. Agriculture is the largest employer here, although the tourism sector is playing an increasingly important role in the local economy. Liberal Democrat International Development spokesman and sitting MP Michael Moore will stand again.

Caithness, Sutherland & Easter Ross

Lib Dem notional majority of 8,168; notional turnout: 59.3%

PARTY	2005 CANDIDATE	NOTIONAL 2005 VOTES	NOTIONAL 2005 % VOTE	PPC FOR NEXT GE
Lib Dem	John Thurso MP	13,957	50.5	John Thurso MP
Labour	Alan Jamieson	5,789	20.9	John Mackay
SNP	Karen Shirron	3,686	13.3	n/a
Others		4,231	15.3	

Coatbridge, Chryston & Bellshill

Labour notional majority of 19,519; notional turnout: 57.4%

PARTY	2005 CANDIDATE	NOTIONAL 2005 VOTES	NOTIONAL 2005 % VOTE	PPC FOR NEXT GE
Labour	Thomas Clarke MP	24,725	64.5	Thomas Clarke MP
SNP	Duncan Ross	5,206	13.6	n/a
Lib Dem	Rodney Ackland	4,605	12.0	n/a
Others		3,808	9.9	

Cumbernauld, Kilsyth & Kirkintilloch East

Labour notional majority of 11,562; notional turnout: 60.8%

PARTY	2005 CANDIDATE	NOTIONAL 2005 VOTES	NOTIONAL 2005 % VOTE	PPC FOR NEXT GE
Labour	Rosemary McKenna MP	20,251	51.8	Gregg McClymont
SNP	Jamie Hepburn	8,689	22.2	Julie Hepburn
Lib Dem	Hugh O' Donnell	5,817	14.9	n/a
Others		4,331	11.1	

Dumfries & Galloway

Labour notional majority of 2,922; notional turnout: 69.5%

PARTY	2005 CANDIDATE	NOTIONAL 2005 VOTES	NOTIONAL 2005 % VOTE	PPC FOR NEXT GE
Labour	Russell Brown MP	20,924	41.1	Russell Brown MP
Conservative	Peter Duncan MP	18,002	35.4	Peter Duncan
SNP	Douglas Henderson	6,182	12.1	Andrew Wood
Others		5,783	11.5	

One of the most aesthetically stunning seats in the United Kingdom, the constituency stretches more than 60 miles from the ferry port of Stranraer in the west to industrial Dumfries in the east, encompassing much of rural south-west Scotland. The constituency, an amalgamation of the former Dumfries and Galloway & Upper Nithsdale seats, offers the Conservatives one of their best prospects for a gain north of the border. Local councillor Peter Duncan, who held Galloway & Upper Nithsdale for the Conservatives for a single term until 2005, will hope to win his rematch with sitting MP Russell Brown, a former parliamentary private secretary to Alistair Darling.

Dumfriesshire, Clydesdale & Tweeddale

Conservative notional majority of 1,738; notional turnout: 68.5%

PARTY	2005 CANDIDATE	NOTIONAL 2005 VOTES	NOTIONAL 2005 % VOTE	PPC FOR NEXT GE
Conservative	David Mundell	16,141	36.2	David Mundell MP
Labour	Sean Marshall	14,403	32.3	Claudia Beamish
Lib Dem	Patsy Kenton	9,046	20.3	Catriona Bhatia
Others		5,026	11.3	

East Dunbartonshire

Lib Dem notional majority of 4,061; notional turnout: 73.0%

PARTY	2005 CANDIDATE	NOTIONAL 2005 VOTES	NOTIONAL 2005 % VOTE	PPC FOR NEXT GE
Lib Dem	Jo Swinson	19,533	41.8	Jo Swinson MP
Labour	John Lyons MP	15,472	33.1	Mary Galbraith
Conservative	David Jack	7,708	16.5	Mark Nolan
Others		4,011	8.6	

West Dunbartonshire

Labour notional majority of 12,553; notional turnout: 61.2%

PARTY	2005 CANDIDATE	NOTIONAL 2005 VOTES	NOTIONAL 2005 % VOTE	PPC FOR NEXT GE
Labour	John McFall MP	21,600	51.9	John McFall MP
SNP	Tom Chalmers	9,047	21.8	Graeme McCormick
Lib Dem	Niall Walker	5,999	14.4	n/a
Others		4,943	11.9	

Dundee East

SNP notional majority of 383; notional turnout: 62.4%

PARTY	2005 CANDIDATE	NOTIONAL 2005 VOTES	NOTIONAL 2005 % VOTE	PPC FOR NEXT GE
SNP	Stewart Hosie	14,708	37.2	Stewart Hosie MP
Labour	Iain Luke MP	14,325	36.2	Katrina Murray
Conservative	Chris Bustin	5,061	12.8	Chris Bustin
Others		5,446	13.8	

Dundee West

Labour notional majority of 5,379; notional turnout: 56.0%

PARTY	2005 CANDIDATE	NOTIONAL 2005 VOTES	NOTIONAL 2005 % VOTE	PPC FOR NEXT GE
Labour	Jim McGovern	16,468	44.6	Jim McGovern MP
SNP	Joe Fitzpatrick	11,089	30.0	Jim Barrie
Lib Dem	Nykoma Garry	5,323	14.4	n/a
Others		4,056	11.0	

Dunfermline & West Fife

Labour notional majority of 11,562; notional turnout: 59.8%

PARTY	2005 CANDIDATE	NOTIONAL 2005 VOTES	NOTIONAL 2005 % VOTE	PPC FOR NEXT GE
Labour	Rachel Squire MP	20,111	47.4	Thomas Docherty
Lib Dem	David Herbert	8,549	20.2	Willie Rennie MP
SNP	Douglas Chapman	8,026	18.9	n/a
Others		5,708	13.4	

East Kilbride, Strathaven & Lesmahagow

Labour notional majority of 14,723; notional turnout: 63.4%

PARTY	2005 CANDIDATE	NOTIONAL 2005 VOTES	NOTIONAL 2005 % VOTE	PPC FOR NEXT GE
Labour	Adam Ingram MP	23,264	48.7	n/a
SNP	Douglas Edwards	8,541	17.9	n/a
Lib Dem	John Oswald	7,904	16.6	n/a
Others		8,024	16.8	

East Lothian

Labour notional majority of 7,620; notional turnout: 64.7%

PARTY	2005 CANDIDATE	NOTIONAL 2005 VOTES	NOTIONAL 2005 % VOTE	PPC FOR NEXT GE
Labour	Anne Moffat MP	18,983	41.5	Anne Moffat MP
Lib Dem	Chris Butler	11,363	24.8	Amy Rodger
Conservative	William Stevenson	7,315	16.0	Michael Vietch
Others		8,115	17.7	

Edinburgh East

Labour notional majority of 6,202; notional turnout: 60.9%

PARTY	2005 CANDIDATE	NOTIONAL 2005 VOTES	NOTIONAL 2005 % VOTE	PPC FOR NEXT GE
Labour	Gavin Strang MP	15,899	40.0	Sheila Gilmore
Lib Dem	Gordon Mackenzie	9,697	24.4	n/a
SNP	Stefan Tymkewycz	6,760	17.0	George Kerevan
Others		7,353	18.5	

Edinburgh North & Leith

Labour notional majority of 2,153; notional turnout: 62.3%

PARTY	2005 CANDIDATE	NOTIONAL 2005 VOTES	NOTIONAL 2005 % VOTE	PPC FOR NEXT GE
Labour	Mark Lazarowicz MP	14,597	34.2	Mark Lazarowicz MP
Lib Dem	Mike Crockart	12,444	29.2	Kevin Lang
Conservative	Iain Whyte	7,969	18.7	Iain McGill
Others		7,630	17.9	

Comprising the northern portion of Edinburgh and the historic port of Leith, this constituency has traditionally favoured the Labour Party. As in many city constituencies, there is a diverse social mix of poorly maintained social housing properties, elegant detached homes and trendy 'loft house' conversions which strongly hint at the seat's industrial and maritime past. Despite this seat's appearance on the Conservative target list, the real battle here is between Labour and the Liberal Democrats, who were separated by just over 2,000 votes at the 2005 general election. Sitting Labour MP Mark Lazarowicz will be challenged by Conservative Iain McGill and Liberal Democrat Kevin Lang. Curiously, the 2009 European elections had the first-placed SNP, Labour, the Liberal Democrats, the Conservatives and the Greens within 4 percentage points of one another.

Edinburgh South

Labour notional majority of 405; notional turnout: 69.4%

PARTY	2005 CANDIDATE	NOTIONAL 2005 VOTES	NOTIONAL 2005 % VOTE	PPC FOR NEXT GE
Labour	Nigel Griffiths MP	14,188	33.2	Nigel Griffiths MP
Lib Dem	Marilyne MacLaren	13,783	32.3	Fred Mackintosh
Conservative	Gavin Brown	10,291	24.1	Neil Hudson
Others		4,436	10.4	

A classic three-way marginal, only 3,897 votes separated the Labour Party from the third-placed Conservatives at the 2005 general election. This is one of the most middle-class and educated constituencies in Scotland, taking in the opulent Morningside and housing many of the University of Edinburgh's staff and students. The Liberal Democrats have long dominated at a local government level and hold the broadly coplanar Scottish Parliament constituency. Sitting MP Nigel Griffiths (former flatmate of Gordon Brown, who had embarrassing photographs of an extra-marital affair published in the *News of the World* in 2009) will fight the seat again for Labour against opposition from Liberal Democrat Fred Mackintosh and Conservative Neil Hudson. With a strong swing from Labour to the SNP forecast and a general weakening of the Liberal Democrat position in Scotland in the two years, the Conservatives are upbeat about their chances of victory here.

Edinburgh South West

Labour notional majority of 7,242; notional turnout: 64.9%

PARTY	2005 CANDIDATE	NOTIONAL 2005 VOTES	NOTIONAL 2005 % VOTE	PPC FOR NEXT GE
Labour	Alistair Darling MP	17,476	39.8	Alistair Darling MP
Conservative	Gordon Buchan	10,234	23.3	Jason Rust
Lib Dem	Simon Clark	9,252	21.1	n/a
Others		6,964	15.9	

The constituency of Chancellor Alistair Darling, the Edinburgh South West seat was formed in 2005 from parts of the old Edinburgh Central and Pentlands constituencies. The seat is a varied social mix; encompassing the infamous high-rise council estate at Sighthill, the Pentland Hills and the communities of Balerno and Craiglockhart, arguably Scotland's wealthiest residential areas. This is one of the constituencies where a direct swing from Labour to the SNP – who narrowly topped the poll here in the 2009 European elections – could result in the Tories gaining a seat with little real increase in their vote. Edinburgh city councillor Jason Rust will hope to take the seat for the Conservatives and provide his party with their 'Enfield, Southgate' moment of the 2010 general election.

Edinburgh West

Lib Dem notional majority of 13,600; notional turnout: 68.3%

PARTY	2005 CANDIDATE	NOTIONAL 2005 VOTES	NOTIONAL 2005 % VOTE	PPC FOR NEXT GE
Lib Dem	John Barrett MP	22,417	49.5	n/a
Conservative	David Brogan	8,817	19.5	Stewart Geddes
Labour	Navraj Singh Ghaleigh	8,433	18.6	Cameron Day
Others		5,598	12.4	

Falkirk

Labour notional majority of 13,475; notional turnout: 59.5%

PARTY	2005 CANDIDATE	NOTIONAL 2005 VOTES	NOTIONAL 2005 % VOTE	PPC FOR NEXT GE
Labour	Eric Joyce MP	23,264	50.9	Eric Joyce MP
SNP	Laura Love	9,789	21.4	John McNally
Lib Dem	Callum Chomczuk	7,321	16.0	n/a
Others		5,376	11.7	

North East Fife

Lib Dem notional majority of 12,571; notional turnout: 62.1%

PARTY	2005 CANDIDATE	NOTIONAL 2005 VOTES	NOTIONAL 2005 % VOTE	PPC FOR NEXT GE
Lib Dem	Menzies Campbell MP	20,088	52.1	Menzies Campbell MP
Conservative	Mike Scott-Hayward	7,517	19.5	Miles Briggs
Labour	Tony King	4,920	12.8	n/a
Others		6,031	15.6	

Glasgow Central

Labour notional majority of 8,531; notional turnout: 43.8%

PARTY	2005 CANDIDATE	NOTIONAL 2005 VOTES	NOTIONAL 2005 % VOTE	PPC FOR NEXT GE
Labour	Mohammad Sarwar MP	13,518	48.2	Anas Sarwar
Lib Dem	Isabel Nelson	4,987	17.8	n/a
SNP	Bill Kidd	4,148	14.8	Osama Saeed
Others		5,384	19.3	

Glasgow East

Labour notional majority of 13,507; notional turnout: 48.1%

PARTY	2005 CANDIDATE	NOTIONAL 2005 VOTES	NOTIONAL 2005 % VOTE	PPC FOR NEXT GE
Labour	David Marshall MP	18,775	60.7	Margaret Curran
SNP	Lachlan McNeill	5,268	17.0	John Mason MP
Lib Dem	David Jackson	3,665	11.8	n/a
Others		3,231	10.4	

Glasgow North

Labour notional majority of 3,338; notional turnout: 50.4%

PARTY	2005 CANDIDATE	NOTIONAL 2005 VOTES	NOTIONAL 2005 % VOTE	PPC FOR NEXT GE
Labour	Ann McKechin MP	11,001	39.4	Ann McKechin MP
Lib Dem	Amy Rodger	7,663	27.4	Katy Gordon
SNP	Kenneth McLean	3,614	12.9	Patrick Grady
Others		5,643	20.1	

Glasgow North East

Speaker notional majority of 8,309; notional turnout: 45.7%

PARTY	2005 CANDIDATE	NOTIONAL 2005 VOTES	NOTIONAL 2005 % VOTE	PPC FOR NEXT GE
Speaker	Michael Martin MP	15,153	53.3	n/a
SNP	John McLaughlin	6,844	24.1	n/a
Socialist Labour	Doris Kelly	5,019	17.7	n/a
Others		1,402	4.9	

Glasgow North West

Labour notional majority of 10,093; notional turnout: 55.2%

PARTY	2005 CANDIDATE	NOTIONAL 2005 VOTES	NOTIONAL 2005 % VOTE	PPC FOR NEXT GE
Labour	John Robertson MP	16,748	49.2	John Robertson MP
Lib Dem	Paul Graham	6,655	19.5	n/a
SNP	Graeme Hendry	4,676	13.7	n/a
Others		5,982	17.6	

Glasgow South

Labour notional majority of 10,832; notional turnout: 56.0%

PARTY	2005 CANDIDATE	NOTIONAL 2005 VOTES	NOTIONAL 2005 % VOTE	PPC FOR NEXT GE
Labour	Tom Harris MP	18,153	47.2	Tom Harris MP
Lib Dem	Arthur Sanderson	7,321	19.0	n/a
SNP	Finlay MacLean	4,860	12.6	Malcolm Fleming
Others		8,097	21.1	

Glasgow South West

Labour notional majority of 13,896; notional turnout: 50.1%

PARTY	2005 CANDIDATE	NOTIONAL 2005 VOTES	NOTIONAL 2005 % VOTE	PPC FOR NEXT GE
Labour	Ian Davidson MP	18,653	60.2	Ian Davidson MP
SNP	James Dornan	4,757	15.4	Chris Stephens
Lib Dem	Katy Gordon	3,593	11.6	Isabel Nelson
Others		3,974	12.9	

Glenrothes

Labour notional majority of 10,664; notional turnout: 56.1%

PARTY	2005 CANDIDATE	NOTIONAL 2005 VOTES	NOTIONAL 2005 % VOTE	PPC FOR NEXT GE
Labour	John MacDougall MP	19,395	51.9	Lindsay Roy MP
SNP	Peter Grant	8,731	23.4	Peter Grant
Lib Dem	Elizabeth Riches	4,728	12.7	n/a
Others		4,512	12.1	

Gordon

Lib Dem notional majority of 11,026; notional turnout: 61.7%

PARTY	2005 CANDIDATE	NOTIONAL 2005 VOTES	NOTIONAL 2005 % VOTE	PPC FOR NEXT GE
Lib Dem	Malcolm Bruce MP	20,008	45.0	Malcolm Bruce MP
Labour	Iain Brotchie	8,982	20.2	n/a
Conservative	Philip Atkinson	7,842	17.6	Ross Thomson
Others		7,606	17.1	

Inverclyde

Labour notional majority of 11,259; notional turnout: 60.8%

PARTY	2005 CANDIDATE	NOTIONAL 2005 VOTES	NOTIONAL 2005 % VOTE	PPC FOR NEXT GE
Labour	David Cairns MP	18,318	50.7	David Cairns MP
SNP	Stuart McMillan	7,059	19.6	Laura Goodchild
Lib Dem	Douglas Herbison	6,123	17.0	Simon Hutton
Others		4,598	12.7	

Inverness, Nairn, Badenoch & Strathspey

Lib Dem notional majority of 4,148; notional turnout: 63.7%

PARTY	2005 CANDIDATE	NOTIONAL 2005 VOTES	NOTIONAL 2005 % VOTE	PPC FOR NEXT GE
Lib Dem	Danny Alexander	17,830	40.3	Danny Alexander MP
Labour	David Stewart MP	13,682	30.9	Mike Robb
SNP	David Thompson	5,992	13.5	John Finnie
Others		6,751	15.2	

Kilmarnock & Loudoun

Labour notional majority of 15,950; notional turnout: 62.1%

PARTY	2005 CANDIDATE	NOTIONAL 2005 VOTES	NOTIONAL 2005 % VOTE	PPC FOR NEXT GE
Labour	Des Browne MP	20,976	47.3	Des Browne MP
Conservative	Gary Smith	5,026	11.3	Janette McAlpine
SNP	Daniel Coffey	12,273	27.7	n/a
Others		6,108	13.7	

Kirkcaldy & Cowdenbeath

Labour notional majority of 18,216; notional turnout: 58.3%

PARTY	2005 CANDIDATE	NOTIONAL 2005 VOTES	NOTIONAL 2005 % VOTE	PPC FOR NEXT GE
Labour	Gordon Brown MP	24,278	58.1	Gordon Brown MP
SNP	Alan Bath	6,062	14.5	n/a
Lib Dem	Alex Cole-Hamilton	5,450	13.0	John Mainland
Others		6,006	14.3	

Lanark & Hamilton East

Labour notional majority of 11,947; notional turnout: 59.0%

PARTY	2005 CANDIDATE	NOTIONAL 2005 VOTES	NOTIONAL 2005 % VOTE	PPC FOR NEXT GE
Labour	Jimmy Hood MP	20,072	46.0	Jimmy Hood MP
Lib Dem	Fraser Grieve	8,125	18.6	n/a
SNP	John Wilson	7,746	17.8	n/a
Others		7,646	17.5	

Linlithgow & East Falkirk

Labour notional majority of 11,202; notional turnout: 60.4

PARTY	2005 CANDIDATE	NOTIONAL 2005 VOTES	NOTIONAL 2005 % VOTE	PPC FOR NEXT GE
Labour	Michael Connarty MP	22,121	47.7	Michael Connarty MP
SNP	Gordon Guthrie	10,919	23.5	Tam Smith
Lib Dem	Stephen Glenn	7,100	15.3	Andrea Stephenson
Others		6,249	13.4	

Livingston

Labour notional majority of 13,097; notional turnout: 58.4%

PARTY	2005 CANDIDATE	NOTIONAL 2005 VOTES	NOTIONAL 2005 % VOTE	PPC FOR NEXT GE
Labour	Robin Cook MP	22,657	51.1	n/a
SNP	Angela Constance	9,560	21.6	Lis Bardell
Lib Dem	Charles Dundas	6,832	15.4	n/a
Others		5,288	11.9	

Midlothian

Labour notional majority of 7,265; notional turnout: 62.6%

PARTY	2005 CANDIDATE	NOTIONAL 2005 VOTES	NOTIONAL 2005 % VOTE	PPC FOR NEXT GE
Labour	David Hamilton MP	17,153	45.5	David Hamilton MP
Lib Dem	Fred Mackintosh	9,888	26.2	Ross Paird
SNP	Colin Beattie	6,400	17.0	Colin Beattie
Others		4,263	11.3	

Moray

SNP notional majority of 5,676; notional turnout: 59.2%

PARTY	2005 CANDIDATE	NOTIONAL 2005 VOTES	NOTIONAL 2005 % VOTE	PPC FOR NEXT GE
SNP	Angus Robertson MP	14,196	36.6	Angus Robertson MP
Conservative	Jamie Halcro-Johnston	8,520	22.0	Douglas Ross
Labour	Kevin Hutchens	7,919	20.4	Stuart MacLennan
Others		8,158	21.0	

Located on Scotland's remote north-eastern coast, the Moray constituency has been held by the Scottish National Party since 1987. As one might expect, this is a sparsely populated rural seat in which the biggest employers are the farming and fishing sectors. Moray is also home to large Royal Air Force bases at Lossiemouth and Kinloss, the troops from which help sustain a relatively vibrant service sector locally. Elgin, with a population of around 25,000, is the largest town in the constituency. At 63.3%, owner occupation levels are relatively low here, partly as a result of extremely high property prices in many of the constituency's coastal areas. The SNP led the Conservatives by 15% at the 2009 European Parliament elections. Sitting MP Angus Robertson, the leader of the SNP's parliamentary group in the House of Commons, will see his greatest challenge come from Conservative Douglas Ross.

Motherwell & Wishaw

Labour notional majority of 15,222; notional turnout: 56.6%

PARTY	2005 CANDIDATE	NOTIONAL 2005 VOTES	NOTIONAL 2005 % VOTE	PPC FOR NEXT GE
Labour	Frank Roy MP	21,327	57.5	Frank Roy MP
SNP	Ian MacQuarrie	6,105	16.5	Marion Fellows
Lib Dem	Conor Snowden	4,464	12.0	n/a
Others		5,213	14.0	

Na H-Eileanan An Lar (Western Isles)

SNP notional majority of 1,441; notional turnout: 65.3%

PARTY	2005 CANDIDATE	NOTIONAL 2005 VOTES	NOTIONAL 2005 % VOTE	PPC FOR NEXT GE
SNP	Angus MacNeil	6,213	44.9	Angus MacNeil MP
Labour	Calum MacDonald	4,772	34.5	Donald John Macsween
Lib Dem	Jean Davis	1,096	7.9	Jean Davis
Others		1,755	12.7	

Ochil & South Perthshire

Labour notional majority of 688; notional turnout: 66.0%

PARTY	2005 CANDIDATE	NOTIONAL 2005 VOTES	NOTIONAL 2005 % VOTE	PPC FOR NEXT GE
Labour	Gordon Banks	14,645	31.4	Gordon Banks MP
SNP	Annabelle Ewing MP	13,957	29.9	Annabelle Ewing
Conservative	Elizabeth Smith	10,021	21.5	Gerald Michaluk
Others		8,074	17.3	

A newly created seat at the 2005 general election, Ochil & South Perthshire is nominally a three-way marginal with only 4,624 votes separating Labour from the third-placed Conservatives. Despite its statistical vulnerability to a Conservative advance, the real battle here is likely to be between Labour and the SNP. Comprised of parts of Clackmannanshire, Kinross and Perthshire, this is a predominantly rural constituency whose largest town, Alloa, has a population of under 20,000. Labour's support is strongest in the former coal-mining Clackmannanshire area while the Tories and SNP are reasonably evenly matched across South Perthshire. Sitting Labour MP Gordon Banks will face off against former SNP MP Annabelle Ewing, who represented a portion of the seat between 2001 and 2005. Gerald Michaluk will challenge for the Conservatives.

Orkney & Shetland

Lib Dem notional majority of 6,627; notional turnout: 54.3%

PARTY	2005 CANDIDATE	NOTIONAL 2005 VOTES	NOTIONAL 2005 % VOTE	PPC FOR NEXT GE
Lib Dem	Alistair Carmichael MP	9,138	51.5	Alistair Carmichael MP
Labour	Richard Meade	2,511	14.2	n/a
Conservative	Frank Nairn	2,357	13.3	n/a
Others		3,736	21.1	

Paisley & Renfrewshire North

Labour notional majority of 11,001; notional turnout: 64.8%

PARTY	2005 CANDIDATE	NOTIONAL 2005 VOTES	NOTIONAL 2005 % VOTE	PPC FOR NEXT GE
Labour	James Sheridan MP	18,697	45.7	James Sheridan MP
SNP	Bill Wilson	7,696	18.8	Mags MacLaren
Lib Dem	Lewis Hutton	7,464	18.3	n/a
Others		7,028	17.2	

Paisley & Renfrewshire South

Labour notional majority of 13,232; notional turnout: 62.9%

PARTY	2005 CANDIDATE	NOTIONAL 2005 VOTES	NOTIONAL 2005 % VOTE	PPC FOR NEXT GE
Labour	Douglas Alexander MP	19,904	52.6	Douglas Alexander MP
Lib Dem	Eileen McCartin	6,672	17.6	n/a
SNP	Thomas Begg	6,653	17.6	n/a
Others		4,631	12.2	

Perth & North Perthshire

SNP notional majority of 1,521; notional turnout: 63.9%

PARTY	2005 CANDIDATE	NOTIONAL 2005 VOTES	NOTIONAL 2005 % VOTE	PPC FOR NEXT GE
SNP	Peter Wishart MP	15,469	33.7	Peter Wishart MP
Conservative	Douglas Taylor	13,948	30.4	Peter Lyburn
Labour	Doug Maughan	8,601	18.7	n/a
Others		7,912	17.1	

Formed in 2005 from parts of the previous Angus, North Tayside and Perth seats, the Perth & North Perthshire constituency is a closely fought Conservative–SNP marginal. Unsurprisingly, the largest employer in this sprawling mid-Scotland constituency is the agricultural sector yet Perth has become an increasingly important centre for insurance and banking in recent years. There is a surprisingly high level of social housing in this predominantly rural constituency (21.6%) with only three in five homes owner occupied. No one party has dominated here in recent times, the Conservatives and SNP polling around a third of the vote apiece to a fifth each for Labour and the Liberal Democrats – a picture broadly mirrored on a local government level. The Conservatives are fielding Peter Lyburn to take on SNP MP Peter Wishart.

East Renfrewshire

Labour notional majority of 6,657; notional turnout: 72.1%

PARTY	2005 CANDIDATE	NOTIONAL 2005 VOTES	NOTIONAL 2005 % VOTE	PPC FOR NEXT GE
Labour	Jim Murphy MP	20,815	43.9	Jim Murphy MP
Conservative	Richard Cook	14,158	29.9	Richard Cook
Lib Dem	Gordon Macdonald	8,659	18.3	n/a
Others		3,773	8.0	

Located just south of Glasgow and better known by its former name Eastwood, East Renfrewshire was the Conservatives' safest seat in Scotland at the 1992 election. Years of Conservative dominance were, however, brought to an end in 1997 when now Scottish Secretary Jim Murphy seized this well-heeled slice of suburbia for Labour. The constituency is largely made up of wealthy detached housing which is broadly contiguous with urban Glasgow, although the south is more rural and agrarian in nature. With most of the population employed in professional occupations and an owner occupation rate of 83.4%, this seat has more in common with the image of the Surrey commuter belt than flinty Glasgow. The Conservatives, who would likely hold this seat if it were not so close to Scotland's second city, are fielding Richard Cook.

Ross, Skye & Lochaber

Lib Dem notional majority of 14,249; notional turnout: 64.6%

PARTY	2005 CANDIDATE	NOTIONAL 2005 VOTES	NOTIONAL 2005 % VOTE	PPC FOR NEXT GE
Lib Dem	Charles Kennedy MP	19,100	58.7	Charles Kennedy MP
Labour	Christine Conniff	4,851	14.9	n/a
Conservative	John Hodgson	3,275	10.1	Donald Cameron
Others		5,312	16.3	

Rutherglen & Hamilton West

Labour notional majority of 16,112; notional turnout: 58.3%

PARTY	2005 CANDIDATE	NOTIONAL 2005 VOTES	NOTIONAL 2005 % VOTE	PPC FOR NEXT GE
Labour	Tommy McAvoy MP	24,054	55.6	Tommy McAvoy MP
Lib Dem	Ian Robertson	7,942	18.4	n/a
SNP	Margaret Park	6,023	13.9	n/a
Others		5,242	12.2	

Stirling

Labour notional majority of 4,767; notional turnout: 68.1%

PARTY	2005 CANDIDATE	NOTIONAL 2005 VOTES	NOTIONAL 2005 % VOTE	PPC FOR NEXT GE
Labour	Anne McGuire MP	15,729	36.0	Anne McGuire MP
Conservative	Stephen Kerr	10,962	25.1	Bob Dalrymple
Lib Dem	Kelvin Holdsworth	9,052	20.7	n/a
Others		7,948	18.2	

Held with increasingly narrow majorities by former Scottish Secretary Michael Forsyth from 1983 to 1997, Stirling is an attractive and historic city nestled between the Highlands and Lowlands. Taking in large tracts of rural land, the agricultural sector is the most prominent local employer, although Stirling city is an important retail centre for the mid-Scotland region. Home to the University of Stirling, this is a well-educated constituency and two thirds of homes are owner occupied. The Scottish National Party has made advances here in recent years, narrowly gaining the broadly contiguous Scottish Parliament seat from Labour in 2007. A large Labour to SNP swing on a Westminster vote is likely to be of most benefit to the Conservatives. Former Labour minister and sitting MP Anne McGuire will face a challenge from Conservative Bob Dalrymple.

Northern Ireland

By any standards Northern Ireland is the most electorally unusual part of the United Kingdom. The major British parties do not generally take part in general elections, leading to the repeated return of 'Others' in all eighteen constituencies, although recently the Conservatives have made fitful attempts both to stand in their own name (they polled just 826 votes of a share of 2.6 per cent in North Down in 2005) and to revive their historic alliance with the Ulster Unionist party. The fact is that the political cleavages are quite different: the principal divide has been between those who wish permanently to remain within the United Kingdom (unionists) and those who ultimately or more immediately wish to be part of a united Ireland (nationalists or republicans). This constitutional dispute, allied closely to the social, residential and religious divisions between Protestant and Roman Catholic communities, accounts for the longevity and intensity of political contests and disputes. In addition there are two major parties on each side of the basic division, and if their battles are added to the mix, it has to be concluded that politics in Northern Ireland have often been bitter, and certainly sui generis. Yet another complexity has been added by the uneasy but as yet lasting power-sharing agreement at Stormont between the two allegedly more extreme parties, the DUP and Sinn Fein.

There has been no doubt in recent elections (whether it be for Westminster, the Northern Ireland Assembly, or the European Parliament) that these groupings have outvoted the Ulster Unionists and the SDLP. In 2005, for example, the DUP advanced from five to nine MPs in the Commons, and Sinn Fein from four to five, leaving the SDLP with three and the once dominant Ulster Unionists reduced from six to just one, their casualties including their leader David Trimble in Upper Bann. At first sight this would appear to represent a further bifurcation, though the cooperation enforced by power-sharing has in effect pulled both the DUP and SF somewhat towards to Northern Irish political centre.

As might be expected from a pattern of four-party politics (and one should not forget that there are others too, such as the traditionally non-sectarian Alliance party, let alone any new groupings) each party has targets from, and vulnerabilities to, most of the others.

This picture is unlikely to be significantly altered by the boundary changes, which were finalised later for Northern Ireland than in the other parts of the UK, but will be in force for the forthcoming general election. The number of seats is unaltered, although they are smaller on average than in England and Scotland, with a target quota for electorates of just 61,000 compared with nearly 70,000 – a technical comparative over-representation of between two and three seats.

Adjustments to the existing eighteen seats have been kept to a minimum, but something did need to be done about the four Belfast divisions, which had only just over 200,000 voters between them. It was decided to retain these seats, but in each case to expand their boundaries beyond the city limits. Apart from this, changes are very minor, and six of the seats are completely unaltered. The only contest which may well be affected by the boundary changes, merely because of its close result last time, is the fascinating struggle in Belfast South (see *One to Watch* below).

In general, the Boundary Commission has preserved the political mixture and nature as the sectors of Belfast seats have been extended beyond the city limits. In Belfast North, for example, which has been enlarged by 12,000 voters, five of the six wards from Newtownabbey district included are in Glengormley, a divided modern estate which itself has demographically become more Catholic in recent years; the other is the overwhelmingly Protestant estate of Cloughfern. The changes maintain the RC share of the electorate at just over 40 per cent, and in this strongly working-class seat Nigel Dodds is likely to retain a majority of 5,000–6,000 over Sinn Fein. Gerry Adams's citadel of Belfast West takes the fewest extra voters, just 4,000, and can perhaps be considered the safest constituency of any in the UK – albeit with an MP who does not take his seat. On the other side of the city in every sense, Belfast East should remain in the hands of the DUP leader Peter Robinson. Although it is much more middle class than West, it will now take in 10,000 voters from the staunchly DUP Dundonald area in Strangford – his wife's seat. He (or another candidate from his party if he should step down to concentrate on his role as First Minister) should win against fairly evenly divided UU/Alliance opposition on a share of at least 50 per cent.

Outside Belfast, boundary changes are more minor. The DUP are likely to hold all of their nine seats in the province, including those such as South Antrim and Upper Bann that were gained from the Ulster Unionists in 2005, where William McCrea and David Simpson have entrenched their position since the last general election. In North Antrim the main interest has been whether the octogenarian Ian Paisley will retire and whether he might be replaced as DUP candidate by his son, Ian Junior, or perhaps by someone outside the family. The former DUP Euro-MP Jim Allister, who turned away to found Traditional Unionist Voice, has also indicated he may stand – but in June 2009 the 83-year-old 'Big Man from Ballymena' told House magazine he may well seek yet another term.

Sinn Fein are also likely to hold their five seats. Although the community balance in Fermanagh & South Tyrone enabled the two unionist parties to poll 47 per cent between them in 2005, this is still amongst the most bitterly divided of all Northern Irish seats and voter discipline is very strong. Michelle Gildernew MP and Sinn Fein have both strengthened their position since her first (disputed) election with a majority of just fifty-three votes in 2001, so she should win again barring the ironically unlikely event of a united unionist candidature. Conor Murphy easily gained Newry & Armagh from the SDLP on the retirement of Seamus Mallon in 2005, and has built up his position as an incumbent since. In West Tyrone, Pat Doherty probably faced his strongest challenge last time in Dr Kieran Denny, who was campaigning to keep Omagh Hospital services; Sinn Fein polled twice the vote of any other party here in the 2007 Assembly elections. Finally, Deputy First Minister Martin McGuinness is now safe in Mid Ulster, despite its chequered electoral history in the heart (and heartland) of the Troubles.

The SDLP may or may not lose the anomalous Belfast South (the only constituency not held at present by the majority tradition in a seat) but their other two are safer. John Hume's protégé and successor as party leader, Mark Durkan, is established in Foyle (a seat named to avoid having to decide between the name of its principal population centre, Derry or Londonderry), especially as the new SF candidate Martina Anderson is not felt to have the appeal of Mitchel McLaughlin. In South Down, many have predicted the retirement of 74-year-old Eddie McGrady, but informed local opinion suggests that the MLA for the same area, Margaret Ritchie (who for sixteen years from 1987 to 2003 was McGrady's parliamentary assistant), would still probably start as favourite against Sinn Fein's Catriona Ruane, another local MA, who represented Ireland at lawn tennis. It is hard now to believe that this constituency elected Enoch Powell as recently as 1987.

The final seat that may change hands is North Down. Lady Hermon is currently the sole Ulster Unionist left in the Commons. In May 2009 she said that she would not be happy about standing as a joint Unionist and Conservative candidate – in the June 2009 elections a seat was won by the new UCUNF (Ulster Unionists and Conservatives – New Force) but this link is not certain to continue to a general election, and she could in any case have a good chance under another label or as an Independent. Although in some ways North Down, as a largely affluent and middle-class seat, might be thought to be the most amenable to British party intervention, in fact its stronger tradition is that of independence, having been held by both James Kilfedder and Robert McCartney in the 1980s and 1990s. British Conservatives should not let their hopes get up too high. They may be involved in a new grouping, but the strength of the 'force' may not be with them.

Independence might not be the most apposite word to sum up the politics of Northern Ireland, given the paramountcy of the division between those standing for unions with Britain and with the Irish Republic. However its politics are sure to remain very distinct from both of those entities, and thus the bloc of eighteen MPs affiliated to no British party (and probably at least five whose principles preclude taking the oath to sit in the Commons) will continue to attest to the unique issues of its history, present and future.

Target seats

SEAT	SWING REQUIRED %	MP	CHALLENGER
DUP from SDLP			
Belfast South	0.3	Alasdair McDonnell	
DUP from Sinn Fein			
Fermanagh & South Tyrone	4.7	Michelle Gildernew	
DUP from UU			
North Down	7.7	Lady Hermon	
Sinn Fein from SDLP			
Foyle	6.5	Mark Durkan	Martina Anderson
South Down	9.9	Eddie McGrady	
Sinn Fein from DUP			
Belfast North	8.0	Nigel Dodds	
SDLP from Sinn Fein			
Newry & Armagh	8.1	Conor Murphy	Dominic Bradley?
UU from DUP			
South Antrim	5.4	William McCrae	
Upper Bann	6.0	David Simpson	

One to watch: Belfast South

Actual majority 2005: SDLP 1,235 (3.9%)
Notional majority 2005: SDLP 188 (0.5%)
SDLP candidate: Alasdair McDonnell MP

The only one of the eighteen Northern Irish seats which was not won by a representative of the majority politico-religious tradition in 2005, Belfast South is ostensibly the mot likely to change hands next time. Although the seat had always previously been held by a Unionist of some kind, at the last general election the SDLP's Dr Alasdair McDonnell benefited from an even split between the DUP and the UUP (after Martin Smyth's retirement) and won – with just 32 per cent of the vote. There is an argument that the DUP have emerged as the stronger unionist party, and should be able to recapture Belfast South; this may be helped by boundary changes which reduce McDonnell's calculated notional majority to just 188. Some 7,500 voters are brought in from Strangford and Belfast East (DUP strongholds currently held by Mr and Mrs Robinson, although the new territory actually included in South, such as Wynchurch ward in Castlereagh district, are better for the SDLP than the notional figures may indicate). On the other hand, McDonnell may benefit from some tactical voting in a seat which includes some of Belfast's most affluent residential areas such as Upper Malone, and this seat is probably seeing more of a demographic shift to Catholic nationalism than any other in Northern Ireland. Finally, it will be interesting to see how the non-sectarian Alliance party fares; in the Assembly elections here in 2007 a seat was won by Hong Kong-born Anna Lo, the first ethnic minority candidate to win in a Northern Irish election. Overall this is clearly – or rather not clearly – the most unpredictable constituency in the province.

East Antrim

DUP actual majority of 7,304; actual turnout: 54.5%

PARTY	2005 CANDIDATE	ACTUAL 2005 VOTES	ACTUAL 2005 % VOTE	PPC FOR NEXT GE
DUP	Sammy Wilson	15,766	49.6	Sammy Wilson MP
UU/UCUNF	Roy Beggs	8,462	26.6	n/a
Alliance	Sean Neeson	4,869	15.3	n/a
Others		2,670	8.4	

North Antrim

DUP actual majority of 17,965; actual turnout: 61.7%

PARTY	2005 CANDIDATE	ACTUAL 2005 VOTES	ACTUAL 2005 % VOTE	PPC FOR NEXT GE
DUP	Ian Paisley MP	25,156	54.8	Ian Paisley MP
Sinn Féin	Phillip McGuigan	7,191	15.7	n/a
UU/UCUNF	Rodney McCune	6,637	14.5	n/a
Others		6,942	15.2	

South Antrim

DUP actual majority of 3,448; actual turnout: 56.7%

PARTY	2005 CANDIDATE	ACTUAL 2005 VOTES	ACTUAL 2005 % VOTE	PPC FOR NEXT GE
DUP	William McCrea	14,507	38.2	William McCrea MP
UU/UCUNF	David Burnside	11,059	29.1	n/a
SDLP	Noreen McClelland	4,706	12.4	n/a
Others		7,685	20.2	

Belfast East

DUP actual majority of 5,877; actual turnout: 58.0%

PARTY	2005 CANDIDATE	ACTUAL 2005 VOTES	ACTUAL 2005 % VOTE	PPC FOR NEXT GE
DUP	Peter Robinson MP	15,152	49.1	Peter Robinson MP
UU/UCUNF	Reg Empey	9,275	30.1	n/a
Alliance	Naomi Long	3,746	12.2	n/a
Others		2,658	8.6	

Belfast North

DUP actual majority of 5,188; actual turnout: 57.8%

PARTY	2005 CANDIDATE	ACTUAL 2005 VOTES	ACTUAL 2005 % VOTE	PPC FOR NEXT GE
DUP	Nigel Dodds MP	13,935	45.6	Nigel Dodds MP
Sinn Fein	Gerry Kelly	8,747	28.6	n/a
SDLP	Alban Maginness	4,950	16.2	n/a
Others		2,908	9.5	

Belfast South

SDLP actual majority of 1,235; actual turnout: 60.8%

PARTY	2005 CANDIDATE	ACTUAL 2005 VOTES	ACTUAL 2005 % VOTE	PPC FOR NEXT GE
SDLP	Alasdair McDonnell	10,339	32.3	Alasdair McDonnell MP
DUP	Jimmy Spratt	9,104	28.4	n/a
UU/UCUNF	Michael McGimpsey	7,263	22.7	n/a
Others		3,322	16.6	

Belfast West

Sinn Féin actual majority of 19,315; actual turnout: 64.2%

PARTY	2005 CANDIDATE	ACTUAL 2005 VOTES	ACTUAL 2005 % VOTE	PPC FOR NEXT GE
Sinn Fein	Gerry Adams MP	24,348	70.5	Gerry Adams MP
SDLP	Alex Attwood	5,003	14.6	n/a
DUP	Diane Dodds	3,652	10.6	n/a
Others		1,512	4.4	

North Down

UU/UCUNF actual majority of 4,944; actual turnout: 54%

PARTY	2005 CANDIDATE	ACTUAL 2005 VOTES	ACTUAL 2005 % VOTE	PPC FOR NEXT GE
UU/UCUNF	Sylvia Hermon MP	16,268	50.4	Sylvia Hermon MP
DUP	Peter Weir	11,324	35.1	n/a
Alliance	David Alderdice	2,451	7.6	n/a
Others		2,247	6.9	

South Down

SDLP actual majority of 9,140; actual turnout: 65.4%

PARTY	2005 CANDIDATE	ACTUAL 2005 VOTES	ACTUAL 2005 % VOTE	PPC FOR NEXT GE
SDLP	Eddie McGrady MP	21,,557	44.7	Eddie McGrady MP
Sinn Féin	Caitriona Ruane	12417	25.8	n/a
DUP	Jim Wells	8,815	18.3	n/a
Others		5,388	11.2	

Fermanagh & South Tyrone

Sinn Féin actual majority of 4,582; actual turnout: 72.6%

PARTY	2005 CANDIDATE	ACTUAL 2005 VOTES	ACTUAL 2005 % VOTE	PPC FOR NEXT GE
Sinn Fein	Michelle Gildernew MP	18,638	38.2	Michelle Gildernew MP
DUP	Arlene Foster	14,056	28.8	n/a
UU/UCUNF	Tom Elliott	8,869	18.2	n/a
Others		7,230	14.8	

Foyle

SDLP actual majority of 5,957; actual turnout: 65.9%

PARTY	2005 CANDIDATE	ACTUAL 2005 VOTES	ACTUAL 2005 % VOTE	PPC FOR NEXT GE
SDLP	Mark Durkan	21,119	46.3	Mark Durkan MP
Sinn Féin	Mitchel McLaughlin	15,162	33.2	n/a
DUP	William Hay	6,557	14.1	n/a
Others		2,774	6.1	

Lagan Valley

DUP actual majority of 14,117; actual turnout: 60.2%

PARTY	2005 CANDIDATE	ACTUAL 2005 VOTES	ACTUAL 2005 % VOTE	PPC FOR NEXT GE
DUP	Jeffrey Donaldson MP	23,289	54.7	Jeffrey Donaldson MP
UU/UCUNF	Basil McCrea	9,172	21.5	n/a
Alliance	Seamus Close	4,316	10.1	n/a
Others		5,795	13.6	

East Londonderry

DUP actual majority of 7,727; actual turnout: 60.3%

PARTY	2005 CANDIDATE	ACTUAL 2005 VOTES	ACTUAL 2005 % VOTE	PPC FOR NEXT GE
DUP	Gregory Campbell MP	15,225	42.9	Gregory Campbell MP
UU/UCUNF	David McClarty	7,498	21.1	n/a
SDLP	John Dallat	6,077	17.1	n/a
Others		6,704	18.9	

Mid Ulster

Sinn Féin actual majority of 10,976; actual turnout: 72.5%

PARTY	2005 CANDIDATE	ACTUAL 2005 VOTES	ACTUAL 2005 % VOTE	PPC FOR NEXT GE
Sinn Féin	Martin McGuinness MP	21,641	47.6	Martin McGuinness MP
DUP	Ian McCrea	10,665	23.5	n/a
SDLP	Patsy McGlone	7,922	17.4	n/a
Others		5,198	11.5	

Newry & Armagh

Sinn Féin actual majority of 8,195; actual turnout: 70%

PARTY	2005 CANDIDATE	ACTUAL 2005 VOTES	ACTUAL 2005 % VOTE	PPC FOR NEXT GE
Sinn Féin	Conor Murphy	20,965	41.4	Conor Murphy MP
SDLP	Dominic Bradley	12,770	25.2	n/a
DUP	Paul Berry	9,311	18.4	n/a
Others		7,650	15.1	

Strangford

DUP actual majority of 13,049; actual turnout: 53.6%

PARTY	2005 CANDIDATE	ACTUAL 2005 VOTES	ACTUAL 2005 % VOTE	PPC FOR NEXT GE
DUP	Iris Robinson MP	20,921	56.5	Iris Robinson MP
UU/UCUNF	Gareth McGimpsey	7,872	21.3	n/a
Alliance	Kieran McCarthy	3,332	9.0	n/a
Others		4,907	13.2	

West Tyrone

Sinn Féin actual majority of 5,005; actual turnout: 72.1%

PARTY	2005 CANDIDATE	ACTUAL 2005 VOTES	ACTUAL 2005 % VOTE	PPC FOR NEXT GE
Sinn Féin	Pat Dogherty MP	16,910	38.9	Pat Dogherty MP
Independent	Kieran Deeny	11,905	27.4	n/a
DUP	Thomas Buchana	7,742	17.8	n/a
Others		6,930	16.0	

Upper Bann

DUP actual majority of 5,398; actual turnout: 61.2%

PARTY	2005 CANDIDATE	ACTUAL 2005 VOTES	ACTUAL 2005 % VOTE	PPC FOR NEXT GE
DUP	David Simpson	16,679	37.6	David Simpson MP
UU/UCUNF	David Trimble MP	11,281	25.5	n/a
Sinn Féin	John O'Dowd	9,305	21.0	n/a
Others		7,057	16.0	

totalpolitics

Britain's leading monthly magazine
for politicians and political insiders

AGENDA-SETTING INTERVIEWS
•
HARD-HITTING DEBATES
•
THOUGHT-PROVOKING FEATURES
•
THE LATEST CAMPAIGN TECHNIQUES
AND TECHNOLOGIES
•
POLITICAL LIFESTYLE, HISTORY AND CULTURE